# THE WILD McLEANS

## Mel Rothenburger

ORCA BOOK PUBLISHERS

First printing, 1993
Second printing, 1995

**Canadian Cataloguing in Publication Data**
Rothenburger, Mel, 1944–
    The wild McLeans

ISBN 1-55143-006-1

1. McLean family.   2. Murderers – British Columbia – Biography.   3. Outlaws – British Columbia – Biography.   4. Frontier and pioneer life – British Columbia.   I. Title
FC3823.1.M234R68 1993   364.1'523'0922
F1088.M234R68 1993   C93-091637-9


Publication assistance provided by The Canada Council

Cover painting by Kelowna artist Don Makela depicts, left to right, Charlie McLean, Allen McLean, Archie McLean and Alex Hare

Cover design by Christine Toller

Printed and bound in Canada


**Orca Book Publishers**
PO Box 5626, Station B
Victoria, BC  Canada
V8R 6S4

For my mother,
Nora Maye McLean Rothenburger,

and for all the B.C. McLeans

# TABLE OF CONTENTS

# INTRODUCTION

When I was a young girl, my grandmother, Margaret (Vodreaux) McLean, used to tell us stories about the family: the heartaches, the shame, and the triumphs. As I grew up, I remembered those stories, and wanted to learn more. Much was written about the family, especially the so-called "Wild McLean Gang," who were hung in 1881. Most of what was written was bad.

There *has* been good and bad in the McLean family; there's good and bad in all of us. The history of the McLeans happens to be more exciting and more violent than that of most families, but throughout the generations the McLeans have shown great courage, an ability to get by with very little, and a tremendous love for their children.

Today people seem to have so much, but not peace of mind. There are murders, suicides, child abuse, and terrible poverty. Years ago things were simpler, but they weren't easier. The McLeans have always accepted what life has offered them, and made the best of it. Many married into Indian families, and so were disadvantaged by the prejudices that were prevalent against people of mixed blood, yet the best qualities of each race made us even stronger.

I've seen many changes since I was born, from the horse-and-buggy days to the space age and computer technology, but the most important thing on Earth is still doing the best we can and getting along. Too many young people blame everything on their parents, yet have no idea what kind of lives their parents lived nor what they had to go through for their kids, and even less idea of their family heritage in general. I hope this book will help some of those young people of the McLean family appreciate the great beauty, bravery and talent — not just the sensational things — that have been typical of the McLeans. A few skeletons in the closet only make it more interesting.

I'm proud of the McLeans. I hope other members of the family, and other British Columbians and Canadians, will enjoy finding out more about them.


Pat Spiers
Prince George

It's been twenty years since I first started researching and writing about the McLeans. During all that time, I've maintained an interest in them, particularly in Donald, the Hudson's Bay Company chief trader, and in his infamous sons, the McLean Gang outlaws, though active research was set aside for awhile for other pursuits. Four years ago I became fascinated with genealogy as a hobby, and renewed my quest for knowledge not only of Donald and his boys, but of other descendants, and of Donald's parents.

The latter involved a long and frustrating series of dead-end trails in England and Scotland. Little was known about Donald McLean's mother and nothing about his father, not even his name. I became a little obsessed with Hudson's Bay Company history and it became required bed-time reading. One night while reading a popular history of the fur trade in Canada, I happened upon a brief account of the so-called Seven Oaks Massacre of 1816 in the Red River colony established by Lord Selkirk. It was one of the most exciting moments in all the time of searching for an answer to the riddle of who Donald McLean's father was. The name of Alexander McLean appeared on the list of those engaged in the Seven Oaks battle between colonists and Métis, causing several pieces of previous information to flash instantly into my head — references connecting Donald's father to Red River, certain dates, diaries, and journals, all of which contained seemingly unconnected information. Now it collectively made sense, providing the basis for a new and successful search in Scotland. While documentary proof — in the form of an actual record of birth — that Alexander McLean of Red River was the father of Donald remains elusive, there is so much other collaborative evidence that there can be no doubt.

It wasn't the only major new information about the McLeans, though it was perhaps the most energizing. The discovery by a local resident of a long-lost set of Catholic baptism and marriage records containing names and dates of many of the key McLean players in the tragic story of the outlaw gang was another example. Going back over all the information obtained in previous research, I was led into other sources, such as the Attorney-General's Papers in the holdings of the B.C. Archives and Records Services, another treasury of detail.

When my second cousin, Pat Spiers, called me one evening and suggested re-publishing 'We've Killed Johnny Ussher!', a book about the McLean Gang I wrote in 1973, I wasn't interested. But Spiers, whose fascination with the McLean family history pre-dates even my own, was persistent. I began to think about it, but had no desire to simply produce a second printing of the *'Johnny Ussher'* book. I wanted to include all of the new material. And I didn't want to fictionalize the story at all, as I had done in *'Johnny Ussher'*. I wanted to tell the story of the McLeans, from their arrival in North America from Scotland through to modern times, as accurately as it could be done, without any fictional characters, dialogue or events. Yet I didn't want this true story — so exciting in its hardships, tragedies, violence and moments of joy and success — to be a textbook. This is a story, after all, that ranges from the opening up of the wilderness of a continent through the fur trade, to the establishment of colonies, the days of the gold rush, the first cowboys, the coming of the railroad, and the global conflicts that introduced us to the twentieth century. It's a story of province- and nation-building, of human failing and shame, of courage and honour, of the clash of cultures, of fighting the odds.

There are, therefore, two main components to this book. The main text is the story itself, tracing the events that overtook key figures in various generations of McLeans. I personally find footnotes an intrusion on a good story, so you won't find quotes and key pieces of information marked with footnote numbers in the text. However, scholars or others who like to know the sources for such things will find a section of chapter notes identified with key words. While the scope of this book doesn't allow inclusion of a full family genealogy, I've compiled a separate one, available in a number of archives and libraries for anyone with a curiosity about the roots of the McLeans.

Essential to any work of this nature is the co-operation of the guardians of information. Archivists and librarians are only human, and some have more or less interest in helping a researcher such as myself find what he's looking for. However, all of the following provided useful material: the Kamloops Museum and Archives, Cariboo-Thompson Nicola Library System, British Columbia Archives and Records Service, Ashcroft Museum, Clinton Museum, Nicola Valley Archives Association, National Archives of Canada, Hudson's Bay Company Archives, New Westminster Library, Historic Hat Creek Ranch, Vancouver City Archives, Vancouver City Library, Oblate House in Vancouver, St. Andrew's Cathedral in Victoria, and University of British Columbia Library (Special Collections). Deserving of special mention for its co-operation is Our Lady of Perpetual Help Catholic Parish in Kamloops, which cheerfully opened its extensive records of baptisms, marriages and deaths for examination. Researchers Petria Englebrecht in South Africa, Julie Poole in Scotland, and especially John Dagger in England were of immense help, tracing what at times was a very thin skein of clues.

Of course, I must thank Pat Spiers, who was, as always, helpful in pointing me toward potentially helpful research, particularly in regard to the more recent, twentieth century generations. And, my mother, Nora Maye (McLean) Rothenburger, has continued her strong interest in the family's history, tapping the sources at her disposal. Williams Lake historian John Roberts was very helpful with some key information. Special thanks to my wife, Syd Jones, and to Kamloops historian Ken Favrholdt for reading the manuscript and suggesting improvements.

This book contains elements of *'We've Killed Johnny Ussher!'* (Mitchell Press, 1973) and *The Chilcotin War* (Mr. Paperback, 1978). Permission from the respective publishers for the unfettered use of material in these two previous books is much appreciated.

Mel Rothenburger
Kamloops

On April 16, 1746, at a place called Culloden near Inverness, the Scottish Highland clans under Bonnie Prince Charlie fought a great battle with the English army of the Duke of Cumberland. Outnumbered almost two to one, and exhausted and hungry after an all-night march, the Scots nevertheless fought a courageous battle for many hours in defence of the Young Pretender. In the front line of the Highland army was the clan McLean, five hundred strong, led by Charles McLean of Drimnin. As the MacDonalds beside them gave in and fled, the McLeans fought on with the Stuarts, Camerons, Frasers and MacIntoshes, routing the left wing of the Duke's army, only to be attacked by numerically overwhelming regiments from the enemy's centre.

Many McLeans, including Charles of Drimnin, died that day under the onslaught of the Duke. Of the five thousand Highlanders, a thousand were killed in battle. The slain McLeans, along with MacLaughlans and MacGillivrays, were buried in a fifty-six-foot-long trench dug in the battlefield. After his victory, Cumberland took an awful revenge, torturing and murdering scores of his defeated enemy, so that even more McLeans died. Then he scorched the Highlands, destroying the clans' castles, killing their livestock and burning their crops. The great estates were confiscated and broken up. Highlanders were ordered not to wear their traditional Highland garb, or else be shot on sight. It was the end of the Scottish clans.

In the late 1700s and early 1800s, Scottish lairds found that the system of leasing their land for agriculture wasn't yielding enough profit, and that there was more to be made by turning out the tenant farmers, known as tacksmen, and grazing sheep instead. There was more money to be made in wool than in potatoes or other crops. This disenfranchisement was called the Clearances. In this way, a generation after Culloden, scores of Highland crofters suffered yet another blow in the total loss of their livelihood. Their only alternative seemed the misery of the cities, where they might find work in the slave-like conditions of industry.

In 1799 a man named Thomas Douglas inherited from his father the Scottish title and properties of the earl of Selkirk. The fifth earl of Selkirk was a student of history, an expert in agriculture and a philanthropist. He knew of the persecution of Highlanders after Cullodon and the suffering of crofters in the Clearances, and decided to do something about it. His great purpose in life became the establishment of a colony in North America where dispossessed Scottish tacksmen could exchange the bleak prospect of life in the grimy cities of the British Isles for new hope and new life on farms of their own. The place he chose was called Assiniboia, in the Red River region of Rupert's Land, the vast fur-trading territory of the Hudson's Bay Company.

# Part 1

DEATH AT RED RIVER

FORT DOUGLAS, Red River Colony, Rupert's Land
Wednesday, June 19, 1816, morning

To Alexander McLean, the leading settler of the colony, Captain of the
Royal Assiniboia Militia, this particular day must have dawned like
any other: with the expectation of battling for survival against the
cut-throat, unscrupulous, lying "rascals" of the North West Company
and their murderous Métis and half-breed henchmen. Such had been
a way of life in the colony for almost a year and a half. Other than
that, it was a fine, dry, warm day. At first, when the settlers had
arrived to build their farms, it was the cold weather, hungry Indians,
rotten grain, wolves, grasshoppers, spirit-breaking frustration, and in-
competent leadership that conspired against Lord Selkirk's grand
experiment. But those worries were soon supplanted by the
Nor'Westers and their Métis, or Bois Brules, allies, who had taken up
the sport of trampling crops, killing horses and cattle, and burning
houses, with considerable enthusiasm. It was for that reason the colonists had lived through the past winter in tents pitched by the river
near the charred remains of their log homes. It was for that reason,
too, that Alex McLean's left hand was a useless lump of scar tissue.

They had been warned two days before by friendly Saulteaux Indians that the Nor'Westers and Bois Brules were planning an attack on
the fort, with the intention of burning it to the ground and slaughter-
ing every man, woman and child who fell into their hands. It had, in
fact, been expected for some time; they were said to be gathering at
the NWC trading post of Fort Qu'Appelle, so the colonists were keeping up a constant watch. Not Alex McLean, nor the colony's governor
Robert Semple, nor any of the colonists, nor even the Nor'Westers
and the Métis, could have any idea that so much blood would be
spilled at Red River that day.

They were a strange alliance, the Scots and Canadian fur traders
of the North West Company and the Cree-French and Cree-Scots half-
breeds, all equally determined to wipe out the struggling colony, but
for greatly different reasons. The Nor'Westers hadn't liked the colony
idea right from the start. They first tried to stop it in London by
buying up shares in the Hudson's Bay Company, hoping to control
the vote on the earl of Selkirk's request for a grant of land to establish a
colony in North America for Highlanders displaced by the Clearances.
When that didn't work, and fears of obstruction of their trade began to
come true, they embarked on a two-pronged offensive: enticing as many
colonists as possible to desert, and killing or scaring away the rest.

Hopes of enlisting the local Saulteaux in this war quickly faded, but the Nor'Westers had a strong ally in the Métis. While the Nor'Westers' hatred of the Hudson's Bay Company and the Selkirk settlement was based on economics, the Métis had a more basic, perhaps more noble, reason. They regarded the land as theirs and the colonists as squatters and thieves. The Métis subsisted mostly on the plains buffalo, which they killed by the thousands in great hunts and turned into pemmican to be sold to the North West Company. Selkirk may have a piece of paper saying he now owned this part of Rupert's Land, but the Métis had occupied it for decades, their Cree and Sioux ancestors for centuries. That so many Métis worked for the NWC formed the basis for a natural alliance against the colonists.

The Hudson's Bay Company, and Selkirk, should have foreseen the problem. But the Company was in a state of such financial desperation and willingness to set aside its usual aversion to colonization, and Selkirk so blinded by his benign ambition to establish a refuge, that potential unpleasantries were brushed aside in favour of promoting the Red River scheme as a "Land of Promise" awaiting all with welcoming arms. The HBC reluctantly saw in Red River an opportunity to economize by providing locally produced food for its Rupert's Land posts, and so granted Selkirk 116 thousand acres — a huge tract of land stretching almost from Lake Superior to the headwaters of the Assiniboine River, and from Lake Winnipeg to the Mississippi, in total almost as big as Great Britain itself.

Alexander McLean was one of those attracted to the idea of carving a thriving new colony out of the wilds of North America. It didn't hurt that he was offered twenty-one very fine Merino sheep, a ten-thousand-acre township, and total financial support for himself, his family and two servants for a full year. This was many times more than any other settler was offered, but Selkirk wanted a man of standing — "not so much with a view to his personal services as for the sake of having one settler of the rank of a gentleman" — among his colonists. McLean's record was not untarnished. In Selkirk's words, he was "of fair and honourable character and a good farmer," but "his conduct in his own affairs has not shown much steadiness."

That would prove to be an understatement, but the offer was accepted and Alex McLean, youngest son of Donald McLean of the House of Drimnin and former tacksman of Kingerar on the island of Mull, his pregnant wife Christina and their four children — the oldest just seven years old — left home for Sligo on the west coast of Ireland, shipping out from there June 24, 1812, on the *Robert Taylor* for the sixty-one day journey to York Factory. Another ship, the *King George*, sailed with them. It was a busy trip. The heavy-handed discipline of the expedition's leader, Owen Keveny, soon chafed on McLean, who

on several occasions offered candid opinions about the limitations of
Keveny's mental capacities. The trip was also marked by an unpleasant feud between the Highlanders and the Irishmen in the contingent,
the former apparently regarding the latter as deserving of less respect
or kindness than a bunch of snakes. Since McLean was Catholic, an
uncommon religion in the Highlands, he may have been friendlier
with the Irish Catholics — except for Keveny — than the rest.

In July the two ships reached Hudson Strait, where they were
slowed by ice floes, or, as the colonists called them, "ice islands." On
August 21, 1812, the *King George* and *Robert Taylor* entered Hudson
Bay. An Arctic storm struck from nowhere with savage fury, tossing
the two ships about like corks for three days. But in one of those
bucking, creaking vessels, Christina McLean gave birth to a new
McLean, a daughter, and a sister for seven-year-old Donald and the
other children. The baby was named Mary. Finally the storm subsided, and the ships approached the icy waters off York Factory, the
HBC's depot on Hudson Bay. It took two weeks to get all the passengers and goods ashore. While the rest of the seventy-one settlers
rested for a few days in log cabins, the McLean family enjoyed the
comparative comfort of the fort and the hospitality of the Edinburgh
surgeon-turned-HBC-trader William Auld, superintendent of the Northern Department of Rupert's Land.

It was seven hundred miles south from York Factory to Red River;
the only special consideration for Christina McLean and her tiny baby
was the use of a canoe instead of one of the awkward and leaky bateaux
used by the others. They followed the Hayes and Hill rivers to the HBC
post of Oxford House, then to Lake Winnipeg and along its eastern
shore and up the Red River to the forks with the Assiniboine. On October 27, the colonists and twenty-one Spanish Merino sheep arrived at the
junction of the Red and Pembina rivers. Waiting for them was Miles
Macdonell, named governor of the colony by Selkirk, and most of the
thirty-nine settlers who had arrived with him a few weeks before. The
Pembina was closer to the plains on which the Métis hunted their buffalo, so food was easier to come by. They all spent the winter there, at a
settlement they named Fort Daer, before returning seventy miles to the
forks and Point Douglas, the site chosen for the main colony.

Selkirk couldn't possibly have picked a man more dedicated, earnest, determined and unsuited for the job than Miles Macdonell. He
was cursed with an unfailing instinct for alienating friends and pro-
voking enemies. If a situation called for a show of strength, he
hesitated; if it begged for tact, he went for the throat. The elements
weren't half as daunting as trying to work with Macdonell, yet Alex
and Christina McLean were among his closest friends. Alex was often
put in charge of Fort Douglas or Fort Daer when Macdonell was trav-

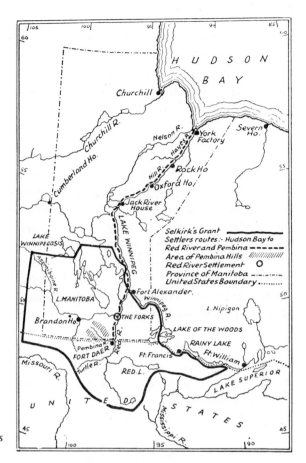

Map of Assiniboia
(HBCA, Provincial Archives
of Manitoba)

elling. Some tongue-waggers in the colony soon began theorizing that
Christina and Miles were a little too close. They said Christina
McLean was the effective leader of the colony, making policy under
the sheets with Macdonell. This may have been nothing more than
scurrilous gossip invented by the enemies of Macdonell and the
McLeans — of which a considerable number quickly became evident —
but the story was commonly believed around the colony.

The stubborn governor demonstrated his loyalty to the McLeans
in the summer of 1813, when he saved their reputations and possibly
their lives. Theft of any kind was a hanging offence, and the crotchety
William Auld decided the McLeans were guilty of exactly that. The
alleged crime: theft of one small, silver teaspoon from the Company at
York Factory. It was, claimed Auld after hearing only one side of the
story, an example of "ingratitude" and "infamy." However, out of respect for Selkirk, he was willing to forego prosecution if the McLeans
returned three other spoons missing from the set.

Macdonell took statements from Alex and Christina McLean, and
from their servant Ann MacDonald. Their explanation was that the

spoon had fallen out of their canteen the day after their arrival in Red River, and that they had asked around for the owner but hadn't found anyone who was missing a spoon. So Macdonell fired a letter back to Auld pointing out that the accuser, a malcontent named Kenneth McRae, had waited months before laying the charge, coincidentally after Macdonell fired him from supervision of the colony storehouse and replaced him with Alex McLean. And then, lacking the courage to lay the charge before Macdonell, McRae had waited until he was in York Factory and made the claim to Auld. The McLeans, said Macdonell, "appear to be condemned on vague evidence, reputation and character wantonly murdered, without that advantage which the laws grant to the vilest criminal, an opportunity of making a defence."

The whole thing was dropped and the records of it burned, but Alex and Christina McLean were left with such bitterness that they would very soon turn against even their benefactor Macdonell, and come very close to destroying the colony.

## [2]

FORT DOUGLAS, Red River Colony, Rupert's Land
Wednesday, June 19, 1816, after 6:00 PM

Looking through his spyglass, Governor Robert Semple could see a large group of horsemen — twenty-five, maybe thirty of them — riding slowly along the plains two miles north of the fort. A man in the watch-house had seen them first, and now the governor and a half dozen colonists were taking turns watching the movement of the group. It was clearly a band of Métis, Canadians, and some Indians, likely Sioux. What, exactly, they were doing, wasn't yet clear.

Between them and the fort, along the old wagon road of the original farms, the tents of the settlers were strung out. The farms were laid out narrow and deep, running up from the river, so that the settlers would be close together. The safety of those in the tents was Selkirk's immediate concern.

"They are making for the settlers," said one of his companions in the watch-house.

"We must go out and meet these people," Semple decided. "Let twenty men follow me."

Twenty-seven men immediately volunteered, and Semple could have gotten more, but he didn't want to provoke a fight, only to find out the intentions of the trespassers. One of those offering to go along was Alex McLean.

If Semple had known as much about the man leading the Métis and half-breeds as Alex McLean did, he might have been more concerned. Cuthbert Grant was young (twenty-three), well-educated, and ruthless, a man who straddled the joint interests opposing the colony: he was both a half-breed and a loyal servant of the North West Company, son of a fur-trader father and a Cree mother. The Nor'Westers had given him the florid title "Captain General of all the Half-breeds in the Country." Much of the time he lived in what the Bois Brules called the "New Nation" on Qu'Appelle River three hundred miles east of the Red, but he was showing up more and more frequently in the colony. Grant was absolutely dedicated to the cause of Métis nationhood, a perfect pawn in the Nor'Westers' avowal to destroy the Selkirk settlement.

Grant had an unwitting ally in Miles Macdonell, who watched his determined wards struggling through crop failures and food shortages, and decided there was something unjust about tons of Métis pemmican being shipped out under their noses to North West Company forts hundreds of miles away. So, on January 8, 1815, Macdonell had proclaimed that no pemmican could be removed from the area without his permission, confiscated North West Company pemmican supplies, then added insult to injury by ordering the Nor'Westers to vacate the region within six months. That was when the Nor'Westers vowed to exterminate the colony; that was the beginning of the Pemmican War.

For the McLeans, a happy event intervened. At midnight on the evening of February 6, 1815, Christina delivered another boy. The family now consisted of Miles, Hugh, Donald, John, Mary and Anna, though before the year was out Anna would be sent home.

If Macdonell had enjoyed the solid following of his crofters, he might have had some hope of success with the embargo, since they outnumbered the Nor'Westers and local Métis. But he was so unpopular that many settlers regarded the whole exercise as an inconvenience they could do without. One of the colony's three bulls was unmanageable and had to be slaughtered, another fell into the river and drowned. McLean's Merino sheep that were to be the basis of a thriving export wool industry were becoming extinct, ending up in the stomachs of local Indians and a growing population of dogs. And the crops were assailed season after season first by one malady, then another — now grubs, then rot, then more bugs. The life was hard enough in the crude log houses, seven hundred miles from York Factory and thousands of miles from home. Add to this the perceived mismanagement of Macdonell, and there were a lot of unhappy settlers. So, when Duncan Cameron of the Nor'Westers began offering them money to desert and resettle elsewhere, or go to Canada or return home, more than a few took him up on it.

Alex McLean was one of the first to whom Cameron offered his bribe, reinforced with threats. And Alex McLean, still seething over the insult of the silver spoons, did not immediately say no. The location for the colony was an interesting choice, since it was virtually next door to the North West Fort Gibraltar, so from the beginning there had been contact between the newcomers and the resident fur traders and Métis. In the beginning, it was not unfriendly. The McLeans, in fact, mixed socially with Cameron and other Nor'Westers, as well as with farmers from their own colony. Of the colonists, the McLeans were the favourites among the Nor'Westers. The going bribe offered by Cameron for desertion was two hundred acres of land, twelve months free provisions, and free passage. To Alex McLean, he added an offer of a thousand pounds sterling, three years' wages for his servants, and placement in "an independent situation."

These overtures did not escape the attention of Macdonell, who was quickly sinking into a permanently blue mood over the whole situation, and his friendship with the McLeans turned to distrust. He began to regret having helped them out of the silver-spoon embarrassment. "That family occasioned me a great deal of trouble. I thought them injured and endeavoured to support them, but there are so many collateral circumstances that I am a good deal staggered as to their conduct," he wrote in a gloomy letter to Selkirk. He resented Alex McLean's failure to stop the Nor'Westers from arresting the colony's sheriff, John Spencer, on charges of stealing pemmican, while Macdonell was away. The governor was becoming convinced that the McLeans were disloyal.

Had the principal settler defected with his family to the Nor'Westers, it could have proven a fatal blow, but Alex McLean did not defect. He listened to the offers of Duncan Cameron and the threats of Cuthbert Grant, but he didn't accept. When the threats started being carried out, Alex and Christina McLean, the silver-spoon bitterness set aside, returned solidly to Selkirk's fold.

It started with a little roughness. As McLean was packing a door along the road on his shoulder one day, Grant and another Nor'Wester, Dugald Cameron, and a few others surrounded him and shoved him around, talking about what could happen to a farmer's family in this dangerous land while the husband and father was away from the house. Raping women and murdering children was to become a standard threat. Instead of being intimidated, the enraged McLean drew a pistol. They let him go, but when Duncan Cameron sent him a contrite letter wondering why McLean had gotten so upset over the misplaced enthusiasm of a few patriotic and overly zealous Nor'Westers, McLean sent him one back calling him and his ilk "barbarians."

There was a lot of that sort of thing from then on. Grant and his Métis would parade around near the settlement looking mean, shouting, warwhooping and loudly singing battle songs. They killed the

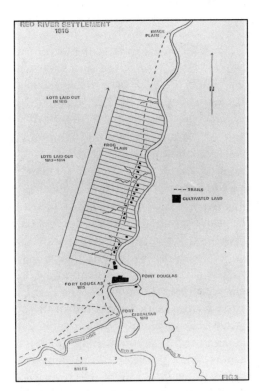

Map of Red River Settlement
(*HBCA, Provincial Archives of
Manitoba*)

colony's last remaining bull and butchered it for steak. Soon horses
and cattle started disappearing. So did colonists, packing up in the
night and going over to the Nor'Westers. Macdonell and the loyalists
didn't take it lying down. They made raids of their own, and pretty
soon there were kidnappings back and forth, which inevitably ended
in armed showdowns. McLean became highly active in these confron-
tations; Macdonell, once again putting his trust in his leading settler,
established a militia for protection and named him captain. In one of
the escapades, McLean and a couple of other colonists temporarily
captured Fort Gibraltar while most of its men were away, liberated a
couple of kegs of rum, and returned to Fort Douglas with a
Nor'Wester hostage. Grant and Cameron soon arrived at the fort with
a large group of men, armed to the teeth, knocked the defenders
around and liberated their compatriot, evening the score.

But escalation was inevitable. By June of 1815, the situation had
reached a point where taking a walk by yourself was like hanging a sign
around your neck that said, "Shoot me." Alex McLean was fired at on just
such an outing. The raids continued. Duncan Cameron threatened to blast
the farmhouses to kindling with a cannon stolen from the colony's own
storehouse with the help of a turncoat settler named George Campbell. He
then issued an ultimatum that Miles Macdonell be turned over to the
North West Company or the entire colony would be destroyed.

After sunset on June 10, a bunch of Métis were seen skulking around the general area of the fort. McLean took another settler and chased after them, discovered he was badly outnumbered and fired off a shot anyway. It was instantly returned and the two sides were blazing away at each other when a messenger from Macdonell arrived to say they should get the hell out of there before they were killed. McLean, his companion and the messenger retreated to the fort, musket balls tracing after them like sleet. A few of the men at the fort started firing at the pursuers, who kept coming, until the fort's three-pounder convinced them to call it a night. Compared to the next day, however, this encounter was little more than a friendly disagreement.

Hopes of getting a rest from the harassment were soon dashed. That Sunday morning Cuthbert Grant took William Shaw, Peter Pangman Bostonois, Seraphim Lamar and a few others, and rode from Gibraltar to a wood near Macdonell's house. From there they fired on James White, the surgeon, who was walking outside the house, but missed. They also missed John Bourke, another long-time colonist. Inside the house, the defenders who had spent the night there, including Alex McLean, began shooting back. McLean stood at a window beside John Warren, trying in vain to see the invisible enemy. As McLean raised his musket to squeeze off a shot, there was a roar and the barrel exploded, mangling his left hand and knocking him off his feet. A piece of the musket flew into Warren's head, splitting it open and cracking his skull. Pieces of his brain oozed out of the hole in his head. Miraculously, Warren would survive and even rally from time to time for more than a month. Alex McLean's hand was permanently maimed and useless. Three others were wounded.

After keeping up the fire for awhile, Grant and his cronies retired back to Gibraltar. The attack was the most dispiriting yet for the colonists, and there was general talk of fleeing to York Factory and taking the first ship home. One hundred and forty of them took an easier way out, accepting the NWC's offer of transportation to Montreal and free land elsewhere. Only thirteen families were now left in the colony. On the night of June 22, the McLeans received a visit in their house from the Nor'Westers. They were there to talk this time, not to shoot. The message: be gone by daybreak, unless they wanted to burn along with their house. Alex McLean, still in bed with his painfully mangled hand, knew they meant it. He and Christina and the children had no choice but to pack a few clothes and utensils, and retreat to the fort. Two days later, they watched from Miles Macdonell's house as their own log home went up in flames along with several others.

Seeing no other way to stop the violence, Miles Macdonell surrendered himself to the Nor'Westers.

OUTSIDE FORT DOUGLAS, Red River Colony, Rupert's Land,
Wednesday, June 19, 1816, shortly after 7:00 PM

Settlers who had been on their farms came hurrying along the road toward the fort, as Semple and his men walked single file toward Seven Oaks, the spot where Grant's horsemen were milling about. Those fleeing for Fort Douglas were unarmed, some carrying children. As they continued past Semple's men they shouted about "the half-breeds," saying they were coming with carts and a cannon and were taking prisoners. Some had already been detained by Cuthbert Grant and taken to Frog Plain, the place north of the settlement where the Métis often camped.

Another mile down the road, more fleeing settlers repeated the information. Semple then told John Bourke, the storekeeper, to return to the fort for a cannon and more men while the advance group waited. Alex McLean, as captain of the militia, was near the front of the line with Semple. There were two military men in the group: Captain John Rogers of the Royal Engineers and Lieutenant Ener Holte, formerly of the Swedish navy and now in command of the colony's gunboat. There was a moment of excitement when Holte accidentally discharged his musket, for which Semple gave him a severe tongue-lashing. Among the others were physician James White, Semple's private secretary Laurence Wilkinson, and HBC blacksmith Michael Heden. And, of course, Semple himself.

Semple, Miles Macdonell's replacement, named not only to be governor of the Red River colony but chief of the Hudson's Bay Company's northern and southern departments, was popular with most of the colonists, but not with Alex McLean. A native Bostonian, Semple was a pompous little man, though an effective leader and administrator.

After Macdonell's heroic but misdirected decision to turn himself over to the Nor'Westers the previous summer, he was taken in irons to Montreal by the same NWC party that accompanied the deserting colonists. Eventually he was released, but, in the meantime, the Nor'Westers ignored their own promise to stop the harassment of the colony. Leaving only four souls to try to protect the crops, the last few families finally gave up and boarded their canoes for Jack River House on the north end of Lake Winnipeg. At this point another staunch friend of the McLeans came into play. Colin Robertson, a former Nor'Wester working for the HBC, who had recruited colonists for Selkirk in the Highlands, happened to meet them at Jack River. Along with the McLeans, now bent on revenge against the Nor'Westers, he convinced the colonists to return to Red River, though several would rather have carried on to York Factory. "They should be erased from the Earth, at least out of this delightful country that they have so long kept in darkness," stated McLean about the Nor'Westers. Robertson and the intrepid colonists got back that fall in time to harvest some of the crops, but their houses were ashes, their belongings plundered by the Nor'Westers and Métis.

The McLeans prepared to rebuild as best they could, facing the fall and coming winter in a tent. For Christina McLean, the final straw was the desertion of the servants, but she resolved to carry on, penning a letter to Selkirk assuring him of that:

> *I'm too fond of revenge to think of ever leaving the country without having some satisfaction of those rascals that was [sic] the cause of my suffering so much, if it should be nothing more than sleeping on the cold ground every night for these three months past without a house to cover my head, a hundred things worse than that, that I cannot think of troubling your Lordship with. Indeed, I have every disadvantage, I have neither a maid or a man servant but I am determined to put up with everything for this year in hopes things will be better next year.*

Shortly thereafter Robert Semple arrived with more than eighty new settlers. The McLeans soon found they much preferred the impetuous and overbearing Miles Macdonell to the egocentric Semple. The dislike was mutual, for Semple blamed much of Macdonell's trouble on the McLeans, and so the suspicion of Christina's infidelity was recirculated among the newcomers by the governor himself. "If she had been my wife I certainly should have been jealous," Semple wrote Selkirk. He regarded Alex McLean as "a fickle unsteady man."

Alex McLean decided Semple had to go, and was supported by Colin Robertson, who remained a steadfast friend to the McLeans. That spring he made Christina McLean a gift of a fine white mare. On another occasion, siding with Alex in a dispute with Bourke, he threw Bourke out of the fort, but Semple overturned the ban. A petition was circulated among the colonists demanding Semple be replaced, but the governor was tipped off and put a stop to it. It was, therefore, out of duty and necessity, not out of affection for the new governor, that Alex McLean joined Semple to march upon the Bois Brules.

[4]

SEVEN OAKS, Red River Colony, Rupert's Land
Wednesday, June 19, 1816, sunset

Cuthbert Grant and his followers had given Fort Douglas a wide berth when they moved northward from the direction of the old Gibraltar site that day, riding at least a mile to the west, then cutting back through the farmland towards Seven Oaks, a grove of trees close to the Red River. There would later be much dispute over Grant's true intentions: he would say he planned no attack at all, but was simply running the blockade set up by Semple, who commanded the river from Fort Douglas and a schooner that prevented NWC pemmican bateaux from getting past without authorization.

In March Semple had taken back the initiative with a bold stroke against the Nor'Westers, over the objections of McLean and Robertson who thought it would only provoke more conflict. Robertson had managed to calm the Métis and there was a truce of sorts, but Semple was insistent. Reluctantly, Robertson took a band of men and seized Fort Gibraltar, arresting Duncan Cameron and expelling the rest. Semple decided to do more than simply take the fort away from the NWC; he dismantled it. For days, the river was crowded with canoes, bateaux, rafts and the schooner moving up and down between Gibraltar and Fort Douglas, as every stick of furniture, bag of grain, bottle of rum, and the very timbers themselves were scavenged from the NWC fort for use in rebuilding Fort Douglas. Even the stockades were removed and reassembled at the HBC fort. What couldn't be used was torched. For a change, the smoke rising into the air above Red River was from Nor'Wester property, not the colonists' or HBC's. When Robertson left, he took with him the much-despised Cameron, in shackles.

Cuthbert Grant was away when this happened. The destruction of Fort Gibraltar angered the Nor'Westers and Métis more than anything before, and they were thirsting for a fight.

Semple grew tired of waiting for Bourke to get back with the cannon and reinforcements. "Gentlemen," he said, "we had better go on." He may have regretted giving Robertson permission to leave Red River only a few days before, as the HBC man's courage and knowledge of the enemy would have been welcomed. Approaching Grant's men, Semple saw that what had looked at first to be two or three dozen riders had grown to as many as sixty or seventy. The Métis, like the Indians, wore war paint, "their faces painted in the most hideous manner." They were dressed in their traditional blue capotes and red sashes, and armed with pistols, muskets, spears, knives and hatchets.

He ordered his men to extend their line, and they began spacing themselves further apart.

Grant waved his own men forward at a gallop and the two forces came together, Semple and his men on foot, Grant and his on their pawing, snorting horses, the latter forming a half-moon, hemming Semple in against the river bank. Clearly, from a military or any other standpoint, Semple was in a bad situation. Colonist James Bruin suggested an attack, but Semple angrily rejected the idea. Grant sent François Firmin Boucher, a NWC clerk and the son of a Montreal tavern keeper, toward Semple to parley.

"What do you want?" Boucher asked.

"What do *you* want?"

"We want our fort," answered Boucher.

"Well, *go* to your fort," Semple shot back.

An angry Boucher replied, "You damned rascal, you have destroyed our fort. You have took down our fort!"

Semple, himself angered that a half-breed should call the governor of the colony a "damned rascal," yelled, "You scoundrel, do you dare to tell me so?"

With that, he grabbed the reins of Boucher's bridle, calling to his men to take him prisoner. It was a fatal choice of actions. Boucher slid off his horse on the opposite side of Semple, hit the ground and ran back to his own side.

Heden, the blacksmith, standing to the right of Semple, watched in horror as the Métis guns were raised against the colonists. *We were within about a gunshot of each other. There was nothing between us but a few willows and bush, everything was visible. As soon as Boucher slid off his horse a shot was fired and Mr. Holte fell.*

It was never proven for certain, but the first shot may have come from Grant himself. It killed the trigger-happy Ener Holte. A second shot hit Semple in the knee and he keeled over, yelling at his men to "Do what you can to take care of yourselves!" But the colonists, who had been spread out in their single-line formation, now clustered in confusion around the fallen governor. The Brules uttered a warwhoop and poured a deadly volley of musket balls into that cluster, and men fell screaming to the ground. A few were able to fire back at Grant's band, others hadn't even loaded their guns. James Bruin fell, and so did Henry Sinclair. Semple lay helpless, in pain, as the Métis and Indians now closed in with tomahawks, bows and arrows, and spears.

Alex McLean, wounded in the first volley, stood up and fired back, then waited to defend himself against the onrushing Brules. A second bullet knocked him back down.

John Rogers, the Royal Engineer, fell wounded but struggled to his feet. John Pritchard, a former Nor'Wester who had often tried to mediate between the two sides, shouted, "Rogers, for God's sake, give yourself up! Give yourself up!" Rogers ran forward, shouting in English and in broken French that he surrendered, begging for them to spare his life. Thomas McKay, a Bois Brules, pointed a gun at Rogers and shot him through the head. Another ran forward and plunged a knife into the dead man's body again and again.

Pritchard, meanwhile, began begging for his life. Seeing a French-Canadian he knew well among the attackers, he began shouting as loud and as fast as he could, "Lavigne, you are a Frenchman, you are a man, you are a Christian. For God's sake, save my life! For God's sake try and save it! I give myself up; I am your prisoner!" In that scene of carnage, a strange subplot was played out as McKay, shouting that Pritchard was "un petit crapaud" (a little toad), prepared to kill him. At the same time, Lavigne, jolted by the sight of his former friend begging for mercy, stood over him fending off the blows of the attackers, all the while yelling that Pritchard had been one of them, that he had helped them out, and Pritchard was likewise yelling and begging. *One Primeau wished to shoot me; he said I had formerly killed his brother. I begged him to recollect my former kindness to him at Qu'Appelle. At length they spared me, telling me I was a little dog, and had not long to live, and that he (Primeau) would find me when he came back.*

For the others, there was no mercy. John Bourke, bringing up the cannon on an ox-drawn cart, tried to get away when the shooting broke out, but he was badly wounded, though he survived. Heden managed to crawl away from the slaughter and came across a colonist, Daniel McKay, along the river bank. They crossed the river in a canoe and made their way back to the fort. A few others, like Michael Kilkenny and George Sutherland, also escaped, swimming the river, and Anthony McDonell was somehow spared, but the knives and spears and hatchets fell upon the rest not killed in the first volley. Semple was found by Grant cradling his head in an arm. "I am not mortally wounded, and if you could get me conveyed to the fort, I think I should live," Semple told him. Grant agreed and left a French-Canadian to guard him. But a man variously identified as an Indian or François Deschamp ignored the guard, yelled at Semple, "You dog, you have been the cause of all this, and shall not live!" and shot him dead.

Alex McLean, blood draining from his body, only a few paces from Semple, died there with him on the plain.

MOOSE FACTORY, Rupert's Land
Wednesday, March 12, 1817

*My Lord*

*I hope the unfortunate situation I am placed in will plead my excuse for addressing your Lordship in the destruction of the Colony of Red River. I have to lament the loss of a beloved husband who, endeavouring to defend us was most barbarously murdered, and I am now left with a family of six children, the oldest not more than eleven years of age and the youngest only eleven months, entirely dependent on the bounty of your Lordship in consequence of the ships not being able to return to England. I have been left here with five of my children, in a most distressing situation, and all the hope that is now left me, is that through your Lordship's Beneficence I may be enabled to bring up my young and helpless family so that they may become useful and respectable members of society which without your Lordship's assistance will be totally out of my power. I have received a bill from Mr. (Alexander) MacDonell on your Lordship for fifty pounds but in consequence of your Lordship's absence from England I am in doubt if it will be paid, and I leave it to your feeling what will be my situation when the ship arrives home, to be left at a great distance from my friends, destitute of the means of supporting myself and family. Trusting to your Goodness and Benevolence,*

*I am, My Lord*
*Your obedient Servant*
*C. McLean*

The cruelty of Cuthbert Grant's Bois Brules at the Seven Oaks Massacre was almost impossible for any person with the least compassion to comprehend. In the first volley of shots, only a quarter of the settlers were killed or wounded, and all the survivors could easily have been taken prisoner, but the Métis and Indians were not in a merciful mood. The dead and dying were jabbed repeatedly with spears, and sliced with big hunting knives, hacked at with hatchets, clubbed with rifle butts. Then they were stripped of clothing and valuables; some were disembowelled, some scalped. Colin Robertson wrote in his diary, "Joseph Lorain, after imbruing his hands in the barbarous murder of Mr. McLean, and took the clothes off the deceased and presented himself with his hands still reeking with blood to the widow, whom only a few hours before he deprived of a husband. . . ."

Of the twenty-eight men in Semple's party, twenty-one were killed and one wounded. Grant lost only one man and one was wounded.

Drawing of Seven Oaks Massacre by W. Jefferys (*HBCA, Provincial Archives of Manitoba, P-378*)

Back at Fort Douglas, all that the remaining colonists could do was watch in horror the one-sided battle two miles away. In less than fifteen minutes it was all over, and when word came back about the tragic result, Christina McLean and her children had to listen to the awful news that Alexander McLean was among the dead. Of those killed, only he and James White had wives and children, but others had brothers and sisters, mothers or fathers, and a collective, heart-breaking scream rent the air. John Pritchard witnessed the anguish. *On my arrival at the fort, what a scene of distress presented itself! The widows, children, and relations of the slain, in the horrors of despair, were lamenting the dead, and trembling for the safety of the survivors.*

In the morning the ghastliness of the massacre was revealed. To Alexander McDonell, left in charge of the fort by Semple, went the sad job of reclaiming the mutilated bodies. Some of the local Indians helped. Already putrefying from the heat, as many as possible were gathered up in carts and hauled to a mass grave near the fort. Only Robert Semple and Alexander McLean were afforded the dignity of quickly carpentered coffins. The Brules and Canadians made a game of harassing the burial detail and kept it from collecting all the bodies; some were left where they died, food for the wolves.

An ultimatum came from Grant: surrender the fort and leave Red River, or be killed. There was a short-lived determination to resist, but reality dictated otherwise. They were allowed two days to prepare to leave, almost two hundred of them, but most of their belongings were to be left behind. At noon on the twenty-second the survivors shoved off in their boats, a sad flotilla of despair paddling away for a second time from the place where they had intended to make a new beginning for themselves and their families. And if being forced from their farms after burying their dead wasn't enough, the next morning they were met by a NWC party of a hundred men led by partner Archibald Norman MacLeod, on their way to rendezvous with Grant. He ordered them ashore for a search, though Christina McLean's baggage was spared from this insult. After two days spent plundering the meagre belongings of the colonists, and declaring his disappointment that the fleeing colonists weren't accompanied by Colin Robertson, whom he would like to have tortured to death, MacLeod let them continue. Then the boat carrying Christina and her children got so leaky it almost sank, and the next day there was a thunder and lightning storm with wind so strong they had to pull into shore again.

They made Jack River, and later the fatherless McLean family was moved to Norwegian Post, and then Moose Factory to await a ship from England to take them home, but the ships didn't arrive. Weeks turned to months, and finally, more than a year after the slaughter at Seven Oaks, Christina and the children, and a new servant named Patrick Chappy provided by Selkirk, sailed for home on the *Prince of Wales*.

The war between the HBC and NWC, and against the Selkirk settlement by the Nor'Westers, continued, but yet another band of hardy settlers returned to Red River to try again, and the colony somehow survived and even, eventually, flourished. The courts in Montreal were kept very busy with lawsuits against and by Selkirk, and in trying charges against the men who had taken part in the massacre.

But in the end, nobody was punished for the murder of Alexander McLean, Robert Semple, or anyone else. By then, Christina McLean and her young family were home, no doubt wishing they had never seen Red River, and hoping never to hear of it again.

# Part 2

## THE COMPANY MAN

HAT CREEK, British Columbia
Tuesday, May 31, 1864

When word came about the massacre up in the Chilcotin, there wasn't any doubt what Donald McLean would do. He'd leave his pregnant wife, his many sons and daughters, his ranch and his restaurant, ride north and kill some Indians.

Writers would say later that Donald McLean liked killing Indians. The truth was he took no particular pleasure in it. There was a story that he'd already killed nineteen of them, but that was a considerable exaggeration. Only three killings are on record, and two of those were accidental. He shot up a couple of other people, but one was white and they both lived. If he hated Indians as much as they said, you wouldn't think he'd have married three of them. When he shot anyone it was out of necessity, except for one insane day in 1849 when he became the meanest man alive.

He wasn't evil, though some people would later say that about him, too. McLean, to the contrary, had a highly developed sense of duty and honour. He was tough, he was utterly without fear, and he was coldly efficient, but he wasn't cruel. He was, in those days when the West was still a wild, dangerous place, a perfect representative of the Hudson's Bay Company, whose aim, pure and simple, was to exploit a resource.

McLean was known among the Upper Country tribes as Kuschte te'Kukkpe — the Fierce Chief. The Chilcotins, whom he was about to go after, had another name for him: Samandlin, the meaning of which is unclear even to the Chilcotins. He well appreciated that the white men in this country owed not only their living but their lives to the natives. But in his mind, shaped by almost thirty years of experience with them, Indians were unintelligent. And they definitely weren't honourable, nor even productive. For centuries they'd lived on this land and done nothing with it. When white men came and showed them how to turn the great natural bounty of furs into handsome profit, they were still incapable of bettering themselves. If anything, they seemed to become lazier over the years, and many a time they starved and froze simply because they didn't bother to catch enough fish to see them through the bitter New Caledonia winters. They'd rather lie than tell the truth, they'd rather steal a horse than earn it. They had no sense of law, and often settled things by shooting each other or, worse, the whites they so greatly outnumbered. They were, at best, unreliable and, at worst, deceitful. That's what Donald McLean thought about Indians.

Donald McLean (*BCARS*)

Keeping them under control was tricky, particularly in the early days, for had they been capable of putting together any kind of confederacy they could probably have wiped out every Scot and Canadian between Fort Vancouver and Babine within a few days. People like Donald McLean, when he'd worked for the Company, had the job of keeping these untamable heathens trapping furs instead of stealing and murdering. Critics of HBC policy irked him no end, and he'd always felt they should spend a while in the country to find out what it was really like. "I wish the glib-tongued speakers and ready-penned writers against the Company were placed for a few years in the un-Christianed Indian country. They would, I suspect, change their sentiments. I know my own, and shall not be easily induced to change them."

And he never had. Of course, the glory days of the Company were ebbing now, and Donald McLean was no longer in charge of Fort Kamloops. He was instead a highly respected country gentleman at Hat Creek, where he and his six-foot wife Sophia lived in their home at the junction of the Hat and the Bonaparte River. Though every few years it swelled and over-ran its banks causing a lot of damage, the Bonaparte wasn't much of a river — if you took a good run at it you could just about skip right across to the other side in three or four strides. Mind you, Hat Creek was barely deserving of being called a creek, and might have been called something else if there was a word to describe something punier than a creek. And, if the truth be told, Donald McLean's house wasn't much of a house. It was a scant twelve by eighteen feet, with a ceiling barely high enough for a tall man like

McLean, much less a six-foot-tall Indian woman, to stand straight up. But it wasn't any different from the dozens of other little log cabins he'd lived in for all the years working for the Company in this difficult, unforgiving, Indian-infested country.

And while McLean was deep in debt, he'd built the place into something in less than four years. Across a fertile hay field from the cabin was McLean's Restaurant, also known as McLean's Station, or simply McLean's. By virtue of the fact the Cariboo Road ran right past its front door, and courtesy in large part of the Barnard's Express stage line, the restaurant did a good business. McLean and his sons had hauled logs down from the hills for the building. It included an eating room, where the Chinese cook presided, a washroom for male travellers, and a licensed bar room for the relaxation of passing cowboys, occasional businessmen, and miners on their way to the Barkerville gold fields. They could get a bunk for the night, too, before continuing on.

His years with the Company hadn't made Donald McLean a rich man, but God had blessed him with many children, so there was no lack of help to keep the ranch and restaurant going. His various sons and daughters lived in other cabins stretching along the creek. There were so many of them that Hat Creek was like a small village.

Donald Jr., now thirty years of age, was the oldest, born to Donald's first wife Ali, a Spokane Indian woman, only a year after he'd arrived in North America from Scotland and was sent to the formidable Snake River country. Elizabeth – dead now for seven years – was next, then Duncan. Twenty-year-old Alex was born in the Spokane. He was a tall, tough and assertive young man with a mind of his own, in many ways like his father. John, Donald's son by a Babine woman, was seventeen, strong, responsible, a veteran of many fur-brigade trips by the time he was in his teens.

Then there were the children from his marriage to Sophia, whom he'd wed legally at Fort Alexandria on the upper Fraser in 1854. Born there was their oldest son, Hector, now ten and a scrappy, stubborn, self-centred kid. Next was Allen, just nine years old, then Christina, eight. Annie was only three, Charlie two. Within a few weeks, there would be a new baby for Sophia to look after. There may have been other children, by other women, but essentially McLean was a devoted father, though a chauvinistic husband. Sophia was tall, pretty, and illiterate, but wonderfully strong, the new matriarch of Donald McLean's family. She raised the youngsters, worked on the farm, and still found the time and the will to grow vegetables and scarlet runners out behind the restaurant.

The Hat was a pleasant spot, with good land for the cattle and horses. The French-Canadian Nor'Westers, back before the merger with the Company, had called it Riviere aux Chapeaux, because of an Indian legend about a hat-shaped rock a fair distance upstream. This rock had two holes that young braves supposedly used as hand-holds —they placed their heads in a third —in summoning their spirits. Indians had some interesting ideas about religion. So when Donald was about ready to head north for Soda Creek, he told Sophia a story. If he wasn't back in seven weeks, he said, she was to go to the old Indian burial ground up in the hills west of the ranch. If a coyote was howling there, it would be lamenting his death. Sophia, being half Indian, liked to view the world in terms of signs and stories, so this story would no doubt satisfy her concerns about not knowing what was happening to her husband on his great expedition to kill her kin.

On this unseasonably hot spring day, Donald, his son Duncan, and his friend Oregon Jack mounted up and started north to put down one more Indian rebellion and to bring some killers to justice.

## [7]

### NANCOOTLEM, Chilcotin Plateau, British Columbia
### Tuesday, May 31, 1864

Four hundred miles from Hat Creek by wagon road and pack trail, Alex McDonald lay on a knoll near Nimpo Lake, trying to decide what to do next.

He, his friend Peter McDougall and their packers had been there two days with their horses and supplies, waiting for something to happen. There was talk of a massacre down on the coast at Bute Inlet. Thirteen men working on Alfred Waddington's wagon road had supposedly been killed by the same band of Chilcotins who were now hanging around somewhere out in the woods. But there was no sign of trouble. It was very confusing; McDonald was uncertain about what to do.

Nearby Nancootlem was a peaceful, pretty spot, like a rest after a long march which, in fact, it was. It was a stopping place on the crude Bentinck Arm trail from the sea, the first Indian village of any consequence after the tough climb up out of the Bella Coola Valley. A few miles apart on the gently undulating plain were Anahim and Nimpo lakes, the latter particularly pretty, with coves edged by evergreens and aspen or poplar. Nancootlem was Chief Anahim's village, picturesque with its lodges and totems carved in imitation of those of the Bella Coola. His people had constructed stockades in the area for protection.

McDonald was employed by Waddington, a Victoria entrepreneur, to carry supplies from New Aberdeen —or Bella Coola —on the coast up onto the Chilcotin Plateau to his own ranch at Puntzi Lake. From there he was to start building a trail south to meet up with the work party making its way up the Homathko River from Bute Inlet.

As scheduled, McDonald's party had left New Aberdeen May 17. It numbered eight men: McDonald; McDougall, a packer; Barney Johnson, an old Bentinck Arm pioneer; Clifford Higgins and John Grant, miners heading for the Cariboo; Charles Farquharson; Fred Harrison; and Malcolm McLeod. There was also a young Alexis Chilcotin named Tom, employed by McDonald as a helper, and McDougall's squaw Klymtedza.

Pack animals were not taken directly from Bella Coola. They were kept instead at Noocultz, the ranch and ferry operated by John Hamilton and his family about two dozen miles up the Bella Coola River from New Aberdeen. McDougall had a big string of pack animals he was taking through to Alexandria, and he and his two men had decided to join McDonald's party. McDonald and McDougall were old friends – McDougall had wintered with his horses at the Puntzi ranch run by McDonald and his partner William Manning. McDougall sold a large quantity of furs to Hamilton for cash, being unable to obtain the quantities of the various goods he'd wanted to take to the Cariboo to sell. Of the forty-two pack animals, only twenty-eight were loaded with goods, worth between $4,000 and $5,000.

The pack train had left Noocultz on May 23, travelling on the opposite side of the river, then up out of the deep valley and over the Great Slide, a huge fan of boulders and loose rock, then toward Nancootlem.

McDonald was in one way a strange choice to be building a trail for Waddington, even though the ranch he operated with Manning was at the junction of the Bute and Bentinck trails. McDonald was unimpressed with Waddington's route and publicly proclaimed the superiority of the Bentinck trail. McDonald knew both routes well. He had accompanied explorer William Downie on an earlier trip to Bute Inlet. And, in February and March of 1863, he had packed his gear on a toboggan and snow-shoed his way down the lakes and through the forests from Puntzi Lake to Bute. He had to agree that while Waddington was deluding himself about the Homathko, the upper plain through the Tatlayoko and Bluff Lake region was good trail-building country. The water travel wasn't as good as Waddington had thought, but the country was fertile and good for stock. McDonald, though, had spent a lot of time in the Bella Coola, trading or tending store for a merchant named Peter Baron, Hamilton's predecessor, and he liked that route better.

As the pack train travelled toward Nancootlem, it had broken again into two parties travelling a day apart. McDougall, Grant and Higgins arrived at Nancootlem on May 28. McDonald, McLeod, Johnson, Farquharson and Harrison joined them the next day.

But in Nancootlem, McDougall's fat Indian wife had heard some strange things from the local Indians. Klymtedza was a young, excitable woman the packer had bought from a Chilcotin family headed by her aging father, Chilhowhoaz. She'd adapted well to the ways of the whites, usually wearing white women's clothes, and working hard for McDougall. Unlike most, or at least many, Indian concubines or slaves of the whites, she was loyal to her master. She got very excited about what she heard from the locals, jabbering at times incoherently, repeating herself, now in her native tongue, now in the Chinook trade language or broken English.

Nancootlem, or Sitleece as it was also known, was her home village. She had visited her family and friends across the lake and learned of a plot against the whites. A nomadic war chief named Klatassine was in Anahim's village, talking of great victories over the whites who had threatened to bring smallpox back on the Indians. This Klatassine spoke of killing many in the Homathko, and of the execution of Manning at Puntzi. He gave away many gifts, and talked with small and large groups of Nancootlem men about the smallpox threat. If the whites were allowed to continue their invasion of Indian land, there would soon be no more Indians left to fight. The whites wanted to kill the Indians and take their land, and this time the dreaded smallpox would be fatal. The white tyhee, or chief, at Bute had said the disease would come in the next "warm," or year. For all those who joined Klatassine to help him wipe out the whites there would be many presents. He was urging Anahim's men to join his own and go down to Bentinck Arm to attack the whites there. When the pack train had arrived, Klymtedza was told, Klatassine exulted at the good fortune. He now had a visible enemy and plunder with which to tempt the Nancootlem warriors.

At first McDougall dismissed his squaw's story as extreme exaggeration. But she had insisted, adding to it from time to time new pieces of information about the alleged plot. McDonald figured they would be better off going forward. The trail back to the Arm was just too tough to travel in a hurry, with all those loaded animals. But Klymtedza was insistent that they leave everything and run. McDougall reasoned that if McDonald's partner were dead as she claimed, they'd be heading into a trap anyway.

The white men were reminded that the brother of one of their party had been killed two years before by Chilcotin Indians near Puntzi Lake. Bob McLeod, besides being Malcolm McLeod's brother, was also Alex McDonald's cousin. He had been leading a pack train to Alexandria when ambushed.

Discretion being the better part of valour, McDonald and McDougall moved their camp to the knoll. The small hill, lightly wooded with poplars, commanded a view in all directions. At the bottom of one side was a large pool, edged with rushes and lilies, and teeming with minnows. Past the hill it drained in a trickle toward Nimpo Lake. The eight white men dug out a protective earthwork twenty feet square at the top of the knoll. By digging down and piling the dirt and a few rocks around themselves in banks, they soon had a secure post from which to stave off any attacks. The horses and pack mules were hobbled nearby.

This situation relieved Klymtedza's fears considerably. With plentiful provisions and a good water supply only a few dozen yards away, they could stay there many weeks. But it was uncomfortable and tedious in the earthworks, and these weren't men who could sit around in cramped quarters doing nothing for long.

Klatassine's plan was apparently to hide in the woods near a broken bridge a few miles further on towards Puntzi Lake. The bridge could be rigged to entangle the horses, and in the confusion the Indians could attack and kill the white men quickly. When two of the pack animals went missing, Tom, McDonald's Indian helper, was sent out alone to look for them. He never returned.

After two days of this uncertainty, the packers and miners had had enough. They wanted to move out, in one direction or the other. McDonald wanted to push on toward Puntzi Lake. But McDougall, "Mac" to the Indians, sided with his klootchman. Klymtedza knew there was no chance of getting through the Chilcotin to Alexandria. If the men insisted on moving, they must withdraw towards Bella Coola, and they must leave their supplies and pack animals behind and ride quickly.

McDougall, though, wasn't about to leave several thousand dollars worth of goods, in addition to valuable pack animals, to the Indians. So, the animals were loaded up and the long pack train started its noisy and obvious journey back toward Bella Coola, McDougall and Higgins leading the way. With McDougall was Klymtedza, who declined the choice of leaving her master to return to her family, where she would have been welcome and safe. Riding behind them was McDonald. Grant was next, with the other men strung out along the trail.

They hadn't gone more than two miles towards Anahim Lake before the wary Klymtedza became frightened. There were Indians running through the woods, she told McDougall. But neither McDougall, Higgins, nor McDonald could see anything through the dense growth of stunted spruce that covered the area like giant strands of grass.

They must leave everything and get to the woods, Klymtedza urged. They must now leave even the horses, for here they would be useless. But once again her warnings were ignored, and the pack train continued on for another three miles.

Then, there was a rapid volley of shots from the woods.

"My God, I'm shot!" McDougall screamed, clutching his chest as he fell. Higgins also fell, shot through the chest. As Klymtedza ran to McDougall she, too, was cut down.

McDonald's horse collapsed under him though he himself was unwounded. Grabbing the reins of a loose animal, he mounted again.

Grant, on foot behind McDonald, shouted at him to run.

"I'll give them all I have, first," McDonald answered, blasting into the midst of several Indians with his double-barrelled shotgun.

## [8]

### THE CARIBOO ROAD, south of Clinton, British Columbia
### Friday, June 3, 1864

Donald McLean's plan was to raise at least two dozen volunteers on his way to meet Richfield gold commissioner William George Cox at Soda Creek. For the handful who had settled around him between Cache Creek and the Bonaparte — Clement and Henry Cornwall at Ashcroft Manor, the colourful William Donaldson at Scotty's Creek just to the north of McLean's, the McDonalds, even Neil McArthur — abandoning their farms this time of year to risk their lives chasing murderous Indians was out of the question. Only to men like Donald McLean and Oregon Jack Dowling was it such a question of duty that they would put everything else on hold. Cox would have an easier time recruiting broke miners and camp followers from Lightning Creek.

McLean not only had a lot of experience with Indians, he knew a lot about Chilcotins in particular. He'd lived with them in the 1840s and 1850s, at Fort Chilcotin and at Fluz Kuz. That whole time had been an uneasy peace, so uneasy that Donald McLean's career, not to mention his life, might have been cut short at any moment. That experience, and the reputation he had gained throughout his years with the HBC in Columbia and New Caledonia, was the reason he was heading up this expedition.

Officially, he would be second in command when he and his men joined up with Cox at Soda Creek. Cox was in charge because he happened to work for the government, and the government wanted one of its own men in charge. McLean had known Cox for at least five years, had hosted him in his home in Fort Kamloops. Cox wasn't much suited for the job at hand. He disliked taking orders, knew little about Indians, and nothing about tracking. If there was a bottle of rum across the table, Cox could find it, but there was no way he'd find his way across the Chilcotin Plateau. Maybe the government should have put a case of rum at Puntzi Lake and let Cox's nose lead them to it, but instead the governor had ordered Cox to take McLean with him.

So it was that McLean was riding north along the Cariboo Road to show Cox how to find Indians. From Hat Creek, the road wound its way among the grassy hillsides some two dozen miles to the Junction, or Clinton. It was called the Junction because at that point the road from Yale intersected the road from Lillooet. It was becoming a busy little place by virtue of this hub location, with hotels, a blacksmith shop, stores and even a library.

But there were few settlements along the way, a fact that had given rise to a whole new form of enterprise in the colony – the wayside house. With the stampede north getting thicker now that the road was finished most of the way, people needed places to rest and drink. And the packers and freighters needed to feed and water their horses. So every five or ten miles a stopping house appeared. McLean's Restaurant was one of the first, but many others had since been thrown up. Most were simple log buildings like his own. Some offered good, hearty food and comfortable lodging; others terrible meals and a floor for a bed with a flea-infested blanket for warmth, but all were busy. Twelve miles north of the Junction was the 59 Mile House, so named because it was that distance from Lillooet, the original starting point for the road. Then, there was the Chasm, a huge wedge missing from the earth. As with many natural phenomena, the Indians had an answer for that one too. An ancient warrior fell in love with a woman from a northern tribe but when he fled south with her they were chased by her father and brothers. Calling upon his god for assistance, the determined lover was rewarded with a cataclysmic opening of the Chasm, which stopped the pursuers in their tracks.

The procession continued on its way to the Seventy, or 70 Mile House, stopping place, built two years before by a pair of wagon-road contractors. After a rest, it was on to Loch Lomond near the Seventy-Four, and then the Eighty-Three post. Ambling along on an eighteen-foot-wide road, eating big meals and spending nights in the relative comfort of roadhouses was something McLean would have had trouble imagining only a few years ago. He was used to struggling through treacherous mountain passes on narrow trails at the head of a fur brigade. Stretching out behind him could be as many as two hundred or even four hundred horses loaded down with furs for Fort Vancouver or Fort Langley, interspersed with forty or fifty packers. Behind the brigade, various hangers-on and family members followed.

On such trips, the scant comfort of the tiny, crude cabins that passed for home in the Company trading posts undoubtedly seemed pleasurable by comparison. Out on the brigade trail, the only shelter was a tent, the only warmth a campfire. Horses and men could get lost and starve. It wasn't unusual to lose two or three dozen horses, and sometimes one or two men on those trails. On one such trip, on the brigade trail between Tulameen and Fort Hope in October 1858, he'd lost almost seventy horses.

The Cariboo Road likely made McLean feel like a tourist in his own country. When he first joined the Company, he could not possibly have imagined the deprivation he would face, a life so different than he would have had on the rugged, wind-swept island of Mull in Scotland where he was born. There were a few short years as a child in the Red River colony, where he might have grown up and become a farmer like his father. But then came that dreadful, unimaginable day in June 1816, when fifteen minutes of horror destroyed lives and unalterably changed others. And there was the confusion that followed for the children, and their mother's tears as she sat in a tent not knowing what would become of her and what was left of her family. Though his mother took them home and established a new start for them, and memories of Red River faded for a growing boy, there remained in Donald McLean's heart a wish, maybe more of a need, to some day return to that place of hardship that had destroyed his father.

The idea incubated there until he reached his twenties, through the time he sailed the seas on a man-of-war, toughening his mind and body. When his mother Christina married again and moved to Lancashire, his life was set on quite a different path from what he might have expected. It was there in Preston, his mother remarried, his sister Anna now also wed, his youth already fading, that he decided to join the Hudson's Bay Company and sail to North America. Enclosing a letter of recommendation from Colin Robertson, his mother and father's old ally during the Red River days, Donald wrote the "Governor and Committee of the Company" in London applying for a position. In due course he was offered employment. He would be taken on as an apprentice clerk on the northwest coast of America "either afloat or on shore." A three-year contract would pay him twenty pounds the first year, twenty-five pounds the second and thirty pounds the third. Finally, almost four months after his application, he was informed that the three-masted barque *Nereide* would sail April 20, 1833, and that he could join her at his convenience.

McLean went off to London where he signed a contract three days before the *Nereide* was due to sail. With his signature, he promised to "faithfully serve the said Company as their hired servant in the capacity of Apprentice and devote the whole of his time and labour in their service and for their sole benefit, and that he will do his duty as such and perform all such work and service by day or by night for the said Company as he shall be required to do, and obey all orders which he shall receive from the Governors of the Company in North America . . . with courage and fidelity."

Among the list of twenty-three men on board the *Nereide* when she sailed out of London May 3, almost two weeks late, were eleven able seamen, a cook, a steward, a carpenter, officers, and "Dd. McLean, Passenger for Fort Vancouver, Apprentice." But his trip into the unknown world of British North America, where the only law was the Company, the only "civilization" a collection of isolated posts hundreds of miles apart, was not destined to go smoothly. The *Nereide*, acquired by the Company that same year, proved to be a leaky little tub, well-suited to her name, seemingly more inclined to sink into the sea than to skim the surface. Her teak hull, pretty as it might have been, simply couldn't keep out the water. Captain Joseph M. Langtry's logs became a monotonous litany of repairs – " . . . leaking because nails not properly driven . . . caulkers busy caulking . . . crew busy pumping ship." Langtry put in for repairs at Plymouth on the English Channel, Lisbon and again at Spithead. The weather was generally favourable with occasional squalls. Considering the quality of the vessel the trip around Cape Horn was one of the more successful parts of the journey. For the crew, there was back-breaking work day after day. For the lone passenger, there was interminable boredom, broken only by a morning walk around the deck, occasionally a sighting of a Danish, Dutch or American vessel, or perhaps time spent with books while enjoying a pipe smoke. Month after month, the *Nereide* wallowed unsteadily toward her destination, soaking up brine all the way. Now trouble of another sort descended on the hapless ship and its captain. At Valparaiso a few of the crew got in trouble on shore and were thrown in jail. Langtry had to make a personal representation to the governor to get them out. They were released only on condition that they not come ashore again. But the very next day, they tried to leave the ship again and when the duty officer stopped them, one jumped overboard and tried to swim for it while the rest tried to steal the cutter. They failed, but Langtry reluctantly resisted sending them back to England to hang for robbery and mutiny; to do so would have left him unable to sail the ship. And so, Christmas Day was spent putting as much distance between Valparaiso and the *Nereide* as possible.

But it was only two weeks' sail to the Sandwich Islands (now the Hawaiian Islands) to take on fresh supplies, giving McLean and his fellow travellers another welcome break from the endless months at sea. Suddenly, there was Diamond Head and the village of Honoruru, with its palm trees, mission house, and brown-skinned Kanakas. And then, after enjoying the delights of that exotic place, there followed the final leg to the west coast of North America.

It was in April of 1834, almost a year after the *Nereide* left London, when the first sighting came. Langtry took his bearings off Cape Disappointment and steered toward the mouth of the Columbia River.

At first a mere haze in the distance, breakers and shoreline gradually becoming clearer, the land beyond taking shape and changing colour from purple to blue to green and brown, a spectacular collage of forest and hills and mountains, all the more impressive for its apparent desolation. After anchoring overnight in Baker's Bay, where some dispatches arrived by boat from Fort George for McLean, Langtry steered the barque into the vicious rip tide at the mouth of the Columbia, past Fort George and up into the swollen neck of the great Columbia River. Here the water was smooth and inviting as they proceeded upstream past strange collections of huts said to be the dwellings of the local natives. Occasionally, there was an eagle overhead, and then a canoe gliding past near the shore. All that day, and the next, and into the next, the *Nereide* made her way up the Columbia toward her ultimate goal, Fort Vancouver, the centre of operations for the Company in the wild Columbia fur department. When they arrived off Fort Vancouver, the brig *Dryad* welcomed them with a salute from her gun, and Langtry returned the greeting with a shot from the *Nereide*.

This was not London, nor even Tobermory, McLean's birthplace. It was a small collection of log cabins surrounded by a stockade of fir pickets. At two of the corners were log bastions. Outside were a few huts, boat sheds and barns; inside the pales, a storehouse, various officers' and servants' cabins, a trading shop or "Indian hall," and various other buildings, and in the centre, a rather large square or courtyard. And all around, as far as the eye could see, wilderness.

This was the first sight for Donald McLean of western North America. John Maclean, another native of Mull, wrote of the prospects for those who contracted themselves to the Company: "They bid adieu to all that civilized man most values on earth. They bid adieu to their families and friends, probably forever, for if they remain long enough to attain the promotion that allows them the privilege of revisiting their native land (twenty or twenty-five years), what changes does not this life exhibit in a much shorter time? They bid adieu to all the comforts and conveniences of civilization to vegetate at some solitary post, hundreds of miles perhaps from any other human habitation, save the wigwam of the savage, without any society other than that of their own thoughts or of the two or three humble persons who share their exile. They bid adieu to all refinement and cultivation, not infrequently becoming semi-barbarians, so altered in habits and sentiments that they not only become attached to savage life, but lose all relish for any other."

Such was the life that faced Donald McLean as he stepped off the *Nereide* on April 23, 1834. Such was the life he would endure, and learn to tolerate and even relish, during the rest of his days.

NEW WESTMINSTER, Colony of British Columbia
Saturday, June 4, 1864

We learn that the British Columbia expedition to punish the
Chilcotin murderers will be under the guidance of Mr. McLean of
the Bonaparte Valley. Mr. McLean is married to a Chilcotin [sic]
woman and both he and his sons are thoroughly acquainted with
that region and with the nature and habits of the tribe. He is well-
known as a man of great energy and determination and is probably
the most suitable man for such a charge in the two colonies.
— The *Daily British Colonist*, Victoria, V.I.

Governor Frederick Seymour, as of three weeks ago the Queen's supreme representative in the mainland colony of British Columbia,
formerly the Hudson's Bay Company district of New Caledonia, was
not happy this particular day.

Seymour, a tall, sincere man who drank too much, had received
from Vancouver Island governor Arthur Edward Kennedy an offer of
assistance in putting down the Chilcotin Indian rebellion. Kennedy
wasn't Seymour's favourite person right now. When news of the massacre had arrived in Victoria some weeks ago, Kennedy hadn't
bothered to send immediate word to Seymour, instead waiting two
days until a regular mail packet steamed its way across the strait from
Victoria. Who could guess what importance a two-day delay might
have played, or how many lives it might have cost? Now, Kennedy
had forwarded an offer of a hundred armed men to help Seymour go
after the murderers. A public meeting in the Vancouver Island capital
— duly reported in the *Daily British Colonist* — urged that Donald
McLean lead an expedition against the Chilcotin Indians, and that
request had been forwarded to Kennedy. Seymour had already appointed McLean as second in command of the Cariboo expedition on
his own, but he now made it clear what Kennedy could do with his
offer of volunteers.

*I had the honour to receive late last night your letter of second*
*instant, forwarding a copy of certain resolutions adopted at a public*
*meeting held in Victoria to consider the state of affairs growing out of*
*the late massacre on the Bute Inlet Trail. May I request that your*
*Excellency will have the goodness to convene in any manner to the*
*people of Vancouver Island my thanks for the resolutions passed at*
*the meeting and the consequent enrolment of volunteers to serve if*
*called upon against the Chilcotin Indians in this colony.*

*There is nothing unfriendly or disrespectful to the people of Victoria in my declining to avail myself immediately of their offer of assistance. I have already pressing upon me for employment in support of the law, the New Westminster Rifle Volunteer Company and the Hyack Fire Brigade, two bodies I believe of admirable efficiency.*

*On the much delayed receipt by me of the intelligence of the melancholy affair at Bute Inlet I at once placed myself in communication with my predecessor as to the measures which should be adopted. His Indian experience and reputation for energy pointed Sir James Douglas out to me as my best counsellor. He told me that a party should be at once sent in the gunboat to the Inlet to pick up survivors and to give information of the Indians' movements. Then a party should be organized to consist of about thirty men, well mounted, equipped and provided with ammunition under a proper leader to go round to Alexandria and that rewards for each man concerned in the murder should be offered, say one hundred dollars to two hundred dollars. He thought the catching of them would be certain but a matter of time – three months or so.*

*In every respect my predecessor's suggestions have been exceeded by my actions and additional steps, equalling at least in vigour any yet taken.*

*We are not at war with the Indians and the energy of the volunteers restrained by oaths as special constables. We apprehend no serious resistance from the small band of assassins.*

> *I have the honour to be your obedient servant.*
> *Frederick Seymour*

By now, details of the massacre were known in some detail by almost everyone in both colonies. The story was not pretty. Waddington, regarded in New Westminster as a shameless opportunist, had sent a work party up to Bute Inlet on the British Columbia coast to work on his toll road, which was to follow a horrendously difficult route up the fiord and onto the Chilcotin plateau. By charging gold diggers to travel his road through Chilcotin Indian territory to Alexandria, where they could then take existing roads and trails to the Barkerville gold fields, Waddington expected to profit by more than $12,000 a year. That scheme was shattered now, to the great concern of its Victoria investors, and to the considerable relief of the New Westminster populace, ever wary of competition from the Island. But no one in either colony would have chosen this particular means to the end.

Thirteen men, members of Waddington's party struggling to blast a road through the formidable obstacle of the Bute, were dead. The killers were a band of Chilcotin Indians led by a war chief named Klatassine, apparently well-known in the Cariboo-Chilcotin as a savage of considerable courage, ferocity and ruthlessness. The events leading up to the

Governor Frederick Seymour
*(BCARS, 23027)*

slaughter, as pieced together by various informants and survivors, had begun in mid-March when Waddington's crew of twenty workmen — mostly ex-sappers from the Royal Engineers — headed north from Victoria to begin work for the season. For many of them it was a welcome and necessary change from a winter of wasting their money on the bars, brothels and gambling houses of Victoria.

When they arrived at the inlet, site of the planned Waddington townsite, they found a camp of Homathko, Klayoos and Euclataw Indians, along with some Chilcotins. The Chilcotins were in poor condition, having long ago run short of food. An English artist named Frederick Whymper, along for the trip, soon found himself in agreement with the unsympathetic attitude of the whites toward the natives. "The Chilcoaten Indians are a dirty, lazy set, and although a few Homathco Indians raise good potatoes at the head of the Inlet, the former prefer half starving in winter to exerting themselves. These people appeared to be very bare of provisions, and disputed with their wretched cayota dogs anything that we threw out of our camp, in the shape of bones, bacon-rind, or tea leaves, and similar luxuries."

Theft of provisions by the Indians was a constant problem for the road crew, but William Brewster, the foreman, got his men organized and headed up the inlet to start work. As work progressed, Indians would have to be hired to pack food and equipment from a ferry crossing to the campsite located nine miles further up in a tough spot called the Canyon. Before taking on some Chilcotins who had followed them up from the townsite, Brewster demanded they return twenty-five sacks of stolen flour. When the Indians told him it was scant payment for entering Chilcotin territory with his road, an angry Brewster threatened to bring smallpox upon them. It wasn't a threat the Chilcotins took lightly: two years before, the white man William Manning at Puntzi Lake had made a similar threat to get them off the land, and that was followed by an epidemic that killed or scarred thousands.

When Brewster had cooled down, he hired the men for packing. While little else about the Chilcotins impressed the whites, their ability for packing did. They fixed a hundred pounds and more to straps that came over their foreheads and hauled goods all day long in this way. But the Chilcotins didn't forget the threat.

Down at the townsite, a new Chilcotin Indian appeared. Like most of the Chilcotins now in the valley, this man, Klatassine, had not been seen by Brewster's workmen before this year. He was a respected and feared Chilcotin war chief, and a near relative of the Nancootlem chief Anahim. "His was a striking face, the great underjaw betokened strong power of will," wrote Reverend R.C.L. Brown, who had seen Klatassine at Alexandria. "The eyes, which were not black like most Indians but of a very dark blue, full of a strange, what might be a dangerous, light, were keen and searching." Probably in his late thirties, he was tall with a big nose and dark brown hair. Unlike many Chilcotin men, he wore no moustache.

Among the Chilcotins, there were certain men who gained power, not through heredity or skill in providing for the band or family, but through bravery in battle. These men were not necessarily well-liked but they were accepted as tyhees, "big men" or chiefs. Since they preferred fighting to fishing, hunting or gathering, they were often poor. But when it came time to do battle with an enemy, it was the war chief who took charge, and everyone including the tribal chieftain became subordinate. With only two or three, or perhaps a dozen warriors, he would seek out the enemy.

Klatassine was one of these men. He had participated in many fights with Carriers, Homathkos and Shuswaps. At the Waddington townsite, Klatassine received the frightening information about Brewster's threat to bring smallpox. He was extremely upset at hearing this, and decided to go up the Homathko so he could consult with his friend, a Chilcotin chief named Tellot. So he headed up the trail with his son Piell, an Indian named Cushen, another the whites knew simply as Scarface for obvious reasons, his young pregnant wife Toowaewoot, and two daughters by another wife. On their way up to Brewster's work camp, they crossed the river in the ferry, tended by a man named Tim Smith, a rough individual who had gotten into several arguments with the Indians. Klatassine, apparently, asked for blankets and food for himself and his family. Smith, with more guts than

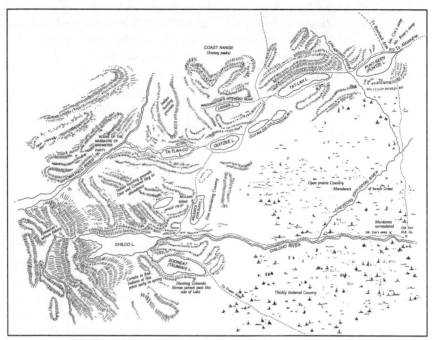

Map of Chilcotin War area. Based on map of "Waddington's Murders" *(BCARS)*

brains, and holding to Brewster's policy, arrogantly refused. There was a scuffle over the goods in question, but Smith retained possession. Klatassine seethed over the rebuke. Chessus and Yahooslas, two Indians who had joined Klatassine's family at the ferry, urged action. Klatassine shot Smith through the head and dumped his body in the river.

The next day, Klatassine and his party continued on to the upper camp and, by evening, his oratory on the white man's smallpox had convinced the entire Chilcotin camp that all the whites must die. They were building a trail that had now entered Chilcotin territory, and before long would go right through it. The whites had no right to be on Chilcotin land; they had offered no compensation for it. The whites would travel the trail, stealing land, hunting the game and taking their fish, bringing madness to Chilcotin men with their whiskey, and the smallpox to all. The whites must be stopped now.

That evening there was the usual intermingling between the white workmen and the Chilcotin employees. A few jokes were shared in their limited ability to communicate with each other, and the Indians appeared to have quite a party, singing and dancing, going in their camp. They wore war paint, but though it made some of the whites nervous there was nothing else suspicious. To the accompaniment of a round single-headed drum, each singer or dancer had his turn to recount famous battles. The music was a volatile lacing of rhythm and scale, the dancing light and graceful. It was a prelude to the planned attack. The Chilcotins always attacked an enemy at dawn, attempting to surprise and kill him quickly, then mutilating the corpses and celebrating on the plunder. Sometimes they scalped their victims and hung body parts from trees. The attack on the road company's camp would be vicious. Some of the Chilcotins quietly recited Christian prayers. Near this same spot twenty years before, a Chilcotin war party had annihilated a band of nineteen Homathkos.

Daylight was just beginning to break over the Homathko Valley on April 30 as cook Charles Buttle dressed and went out to ready the fire for the work party's morning meal. The ex-miner and Boundary Commission sapper must have things brewing by the time the men awoke. Except for the prattle of the river it was a quiet morning. The dancing and singing at the encampment of the Indians (or "Siwashes" as the whites called them) had ceased a couple of hours ago. The only sound in camp was the knocking together of wood sticks and the dull clang of pots and pans as Buttle stooped beside the fire. A black terrier kept by the work party wandered up and sniffed around. Intent on his work, the cook was unaware of any movement in the surrounding bush; the explosion of animal-like gasping whoops must have chilled him. Uncomprehending, Buttle had only started to turn and rise when two bullets caught him in the back, killing him instantly.

Klatassine sprung in among the tents with his dozen warriors while the squaws and children came up to the edge of the camp to watch. Simultaneously the Chilcotins headed for the tents of the workmen. The attack took only a few terrifying minutes. Musket balls and knives ripped into the tents of the sleeping men. Scant seconds after the attack began, Klatassine's men employed their most deadly tactic — the supporting ropes of each tent were cut and the canvas flopped down on top of those still inside. Wherever there was movement, the knives, hatchets and musket butts fell.

But there was more to do. Brewster and his "axe men" were camped further up river where they were blazing a trail. Cushen gathered up five of the other men and set out to look for the foreman. They left behind them a disorganized scene of butchery. The bodies of the dead roadworkers were being stripped and quartered; the procedure remained as it had through generations of battle between the Chilcotins and enemy Coastal or neighbouring Interior tribes.

Two miles up the trail over treacherous terrain, the camp of Brewster had remained innocently out of earshot or any suspicion of something amiss. Two of his men were shot dead; a third, wounded, jumped into the river and drowned. Brewster was shot in the chest, smashed in the head with his own axe, his penis was cut off and jammed in his mouth, his heart cut out and eaten by the attackers to steal his strength.

Three survivors from the main camp somehow made their way back down to the inlet and safety. When word reached Victoria, there was predictable alarm coupled with outrage.

The *Colonist* called it "the most startling thing of the kind" ever to take place in either colony.

> There is something almost fiendish in the manner in which this treacherous massacre was perpetrated. . . . Let justice follow inevitably on the footsteps of Indian crime, justice uninfluenced on the one hand by a morbid sentimentality, on the other by a reckless and brutal indifference to savage life and we shall not likely have again to recount so heart-rending a story as we present this day to our readers.

The mood of the Vancouver Island colonists, in the wake of the news, was hardly one of intelligent reflection on the causes of the massacre. Simple plunder was assumed to be the principal reason. But over in New Westminster, Seymour, in whose jurisdiction the killings had occurred, had the unenviable job of somehow dealing British justice to a band of Chilcotin Indians who apparently believed themselves embarked on a holy mission to save their people from extermination. After consulting with Douglas, Seymour came up with his two-pronged expedition. Volunteers were back from the Bute where they had recovered the bodies and picked up the remaining settlers. Now he would press ahead with plans to take a force to North Bentinck Arm. The crotchety old Admiral John Kingcome of the Royal Navy came through with approval to use one of the big warships stationed at Esquimalt for the expedition. But until the colony's superintendent of police, Chartres Brew, got a new force picked and supplied, the main thrust would be from the Cariboo.

# [10]

## THE CARIBOO ROAD, south of Soda Creek, British Columbia, Sunday, June 5, 1864

McLean and Cox were supposed to meet up at Soda Creek, which was as far north as the Cariboo wagon road extended. Eventually the road was to continue up to Alexandria and on to Quesnellemouth, then east all the way to Barkerville, but for now the fastest connection between Soda Creek and Alexandria was by the Quesnel River steamer *Enterprise*. Cox would take whatever Barkerville volunteers he could find along the pack trail to Alexandria, recruit as many as he could there, and bring them down to Soda Creek on the boat. With the two parties joined, Cox and McLean would travel the well-established trail west onto the Chilcotin plateau. Once there, it would be McLean's job to find the Indians responsible for the massacre. To do so, he would have to rely on the co-operation of friendly Chilcotins, and that's where his knowledge of their language, customs and haunts would be indispensable to the inexperienced Cox. Otherwise, looking for a couple of dozen bush-smart Indians in thousands of square miles of densely forested plateau would be tougher than finding a flea on a dog.

To understand Donald McLean's attitude toward Indians, it helps to know something more about the Hudson's Bay Company's attitude. By the time McLean reached Fort Vancouver in the spring of 1834, the Company had been doing a very profitable business in North America for 164 years. In that time, the "Company of Adventurers of England Trading into Hudson's Bay" had extended its domain from one side of the continent to the other, from the Russian territories south to Spanish California. It was supreme ruler of Rupert's Land and the vast region stretching to the Pacific. And it was there for one purpose: to make money for its shareholders. The Company's objective wasn't to colonize, nor to educate or even convert or otherwise improve the lives of the natives the Company found there. It was to trade with them for the furs of fox, marten, lynx, otter and, above all, beaver, to be sent home to England to grace the shoulders and heads of stylish ladies and gentlemen. Whenever the Company explored new territory, it looked first at the prospects for setting up trade with the Indians. A century and a half after King Charles II had granted an exclusive charter to his "Deare and entirely Beloved Cousin Prince Rupert" and his seventeen partners for trade and commerce in America, the Company maintained a strict, formal business relationship with the natives.

The natives, for their part, could be either friendly and co-operative or openly rebellious, even murderous. The Company's general strategy was to rule with an iron fist and encourage dependence on the HBC. The Company was an understanding but unforgiving parent, the natives were wayward children. The Baymen had little respect or fondness for them. Being in the great minority, the whites often held onto their dominant position tenuously, but there was never any question of changing the policy of cultivated dependence. The fur trade required strong backs, not agile minds. As Sir George Simpson, the Little Emperor, HBC governor in North America for four decades starting in 1820, put it, "an enlightened Indian is good for nothing."

Yet almost all of the Company's employees took Indian women

for wives, "according to the custom of the country." Not formally, usually, for it wasn't until the mid-nineteenth century that missionaries showed up in any significant numbers to perform the ceremonies. Even so, these HBC men inevitably established households and raised families with young Indian women. In the early years the Company actually forbade such liaisons, only later encouraging them when it realized there were economic benefits. Some took up with Indian women though there might be a wife waiting at home in Scotland. Some would eventually desert their Indian families when they brought their real wives over; others became so acclimatized to the new way of life that they never did re-unite with their legal wives. And others, like Donald McLean's father, came to North America and were killed, leaving widows and sons and daughters to return home to start all over. As the Baymen took Indian wives, "strangers in blood," an entire generation of mixed-blood offspring was produced, different from either parent, with special characteristics, strengths and social problems.

The best possible candidate for an HBC posting was a young, literate Scot, used to a hard country life and unencumbered by family ties. Donald McLean fit that description perfectly. When he arrived at Fort Vancouver, the first man he reported to was Chief Factor John McLoughlin, the "Great White-Headed Eagle," a capable, genial administrator who lived with a half-breed named Marguerite. McLoughlin not only was untroubled by his lack of formal marriage to Marguerite, he was insulted by any suggestion that the alliance required a piece of paper to make it valid. If Donald McLean had thought about it, and it seems unlikely that he didn't, he would have realized the probability that by signing his contract with the Hudson's Bay Company, he was forsaking the prospect of a "normal" marriage to someone of his own ilk in favour of life with an Indian wife. It took little time to prove out.

Following the amalgamation of the Hudson's Bay Company and the North West Company in 1821, to put an end to the cut-throat competition that had threatened to ruin both of them, there were basically three levels of employees in the field. The upper-level "commissioned gentlemen" included chief factors and chief traders. The chief factors were given the more responsible duties such as supervision of entire fur-trade districts, while chief traders were assigned responsibilities such as running single posts. A step beneath the field officers were clerks and apprentice clerks. They were usually young and were relatively well-educated. The training was demanding, and those with seniority and promise provided the greatest supply of promotions to field commissions. After five years' service they were eligible to become clerks and might be given charge of small posts or expeditions. While as an apprentice the employee earned from twenty pounds to fifty pounds a year for keeping accounts and correspondence at the posts, his pay could reach 150 pounds a year as a clerk. With fourteen years' service he could be appointed a chief trader.

Beneath these ranks were the various workers, the engagees, who had little hope of rising up the ladder of promotion. This lower-class group of employees had within it grades and classes ranging from the highest, post master, down through interpreters, guides, steersmen, bowmen, voyageurs and labourers, to the lowly apprentice labourers. Post masters, though they were barred because of lack of education from further promotion, had the confidence of their superiors, and they kept accounts at smaller posts and were even given temporary management of posts on occasion while higher-ups were away.

Although he had been hired as an apprentice clerk, McLean was broken in as a post master with the Snake River Expedition. He was referred to as "Donald McLean C" — the C being used to distinguish him from other HBC employees of the same name — and he retained that designation throughout his service with the Company.

Within a year he had taken as his wife Ali, of the Upper Spokane, or "salmon people." She was the equivalent of Indian royalty, descended from a great Spokane warrior chief named Pelkamu'lox, which translates roughly into English as Rolls Over the Earth. This man, whose father had been of the same name, ranged from the American plains up into New Caledonia, where he often wintered in the Okanagan. As it happened, bloodlines made Ali a cousin of the Kamloops chief Nicola, whose native name was Hwistesmetxe'qEn, or Walking Grizzly Bear, a man McLean would later come to know well. Even this sprawling untamed country sometimes was a small world. For years Ali was to be his faithful wife and mother to several of his children.

There was a series of assignments ranging around the Pacific Northwest. By now McLean had become a true Company man, in it for the long term. For about four years, from the summer of 1835, he was with the Snake River operations in some of the nastiest country in the Company's domain. He served at Fort Hall, then at Fort Colville under Chief Trader Archibald McDonald. In 1840 he was appointed clerk at Flatheads, on the Flathead River, at a salary of sixty pounds a year. This was a position more suited to the talents of McLean, whose administrative abilities were becoming evident. During all of this time, he scouted the wild rivers, shot buffalo on the plains, guided for explorers, and lived as lonely and hard a life as one could imagine. And he learned to think and speak like an Indian.

Samuel Black, a former Nor'Wester described by Sir George Simpson as "a cold blooded fellow who could be guilty of any Cruelty," was murdered at Kamloops in February 1841 and McDonald was absent from Fort Colville that summer. During this time McLean took charge of the post. Black's death made some shuffling necessary, and McLean was transferred up to Fort Alexandria in the New Caledonia district the following year. Taking his family with him, McLean embarked on the arduous journey. By trails and rivers, they made their way west and north, up the Snake River, across the Bitteroot Range through the Lolo Pass, then followed the Clearwater River back to the Snake, which they rode down to the Columbia. Going up the Columbia, they broke off and went up the Okanagan trail to Thompson's River Post and eventually to Alexandria. The entire journey covered about a thousand miles.

## [11]

BELLA COOLA, Colony of British Columbia
Sunday, June 5, 1864

The settlement of Bella Coola consisted of sixteen white people living in log houses along the river and among the totems and thunderbird-painted lodges of a large Indian community they called Great Village. The Indian name for it was Koomkootz and it was a fairly impressive place, established on both sides of the river. The North West Company explorer Alexander Mackenzie had reached it in 1793 during his overland search for the Northwest Passage, and Captain George Vancouver visited it that same year by sea. Eventually a few whites had become established, trading with the Bella Coolas and farming. Bella Coola had much in common with the Waddington townsite geographically. It was situated at the head of a deep fiord, the North Bentinck Arm of Burke Channel on the British Columbia coast. A lush green valley reached inland along the Atnarko or Nookhalk, or Bella Coola River, shadowed by rough peaks frothing this time of year with waterfalls. Numerous rockslides fanned out from the crevices. It was Mackenzie who had given Koomkootz, at the head of the inlet, the name Great Village. He had also called it Rascal's Village. Later, with the white intrusion, it became New Aberdeen, and then Bella Coola. But none of the names entirely disappeared, and they were used interchangeably.

Mackenzie found the Bella Coola Indians to be a proud, artistic, and industrious people, excellent rivermen and fishermen. Lieutenant Henry Palmer of the Royal Engineers, when he visited the Bella Coola Valley during an 1862 road survey, found them quite different:

In moral character the Bella Coolas are degraded specimens of the red Indian. Prostitution, polygamy, and other worse vices at which civilized men shudder are of frequent occurrence amongst them. Thieving is an art that all attain to perfection. . . . To their immoral habits of life, and partly also to wars with the Hydahs, the bloodhounds of the northwest coast, may be attributed the gradually progressing extinction of the race, clear evidence of which is afforded by the sight, at different points further up the river, of the ruins of deserted lodges, once the habitations of large families of Indians that have gradually dwindled away by death. . . .

But it was the smallpox encountered by Palmer and other explorers that was undeniably the main factor in the degeneration of the Bella Coola Indians.

Overnight, between June 4 and 5, 1864, the white population had boomed to twenty men and four women, and every one of them was inside the store owned by A.H. Wallace, the customs house officer. They were there in order not to repeat the mistake made by Alex McDonald, that is, underestimating the enemy. The enemy was a bunch of Chilcotin Indians lurking around in the village, trying to talk the Bella Coolas into revolting against the whites. Wallace had first-hand knowledge of what the Chilcotins were up to. Several of them had barged into his store demanding powder and balls. When he refused, claiming he had none left, one of the Indians drew a knife and slashed at him. The frightened and angry Wallace had run into a back room and returned with a long sword, charging at the invaders, "who incontinently left."

Among those now in Wallace's store, besides Wallace, was another storekeeper, Peter White, who had lived in Bella Coola through the smallpox epidemic and had witnessed the decimation of the local Indians from four thousand to a fraction of that. Also there was John Hamilton, who ran the trading post twenty-two miles upriver, and his wife and daughter. He'd had his own run-in with the Chilcotins only the day before, when Chief Anahim himself had paid for gunpowder with two five-dollar gold coins. Hamilton didn't find out until later that the money was from Alex McDonald's pack train.

The most important guests of honour in the store, however, were John Grant, Fred Harrison, Malcolm McLeod, Barney Johnson and Charles Farquharson, survivors of Klatassine's attack on the pack train at Nancootlem. Grant had ridden into Hamilton's Boat Encampment trading post shortly after Anahim's strange visit. The packer looked awful, bloodied from gunshot wounds and weak from hunger and his struggle back down into the valley from Nancootlem. There was a rush to pack a few belongings, and to jump into a canoe for the ride down river just as a band of Chilcotins reappeared, apparently intending attack but foiled by the quick exodus. And later, a return trip by the Bella Coola white men to find the trading post plundered and, hiding in the bush, Harrison and McLeod. The next morning a badly wounded Barney Johnson showed up, leading a horse ridden by Charles Farquharson. The greenhorn Farquharson had escaped injury in the attack, but became completely lost until the bush-wise Johnson found him and led him back toward the coast.

Now, back at Bella Coola, all of them were sealed inside Wallace's store, with plenty of food, water, weapons and ammunition, determined to wait there until they starved to death, the Indians left, or help arrived.

## [12]

SODA CREEK, Fraser River, Cariboo
Monday, June 6, 1864

While William Cox waited for transportation down the Fraser River from Quesnellemouth, Donald McLean stewed impatiently at Soda Creek. The *Enterprise* was laid up for installation of a new shaft, delaying Cox.

McLean made good use of the time at Soda Creek, the end of the line for the wagon road that was eventually supposed to continue north through the Australian Ranch and Alexandria to Quesnellemouth, and east from there all the way to Williams Creek and Barkerville. A tiny settlement with a couple of hotels and not much else, Soda Creek was thus enjoying something of a boom as a junction between road and river travel for freight and travellers. Outfitting the expedition for the trek west into the Chilcotin had to be done there and at Quesnellemouth, a prospect that didn't please the economy-minded Frederick Seymour. Due to transportation costs, prices for staple goods increased dramatically the closer you got to the goldfields. At Alexandria, halfway between Soda Creek and Quesnellemouth, flour was twenty-eight cents a pound, sugar fifty cents, "Cariboo strawberries" (beans) were thirty-five. The same flour was thirty-six cents a pound at Williams Creek, while sugar sold for sixty-two and a half cents, beans for forty-five. After the initial rush of '62, and now that the road was edging closer and closer toward the gold fields, prices were in some cases only half what they had been, but Seymour fretted back home in New Westminster nonetheless. As Cox and McLean assessed the needs of their respective expeditionary parties, it was estimated the total force would need three thousand pounds of flour, eight hundred of "Cariboo turkey" (bacon), three hundred of sugar. Though apples were scarce, they'd take what they could get their hands on. And they would need salt, coffee, yeast powder and pepper. But there was also clothing – shirts, boots, sox – and necessities like soap, pipes, ammunition, and horses. This was going to be a very expensive posse.

While preparations were being made as best they could be, the posse members had a fresh rumour to contemplate. Supposedly there had been another murder, this time of William Manning, McDonald's partner at Puntzi Lake. The story was being circulated from among some Chilcotin Indians, members of the tribe of Chief Alexis, trading at Soda Creek. Alexis was letting it be known that his Chilcotins were not part of the rebellion and he didn't intend to interfere in what he considered a matter strictly between the whites and Klatassine's group. That was good news indeed, for the only hope of catching the killers was to gain the co-operation of some of the Chilcotins themselves. Just as importantly, it meant Klatassine wasn't meeting with unanimous support in his apparent plans to wipe out the whites. McLean hired an Indian to ride into the Chilcotin to find out whether or not the report of Manning's death was true.

The Chilcotins hanging around the Fraser River settlements were a sad, defeated-looking lot, quite different from those McLean had lived and worked with during his time there. It was the smallpox that had changed them. Though as far as he was concerned Indians were, at best, untrustworthy, they were not naturally so shamefully ragged. The white man's disease had decimated them in numbers and in spirit. Its roots were in the gold rush – a miner with smallpox who had arrived in Victoria from San Francisco in April 1862. It very quickly reached Indian camps near the colonial capital and though it wasn't the first such epidemic to strike the Indians, this one became the most disastrous. The Vancouver Island natives trading in Victoria took the disease back with them, and it became a lethal fire jumping from whites to Indians and from tribe to tribe.

Within a month the smallpox made its appearance in the Chilcotin, attacking the Nancootlem band of old Chief Anahim. In July Lieutenant Palmer, who had surveyed the routes to the goldfields via New Westminster, was engaged in his survey of the North Bentinck Arm route to Alexandria, which continued past Nancootlem and joined the Bute Inlet trail at Puntzi Lake. He noted the fast spread of the disease:

> During my stay here this disease, which had only just broken out
> when I arrived, spread so rapidly that, in a week, nearly all the
> healthy had scattered from the lodges and gone to encamp by
> families in the woods, only, it is to be feared, to carry away the

seeds of infection and death in the blankets and other articles
they took with them. Numbers were dying each day; sick men
and women were taken out into the woods and left with a blanket and two or three salmon to die by themselves and rot
unburied; sick children were tied to trees, and naked, grey-haired
medicine men, hideously painted, howled and gesticulated night
and day in front of the lodges in mad efforts to stay the progress
of the disease.

In October of that year, James Young, a newspaper correspondent
from Ottawa travelling with two companions from Alexandria toward
Bella Coola on Palmer's trail, discovered how extensively the disease
had spread into Chilcotin territory. He had been told by Malcolm
McLeod's brother Bob, a packer, of the devastation of Nancootlem,
but it was no preparation for seeing it. He entered the village with
A.L. Fortune, a recent arrival in Kamloops with the gold-seeking Overlanders party. Fortune was determined to look in the Indian dwellings
for the source of the nauseating smell assaulting their nostrils.

We followed, and saw in many of the houses corpses that had
been deserted when their owners were still alive. We saw signs of
a fight against a relentless enemy, a sudden conquering fear, and
a flight by all those who could flee, leaving their dead unburied,
and their sick to become dead, uncared for. Shortly we could
stand no more, and departed as fast as we could.

Young found similar scenes all the way down to Bella Coola, and
his experience was repeated by many white men living or visiting in
the Chilcotin territory. Few natives who caught smallpox survived,
usually dying within a couple of days. If they lived longer, they broke
out into a rash, which soon developed into quickly spreading pus-
tules, and then came fever and delirium. Sometimes they tried sweat
baths, or lay in the cold waters of a stream or lake, to no avail. They
died in agony by the hundreds and the thousands. They soon gave up
trying to give their dead proper burial, simply dragging the bodies
into the woods or walking there themselves before dying. Two years
later, the epidemic had burned itself out, but it killed twenty thousand of British Columbia's sixty thousand Indians. Of the fifteen
hundred Chilcotins, barely half survived. It should not have been sur-
prising, therefore, that they were neither especially noble-looking
creatures, nor very honest with white men. Their relationship with the
whites had always been sensitive at best. After his transfer out of Fort
Colville, and a short stay at Fort Alexandria, McLean had been posted
to Fort Chilcotin. An outpost west of Alexandria established in an
attempt to more effectively enlist the independence-minded Chilcotins

Fort Alexandria, where Donald McLean was in charge for several years
(*BCARS, 93603*)

in the fur trade, it was never very successful. Seventy miles to the
north was Fluz Cuz, another, even smaller and more isolated post, the
raison d'être of which was to collect beaver pelts in the area west and
north to Alexandria and the Nechako. McLean was in charge of both
Chilcotin post and Fluz Cuz, but lived at Chilcotin. For four years he
served out on the plateau, coming to know the Chilcotin Indians as
well, and becoming as familiar to them as any white man. McLean
knew most of the chiefs and subchiefs, their habits and personalities,
and their territories. He thought little of the Chilcotins, who always
seemed to be looking for trouble, and thought Fort Chilcotin was "in
my humble opinion a dead loss" to the Company not worth risking the
lives of its employees. Life, as always, was tenuous.

The tribes of the region were often at war with neighbouring na-
tions and among themselves, and it was one of these civil wars that
almost got McLean killed while he was at Fort Kilmars, or Babine.
The problem centred around the loss of a child and reprisals carried
out by one tribe against another. Since peace was essential to fur-
trade profitability, it was McLean's job to restore harmony. His force
of three men wouldn't have proven very effective against the "rascals,"
or "black vagabonds," as he had taken to calling them. "God help
me," he penned to his superior, Chief Trader Donald Manson at Fort
St. James. And, seemingly, He did, since a Jesuit missionary named
Father John Nobili happened into the district. Nobili was following up
an earlier visit by Father Modeste Demers, the first Catholic missionary ever to visit the region. Demers was a member of the French
Roman Catholic religious order, the Missionary Oblates of Mary Immaculate. The Oblates were to play a tremendously influential role in

New Caledonia and later British Columbia, but, on this occasion, it was the combined influence of the Jesuit Nobili and McLean that calmed things down. The crisis passed.

Fort Babine was even further north than the Chilcotin post, in even wilder territory. For two years McLean was in charge of Babine, which had an outpost of its own in Fort Connolly on Bear Lake. His strength, management abilities, and absolute fearlessness were by now well recognized, but so was another part of his temperament — his refusal to back down from superiors if he felt he was right. Though his letters were marked by the usual exaggerated politeness — "I have the honour to address. . . . ," "With sentiments of respectful esteem. . . . ," "Your Most Obedient Servant. . . . " —they could become edged with enough disappointment to make it clear he disagreed with some of their decisions. He often complained about the lack of necessities provided by the Company. "It is really too bad to be so ill supplied with medicines. The gents at Vancouver and elsewhere take but little trouble about us poor devils in this quarter but doubtless they take good care of themselves."

But these were men among men, with shoulders broad enough, and minds acute enough, both to accept and to offer such criticisms with seldom a hint of outright hostility, though that wasn't unheard of. McLean was directly responsible, at that time, to Manson, who bossed the entire New Caledonia district. He was older than McLean, less educated, a no-nonsense autocrat of great stamina. The two men frequently found cause to disagree, yet they and their families forged a close bond, and Manson was, without fail, supportive of McLean with those in the upper levels of the Company.

Early in 1849 Manson brought McLean in out of the cold and put him in charge at Alexandria. McLean had been in charge there before for short periods, but this was to be a longer stay, and it was a much more important posting, for Alexandria was the supply depot and the marshalling point for the New Caledonia brigades. Furs were brought there on the rivers by boat, and transferred to the big horse brigades that left each April for the trip down to Fort Kamloops and then south over the Cascade Mountains to Fort Langley on the lower Fraser.

Almost immediately McLean was called upon to exercise the Company's ruthless brand of justice. It involved a handsome young Canadian-Cree half-breed named Alexis Belanger, an orphan who had joined the Company in 1829 at the tender age of thirteen and been put to work in New Caledonia. He had a talent for language and picked up enough Carrier dialect to act as interpreter at Fort Babine. His career, however, had its ups and downs, brought on by his unpredictability. One incident involved Belanger's wife who, much to the interpreter's consternation, bedded down with his superior. Belanger had to content himself with beating his wife but a year later he was fired from his position.

In Chief Factor Peter Skene Ogden's opinion Belanger was a "worthless scamp," but the half-breed turned out to be hard to replace. Belanger, who was not only lazy but indulged in a little theft to supplement his meagre salary, was rehired, fired, rehired, and so on. In 1848 he was hired again to steer one of five Stuart Lake brigade boats going to Alexandria. This wasn't his favourite territory, as he was in the "bad books" of the local Indians there, particularly the Quesnelles who traded at Alexandria. It was November and Belanger was steering the last boat as the brigade poled past Quesnellemouth on the return trip. The boat had shoved off from the left bank of the Fraser and was crossing the stream to avoid the strong water at the junction of the Quesnelle and Fraser rivers. On a cliff over the river, a coal-blackened face peered down at the brigade. It belonged to Tlhelh, a young brave of the Quesnel band who had lost his wife in a battle with wandering Crees at Tête Jaune Cache and was sworn to avenge her death. Belanger, being half Cree, became his target at the urging of his maternal uncle, Nadetnoerh.

The Indian's gun, an old musket with a short barrel, was aimed at Belanger. The first ball struck the water by the side of his boat. The second pierced his chest.

"I think I've been shot," Belanger observed as he slumped over the Indians next to him. He was rushed down to Fort Alexandria but died eight days later.

An employee of the Company had been murdered; the killer must be brought to justice. Donald Manson ordered McLean to get him. There was no thought of bringing the Indian in for questioning, or holding the equivalent of a trial. Tlhelh was to be found and shot. McLean knew he could expect no co-operation from the natives. He and a clerk named Montrose McGillivray took a posse of sixteen and trekked up to Quesnellemouth in January 1849. The story of what happened there was to be repeated many times until it became a part of the McLean legend. Later it would become the basis for the contention that McLean was a cruel and bloodthirsty man. All of the respect and admiration of his contemporaries would be replaced by the hindsight of writers removed by a generation of time and condition.

At Quesnellemouth, McLean and his men found the village deserted, but on the opposite side of the river three huts seemed to be inhabited. Crossing the river with his men, McLean entered one of them to find Tlhelh's uncle, the Quesnelle chief, with his half-breed daughter-in-law and baby.

"Where be Tlhelh?" McLean is said to have demanded through his interpreter, Jean-Marie Boucher. "Tlhelh tatqa?"

"Tlhelh huloerh," replied Nadetnoerh. "Tlhelh is not here."

"Where is he? Better tell me quick," McLean warned.

"How can I know his whereabouts?" asked the old man who had goaded Tlhelh into the pointless murder. "All I know is that he is not here."

Angered by the shielding of the fugitive, and having been told that Natednoerh was partly responsible for Belanger's murder, McLean was determined not to let him get away with it.

"Then for today you shall be Tlhelh," he proclaimed. There followed a lot of shooting and, presumably, a lot of scrambling to get out of the way. With two pistols, McLean fired at Nadetnoerh. Both shots missed their mark, but a third, from his musket, killed the Indian. One of the stray bullets crushed the baby's head and wounded its mother in the shoulder. In the melee, the son-in-law was also cut down.

In another hut, an old man bolted his door and defied the raiders to enter. A hole was cut in the roof and McLean climbed up to reconnoitre. He stuck his head in the hole and jerked it back just in time to avoid having it blown off by a rifle shot. McLean and his men left, not realizing they were leaving behind a wounded woman.

Back at Alexandria McLean called in the Indians from around the fort and explained that while Nadetnoerh had been executed, the killing of the son-in-law was a mistake. They accepted McLean's explanation, but he ordered extra guard duty at the fort just in case. It was five days before McLean learned about the death of the baby and the wounding of its mother. "News has arrived from above that a woman was severely wounded and her child killed by our fire. Should that be the case I am sorry that it should have happened as it was not my intention to injure the women or children," he wrote in his journal. He sent two men to get the woman and bring her to Alexandria, and had her cared for. Though she was "in a low state," she recovered.

Upon receiving word at Fort St. James of the escapade at Quesnelle River, Manson called for a celebration in the hall of the fort. When Indians killed an enemy, it was customary to create a victory dance. In this case, Manson turned the tables, making up a dance of his own. "Tlhelh tatqa?" he asked, and the dancers would reply, "Tlhelh huloerh!" He also notified Sir George Simpson and his Council of the fine work, saying, "Messrs. McLean and McGillivray while under my command have always given me entire satisfaction, and in this last important duty I feel much indebted for the handsome manner in which they have executed my orders, so far as it was in their power."

Meanwhile Tlhelh managed to elude capture with a little help from his friends, namely the Lhthau'tenne (people of the Fraser River or Alexandria) and the Nazhoh'tenne (people of the Blackwater River).

More than a year after the shooting of Belanger, he had still not been taken into custody. McLean was too busy with other duties to undertake another full-scale expedition to find him, and his frustration with the situation grew as the months passed. It was a job unfinished. Bits of intelligence filtered down to him from time to time so that he knew the general area where Tlhelh could be found. McLean threatened death to those who concealed him but many tribesmen remained friendly to the fugitive. "If my will was only concerned, the black, ungrateful, bloodthirsty, treacherous, and cowardly scoundrels should have prompt justice for it; hang first, and then call a jury to find them guilty or not guilty," McLean stated in a letter.

Finally a group of Quesnelle Indians "begged for peace" and agreed to provide McLean with a guide if he wanted to go after the fugitive again. He told them to bring him Tlhelh's head. But it was the chief of the Nazkhos who took ten men and went after Tlhelh in earnest, in return for a promise of a hundred skins, worth about sixty dollars. They tracked him to the Cottonwood River and returned to Alexandria late in March, presumably with Tlhelh's head, "good proof of the scoundrel being dead."

Shortly after that McLean did a stint as clerk at McLeod Lake post but was moved back to Alexandria after about a year. He remained there except for southward trips with the New Caledonia brigades in the summers of the years 1851 to 1854. He was in Alexandria when recognition was granted for his length of service to the Company. A letter dated March 30, 1853, found its way through the slow but inexorable mail system of the HBC to Donald McLean Esquire, "hereby appointed Chief Trader":

> *By virtue of the Charter to us given by King Charles the Second by the Letters Patent under the Great Seal of England bearing the date the Second Day of May in the 22nd year of his Reign. We do hereby appoint you Donald McLean a Chief Trader, as well in our Territory of Ruperts Land, as in all other places where Trade is authorized to be carried on by said Charter. You are therefore in virtue of this Commission, to perform all the duties which now or hereafter may be by law, performed by Chief Traders. And we do hereby order and direct all our Clerks and other Servants strictly to obey such orders as you may think proper to give them. And you are to observe and follow such orders from time to time as you shall receive from us – the Governor, Deputy Governor, and Committee of the Company of Adventurers of England trading into Hudson's Bay or our successors for the time being, and all orders issued by the Governor and his Council for the time being, of the District or Department in which you may act.*

*Given under our common Seal at our House in London this Thirtieth
day of March One Thousand Eight Hundred and Fifty Three.*

> *By Order of the Governor,*
> *Deputy Governor and Committee,*
> *(signed)*
> *Archibald Barclay, Secretary*

On this occasion Donald McLean forgot his past differences with
Donald Manson. In the same year, 1853, Simpson had cautioned
Manson to "put a check on the club law" in the district. ". . . We hear
that McLean and Odgen [sic] use their fists very freely and I think you
should caution them on the subject." But McLean felt gratitude to
Manson for the promotion. "It is to your kindness that, in a great
measure, I owe having been promoted, and believe me, I will ever
remember it," he wrote on February 6, 1854.

The promotion came after a longer period than usual with the
Company, but that wasn't the only reason it was especially welcome.
His new rank entitled McLean to significant financial benefit. He was
no longer a servant; he was a half-shareholder, a wintering partner,
entitled to a direct stake in the profits of the Company.

Company business, though, wasn't all that concerned McLean, for
those years were among the most turbulent for him. His daughter
Elizabeth, whom he loved dearly, struggled with illness. Ali, her
mother and his first wife, was gone, her place taken by a Babine Indian woman. And now, there was a third woman, Sophia Grant,
daughter of HBC employee Peter Grant and his Indian wife, Anne.
Grant had died in 1849, and his widow stayed around Alexandria.

On August 29, 1854, a marriage ceremony was conducted at Fort
Alexandria by Donald Manson. It was common for chief traders and
chief factors to perform marriages, though by now visits by the Oblate
missionaries were fairly common. Though other records say she was
born at Bear Lake in the Babine country, the certificate of marriage
refers to Sophia as being "of Fort Colville."

Somehow McLean managed to keep his family together; his children remained with him as their numbers grew, for despite the
rigours of life in the fur country, and all the physical and mental
toughness it bred, McLean was a devoted father. Besides Donald Jr.,
Duncan, Elizabeth and Alex from his union with Ali, he had John
Allen by the Babine woman. One son died early, moving Donald
McLean to put pen to paper in expression of his utter grief.

> *Oh! what is it, late yester night*
>    *My Boy was alive and well*
> *And now his spirit pure and bright*
>    *Has gone where Angels dwell*

It would not be the last time, tragically, that McLean would have occasion to write about the loss of a loved one.

Another stage in McLean's career with the Hudson's Bay Company was nearing. In 1855 Thompson's River Post, or Fort Kamloops, was a slowly growing depot in the Company's New Caledonia District. At one time the Company had considered closing it because its yield of furs wasn't great, but it was important as a stop-over and for protection of the New Caledonia brigades against possible Indian uprisings. It also supplied the horses for the colder, northern posts. A fifteen-foot high palisade with bastions at the corners surrounded the fort's buildings northwest of the junction of the North and South Thompson rivers. The lord of this little empire was Paul Fraser, appointed as a clerk to take charge in 1850 and promoted to chief trader in January, 1854. He was an unpopular leader. In late July of 1855, on the way to Fort Langley with the Kamloops brigade, he was killed when a tree was cut down and fell on his tent. It was five in the afternoon and Fraser lived another hour but never spoke. There were suspicions that his death wasn't accidental. The next day Manson, who had been travelling with Fraser, put Donald McLean in charge of Kamloops.

## [13]

Mr. Moss, who has just arrived from New Westminster last night informs us that intelligence has been received from Mr. McLean from Soda Creek confirming the report of the murder of Mr. Manning and his party at Benchy [sic] Lake by the Chilcotin Indians. Mr. McLean sent through a number of Indian scouts to the spot who brought back proofs of the melancholy tragedy. McLean was still at Soda Creek awaiting the arrival of Commander Cox. He had only taken up fifty rifles and the same number of revolvers but an additional supply of arms would be obtained. Upwards of eighty men volunteered at New Westminster for the Bentinck Arm Expedition but only forty would be accepted, that number being deemed sufficient. The Government acquired a number of pack mules from Mr. Ladner and dispatched the *Reliance* to Yale to bring them down to New Westminster where they will be shipped aboard H.M.S. *Tribune* which will convey the party to Bentinck Arm. The *Tribune* will come down to Esquimalt tomorrow and will take the outside passage to the Arm. The *Columbian* asks us to notice that the *Tribune* drawing nineteen feet eleven inches got safely up to the Capital but had missed to mention that she touched bottom on the way up. She may have more difficulty coming down with the current. — The *Daily British Colonist*, Victoria, V.I.

---

THE CHILCOTIN PLATEAU, west of Alexandria
Thursday, June 9, 1864

By the time the citizens of Victoria were hungrily reading that latest dispatch on the progress of the Chilcotin War, Donald McLean was no longer in Soda Creek waiting upon Cox. He and Cox, in fact, were a day and a half out of Alexandria toward Puntzi Lake, the scene of Manning's murder. McLean had become so impatient at Soda Creek that he'd been on the verge of forgetting the whole thing and going home. But word had come back about Manning, apparently shot down on his doorstep by a reluctant Chilcotin assassin named Tahpitt, taunted into it by Anahim himself. Manning, the first white settler in the central Chilcotin, had been there only two years but refused to believe the warnings from his Chilcotin klootchman Nancy that his life was in danger. Tahpitt simply walked up behind Manning and shot him with a musket. Manning was probably dead before he hit the ground but Tahpitt chopped up his face with a couple of hatchet swings for good measure. There was no lack of witnesses, most of whom joined in hacking at the body while others plundered the house. Manning's plough, which they had been forced to watch turning up the land of their campground, received special attention. To the Chilcotins it was the symbol of the white intrusion on their territory, so several Indians attacked it together; it was soon a piece of junk. While all this was going on, the unfortunate wretch Tahpitt sat on the ground sobbing, belatedly repentant, his face covered by a blanket. For the others, however, this was occasion to party, and a jubilant potlatch continued into the night, with Klatassine himself, along with his followers, joining the Tatla and Puntzi Indians in singing, dancing, eating, smoking and story-telling. And Klatassine told the tale of his own great victory, urging the men to join him in a sacred war to take back their land before the white man's curse killed them all.

This vivid reminder of the brutality of life and death on the plain rekindled McLean's determination. He sent a letter to Seymour assuring the governor that "no danger or difficulty" would deter him from using his "utmost efforts to secure the object of the expedition."

Then word came from Cox that the gold commissioner had managed to get a raft built and was transporting himself and his volunteers down the Fraser to Alexandria from Quesnellemouth. So

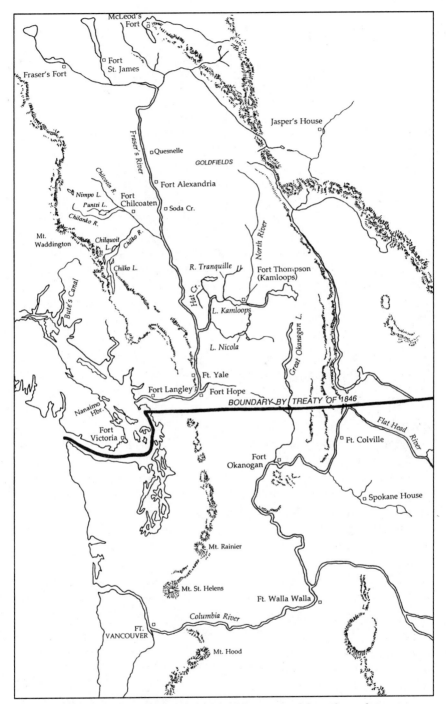

Donald McLean's domain, about 1860. Adapted from Map of the Colony of New Caledonia and the British and American West Territory of the Rocky Mountains. James Wyld, London *(HBCA, G3/137)*

McLean and the handful of men he'd managed to enlist went up from Soda Creek and the two forces became one. How different Alexandria was from the days when Donald McLean had been in charge, when it was a major fur depot for the brigades. It had suffered from the gold rush, which sucked trade away to more strategically located settlements. The previous summer the Company had bought a restaurant and other buildings across the river on the east side in an effort to catch some of the business from miners travelling to and from the goldfields. The decline of Alexandria was visual proof, if any were needed, of the decline of the Company itself. The halcyon days of the fur trade were gone. The Company no longer held a life-and-death monopoly from Hudson Bay to the Pacific Coast. The monopoly, in fact, was officially dead. The Columbia district was now the Oregon Territory of the United States, given away by Britain in the Oregon Treaty of 1846. New Caledonia, north of the 49th parallel, saved for Britain in the same treaty, was the colony of British Columbia. Vancouver Island was a colony, too. James Douglas, once governor of both the new colonies, was gone, retired to spend his few remaining years a spent old man. Gone too were Ogden, McLoughlin, McGillivray and Manson, all retired or dead. The new Bay men, like the able Joseph McKay who had replaced McLean at Kamloops, were reduced to little more than general-store clerks. But this was the new way, with wagon roads and stopping houses — it was called "civilization." When William H. Fitzgerald, appointed by Cox in charge of supplies, paid for the goods needed for the expedition, he did so not by barter but in coin.

McLean requisitioned a blue serge shirt, a lamb's wool undershirt, a pair of shoes, a fine-tooth comb and a bottle of whiskey from Fitzgerald's stores, and pointed the Alexandria Expedition, as it was called, toward Puntzi Lake. He would, to the best of his considerable abilities, endeavour to punish Klatassine and his Chilcotins for trying to stop the now-inevitable advance of civilization.

After a short climb out of the valley of the Fraser River at Alexandria, the country suddenly and dramatically flattened into a gently rippling plain, cratered with innumerable lakes and freckled with marshes and meadows. Poplars, berry bushes and tall grass formed oases among the evergreens. As they progressed westward, the vegetation became more luxuriant and the Coast Mountains gradually rose above the horizon like a frozen sunrise. It was an impressive land, but at the same time tedious in its similarity. Even the appearance of a black swath of burned-out forest offered temporary though eerie relief. As the long train passed between the tall, sharp stumps, the occasional rasping of a charred branch was the only sound from this dead countryside.

To Cox's credit, he made it clear from the start that he intended to defer to McLean on anything to do with the country or the Indians. He at least realized his limitations in a strange place. He was there to represent the wishes of Frederick Seymour, who had given him wide discretion. In the Chilcotin wilderness there could be little interference, and certainly little advice, from New Westminster.

Cox and McLean had under them a questionable representation of humanity. These men were rough and tough, most of them American traders or miners, inexperienced in Indian fighting but hardy and ready for combat, enticed by the offer of forty dollars to sixty dollars monthly wages. They were also not inclined to accept discipline very easily. It was Cox's job to mould them into at least a semblance of order, but he himself had never readily accepted any orders that contradicted his own inclinations. He was a fat, balding Irishman with a huge moustache, an Indian wife he preferred to the one back home in Ireland, and an easy-going nature on the surface but a will that could become as stiff as sap. He'd gotten on well with Douglas but often didn't get the proper authority for things, and Matthew Baillie Begbie — the hanging judge — often found it necessary to annul his decisions. Cox once settled a mining dispute by having the two rivals race from his office to the claim they both wanted. The winner got the claim.

Cox simply did not like being told what to do, as if an order represented an insult or a question of his own competence. As a result, he did his job well when it was of his own doing and poorly when he chose not to co-operate. He was a fine horseman though, at home in the rugged Cariboo, and if he was capable of anything it was enforcing his will, even upon the likes of the roughnecks now under his command.

The third in command was a tough, competent, tall and thick-set civil servant named John D.B. Ogilvy, known by McLean from the time they were both in the service of the Company. Once, in Ogilvy's house at Fort Hope, McLean and Ogilvy had stood sponsor for a baptism, the child of one of Sir George Simpson's sons. Afterward McLean paid the clergyman, a Wesleyan missionary named Ebenezer Robson, with a twenty-dollar gold piece.

Only a couple of days out of Alexandria a Cariboo miner got into an argument and drew a knife and a revolver. The fracas was broken up before it really got started, but Cox gave him ten minutes to leave camp. After that, Cox said, the men the miner had threatened could do what they wanted with him. The man left without his weapons, blankets or provisions on a frightening trek back to Alexandria, if he could find it. It was the first and last such incident.

These, then, were the kind of men now populating the place, the men for whom the Chilcotin and all of British Columbia and Vancouver Island must be preserved against the claims of Klatassine. Their greed and their crudeness were another product of the rush for gold, itself the result of every man's dream of riches. There was some kind of small irony in the whole situation with regard to McLean's position in all of this. It was Donald McLean, after all, who was mainly responsible for the gold rush that had come to a head with the massacre of Waddington's men. The rush would have happened anyway, but McLean was its main player in the early stages, for he was the Company man to whom the first gold from the Fraser River had come, the author in large degree of the Fraser River panic and the Cariboo rush that was an extension of it. In the wake of all this came the Cariboo Road, and the attempted construction of a competing road through the Chilcotin to the gold fields at Barkerville and Richfield. Had Old Waddy not come up with his get-rich road-building idea, there wouldn't have been a massacre.

The chain of events had started more than a decade before. Since 1852 McLean had been aware of the existence of gold in New Caledonia. While taking a drink from the Thompson River beside Nicoamen, an Indian had found a nugget and taken it to him at Alexandria. The Indians were furnished with iron implements and soon small quantities of gold were being brought in regularly. But while McLean and the HBC encouraged their own employees and the Indians to dig gold and bring it to the Company, they weren't anxious for its existence to be widely known. It was felt a large influx of gold seekers would disrupt the fur trade. Chief Factor and Vancouver Island Governor James Douglas, in charge of HBC operations west of the Rockies, hoped the Company could monopolize the gold digging on the mainland, and the tide was resisted for a time. McLean, the first white man to see gold from the district, helped keep the secret, but eventually it had to get out.

In the autumn of 1855, news reached the ports of Puget Sound that gold had been discovered near Fort Colville at the mouth of the Pend d'Oreille River, in McLean's former stamping grounds. The rush was on and by 1857 the search for gold had spread northward to New Caledonia.

In the midst of all this activity McLean was dealt a series of personal blows. First came the death of his stepfather, William Robert Browne, who succumbed at the age of sixty-six, at Portsea in the south of England, to chronic liver disease. A month and a half later, in August, 1856, his mother Christina died at seventy-four. For three years she had been insane, a resident of the Union Workhouse asylum at which her husband was chaplain The official cause of death was "sloughing of nates." Donald McLean had been sending money for the care of his destitute mother for years, and also generously supported his sister Anna, though she was married to a successful wine merchant in London. A little more than a year after his mother's

Elizabeth McLean, daughter
of Donald
*(KMA, 5803)*

death, Donald's beloved daughter Elizabeth and son-in-law William Manson gave him a grandson, named Donald in honour of both grandfathers. But the pregnancy proved too much for the frail Elizabeth, who died less than three months after giving birth.

The tide of change sweeping over New Caledonia and the fur trade didn't stop for such tragedies. The course of history in the country was about to be dramatically altered. John Houston, a Scottish sailor who caught gold fever in California, discovered gold in Tranquille Creek, a little stream feeding Kamloops Lake, in the spring of 1857. He sold his findings to McLean, who by then was in charge of the post in Kamloops. The rush to the Thompson and Cariboo now began in earnest. Since the time when the first gold was found by Indians, it had been shipped to Victoria and then by the HBC steamer *Otter* to San Francisco for minting, and this provided the U.S. with an excellent source of news about gold.

In December of 1857 the governor issued proclamations regulating the digging of gold on the mainland. Although the news was spreading quickly, most heard too late in the year to do anything about it. The Fraser River rush started the next spring, and almost thirty thousand miners and camp followers took $573 thousand in fine gold dust from the river that year despite frequent attacks by Indians, attacks that sometimes had fatal consequences.

In the spring of 1859, the HBC policy of attempting to stifle the gold rush was broken for good. A party of Americans headed by Peter Curran Dunlevy arrived at Kamloops, and while they were at first refused supplies the Americans' persuasiveness finally prevailed. In what might have been a hot confrontation, Dunlevy convinced McLean to acquiesce. McLean realized that the miners would steadily increase in numbers, and the HBC might as well get their trade.

The fears of Governor Douglas were realized. Americans flocked into the fur trade area, and the HBC waited for the explosion that was sure to come. As the gold rush led to increased immigration, the governor became concerned not only about the effect on the fur trade and the weakening of the British foothold, but about the threat of Indian warfare spreading from south of the border. The Cariboo goldfields alone were to account for about $93 million in production by placer, and almost $100 thousand in platinum. After British Columbia became a colony in 1858, Donald McLean was the first person in the new colony to receive a trading licence.

There was more to the story. With excitement caused by the gold rush, McLean was given added responsibilities in the supervision of establishing two new posts — Fort Dallas and Fort Berens — and in assisting in construction of the Harrison-Lillooet route. The new forts were expected to take advantage of the gold-rush traffic, and Fort Dallas in particular was recommended by McLean. Douglas made the decision for the projects. Things went smoothly at first but months passed and Fort Dallas and Fort Berens never became operational. A.G. Dallas, who took charge of the Company's business west of the Rocky Mountains after Douglas resigned, complained to McLean that the chief trader had sunk too much money into the work, although acknowledging McLean was acting on instructions. The construction was abandoned in 1859 after expenditures of $16,500 and some sharp words between Dallas and McLean.

McLean got into one more disagreement caused not by himself but by Dallas. It involved Jean Baptiste Lolo, a sixty-two-year-old French Canadian-Iroquois half-breed who had run a packing outfit on contract to the Company since McLean's Fort Alexandria days. Even then Lolo had been known as St. Paul. Over the years he earned quite a reputation as a character, and a man of considerable influence. In 1859, when Lieutenant R.C. Mayne of H.M.S. *Plumper* was touring the colony, McLean introduced him to St. Paul. Mayne was so impressed by this man, who looked like an Indian and spoke English with a French accent, that he officially named the mountain that overlooked the Hudson's Bay Company fort at Kamloops after him. When Douglas ordered agents to stake out land claimed by the Company, McLean did an inventory and found that St. Paul's house was on ten acres the HBC regarded as its own. After Douglas quit the Company but continued as governor of the colony, he put the wheels in motion for the establishment of Indian reserves. Dallas told McLean to press Douglas on the Company's ten-acre claim. Douglas rebuffed McLean, saying that "in my own private opinion" the land rightfully belonged to St. Paul and that he couldn't be ejected. McLean came across as wanting to kick a poor native off his land.

Dallas wanted McLean replaced as the man in charge of Thompson's River District and Sir George Simpson authorized his transfer to a post east of the Rocky Mountains. On June 5, 1860, McLean was instructed by W.F. Tolmie to join the New Caledonia Leather Party and travel to Peace River to take up a new position. McLean was not anxious to do so because of his large family but said he'd take up the Peace River appointment the next year. However, he was told to hand over charge of his district to Chief Trader Joseph McKay and to report at Victoria for further information.

A decision from the Company on his future was slow in coming, so McLean made a decision of his own. In his travels around the Fort Kamloops trading area, he was well-acquainted with potential farming and ranching sites and had already been thinking of taking up some land for himself. He liked the Bonaparte River-Hat Creek area fifty miles west of the fort, both because it offered good soil and weather, and because of its location on the route of the Cariboo wagon road soon to be constructed, connecting the coast with the Barkerville gold-fields. Though he had spent most of his life as a fur trader, he wasn't unprepared for such a move. His long experience, cunning and knowledge of New Caledonia had made him an excellent manager. All of the major posts had horse and cattle herds. At Thompson's River Post he'd worked hard with his sons and fellow HBC employees to fence more land, grow more varied crops and improve cattle ranching and horse breeding. His work also included supervising trail improvements for the brigades. In 1859 he started the "Experimental Farm" under William Manson, Donald Manson's son, at the Calumet near Dairy Creek about fifteen miles up the North Thompson on the west side. Here crops were planted and butter was produced, with varying success. Donald was a connoisseur of horse flesh, and much of his time was devoted to improving the stock. With him in the Company were his older sons Donald, Duncan, Alex and John.

Horses, in fact, had become more and more important to Thompson's River Post. As the dominance of the fur trade began to decline, the post continued to be the strategic local supplier of horses for the district. Of course, farming and raising horses were subject largely to the whims of the weather, and a harsh winter would bring the post and its dependents near starvation. Salmon supplies would become low, so horses not already dead from cold would be shot and eaten. McLean had been able to develop a good herd of horses and some cattle of his own, which would serve as the beginning of his plans for Hat Creek.

So on a cloudy day in August, 1860, the McLean family began the move to their homestead. It was no small undertaking. Donald Jr. and Duncan and some Indian helpers moved out first, taking the stock on the tricky drive along Kamloops Lake to the Thompson River, then continuing west to Cache Creek. From there, it was only a few miles north to the spot Donald had picked out at the confluence of Hat Creek and the Bonaparte. A second procession included Sophia and the younger children, with a pack train loaded with belongings. Finally, Donald McLean officially turned over command of the post to McKay and headed off to join his family. He was still technically an employee of the Hudson's Bay Company, but he wasn't about to wait around while they decided what to do with him, then have to move his family and all his possessions someplace that might be hundreds of miles away.

## [14]

### VALLEY OF THE CHILKO RIVER, Chilcotin Plateau
### Saturday, June 11, 1864

When the expedition reached the valley of the Chilko River some seventy miles west of Alexandria, Cox took the opportunity for a short bivouac. Here he hoped to find Alexis and employ the Chilcotin chief as a guide, since the area from the convergence of the Chilko and Chilcotin rivers to Puntzi Lake was his most frequent habitat.

The recruitment of Alexis had been Cox's, that is McLean's, primary strategy from the start. As Seymour explained it, Cox was to "at once proceed to the headquarters of Alexis, the great chief of the Chilcotin tribe, show his warrant, and explain that the Queen's law must have its course. He will support his application for redress by showing my proclamation, offering a reward of fifty lbs. for the apprehension of each of the murderers."

McLean knew it wouldn't be that easy, and Cox quickly found out the same thing. "Alexis was not to be found, he having with his family fled to the mountains, reports having been freely circulated that we were coming to this region for the purpose of exterminating the Indians, friendly or otherwise."

The "rumours" had been picked up in Alexandria by members of Alexis' band as the expedition prepared to move out. The miners and drifters recruited by Cox from the goldfields had talked loosely of their mission, the intent being, according to many of them, to go out and shoot as many Indians as possible. Alexis was not about to take any chances, even if he did consider himself a neutral. He decided to leave his village a few miles north of the Chilcotin-Chilko forks and go on an extended hunting trip in less accessible territory.

All Cox and McLean could do was to push on and hope to contact Alexis somewhere along the way.

## [15]

PUNTZI LAKE, Chilcotin Plateau
Sunday, June 12, 1864

The expedition continued another forty miles to Puntzi Lake, the junction of the Bentinck Arm and Bute Inlet trails, and the scene of William Manning's murder. They arrived four days after leaving Alexandria. Many of the men were near exhaustion, not having been in shape for the march.

Puntzi is a tadpole-shaped lake about five miles long at the head and three more at the tail. The north-west shore alternates between groves of giant cottonwoods and stands of dwarf poplars and aspens, with large spreads of juniper on the rocky slopes. Occasional sandbars or peninsulas break a shoreline otherwise thickly forested.

A mile from Manning's ranch, as the expedition made its way along the north shore, a group of Chilcotin lodges was sighted. It was the village used by the Indians after being expelled from the choicest spot by Manning, the village from which Tahpitt had walked to kill the rancher.

The village came into view quite suddenly as the trail crested on a hill. The whites were sighted by the Chilcotins, but the Indians did not immediately flee. In fact, thinking it was another pack train, they were preparing to let it walk into a trap.

If Cox had been a smart Indian fighter, he would have broken off a party of men and sent them behind the hills ringing the lake and closed off any escape by the Indians. But he was not a smart Indian fighter and instead ordered the expedition into full armed view on the hill. Within minutes the Chilcotins had deserted the village for the bush. Cox, instead of capturing at least some informants and perhaps some of the murderers, had nothing but a collection of empty huts.

McLean, through this, could surely only mutter to himself about the incompetence with which this first contact with the Chilcotins had been handled. While Cox had orders to avoid a direct "clash" with them, even Seymour would have been able to see the advantages of a more tactical action. Cox had the potential to become an annoyance.

After an examination of the deserted village, Cox called up William Fitzgerald. Two Chilcotins had described to Fitzgerald in Alexandria the location of Manning's body. With Fitzgerald, McLean and several other men, Cox continued on to the charred remains of McDonald and Manning's ranch and searched out the stream. It took less than a half-hour of thrashing through the cold-running water to find the body under the roots and branches.

Considering that the body had lain there for probably three weeks, it was well-preserved. The cold water and the covering of roots, which kept the sun off, retarded decomposition. The bullet wounds were easily identified — holes in the right breast and left shoulder blade where the ball had entered and exited. The head was completely crushed.

The body was removed and an inquest held. As it was interred on the land Manning had paid for with his life, Donald McLean read a burial service commemorating the courage of white settlers in opening up new land against formidable odds. None of them knew it, but Manning's wife and children had only just arrived in Victoria, anxious to join him.

William Manning and Donald McLean were the same kind of pioneer in some ways. They represented the old accommodating the new. Just as the fur trade was being destroyed by the stampede to the Fraser River and now Williams and Lightning creeks, so the gold rush would pass and the fever subside. A few would strike mother veins and become rich, others would return home heartbroken, and still others would die. Men like Manning and McLean would stay, recognizing there were other kinds of wealth to be mined, less literally, from the land. The land so jealously protected against settlement by the Company was finally to yield its true bounty from the water and the soil. Like McLean, Manning had taken up his farm only two years before and, like McLean, he had positioned it to intercept travellers, doubling the potential of success. But while McLean had seen Douglas' new Cariboo Road constructed past his doorstep, Manning had died before Waddington connected the coast with Alexandria.

Hat Creek, though well-located, was no easy proposition. The creek tumbled down out of the hills through Marble Canyon to the Bonaparte, where there was excellent soil and grass, but the winters could be harsh and the summers dry. The first small cabins were built along the creek to get through that winter of 1860, and there was a steady stream of trips back and forth to Kamloops all winter to keep up supplies.

It was a difficult winter. Donald and his son John, thirteen years old at the time, helped Joseph McKay, the new chief trader, bring up a brigade from Hope, but it was a rough trip and nine horses were killed. John managed to get himself lost in the mountains and Donald had to leave the brigade to find him.

In March 1861 Dallas wrote McLean advising him that there was "no prospect of profitable employment" west of the Rocky Mountains. Morever, if he wanted to stay with the Company, he should report at Fort Garry in Red River Settlement, in June, for the meeting of the council of the Northern Department of Rupert's Land, where his appointment would be fixed.

So there it was – after a lifetime of faithful and competent service to the Company, he was being ordered to pack up and move like some apprentice clerk. He must have thought about returning to the place of his childhood, the place his father was killed, but he was tied to British Columbia now. McLean wrote back, in his elegant, swirling hand, that he couldn't go to Red River, and officially offered his resignation. The Company, when the letter reached headquarters in London, officially accepted.

The restaurant was built that same season, a simple rectangular building, fifty-five feet by twenty-two feet. The fir and Ponderosa pine from the nearby hills made for good building logs, and McLean knew how to build. Using an axe and a saw was just one of the things you learned working for the Company. He built the restaurant Company style, joining sections of logs together with squared vertical ties and chinking with bark strips.

Hat Creek tested all of McLean's experience and knowledge, not only in construction, but in ranching and farming. Though grass and water supplies were excellent, the summer could sometimes bring drought conditions, a problem he partly solved by constructing a flume system from the creek to his fields. He was, in fact, the first in the colony to use flood irrigation. One summer almost the entire crop of barley and vegetables was lost, for though the irrigation system delivered the water wonderfully well, it was so cold it killed the young plants.

McLean also did some prospecting, and found enough minerals in the summer of 1863 that he formed the Bonaparte Gold and Silver Mining Company and dug a twelve-foot shaft. One of the boys built a roadhouse up the canyon at Pavilion. The Cariboo Road reached Hat Creek that year. William Hood of Cache Creek, hired to build the section from Cook's Ferry (Spences Bridge) to Clinton, took it right through Donald McLean's ploughed fields past the front door of the restaurant. McLean complained to the colonial government in New Westminster: " . . . Although it is not my wish to throw the slightest impediment in your way, I am not sufficiently rich to admit my suffering the loss of seed and labour without wishing to obtain compensation for all loss sustained." The Lands and Works Commission put the issue to arbitration, decided to leave the road where it was rather than incur the expense of diverting it, and paid McLean for his troubles. McLean won twice: not only was his roadhouse perfectly located, but the government paid him for the road.

He foresaw that, even after the rush subsided, which it surely must, many who came looking for gold would stay to settle. They would want land; the wilderness now occupied by the Indians would soon be filled with whites. Some day the whites would even outnumber the Indians. McLean meant to protect his investment and used a smart and perfectly legal means of doing it. Originally, when colonization had started, he'd intended to settle near Fort Kamloops and had tried to get permission to stake out five hundred acres. But in 1859, before the Land Proclamation of British Columbia provided for the sale of Crown Lands, there was no system for establishing private ownership in the interior of the colony. The British Columbia colonial government set up a method of land settlement called pre-emption, whereby a person could occupy land and begin working on it before obtaining an official Crown grant. It hastened settlement by removing the need to wait for surveys and legal titles to be obtained before developing a farm or ranch. While Donald McLean was waiting at Hat Creek for a decision on his fate with the Company, he had his friend and former employee Neil McArthur pre-empt 160 acres — the maximum allowed — at the site of the roadhouse and ranch. After officially leaving the Company, he pre-empted another 160 acres of good range several miles south, where the Bonaparte River flowed into Cache Creek. That land was known as McLean's Farm, as opposed to the Hat Creek roadhouse, which was called McLean's Restaurant and other names. He also pre-empted 160-acre parcels adjacent to the Hat Creek land in the names of Duncan, Donald Jr., John, Alex, and even Charlie and Allen, though the latter two were still young children. Not including McArthur's Hat Creek claim, Donald McLean and his family had well over a thousand acres under pre-emption, the makings of a ranching and farming empire. It was a hard life, but the work must eventually pay off. They were now officially no longer a fur-trade family. They were ranchers, farmers, and hoteliers. Others soon began to move in around them, but they were the pioneers.

## [16]

PUNTZI LAKE, Chilcotin Plateau
Monday, June 13, 1864

After they buried Manning, the expedition's leaders — Cox, McLean, and Ogilvy — talked about what to do next. It was clear that the nature of the surrounding territory, thickly timbered and covered with bushes, made it more important than ever to gain the services of Alexis as guide and interpreter. Without someone of his stature to act as intermediary with the rebels, it would be almost impossible to make contact with them. The expedition was supposed to talk, not attack. The speed with which the Indians were able to flee their village that day demonstrated the Indians' key advantage — they were in their own environment. The trails were innumerable and impossible to sort out.

Cox had no desire to take his men tramping through the bush, where the enemy might jump them at any time. McLean proposed to take his son Duncan, an Indian scout named Jack, and another volunteer and go to Chilcotin Forks to find Alexis or at least members of his family or immediate band. On this morning, before the sun was up, McLean's scouting party slipped out of camp, making it safely away from the area unharassed.

It was a dangerous mission, for they might easily be slaughtered by Tahpitt's Puntzi Lake band, who were probably in a vile mood at having been chased out of their lodges. But McLean believed a small party was best anyway, and he had no fear of the Chilcotins. McLean had no fear of anything. His somewhat simplistic sense of honour and justice drove him to unthinkingly risk his own safety time after time. But he knew no other way.

When the Fraser River gold rush brought the California miners streaming into New Caledonia, law and order hung by a tenuous thread. The Company was still the only law. In May of 1858 the miners poured into Victoria and onto the mainland, walking, riding or boating their way up to Fort Hope on their way to the Fraser. On June 8 of that year, Donald McLean happened to arrive from Thompson's River Post with a load of furs. At the same time, a man had arrived from down-river with a boatload of Chinese. When the Americans in camp saw this, they refused to let the Chinese land. No Chinese will land at Fort Hope, they declared, ignoring the white boatman's pleas. They would have strung up those Chinese, and the boatman too, if they'd tried to land. But Donald McLean and his young son Alex stepped between the crowd of Californians and the boat.

"Who says these Chinese are not to land?" Donald McLean demanded, telling them he represented the Hudson's Bay Company, which owned the country, and that he, Donald McLean, said they could land.

He then told Alex to get some Indians from the local rancherie, which Alex did. Holding the mob at bay with a pistol until Alex returned with the Indians, Donald then told the Indians to take the Chinese miners' baggage up to the fort. Next he told the Chinese to land and go into the protection of the fort, and dared the miners to try to stop them.

Not one of those toughened miners tried.

Three years later, though now out of the Company's service, he prevented a lynching by a group of American cowmen who were driving a herd of cattle to the Cariboo mines. When they reached Kamloops, some money was discovered missing, and they decided to hang one of their crew, thinking that if he were not guilty of that crime he must be guilty of some other. McLean, who happened to be in Kamloops at the time, convinced them that under British law they needed proof.

Clearly, law and order was changing. When it was just the Company and the Indians, maintaining the law consisted mainly of disciplining an occasional Indian for horse theft, or a Company employee for dereliction. Now the full force of British law must be upheld among almost forty thousand rowdy immigrants, by Chief Justice Matthew Begbie and a handful of justices of the peace.

As people began to settle around McLean at Hat Creek, they regarded him as the law. He was the most respected man in the area, in all of the Upper Country in fact. Local geographical points were established in relation to their distance from McLean's Restaurant. A farm or a creek would be described as being "twelve miles south-west of McLean's," for example.

Within a year or so of establishing at Hat Creek, the McLean family had several neighbours. A Scot named William Donaldson built his own crude log roadhouse four miles north, and Ranald and Allan McDonald also to the north. There was Oregon Jack Dowling on Gaspard Creek and the Cornwall brothers eleven miles south. They were interesting neighbours. Donaldson generally wore a Glengarry bonnet as he stirred up a huge new pot of batter for the tasteless flapjacks he served his customers. The Cornwalls' favourite amusement was to go on a full-fledged fox hunt, complete with imported fox hounds, a huntsman and all the trappings, except that there were no foxes around the manor, so they went after coyotes. The McDonalds were sons of Archibald McDonald, McLean's old boss at Fort Colville, and Ranald had been one of the first white men to visit Japan. Oregon Jack, so-called, naturally, because he was from Oregon, was colourful but probably the most normal of the lot.

The settlers relied on themselves — that is, McLean — for law and order. If stock was missing, a saddle stolen, or if somebody was feuding, it was McLean they asked for help. Of particular value was his experience with Indians, or Siwashes as they were known by the whites. On more than one occasion he was asked to track down a renegade, and then interpret for the whites as the suspect was grilled about a crime. Even the Cornwalls, who arrived in 1862 and had the most impressive operation in the area other than McLean's, relied on him in such situations.

As tough as he was, Donald McLean was also hospitable. After the near-lynching in Kamloops, one of the Yankee cowmen who had been involved in the dispute showed up on the Bonaparte one day with 150 cows, heading for Barkerville. It was late in the season, and Donald advised the man, Major John Thorpe, not to try to go any further until spring. He offered to let Thorpe winter his herd on the McLean property, and Thorpe gladly accepted. The cows ranged both at Hat Creek and at McLean's Farm on Cache Creek, and despite it being one of the worst winters in years, not an animal was lost. A single, sixteen-year-old cowhand named Andrew Jackson Splawn stayed with the herd till spring, following McLean's advice on how to move the herd around to keep them alive. Splawn admired Donald McLean. "A good brainy Scotchman he was, even if he did have a squaw for a wife and a dozen half-breed children."

A miner named John Clapperton stopped in one day in 1862. When next he saw young Charlie and Allen McLean, they would be holed up in a log cabin trying to avoid the hangman.

It wasn't just miners and cowmen who passed through Hat Creek. Governor James Douglas himself paid his old chief trader a visit there, concluding: "from the appearance of the crops there is every prospect that his labour and outlay will be well rewarded."

There were men of the cloth too, like Father Charles Grandidier, one of the new French Oblate priests sent to work among the miners. Donald found the young missionary on the road from Port Douglas one day, looking like a wet cat, hungry and exhausted from having walked the entire distance of more than a hundred miles. The God-fearing McLean, ever remembering that it was a missionary who saved his life at Fort Babine many years before, took him in, then provided him with a horse for the rest of the trip to Williams Creek and Barkerville.

You didn't have to be a Catholic to receive the McLean hospitality, though it wasn't always returned. In July of 1863, a mouthy but energetic Methodist clergyman named Ebenezer Robson stayed at the roadhouse. He complained about the flies, the food and the beds, a strange way to show gratitude, considering McLean's was regarded as the finest roadhouse on the Cariboo Road. Even more strange since it was Donald McLean who had generously paid Robson a twenty-dollar gold piece for that baptism down at Fort Hope a few years before.

Anglican Bishop George Hills stopped at McLean's, admiring the cattle and horses, and an especially impressive bull brought up from Salt Lake City. He also admired Donald McLean's family, though he found the younger boys "wild as colts."

There were the tourists too, looking for adventure and something to write up for the British journals that were starving for stories about the gold rush, like William Champness, a traveller and diarist who called McLean's "the best farm in the colony," and wrote about it in a journal published back home in England.

But not all travellers were pleasant, nor law-abiding. In August of 1863 a man named Thomas Clegg was carrying forty thousand dollars in notes, belonging to E.T. Dodge & Co., south through the Cariboo when he was jumped by two miners, William Armitage and Fred Glennard, twenty miles north of Hat Creek. Clegg's companion, a Captain Joe Taylor of Seton Lake, escaped, but Clegg was gunned down and robbed of his fortune. McLean was quickly on their trail, searching up and down the Cariboo Road with some of his boys and a handful of local Indians. Coming upon the killers, the posse was shot at, but McLean fired back and wounded one of the badmen. The pair got away into the night, and McLean couldn't track them in the dark. The outlaws split up, with the wounded Glennard heading for the hills near McLean's ranch, hoping later to get to Savona's Ferry at the west end of Kamloops Lake and get away to the international boundary line. He shot one of McLean's calves for food, but wasn't seen again after that. His partner wasn't so lucky.

McLean and his helpers caught up to Armitage seven miles north of the restaurant and took him down to Lillooet for trial. Armitage, despite having Clegg's pistol on him when captured, professed to be a mere bystander to the murder. His offer to lead them to Glennard if the judge went easy on him was ignored; he was hanged.

Clegg's murder was a sensation in the press for a few weeks. Though Glennard wasn't caught, the money was retrieved. If not for Donald McLean, both killers would have gotten away clean with the money. If not for Donald McLean, that part of the booming Upper Country would have been without law and order.

## [17]

ESQUIMALT HARBOUR, V.I.
Wednesday, June 15, 1864

At 11:30 AM, H.M.S. *Sutlej* sailed for Bentinck Arm, sent off by a large cheering crowd and the band of the Russian flagship playing "God Save The Queen" and other British national airs. Admiral John Kingcome himself was in command. Governor Frederick Seymour travelled on the *Sutlej*, but his personal steam yacht, *Leviathan*, was already on its way to Nanaimo to pick up two Homathko Indians who would act as guides. From there the *Leviathan* would take them to Bentinck Arm to join the expedition and identify the murderers when they were found.

The *Sutlej* was an impressive warship. The big frigate was nine years old, launched at Portsmouth as a sailing ship, but converted to screw propulsion and lengthened four years later. Designed for fifty broadside guns, the number was now thirty-five plus a chase gun. With 515 officers and men, she'd arrived at Esquimalt for service in the pacific Northwest almost a year ago to the day.

The *Labouchere* and the old HBC steamer *Beaver* were also to sail into Bentinck Arm to impress the Indians there with a show of strength.

Brew's new volunteers, some of whom had been with the first Bute Inlet expedition, were as well suited to the job as any available. He pared them from the dozens who had asked to join and was pleased with their calibre. Most were former Royal Engineers who had come from England with Colonel Richard Moody. When the Engineers were disbanded in late 1863, most remained in British Columbia, taking up occupations ranging from small business to farming to blacksmithing. Thomas Elwyn would be second in command. Among the volunteers was William Buckley, one of the Bute Inlet survivors.

This small force of special constables was favoured over professional soldiers, in keeping with Seymour's intention not to put the expedition on a war footing. His decision to go along with Brew to Bella Coola and into the Interior to join up with Cox was mostly for the purposes of moral suasion. It would make a grand show, the governor tramping about the wilderness personally seeing to it that justice prevailed, and he could then continue on to the goldfields for a personal inspection. Despite the control Douglas had tried to exercise over the influx of miners into British Columbia, he never had direct contact with them. Seymour thought a visit would be a good thing both for his own edification and for the entertainment of the miners.

Brew had made all the arrangements for the expedition after Seymour finally wrung assurances from Kingcome that naval support would be available. The first plan was for the *Tribune* to pick up the volunteers and their supplies and pack animals at New Westminster. Unfortunately, that arrangement was abandoned when the *Tribune* ran aground in the Fraser River getting to the British Columbia capital, and there was concern about its ability to get back down to the sea fully loaded. Another problem was that a train of pack mules hired from upriver failed to arrive. So Brew went to Victoria and bought seventeen pack horses and got them loaded on board the *Sutlej* June 14. The *Forward* went over to New Westminster and brought back the forty volunteers the same night.

Victorians had at first been indignant at Seymour's rejection of their proposals to send an expedition of their own, but grudging approval was allowed Seymour's actions and the ability of the men who had been picked. Editorialized the *Colonist*:

It is needless to say that it would be difficult to obtain a better set of men than these.

The Royal Engineers have had abundant roughing experience while on the other hand they possess habits of discipline and obedience which are the very greatest importance in an expedition of this kind and which we fear might be sadly wanting among some of our Victorian volunteers. It is not desirable that every Indian north of Victoria should be killed but it appears to be the idea of some of our heroes that are 'spilling for a fight' amongst us that all they had to do was to elect their own officers and start out on a general hunting expedition in which the Indian race generally were to be the game. If we wanted to bring about an Indian war, we couldn't do better than indulge this highly irresponsible and anti-discipline element, while, however, there were at the same time a goodly number of valuable men ready to start from Victoria. We believe all things considered, that it is fortunate Governor Seymour, by having so effectual a force ready to leave, is able to dispense with extraneous assistance.

# 18

PUNTZI LAKE, Chilcotin Plateau
Sunday, June 19, 1864

*His Excellency*
*Governor Frederick Seymour*

*I have the honour to report for the information of his Excellency the Governor that in accordance with your instructions I left Alexandria on the 8th instant in command of the Bute Inlet expedition, our force including myself, consisting of 50 men and an indian boy, and provisions for one month.*

*Alexis, a Chilcotin chief whose good services as a guide I was led to calculate upon was not to be found, having with his family and tribe fled to the mountains, reports having been freely circulated there we were coming to this region for the purpose of exterminating the indians friendly or otherwise.*

*12th arrived at Punt-zeen lake and discovered in a ditch the murdered body of Wm. Manning, one side of the head was completely crushed in and a musket ball had passed through the body. I held an inquest and had it decently interred.*

13th dispatched Mr. McLean his son another man and indian Jack to Chilcoaten Forks to secure if possible the services of Alexis an indian chief not only as an interpreter but a guide the country here being so thickly timbered and covered with brush that it would be a difficult & dangerous task to follow with any certainty of success the indian tracks and trails they are so numerous and intricate, purposely made so I presume – about midday a Scouting party returned to camp reporting having seen an indian's dog on the ridge of a wooded hill. I at once dispatched a party of 8 of our best men with an indian boy to follow the dog & bring to camp any indian they might fall in with so that I could make my mission known amongst them. This party had entered the wood about half a mile or so when the indian guide made signs indicating that indians were near when our party were instantly fired upon by indians lying under cover the latter entrenched themselves behind trees reloaded & fired again. The fire was as quickly returned the indians started again & retreated, covering themselves as they did so by passing from behind one tree to another whooping as they flew.

One of our men was wounded in the thigh. I believe the indians escaped unhurt although our party appear to think they wounded one of them. On the firing being heard at camp I sent a second party of 8 to the assistance of our men and Mr. Ogilvy & myself went with 6 men in another direction so as to Surround the indians but having taken shelter with bush we all looked and searched in vain for them – this day we constructed good breastworks for our protection during the nights.

14th about 11 of 11 AM heard firing in the same direction as above & saw 5 indians come in front of the hill & discharge their pieces into the air as I presume, defying us and a trap. I concluded not to risk the lives of my men in any way until the arrival of Alexis as the indians hold complete advantage over us in the bush.

16th Mr. McLean and party returned amid reports having met with Alexis' tribe and family at Chilcoaten Forks – all were in arms at the approach of McLean but he assured them of our peaceful intentions and they promised to send for Alexis to the mountains and stated that we might expect his advent in 4 or 5 days – the above tribe informed Mr. McLean that the murderers 10 in number were banded together and were lurking about the country ranging between Bute inlet and the point I now write from.

I am now sending for fresh supplies, as it's possible we may be here or elsewhere in this vicinity for some weeks as the murderers among these tribes have retired into the woods and their position must be discovered before we can think of taking them with certainty and for this duty we require Alexis who is well acquainted with their haunts and hiding places.

I believe our force is sufficiently strong to perform our task, the indians

*friendly and unfriendly do not number more than 70 at the furthest.
I expect Alexis to arrive here tomorrow. Should he disappoint me
which is unlikely I shall proceed toward Bentinck Arm about 65 miles
and obtain "Anaham" an influential and good indian, as a guide.*

*I have the honour to be Sir
Your most obedient and humble servant
William Geo. Cox*

## [19]

NANCOOTLEM, Chilcotin Plateau
Tuesday, June 28, 1864

Seymour and Brew were resting their men and horses after climbing
up out of the valley of the Bella Coola onto the plateau when John
Ogilvy and a dozen men arrived with Cox's report of the 19th. The
Bentinck Arm expedition was literally catching its breath. After landing
at Bella Coola ten days earlier to relieve the "siege" of the white population, the expedition had pushed on up the valley under the competent
leadership of Brew, a no-nonsense Irishman who always stayed focused
entirely on the task at hand. The sweating, cursing, snorting, stumbling
train of nineteen horses and seventy-five men had just climbed the Great
Slide of Mount Deluge on a trail with few zigzags for relief.

The governor read Cox's report and immediately decided to ig-
nore the suggestion that the Alexandria force be left to handle
everything, telling Brew they would continue as planned to Puntzi Lake
to connect the two forces. He wrote a letter to Cox asking him to meet
them half way so they could discuss strategy. Ogilvy started back to Cox,
leaving Brew and Seymour to follow behind with their men.

The Bentinck Arm trail now emerged onto an elevated rolling area
almost level with the summits of the mountains. The big pines, cedars
and firs of the valleys were gone, there now being stunted firs, sparser
brush and grass grasping sandy soil. The trail descended gradually
five hundred feet to the Hotharko, a small tributary of the Bella Coola
or Atnarko, following its valley for several miles east and north.

At the forks of the Hotharko was a steep one hundred-foot high
bluff of basalt columns known as the Precipice. The trail here was
extremely steep, the top of the Precipice 3,840 feet above sea level.
From there the country became much like that Cox's party had
passed over to get to Puntzi Lake from Alexandria — a broad plain of
forest broken only by marshes and lakes. Poor grass, wild roses and
strawberries and knnik-knnik or uva ursi, the native tobacco, formed

the main ground-cover. The evergreens remained stunted, but small cottonwoods formed groves along the banks of streams.

Mishaps plagued the expedition in fording torrents, crossing rotten bridges or negotiating the steep, sometimes almost non-existent trail. It was a pretty bedraggled party of volunteers that neared Nancootlem, and one of the men complained that "the whole business is botched from the first from want of a proper leader."

By now twenty of the thirty Bella Coola Indians who had volunteered at Bentinck Arm to help the expedition had deserted and three horses had disappeared, a total Seymour called "a comparatively trifling loss."

It was known that Anahim had a palisaded fort at his village. Though Brew didn't believe Anahim himself was involved in the rebellion, he was tired of the march and hoped the whole Chilcotin would make a stand there. He was disappointed to find the fort empty, and Anahim's village deserted. He didn't order the fort or lodges burned; if his opinion of Anahim proved wrong, the decision to leave the fort could prove dangerous later.

The first sign of McDonald's party was an aparejo, some straps, a half keg of nails and some augers. A little further the expedition came across some broken boxes, with matches and candles strewn around. Mosquitoes and black flies buzzed about.

Then, beside the road near a tree bigger than the thin dwarf spruce usual to the area, was a body or, at least, part of one. It was hard to know which had mutilated it more, the Chilcotins or the wolves. Both legs were off near the knees. Only the thigh-bones, ribs, back and head were left — the rest apparently having been eaten by wolves. Both hands were gone, but the fingers of one were found near the torso. A knife was deeply imbedded in the skull. An examination of the clothes beside the corpse showed that one shot that passed through the left arm near the shoulder and probably exited through the right wrist had been fired from close enough range to singe the shirt. Other holes were found in the shirt and pant legs. These were the remains of Alexander McDonald.

Only fifteen yards away was an even more grisly sight. Near an Indian tomb of logs and stakes, an expedition member was startled to see a Chilcotin sitting on the ground. A moment later he saw that the Indian was quite dead, the body also having been eaten at by wolves. A wreath of feathers sat on the head, a ring hung from the nose, and in the mouth was a pipe.

They didn't know it at the time, but this was the body of Chacatinea, one of three Nancootlem Indians who had joined Klatassine for the attack on the pack train. After Chacatinia and Klymtedza had been buried and the Chilcotins had left the scene, the wolves had moved in for a free meal. They not only tore apart the bodies of the white men, but managed to drag out Chacatinea's body from its grave. They had dragged it a few yards but had apparently been interrupted and left it, quite by accident, in a sitting position. A Bella Coola Indian happening by spotted the body and, rather than burying it, insulted the corpse by leaving it in its sitting position and putting the pipe in its mouth.

A dead horse was next to come in sight. About two hundred yards further the body of Higgins was discovered. He had been shot in the chest and arm with musket balls, and in the stomach with buckshot. Higgins had been dragged off the trail by the feet. His head lay in a hollow surrounded by hair. The back of the head was smashed, obviously having been struck repeatedly with axes, knives or musket butts.

Next there were several more dead horses and more candles and other goods scattered around. Near a small pond beside the trail lay the body of McDougall, riddled with bullets and horribly mangled like the others.

In the woods and along the trail for half a mile were boxes of carpenter's tools, yeast tins, ropes, candles, gutted pack saddles, broken agricultural instruments, kegs of nails, and personal papers and money.

The bodies were interred by the volunteers.


[20]

PUNTZI LAKE, Chilcotin Plateau
Wednesday, July 6, 1864


The convergence of the two expeditions was cause for celebration. Cox's men — "virtually besieged by an invisible enemy" as Seymour described their situation — gave the governor a hearty and prolonged cheer.

Brew's men set up camp near the fort, and the leaders gathered to discuss events to date and to plot strategy. Though Brew and Cox were ostensibly the two leaders of rank, with Elwyn and McLean the respective seconds, Seymour dominated the decision-making. He was surprised and a little disgusted to find that, although Cox had been at Puntzi for two days before Brew and Seymour even left for Bentinck Arm, he had accomplished virtually nothing. Cox insisted that he had had to wait for Alexis, who had not shown up as promised, but Seymour wanted some action. He ordered Cox to take his unit and scout the area beyond Tatla Lake towards Bute Inlet instead of waiting for friendly Indians, who might or might not show up to help. And there would be no waiting; Cox would leave the next morning. Since provisions were low, Brew decided to send another party back some 150 miles to Bella Coola for supplies. That would leave only ten men at Puntzi Lake.

Though the members of the two expeditions had hailed each other and welcomed the chance to swap tales, they were two very distinct camps that night. Cox's band of miners took the opportunity to celebrate. Brew's New Westminster volunteers were more sombre. The difference between the two would be difficult to reconcile if they were to be together over a lengthy period of time. Seymour recognized the possible problem right away, and tended to side with Brew's men. "The few hours that the two parties had passed together sufficed to show the difference in their character. The men raised in the gold district, mostly Americans, passed the greater part of the night in dancing and playing cards to an accompaniment of war whoops and the beating of tin pots. The New Westminster Expedition, almost exclusively English, and comprising many discharged Royal Engineers, spent the evening in their usual quiet soldier-like manner. No spirituous liquor was in either camp, yet the amusements were kept up in the one long after total silence prevailed in the other, and a slight estrangement commenced between the occupiers of the fort and those encamped on the plain below, which was never entirely healed."

If it were true that there was no liquor, it must have been because the Cariboo posse had drunk it all, since they had left Alexandria with a plentiful supply. And, there being no liquor left, it must have made the expedition doubly trying for the normally hard-drinking governor.

## [21]

### CHOELQUOIT LAKE, Chilcotin Plateau
### Sunday, July 17, 1864, early morning

Donald McLean was up before day broke on the tents pitched near a stream running into Choelquoit Lake. There was, as yet, no banging of cooking utensils, no chatter of men rising from sleep. There was only the crackle of the campfires that had been kept burning through the night, and the gurgle of the creek.

He knew the Chilcotins were near, that their camp was probably within a few miles of their own. They had had several brushes with the Indians in the past several days, had even sighted Klatassine himself, but had come up empty each time.

Were it not for the retired fur trader, the expedition wouldn't have done even as well as it had, for Cox's inexperience and conceit had continued to be a trial. While McLean stayed largely in the background as Cox issued the orders, it was McLean's advice, rather than

Cox's ignorant snap judgments, that resulted in any positive action.

Since the day they left Puntzi, virtually kicked out into the cold by Seymour (and quite rightly so), they had been closely watched by the Chilcotins. Wherever Cox's men went they were close by, though the volunteers hadn't seen any Indians for the first few days. McLean and the Indian Jack guided the expedition twenty-five miles south of Tatla Lake into Klatassine's favourite hunting and fishing territory, the mountainous range covering thirty miles from east to west between Mosley Creek, a branch of the Homathko, and Chilko Lake, which stretched like an inland sea almost forty miles itself to the foot of the Coast Mountains. Dozens of Indian trails criss-crossed the area, and the expedition's scouting parties covered twenty or thirty miles a day in their search.

One day one of the scouting parties came upon a new trail in hilly country that was followed for several hours. They discovered a village of deserted Indian lodges and, in a thickly wooded area, found a cache of flour, bacon, saddles and other goods from McDonald's pack train.

Cox consulted with McLean and they concentrated their efforts in the area surrounding the deserted village for a few days but came across no further sign. By July 16 the miners were growing impatient with an expedition that was turning into a ridiculous failure. Cox decided to take them back to Puntzi Lake, and Seymour be damned.

They had broken camp and started their first day's journey back toward Puntzi when one of the volunteers discovered that he'd forgotten something in the camp. He rode back to the site. As the volunteer broke through the brush into the clearing he stopped short. Squatting by the dying embers of a campfire were several Chilcotins puffing on a calumet. They saw the white man as he wheeled his mount and charged back down the trail. They were almost as surprised as he was, for they had thought it was safe to come and examine the remains of the camp. The Chilcotins hurriedly, but calmly, stood and walked out of the clearing. In the bush they split up and went in different directions.

Cox's volunteers were back a few minutes later beating the bush for the half dozen Indians, but it appeared they once again had vanished. One party of a dozen miners was getting discouraged when they picked up the footprints of a lone Indian. Hurrying up on them, they sighted their quarry, a tall, muscular Chilcotin loping along across a pasture-like opening in the forest. Three shots were fired but they missed. The volunteers didn't know it, but the man was Klatassine, who broke into a dead run toward a lagoon, or pengontsodl. When the whites galloped up to the lagoon, there was no sign of the Indian.

Based on that sighting, McLean now wanted to go out for a reconnoitre of the area unhindered by the greenhorns in the expedition.

They could sleep while he got something accomplished.

He let Duncan sleep, too, though Duncan was certainly not a greenhorn. He, like Donald's other older sons, was thoroughly competent in the bush. He had worked for years with his father for the Company, as had Donald Jr. and Alex. They worked as labourers, packers, and interpreters, and were among the strongest and most dependable of men. Unlike the "gentlemen" hired in London, they would never have the opportunity to rise even to the level of an apprentice clerk; it was against Company policy to allow half-breeds in the more responsible positions. But the McLeans were no longer Company men anyway.

As the weeks had passed, men had come and gone to keep the Chilcotin Expedition up to strength. As one group was returned to Alexandria, a new roster of recruits was brought out. Donald McLean had sent word home to Hat Creek for Donald Jr. to come up and join them. Donald Jr. was the giant of the family, tall and lithe, but with excellent stamina. At thirty, he was the oldest of the boys. Within days, or perhaps it had happened already, Sophia would be giving birth to another McLean.

Donald McLean strode over to where Jack, the Indian scout from Alexandria, was sleeping, and shook him awake. Nobody was supposed to leave camp without permission or, in McLean's case, without notifying Cox. McLean felt strongly the presence of the Chilcotins on this morning, and wanted to get moving. Jack was nervous about the two of them going out alone, but McLean insisted.

Sun was beginning to spill over the outlines of the mountains in bright ribbons as they crossed the stream and started up a hill. It was going to be a clear, warm day. The hill was steep, the only one of any consequence in the immediate area, the only one from which one could get a good view of the surrounding terrain. Near its summit there was a ravine that broke into a bare spot. Otherwise the hills were low; that's what made the campsite easy to protect.

Jack was cautious from the time they left the camp. McLean was, as usual, unconcerned. Death didn't worry him. He had contemplated it often, shaken hands with it and walked away. Many others he had known had not escaped Death's embrace, succumbing to tragic accidents, murder, disease or exhaustion. During the winter of 1849-50, a bitterly cold, miserable winter, when the cattle and horses were dying in the snowdrifts of cold and starvation, or being eaten by the camp dogs or killed for food by the Indians, a strange sickness had fallen on Fort Alexandria. The fur trade during that winter all but disappeared; the Indians were too busy dying from the cholera-like mystery disease, the whites too busy coughing and vomiting and trying not to die like the Indians. McLean was in despair, worried about being blamed for an unproductive season and himself so weak he was unable to swallow dried salmon without immediately puking it back up. So shaky was his hand that he could barely maintain the post journal, and waited for his old friend Death to come calling. "Death," he wrote, "is a creditor that must be paid." For eight weeks he waited, yet somehow he denied Death once again. Why should today be different from any other?

A rocky trail led up the hill by the ravine, and he and Jack followed it.

A Chilcotin, who has been identified variously as Anukatlk, Shililika, Sachayel and Hatish, watched as McLean and Jack approached the top of the hill. His rifle was trained on the big, handsome white man. McLean had become a familiar figure to the Chilcotins as they watched the activities of Cox's party. He was still remembered from the time he had spent among the tribes of the area two decades ago. McLean was said to have magic, for at least twice before, in years past, he had been shot in the heart only to ride off unharmed.

Anukatlk, who had joined Klatassine after the massacres, was one of several scouts who were out that morning. He had settled down near the trail to keep watch, for it had been expected that the whites would send out a party in this direction. But Anukatlk didn't expect to see two men out by themselves on foot, and certainly not the great chief McLean.

McLean was alert but confident, as ever, as he advanced up the trail followed by Jack. The Indian tugged at McLean's coat sleeve.

"Indians near." He wanted to go back for help.

McLean rested his rifle butt on the ground for a moment, wiping his brow and straining his senses to pick up any sign of the rebels.

"Don't be foolish, Jack," he said quietly. "We'll be alright."

He continued up the trail, and the nervous and reluctant guide caught up to him. They were at a distinct disadvantage. The trail was steep and there was good cover all around. There is a tendency for a greenhorn to lower his eyes and concentrate on pumping his tired legs up the grade, so that the proper caution is not taken. McLean, though, was ever wary. When they rounded a slight curve in the trail, it was he, not Jack, who immediately sighted a screen of fir bows piled against a tree trunk off to one side in the bush. At the same time as his eyes fell upon the hiding place, McLean's arms were raising his rifle and cocking it to fire.

But there was no one behind the screen, for Anukatlk was hiding in a clump of willows on the opposite side of the trail. As McLean wheeled toward the screen of boughs, expecting to see a gun poke through it, he exposed his back to Anukatlk.

Jack's first reaction was not to the blind, but to the click of a gunlock somewhere in the brush. He threw himself to the ground as

Anukatlk's rifle boomed.

McLean fell. A second bullet passed over the guide, who tumbled a few feet down the hill, regained his feet and looked back in time to see some Chilcotins sink below the crest of the hill. Jack plunged full speed down the trail to the camp. He almost collided with a horse ridden by Harry Wilmot, who had been on watch and had heard the shots.

Duncan McLean, arising to find that his father wasn't in camp, was running across the meadow on foot.

Wilmot urged his mount up the trail, knowing he too might come under attack. He came upon Donald McLean lying face down, and when Wilmot turned him over it looked as though he might still be alive. But there was no pulse.

The volunteer remounted and rode back for help. As he reached the flat a few hundred yards later, Duncan McLean rushed up puffing in an obvious state of distress. He asked if Wilmot had found his father.

Wilmot's first reaction was to avoid the truth, but the young McLean insisted.

Wilmot told Duncan his father was dead.

Duncan's face contorted, he moaned in anguish and fumbled for his revolver. Wilmot's fast action in leaping from his mount and grabbing the weapon saved the young man from suicide, for he had the pistol cocked and was about to point it towards his head. Duncan fainted.

Cox was already rushing out of the camp with twenty men on foot, for he had heard the shots too, and then Jack had come tearing in. He ordered two of them to help Duncan back to camp, while the rest, including William Buckley, went forward with Wilmot and Jack.

As they filed up the slope, one of the volunteers tripped. His rifle fired and the ball went through his leg. He screamed and fell down thrashing. The men in front of him flattened themselves.

"They're behind us!" one of them cried.

"Where?" asked the fellow who had shot himself.

Two more men hauled the unfortunate victim back to camp while the rest continued on.

Passing McLean's body, Cox peeled off more men to carry it back. The remaining volunteers reached the summit of the hill and scanned the topography of the surrounding country. Cox sent a message to Ogilvy to bring up more volunteers and to form a ring around the hill.

Fitzgerald sighted in his telescope a group of Indians huddled near a big rock several hundred yards away. Shots were fired at them. One ball struck a tree five feet above Klatassine's head and the chase was on.

Cox thought he had them this time, but Indian cunning once again foiled the whites. While the area had all but been encircled by volunteers, a long lagoon at the bottom of an almost perpendicular, rocky bluff left a gap in the snare.

Klatassine and his half dozen men scrambled down to the water and plunged in. Before the whites realized what was happening, the Indians swam the sixty yards to the other side and were through the line. A few parting shots followed them, but further search was useless.

The camp was both restless and morose that evening. McLean had been highly respected, and his death was the crowning disaster of what had become to many of them a fruitless exercise. An examination of his body revealed the reason for his previous escapes from attempts on his life. He wore a special breastplate, but it had done him no good against the back shot.

McLean, who had read the burial service for Manning, was now the subject of words of praise as he was laid in the ground in a field near the camp. Cox renamed the lake after McLean. A shallow layer of dirt was shovelled over the blankets that covered the fallen hero, then rocks and logs were placed in the grave. Finally, more dirt was smoothed carefully over, all level with the ground. That night flames licked over the field for several acres and a pall of smoke hung in the air. Neither wolves nor Indians would be able to find and disturb the remains of Donald McLean.

## [22]

BONAPARTE RIVER
Wednesday, June 1, 1865

*To His Excellency*
*Frederick Seymour Esq.*

*Sir:*

*I have the honour to acknowledge the receipt of your letter announcing to me, that you had bestowed on me a pension of 100 lb. a year for five years.*

*In reply I have merely to say that I have to thank the Legislative Council for the value they entertained of my husband's services.*

*I would wish to have the pension paid quarterly and by the magistrate at Lytton if it would be convenient to you.*

*With many thanks for the high opinion you entertained of my late husband.*

*I have the honour*
*to remain*
*Your Most Obed. Servt.*
*Sophia McLean*

They never did convict anyone of Donald McLean's murder. After McLean's burial Cox headed back to Puntzi, where Seymour decided he'd had enough of the wilderness experience and headed on to Barkerville. Brew and Cox each beat around the bushes for a few more weeks until Cox got a message from Klatassine that he wished to talk. Sure, said Cox, come on in, we'll talk.

Klatassine was discouraged by the refusal of Alexis and Anahim to join him; he was short of food and ammunition and slowed by a camp full of women and children. Under the impression that he would be taken to meet Seymour, and having sent gifts to Cox as a sign of trust, he and several of his followers and their families, accompanied by Alexis, showed up at Cox's camp near the old Fort Chilcotin site, long ago abandoned by the Hudson's Bay Company. When Klatassine found he was to be taken prisoner, he was greatly angered. Even Alexis accused Cox of being a liar.

On October 26 Klatassine, Tellot, Tahpitt, Piell and Chessus, the main instigators of the rebellion, were hanged in Quesnel after being tried by Judge Matthew Begbie. Before he died, Klatassine said, "We meant war, not murder." The Chilcotin War, after an expenditure of sixteen thousand pounds, was officially over. Though Klatassine's attempt to wipe out the whites and take back the Chilcotins' land failed, the road that caused it all was never built.

Seymour looked upon his small part in the Chilcotin expeditions as quite a personal accomplishment. He lavished great praise on all concerned when the colonial legislature opened for a new session. Of Donald McLean he said:

> The ruggedness of the coast range, aided by the absence of all means of transport, seemed to debar us from access to the Chilcotin country from the sea, but an expedition under a gentleman of great reputation for courage and skill in dealings with the native tribes of the colony had left the Upper Fraser for the Interior.

The Chilcotin War remained one of Seymour's greatest sources of pride in the years to follow. He was certain it had insured that the Indians would never again attempt to rise up in force against the white population. In one of his letters to Colonial Secretary Edward Cardwell, he summed it all up:

> That Europeans should thus run down wild Indians, and drive them to suicide or surrender in their own hunting grounds, in the fruit and fish season, appears to me, I confess, little short of marvellous.

But for the family of Donald McLean, hardship was only beginning.

# Part 3

THE BOYS

LONG LAKE, Nicola Valley, British Columbia
Saturday, December 6, 1879

The Nicola Valley stretches south from Kamloops for some forty-five miles through a series of elbow-shaped lakes formed by glacial deposits ten thousand years ago. It has a sparse kind of a beauty better appreciated once you get to know the place. The upper hills are thick with Ponderosa pine but the lower slopes are quite bare, here and there broken by vein-like clefts worn away by the creeks spilling down towards the lakes and the Nicola River. Where the creeks haven't run dry, massive cottonwoods and spindly poplars hug the beds, giving the country a marbled kind of look. Frequent rock outcroppings speak of the valley's ice-age past.

In 1879 the land was still thick with bunch grass that would touch the shoulders of a tall horse. In summer the blades of the grass were deep green, gradually tinging blue as the weeks passed; the crowns of the stocks turned to straw by late July. Those summers could blister a man's body and mind so that at the peak of the hot season, from mid-morning to early evening, it was nearly impossible to work outside to any purpose. In winter it was a different story. Temperatures could plunge to thirty degrees below zero or worse, accompanied by deep snow. But there was the bunch grass, giving life to the cattle and horses kept by the handful of ranchers who had moved into the valley during the past ten years. The Nicola, a natural habitat for deer and other game as well as a wide variety of fowl, was near perfect for ranching and farming. Already the grass was being reduced by heavy grazing near the wagon road that now connected the valley to Kamloops. In the days of the Hudson's Bay Company, Donald McLean and other fur traders had travelled the Nicola with their brigades on their way south to Fort Langley. The fur trade was long gone, and so was the gold, but the gold rush had by-passed the Nicola anyway. Now it was cattle country.

The winter of 1879-80 was one of the bad ones; in fact, the worst yet. In early December, at least a month away from the coldest time of year, it was already twenty below. The wind that swept down the valley over the snow drifts, rustling the stiff bunch grass, was even colder. It would be a long time to break-up for the ranchers and their stock.

A dozen miles from Kamloops, within sight of Long Lake, four riders sat on their mounts. They were just sitting there, holding their horses still, waiting. They were known around the area as the McLean Gang. For the past year and a half, they had done pretty much as they

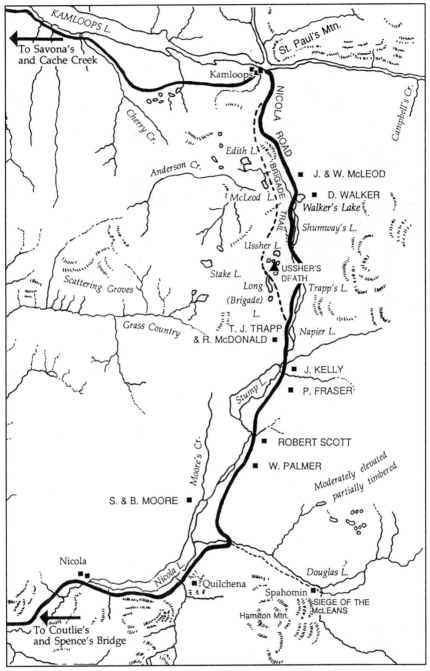

Nicola Valley and the flight of the McLeans. Adapted from Map of a portion of the Southern Interior of British Columbia, Embodying the Explorations made in 1877 by G.M. Dawson, and in 1882-84 by Amos Bowman (*KMA*)

Allen McLean (*BCARS, 3387*)

pleased anywhere in the Upper Country.

Their leader was Allen McLean, at twenty-four the oldest. He was fearless, cool and decisive, not to mention a very good shot —important traits in the outlaw business. He also had an enormous appetite, though the rigors of his trade kept him in superb physical condition. Allen was tall, wonderfully strong, and sported a jet black beard. Even slouched in his saddle, dressed in bulky winter attire, he looked impressive. Somehow Allen's heart had gone cold, yet his temper had a low flashpoint. Recently, raging at a horse that wasn't fast enough, he had pulled out a knife and stabbed it in the neck. As it bled profusely, he turned it loose to whatever fate a slow horse deserved.

Nearby was seventeen-year-old Charlie on a handsome black gelding. He too was tall and muscular, but, while Allen's face combined piercing eyes with softer Scottish features, Charlie's was squat and sharp. His high cheekbones and steel jaw gave him an expression that was hard, furtive. He had his father's eyes, his father's scowl. Charlie always appeared like a man gnashing his teeth in anger over some unexplained incompetence. His melancholia, however, should not be mistaken for lethargy; in a fight he could show considerable enthusiasm, as one Indian who now had to function without a nose could attest.

Archie, the third McLean brother, was barely in his teens, but he was big. He was the fairest of the group, not just in complexion but in brightness of outlook. Arch was in good humour just about all the time, no matter what the situation, almost to the point of being ridiculous. But on rare occasions he betrayed his youth —when angered, he would sometimes cry. At fifteen he could out-drink most, and he could certainly out-ride them. He was a superb horseman, better even than Charlie. One of his favourite amusements had been jockeying in the various horse races held around the Upper Country, before he'd gone on the run in a much different way.

His sullen partner, just Charlie's age, was Alex Hare, who sometimes called himself Dane English. He was a breed, like the rest of them. Hare lacked the height of the McLeans, being broad and dark, but he was muscular, with high cheekbones and a brown complexion that made him look more

Charlie McLean (BCARS, 3389)

Indian than white. The McLeans were among the only people he could call friends; he and Archie knew each other from their days together at the Cache Creek Boarding School, an experience that set them apart from Allen and Charlie in that they had learned to read and write. Literacy was an important discovery for Archie in particular; though he could write little and read poorly, it was enough to enjoy Jesse James stories. Their time at the boarding school, though, had been chaotic —the two teachers running the place had been forced to

Archie McLean (*BCARS, 3390*)

resign when the boys found a way of sneaking into the girls' dormitory after lights out. It's hard to imagine that Archie didn't have something to do with that situation.

Like the other three, Hare was well-armed; a six-shooter initialled "A.J.H." — Alexander Joseph Hare — and a razor-sharp bowie knife were in his personal arsenal.

Aside from being loaded for bear, these four young delinquents had something else in common: a consuming hatred for most of the white merchants and settlers in the Kamloops area. On this particular morning, they were watching someone on a horse riding toward them on the old trail not far off the Nicola Road. The man was travelling at a steady pace, apparently unworried, maybe even anxious to catch up to them. They waited patiently as his form, at first a dark speck against the snow-clad landscape, grew clearer.

William Palmer knew who the four riders up ahead of him were, and as he got closer his determination waned considerably. The thirty-four-year-old rancher had been at Stump Lake further down the Nicola for five years, and he knew all about the McLeans. They were the last people he wanted to meet up with.

Palmer wouldn't have been out on the trail, except that his big black gelding had been missing for four days. He'd bought the horse from a Mexican and it was well-known in the area, running with other stock on the range. Palmer had been moving north since the day before in hopes of finding it. Earlier that day he'd passed through the sheep ranch of Peter Fraser, at the north end of Stump Lake, and seen Fraser's herder, Jim Kelly, with Napier Lake stockman Richie McDonald and Johnston Stevenson, an easterner who'd recently taken up land near Douglas Lake. They were near Kelly's cabin. The herder's two sheep dogs announced his arrival.

Palmer had stopped to chat and to ask the time. Kelly carefully took out his silver pocket watch, the chain of which passed around his neck and into his pocket. It was half past nine. Discussion naturally turned to the activities of the McLean Gang. Kelly told them the boys had broken into his house and wrecked everything, stealing his bread and a half-bottle of brandy. Steven-

Alex Hare (*BCARS, 3386*)

son said he had been threatened by them. In fact, he was on a long death list the boys had been announcing around the country lately.

Palmer had moved on toward Kamloops, for several miles seeing no sign of his gelding, but now seeing it he wished it were somewhere else. There it was, twelve hundred pounds of prize horse, with Charlie McLean, now dismounted, holding it by the bridle. There was no mistaking the horse: it had a white face and a little white on the left eye. At first, when they saw him, they levelled their guns and rode on a little, up a rise toward the lake. He'd lost sight of them for half a mile, but now that he was almost on them they were simply waiting for him. He was now close enough to hear the click of gunlocks. Since he couldn't very well avoid them now that he was so close, he continued on until he was within talking range. As he would later testify in court, he was not greeted hospitably. Allen pointed a pistol, Archie a shotgun. Both were cocked and ready to fire.

"Don't shoot, boys!" Palmer shouted. "I'm not after you."

"You hadn't better be," was Allen's advice. "We're after fetching the Moores to time, and we'll kill any other sonofabitch who comes to arrest us."

It wasn't a particularly good start to the conversation, but not unusual considering the disposition of the McLeans these days. The reference to the Moores was to Ben and Sam Moore, Irish brothers who each had pre-emptions at the head of Nicola Lake. The Moores were one thing Palmer and the McLeans had in common. Palmer and his wife Jane hated them as much as the McLean Gang did — they were bad neighbours. When the Palmers had built their first house, the Moores knocked it down, claiming it was on their land. Then there was a disagreement over water. One day the Moores caught Palmer as he was digging a ditch, beat him up and stabbed at him with a knife. And Palmer charged Sam Moore with stealing a steer. John Clapperton, the Nicola JP, generally sided with the Moores.

The McLean boys, though, didn't like Palmer any more than they liked the Moores, who were on their death list along with Stevenson. Apparently the boys had heard the Moores were trying to execute one of the many arrest warrants on them. It was odd that Palmer wasn't on that list. Maybe they were grateful for the use of such a fine horse.

"Why did you ride up so fast?" asked Charlie, his voice a hot flash that seemed to singe by the rancher even in the frigid air. At least none of them seemed drunk; they had a reputation for enjoying strong whiskey, and even young Archie was said to enjoy an occasional drink.

"I just wanted some company," Palmer told him weakly. "I'm going to Jones' and Mellors'." G. William Jones and Jim Mellors had a ranch near Kamloops.

As Palmer spoke, his black seemed to recognize his voice. The horse's ears perked up and he stirred, turning to look at Palmer with big, dusky eyes. *I dare not recognize my horse.*

Charlie pulled the horse around and walked off into some brush. Palmer noticed that Archie's buckskin looked like a horse owned by George McRae, another rancher.

He told them that if they were headed toward town he'd ride along with them.

"We're not going anywhere near Kamloops — until we ride in to burn it down," said Allen.

That put an end to the conversation. Palmer was ordered to leave, which he was perfectly happy to do. The guns were lowered, but the outlaws kept an alert eye on Palmer as he rode on.

Probably the McLeans and Hare knew that Palmer knew whose

Kamloops in the early 1880s, before the coming of the railway (*KMA, 340*)

horse they had. But they had no reason for concern, since they'd been stealing anything they wanted with virtual impunity for so many months. There was nothing Palmer nor anyone else could do about the situation.

Palmer, though, wasn't about to simply walk away from his horse. A half mile away he almost decided to go back and confront them about it, but decided they'd probably shoot him. Instead he hurried toward Kamloops, where he intended to report the theft to Johnny Ussher, the British Columbia Provincial Police constable who was the only law within a hundred miles. Ussher wasn't even a full-time constable, sometimes complaining that he was so busy with other things he didn't have time for police work. But Palmer was determined to get some action and to get back his gelding.

The Nicola Valley ends abruptly above Kamloops. If a traveller has a moment he can pause at any number of vantage points to enjoy a very pretty view of the townsite, where the powerful North Thompson River meets the more sedate South Thompson. On the north-east shore, under the shadows of Mount Peter and Mount Paul, is the Indian reserve, several thousand acres of it, and the site of the original fur-trading post. In 1879 Kamloops was still a tiny community serving the burgeoning ranching industry. It waited only for the arrival of the promised rail line from the East to become a major centre. Its buildings were concentrated along a narrow strip of land squeezed between the Thompson River and the hills west of the confluence.

Besides the white and a few Chinese residences, the town had a handful of stores, hotels and blacksmith shops. There was no school for the children, and there were no resident clergymen, not even a whorehouse, but these would come soon. There was the Shuswap Mill in town on the river, and a mill at Tranquille to the west. Johnny Ussher lived with his new wife in a house next door to the old log jail. When Willie Palmer descended into the Thompson Valley, that's where he headed.

## [24]

By the time Ussher got on his way, it was well after lunch the next day. His wife was sick and he was reluctant to leave her by herself, but he had to act on Palmer's complaint. First he got a new warrant from John Edwards, a local justice of the peace. Edwards was a full-time rancher and businessman but, like other JPs, filled in when there was no circuit judge available, which was almost always. Then Ussher had to listen patiently as John Tait, another JP, lectured him about taking a big posse. Ussher declined the advice, believing from his own experience with the McLeans that it wouldn't be needed. Instead he'd take along Palmer, sworn in as a special constable by Edwards, and pick up a couple of men on the way.

Before he left town, he had one more important chore to take care of. He went with Palmer and Ed Grant, another special, out to Hector McLean's cabin above Kamloops Lake and arrested him on a two-week-old warrant for theft. The complaint had come from Cache Creek rancher Tom Cavanaugh, who alleged that Hector and some of the other boys had stolen his saddle. Hector was back in Kamloops after working in the Bonaparte for a few weeks. Some people liked Hector; he was generally a reliable hand. Ussher himself had always been on friendly terms with him. Others believed him to be the worst of the bunch. When Ussher explained to Hector why he was taking the precaution of locking him up, the older brother made no complaint, though he warned the constable about their threat.

"They say they'll shoot the first sonsabitches that come to arrest them."

Grant suggested Hector go with Ussher to help.

"I'll go any place with Johnny," Hector offered.

Ussher said it wouldn't look right for the boys' own brother to be riding with the posse, and that Hector would have to wait in jail under Grant's guard.

That done, the warrant in his shirt pocket and with a mouse-coloured horse he'd been renting from Grant, Ussher was ready to go after the McLean Gang. He wore no uniform, dressed instead in several layers of clothing to protect against the cold: shirt, vest, coat, overcoat, boots, overshoes, heavy woollen socks and pants, hat and a bandanna tied around his head to cover his ears.

Their first stop was to enlist Amni Shumway, a freighter who had a small acreage just south of town. Shumway was a good tracker and had been in the area for three years so knew it particularly well. He was a reluctant participant but Ussher assured him there would be no gun play. If there were, Shumway needn't be involved. So he borrowed a saddle horse from Jim Mellors, and Ussher swore him in as a special constable.

Whether he fully appreciated it or not, John Ussher represented almost single-handedly the credibility of law and order in British Columbia that Sunday afternoon as he headed south into the Nicola with his little posse. He was the only British Columbia provincial policeman from the North Thompson Valley south to Osoyoos on the border line, and from the Shuswap region west to the Similkameen. There were only a dozen "Provincials" in the whole Interior, and Ussher, as official in charge at Kamloops, was also government agent, jailer, court registrar, tax collector and assessor, mining recorder and gold commissioner. These various offices, not to mention his private business enterprises, made him a busy man. It had always been left up to him to do what he could to maintain a semblance of law and order in the district. Most of the police work was routine stuff. Even arresting the McLeans bordered on the routine. During his brief career as constable, Ussher had made less than a dozen arrests, and most of the warrants had the name McLean written on them. Having hosted them in his decrepit old jail a number of times, Ussher had no concern about hauling them in again.

Allen was telling people he wanted to follow in his father's footsteps and die fighting, that he would not let himself be arrested again and wouldn't be taken alive. Ussher believed that was just bluff to scare off anyone who might come after them. So was the death list, though the boys had some grievances that couldn't be denied. Ussher felt particularly sorry for young Alex Hare. Alex's father, Nick, had owned and run the Cherry Creek Ranch about twelve miles west of Kamloops since 1865. Though he was a good cattleman, his neighbours were pretty sure that whenever a cow went missing it ended up in Nick Hare's meat locker. Somehow Alex's Indian mother was no longer in the picture and, after Nick took a new wife, things blew up and young Alex was thrown out. When that happened, Ussher took him into his own home for awhile.

His acquaintance with the McLean Gang didn't make it any easier to catch them, though he was the only one who ever did. Arrest warrants were easier to issue than to do something about, and Ussher had a drawer full of them. Both Senator Clement Cornwall of Ashcroft and John Edwards of Kamloops, as justices of the peace, had signed warrants. Though the government allowed the use of special constables, it refused to pay them travelling expenses. JPs were even reluctant to issue arrest warrants because the impecunious government so often would return expense vouchers unpaid. Nevertheless, "specials" had, from time to time, been sworn in and tracked the gang. Jim Kennedy of Nicola, serving as a special constable, had accompanied Ussher for four days and five nights in one attempt to find the McLeans. That was back in October, and Kennedy was still waiting for his four-dollars-a-day pay. Once a special had caught up with Charlie. But Charlie emerged boldly from his hiding place, threatening to shoot the constable if he took another step. That was the end of that attempt at justice.

As for the state of the jail in the west end of Kamloops, little had changed. Consisting of a small whitewashed building with wooden veranda, it contained a courtroom, a tiny office and a cell room and had a fenced-in prison yard in back. The place was a joke. Ussher's pleas for better facilities and improvements to the law-keeping system in general went unheeded. People like the McLean boys walked out just about as effortlessly as they walked in. A bent rusty nail had served the purpose of a key for one earnest prisoner. In the fall of 1878, a grand jury found the building insecure, but the government refused to pay the hundred dollars Ussher said would fix it.

Recently it had happened all over again. Ussher had brought in Archie, Allen and Charlie on charges of horse stealing and highway robbery and clapped them in jail to await trial when the judge, Peter O'Reilly, visited Kamloops on his next round. For four days it was the happiest jail in the province, with the boys laughing and singing all the time. Their sister Annie came to visit them, and they talked in Shuswap and Chinook. Then, one day while the boys were out in the prison yard and Ussher wasn't around, a rope came sailing over the wall. When Ussher checked on his inmates, they were gone. No doubt Alex Hare and Hector McLean had been mixed up in the escape.

The constable hadn't been able to catch them again. Until some means was devised of keeping them locked up there probably wasn't much sense in trying too hard anyway. A little over two weeks ago, George Caughill had been sworn in as special constable and, with another special, Jim Jamieson, had set out on a determined effort to capture the McLean brothers. A collection was taken up from several Kamloops residents, including Ussher, to raise sixty dollars to cover their expenses. Charles Semlin, a Cache Creek JP and former member of the provincial parliament (and who would, years later, become premier), telegraphed Premier and Attorney-General George Anthony Walkem complaining about the McLeans. Noting that the brothers and Hare had banded together and that thefts by them were becoming more frequent, Semlin urged that a reward be offered for their capture, particularly as there was no constable in Cache Creek. Walkem immediately posted a reward of $250 on behalf of the government.

In acknowledging the reward, Semlin noted that Caughill was trailing them:

> *If he cannot come up with them in the mountains or if they shoot him then the only way left is to turn the Indians loose and let them take them alive if they can, if not. . . . These boys are a hard lot and good men may come to grief before they are safely lodged. The weather today is very inclement and makes scouring and sleeping in the mountains anything but pleasant.*

Semlin sent word of the reward to Ussher. While previously there had been little incentive for people to risk their necks with no reward for their trouble, it was now becoming more worthwhile. John Tait, on behalf of the Hudson's Bay Company, offered another $250. If the Company refused to honour his pledge, he said, he would pay it himself. Fifty dollars of Ussher's own money sweetened the pot a little more.

The tenacious Caughill, back in Kamloops after some unsuccessful tracking, vowed to "proceed on their capture as long as my time and money will hold out." He had come close to them, talking to people they had robbed and obtaining descriptions of the missing property. He had a half-breed named Simpson hanging out as a spy with the Siwashes in the Nicola Valley, hoping to find out where the McLeans were. Unbeknownst to Palmer, Caughill and Jamieson left Kamloops for Nicola the morning of the sixth, just as Palmer was riding in to tell of his stolen horse and his brush with the gang. Poor Caughill. He had probably narrowly missed both Palmer and the McLeans.

Because Palmer had run into the boys so close to town, and because he was so insistent that something be done immediately, the opportunity to execute the paper on them couldn't be passed up. The McLeans and Hare, "one horse of the goods and chattels of William Palmer feloniously did steal, take and lead away. . . . "

Ussher, with Shumway showing him the way, very soon cut the McLeans' trail at a break in Jim Mellors' fence. Four sets of tracks in the snow led a couple of more miles to Anderson Creek. A short distance farther, the tracks left the creek and continued south toward a rise known as Brigade Hill. It looked as though they were now following the route of the old Brigade Trail of the Hudson's Bay Company that led over the Long Lake Range and south into the Nicola. They might be heading to Jacko Lake, named for old-timer Alex Jacko. But night-fall forced Ussher and his helpers to abandon the hunt for the day.

"I think we'd better get more help," Palmer said to Ussher.

"I don't think it's necessary to get too many men," the constable persisted. "I don't think there will be any trouble arresting them."

But they backtracked to John McLeod's place in hopes of persuading him to join them. Other than his pistol, the only weapon McLeod had that fired was an old shotgun, but when Ussher told him about the reward, that part of it would be his if they succeeded, he agreed to meet them the next morning at former HBC packer Donald Walker's place. McLeod said they could get firearms at Tom Trapp and Richie McDonald's ranch.

Palmer, Ussher and Shumway spent the night at Dominion Government Camp, the cabin used by Bill Roxborough, who was in charge of looking after the mules and horses used for Canadian Pacific Railway survey crews during summer months. The railway, eight years after it had been promised as an enticement to get British Columbia to join Canada, was finally coming through. The possibility of routing the line through the Nicola Valley was being examined at that time, so the CPR's stock was wintered there. Roxborough agreed to go along with the posse the next day.

## [25]

LONG LAKE RANGE, Nicola Valley, B.C.
Monday, December 8, 1879, 7:00 AM

Ussher had his posse on the move again. McLeod beat them to Donald Walker's by almost two hours and was there waiting for them.

It was a disparate bunch, these four special constables and their Provincial. Ussher himself was an unlikely looking lawman. He was small and skinny, a very definite contrast to his quarry, and had an easy-going, sanguine outlook. His life had been marked by moderate but progressive success. The son of a Reformed Episcopal Church minister in Montreal, he'd gotten a stake —as had many others in the area —in the Cariboo gold rush. Ussher had been ranching in the Kamloops area for eight years, first on the North Thompson River, then southeast of Kamloops. For four years he had been a government agent and was doing pretty well for himself. He was a partner in the Shuswap Milling Company with John Andrew Mara, provincial legislature member for Yale, and with Jim McIntosh, whose sister, Annie Clara, he had married just a year ago. He was able and popular as a govern-

John T. Ussher
*(photo courtesy Leslie Sagwell)*

ment agent, but his work lately had been plagued by the problems of the government, and at forty he was past willing to do the politicians' dirty work. Instead of chasing a bunch of boys who should never have been allowed to reach the edge of serious trouble, Ussher undoubtedly would have preferred to be home catching up on paperwork.

Palmer, who wore an austere beard, was a good rancher and a solid citizen, but he had a temper that could quickly boil to the surface when he didn't get his way. He and his pretty but vain shrew of a wife, Jane, apparently had a stormy marriage. George Cavanaugh, a neighbour who worked for the Palmers from time to time, told stories. On one occasion, he said, Jane Palmer showed him marks on her neck, claiming her husband had whipped her. On another, Willie Palmer had accused Cavanaugh of stealing tools while he was building the Palmers' house. According to Cavanaugh, Jane Palmer once caught Willie on a couch with another woman.

Shumway was a quiet man, never talking about his past, but those who knew him gathered that his life had not been happy. A Mormon, he'd had some sort of trouble in his native New York and other places south of the border. Then, his wife died and he'd lost his family. He was seven years older than Ussher. His son, Amni Jr., if he were still alive, would be about the age of the older McLean boys.

Though John McLeod was only in his mid-twenties and had been sheep ranching with his brother Bill above Shumway Lake for little more than a year, he was a valuable addition to the posse. He had been a policeman in Glasgow, Scotland, as well as in Victoria. McLeod knew the McLeans, especially Allen, who had been around the area ever since the McLeod brothers had come to the Upper Country. Allen had mooched dinner at their sheep ranch the previous summer.

Roxborough was there strictly by accident of the fact he wrangled for the CPR. Not much is known about him, but he seemed more concerned about his stock than about chasing outlaws. To Roxborough, the ride was a chance to look for strays. Like Shumway, Roxborough would be a non-combatant in a showdown but, of course, Ussher wasn't expecting it to come to one.

"Meet you up the trail," Roxborough said now, explaining that he'd seen some mules head into the bush nearby; they probably belonged to the railroad. He spurred his horse off to the right through some trees.

They were a long way from Government Camp now, fifteen miles from town, off the trail and half a mile from the top of a rise near Brigade Hill. Palmer sighted what he thought was smoke, but after looking at it for awhile they decided it was snow powder blowing off the trees. Still, if the McLeans were camped, this would be a likely place. They could have picked just about any spot and had a clear view of anybody who might ride up toward them.

The McLeans and Hare hadn't gone far since their meeting with Palmer near the wagon road. They had no desire to go to Kamloops, and no pressing business anywhere, so they wandered around and up onto a plateau above the valley. It's a pleasant area that contains meadows and pothole lakes, quite different from the dry valley below. Only a couple of miles from where they and Palmer had their aimless conversation, they camped at a spot they had been using for several days. They had three more horses there, and Allen decided Palmer's black was going to be more trouble than it was worth. He ordered Charlie to turn him loose.

Camp was not far from Brigade Hill, on a shady flat near a ravine with good water nearby, and a good view of anyone approaching either along the old Brigade Trail or climbing up from the valley. It was just where Ussher thought the McLeans might be. The difference was that he didn't know it for sure. The McLeans, on the other hand, knew by now that their old friend Johnny Ussher was coming with a posse to try to do what others couldn't.

"Should we leave?" Charlie asked.

"No, we won't leave our grub behind," said Hare.

Allen returned from getting a drink at the creek when he saw the posse. He and Archie took off their coats.

What happened next is clouded by time and the limitations of men's abilities to process information that comes too quickly, but the general sequence of events is clear. Shumway was in the lead, still tracking, with the others behind, when he came onto the open flat. Suddenly, he glimpsed several horses in one of the larger groves ahead of them. Motioning quiet, he waited for the others to catch up. It was eleven AM.

Four horses were saddled, looking like they'd been ridden hard. Two other horses stood nearby. A campfire had been allowed to burn low. There was no one in sight. The posse members seemed unsure of what to do next, but Ussher told them, "They'll never fire a shot. Come on, I'll take the lead."

With this he spurred his horse closer to the camp, reined up and started to dismount. Palmer kept up with him, then the others came behind, pulling up about thirty feet from the campfire. McLeod pulled out his shotgun and carried it under one arm. The two horses that were separated from the others looked like government stock, so Shumway went over to them to look at brands, some distance from the other posse members. He'd been told that Alex Hare was using a government horse.

"Okay, boys, come on out, we've got to take you back to town!" shouted Ussher.

"I don't see my horse," Palmer said to McLeod. But at that instant he did see Charlie McLean hiding behind a tree on the other side of the fire, his rifle ready.

Seeing that Palmer had discovered him, Charlie gave a sharp whistle. Suddenly the rest of the gang appeared from hiding, all of them throwing down their hats. It looked as though they had planned out their signals and strategy beforehand. At the same instant, Allen sent a bullet at Palmer for unloosing the law on them.

It brushed through the icicled beard of the startled Palmer. "That's a close shave," the rancher breathed, intending no pun. He struggled to control his frightened horse.

The ball carried on unspent, tearing into the face of the open-mouthed McLeod, entering one cheek and exiting through the other. He choked and spit blood, but the ball had miraculously missed his teeth.

"I'm shot," he wheezed, reporting the obvious.

Despite his wound, McLeod tried to work the borrowed shotgun, but the other McLeans were opening up now and another bullet hit him in the leg, shattering his knee. Three more hit his horse.

Palmer was trying to sight on Allen, who dodged from tree to rock, reloading and firing as he went. Palmer fired and Allen jumped behind a tree, then appeared and fired again. Palmer pulled the trigger two or three more times but the pistol wouldn't go off. He saw pistol smoke from behind the tree where Hare stood, but couldn't get Hare in his sights, either.

Ussher's horse reared and stumbled as the blasts from guns rang through the air and bullets whistled past him, but he managed to control it. He had spotted Alex Hare circling the gang's own horses, revolver in one hand, bowie knife in the other.

"Stop this shooting, boys!" the lawman shouted. "I want to talk!"

But the shooting continued. Ussher, on the left flank now, was out of the line of fire. Calming his horse, and leaving his pistol strapped on the saddle horn, he dismounted and walked forward unarmed to within ten or twelve yards of the fire, again calling on the boys to surrender. He was certain they were bluffing, trying to scare them off.

Hare, after discharging his pistol in the direction of Palmer and McLeod, came out to meet Ussher while guns blasted in the battle beside them.

"Surrender, boys!" Ussher was yelling.

Palmer saw Ussher go towards Hare and reach out his left hand toward him, grabbing his right shoulder. It was impossible to know, but it didn't look as though Ussher was trying to restrain Hare; it seemed more like a steadying gesture, perhaps one of friendship. Palmer distinctly saw that Ussher's fingers were out-stretched and spread rather than in a fist.

Whatever Ussher was trying to do, Hare either took it as a threat or was too excited to judge it correctly. He swung at Ussher with his knife, and now the two men grappled. Ussher fell on his back in the slippery snow; Hare leaped on him, holding him down with his left hand and flailing away with the knife in his other. The scrawny constable was no match even for a boy less than half his age.

"Don't kill me, boys!" Ussher pleaded.

"Kill the sonofabitch!" came a voice from somewhere in the melee.

Archie McLean ran out from behind another tree to help his partner. He put a pistol a foot and a half from the struggling Ussher's head. The constable was partly on his back, partly on his side, looking toward Archie.

What happened at the next instant would later be disputed, though the end result was the same. Palmer saw the pistol pointed at Ussher. *I heard it fired. Heard the report and saw the flash. Ussher's both feet raised spasmodically. I knew then that Ussher was gone.*

Archie McLean would admit he pointed the gun at Ussher, but would claim it didn't fire. *I did not kill Ussher. I did not fire into his forehead. I pointed my pistol, but it snapped.*

McLeod, from a different angle, saw much the same as Palmer. *When Ussher was shot he gave a convulsive spring. I thought, "That's the last of him."*

Shumway had advanced toward the battle when he heard the shouting, but being weaponless he didn't venture too near. He didn't have a clear view of the fight now going on, and there was so much confusion it was hard to tell just exactly what was happening or being said. He didn't hear the fatal shot, but there was no mistake that a coup de grâce had been given. *Smoke rose from the pistol. Ussher's feet gave a jerk. Hare sat on Ussher's body and raised something in his hand with which he struck a blow towards Ussher's head.*

Alex and Archie both raised their guns and swung blows at Ussher.

All the time the fight between Hare and Ussher was going on, Allen was forced to keep back under cover, guarding against the rest of the posse with Charlie. It was Allen who yelled, "Kill the sonofabitch!" and it was that shout that spurred Archie to forsake his own cover and run to help Hare.

Allen McLean later blamed Hare. *When the boys threw down Ussher I said, "Come back, boys, don't touch him." They came back, but Hare went up to him again to get his coat, and said, "The son of a bitch isn't dead yet," and stuck a knife in his throat.*

Palmer's horse, excited by all the racket, almost tore the reins from his hands. He managed to pull off a mitt with his teeth so he could turn the chamber of his pistol to get it working again. Now he caught sight of Allen reloading his gun so he rode towards him and fired. Allen shouted and jumped behind cover as Palmer fired a second time.

"You sonofabitch!" Allen screamed at him.

Charlie McLean advanced, firing back.

Archie now ran back toward the campfire, shouting, "Come on, you sonofabitch!" at the wounded McLeod and firing again.

McLeod, his face drenched in blood, was in no position to take up the challenge. In great pain from the knee wound, he found it impossible to dismount, which would turn out to be a good thing. His Colt — initialled J.McL. — lay useless in the snow. Neither was he having any luck getting his shotgun working.

Palmer was having the same trouble with his own gun. And all Shumway could do was stay behind cover.

It was no use. "We are here long enough, boys!" Palmer called to McLeod and Shumway. Bullets whined by them as the battered posse galloped off.

Some thirty shots had been fired within a few minutes. As the posse left, the McLeans retrieved their hats and waved them, and cheered.

Roxborough, the fifth member of the posse, came as close to the battle as he wanted to. After he had separated from the others to look for the mules he had seen in the bush, he lost sight of the rest of the posse members. He foraged around for a time, working his way along the valley's ridge. Then he heard firing, and knew what must have happened. He rode a half mile in the direction of the shooting.

Suddenly, a man appeared from behind a tree.

"I'm Allen McLean," the man announced in a boastful voice, "and I don't care who knows it!"

As Roxborough hastily turned his horse, Allen raised a pistol and fired. He missed. Then the other members of the gang appeared.

"I'm Alex Hare," said one, "and I don't give a damn who knows it, either!" He, too, fired and missed.

Finally, Roxborough got his frightened horse away before any damage was done and hurried back toward Kamloops.

The gang, still in a blood frenzy after the kill, struck camp. Hare made himself busy stripping Ussher's body of the coat, gloves and boots.

"Poor Johnny," he said, the enormity of their actions perhaps starting to sink in.

"Don't call him poor," said Charlie. "He wouldn't call you poor if he had you in jail."

They let George McRae's buckskin loose in favour of Ussher's mouse-coloured mount. Instead of smothering the campfire, they dumped everything into it that wasn't needed.

It was during this activity that Allen McLean discovered he'd been shot. It must have been Palmer's bullet that got him, hitting him in the side. It wasn't a crippling shot, and Allen had carried on without noticing it. But it would need tending to.

"Let's go down to Trapp's," Hare said. "There's a shotgun and Henry rifle there."

It may have been at that moment the boys decided, perhaps without need of further words, what they would do. They had a plan they'd talked about many times before, had even let it be known around the area. This day had, at last, made the plan possible or, more accurately, left it as the only option. It involved nothing less than stirring the Indians into a full-scale uprising and killing the white settlers. For that, they would need all the firearms they could get.

As they galloped away, the poplar grove that had echoed so loudly with gunfire and desperate shouts that morning became still and quiet once again. A few yards from the crackling campfire, looking lonely, vulnerable and bloody, lay the body of the man who had tried to be their friend.

## [26]

NICOLA WAGON ROAD, south of Kamloops
Monday, December 8, 1879, 12:00 noon

Bloodied and beaten, what was left of the posse retreated hastily toward Kamloops. Palmer, Shumway and McLeod could consider themselves lucky they weren't lying back there in the snow with Ussher. Shumway was of the firm opinion that had the McLeans not been so excited they could have bagged the entire posse, could have killed all of them with their knives if they'd wanted to. Even now the gang might easily catch them and finish them off.

McLeod was in great pain from his messy wounds. His horse, in no better shape, laboured along. The three men had no idea, and likely gave little thought to, what had happened to Roxborough, but they weren't about to go back and find out.

As stunning as Ussher's murder was, the clarity of hindsight suggested the McLeans' savage response to the posse shouldn't have been such a total surprise. Obviously, the boys' warnings that they wouldn't allow themselves to be arrested, that they would kill or be killed, deserved more serious consideration than anyone had given them. Palmer himself had heard Allen say it one day when Allen stopped by for breakfast ('stopping by' for breakfast at the ranch cum restaurant of his choice had become a regular practice for him). Like everyone else, Palmer had written off the threat as typical McLean swagger.

"They'll never fire a shot." Ussher truly believed they would do him no harm; all he had to do was reason with them, lecture about the need to stop all the fuss and come along quietly. The boys were past lecturing. Everything they'd done during the past several months, an accelerating litany of crime and violence, should have made that obvious, but maybe people didn't want to believe their eyes and ears. Tait had told Ussher to take more men. Palmer had told him. John McLeod had told him. Everybody had told him, but Ussher, the man who was supposed to enforce the law, was the only one who thought the gang would cause no trouble. Ussher and his posse were fools to think they could ride into the boys' camp, put the cuffs on them and take them back to town like docile cattle the way it had been done before.

The road to murder for these wild youngsters had started more than two years before. It had started with Charlie, when he bit the Indian's nose off in a nasty fight on the Kamloops Indian Reserve. That was in April 1877. The Indian, Baptiste, filed a charge of grievous bodily harm. Charlie was eventually arrested and Tait, as JP, sentenced him to three months in the Crowbar hotel without waiting to hear evidence for the defence. The unpaid frontier JPs often had a tenuous grasp of the rudiments of law, and Charlie suffered for it, though he was probably guilty anyway. He and a friend and cattle thief named Antoine Lamprone, who was serving a similar sentence, broke jail with help from Lamprone's friends. Charlie roamed about the country, far and wide, with and without his brothers. At one point they had lawmen on both sides of the border after them when they crossed the line into the U.S., stole some cattle, and shaved off the hair of a klootchman, a sign of contempt. Chief Justice Matthew Begbie, stern enforcer of law and order, had promised to do something about them.

A warrant on August 20, 1878, brought no result; neither did one on November 20. Then the homeless Alex Hare, an old schoolmate of

Archie's, joined them after getting kicked out of his father's place. Alex admired the McLeans, especially Allen. They all loved horses, guns, fights, and a bit of liquor. Most of their scrapes they got away with. They were, after all, only boys. When they held a grudge against somebody, that person was likely as not to find some of his stock stampeded. A time or two, they were caught, but never for long. The gang grew bolder, and their respect for the law grew weaker.

In mid-November, 1879, Alex Hare went on a horse-stealing and robbing binge. Things got worse. The gang stole provisions and a saddle from teamster George Wilson. They got away with four horses and saddles from cattle baron Johnny Wilson's ranch at Savona. From the Kamloops reserve they took a horse and saddle. They broke into the store room of James Uren's hotel at Savona's Ferry and took provisions; and into a building on Thaddeus Harper's ranch east of Kamloops, and took two blankets, a sack of flour, and a Henry rifle. From George Caughill, the very man who was trying to capture them, they stole a saddle. Another saddle was taken from Tom Cavanaugh of Cache Creek. Others, including James Birmingham of Cache Creek, found clothes missing, thanks to the gang. All told, they had stolen more than a dozen horses. They also gathered a plentiful supply of sixteen-shot repeating rifles, revolvers and knives, not to mention money and livestock.

Allen McLean's downward slide into hell should have been foreseen. He was the most dangerous, because he led by violent example. He had a presence that exuded strength and wild freedom that said, don't cross this one. But though you might admire him, it didn't mean you had to like him, and there was ever more reason not to like him.

Last March Nicola Valley rancher Edward Sullivan had seen Allen and his woman stealing hay from his stack. The next morning McLean came to the house swearing at Sullivan and pushing his wife around. When Sullivan asked him to leave, he refused, threatening to shoot him. Nothing more came of it, and it was one of the least violent of the escapades that would follow, but his willingness to physically abuse a woman showed how short on moral fibre Allen McLean had become.

The McLean Gang were also guilty of highway robbery. Only a couple of weeks ago the boys accosted a Chinaman on the road west of Savona's Ferry, beat him to a pulp and threatened him with death if he didn't have more money next time. They took what cash he did have, plus a bottle of whiskey, and rode off. The poor victim was afraid he would die from the beating. The savagery of the attack was what had finally started waking people up. People were afraid to leave their homes for fear of being robbed.

Palmer, McLeod and Shumway — and Roxborough if he ever caught up — now carried with them news that would make beatings and robberies seem like the good old days.

DUNBALLOCH, Napier Lake, Nicola Valley
Monday, December 8, 1879, shortly before 1:00 PM

Stock raiser Thomas John Trapp heard his dogs barking outside the
ranch house. Maybe his partner, Richie McDonald, had returned.
Looking out the back window, he saw four men on horseback coming
down the hill.

Trapp hastily hid his money, which he kept in a satchel, then
waited a few minutes. Not seeing anything of the riders, he went to
the front door and out onto the porch.

"Quiet, Banjo," he admonished his favourite hound, who was
making the most noise.

Alex Hare had dismounted and was walking toward him with a
pistol in one hand.

"Hello, Alex," said Trapp. "Sorry to see you boys out in this weather."

"We want your rifle and your shotgun," Hare ordered. "We must
have them. We've killed Johnny Ussher."

The words, spoken so matter-of-factly, chilled Trapp. Was it the
truth, had they finally killed? Or was it just more bragging? The
thirty-seven-year-old bachelor ran his fingers through his thinning hair
and noticed his hand trembled slightly.

"Sorry, you can't have them."

Archie pointed a cocked six-gun at Trapp's chest, while Charlie
levelled a rifle at him.

"Give us your guns right now if you don't want to get shot," Archie demanded.

"Boys, if you want them that bad, they're inside. Go and take them,
but you can do no good by shooting me. I never did you any harm."

"We'll need cartridges for the Henry, too," Archie said as he dismounted and entered with Hare.

Trapp told them he didn't have any. Archie repeated the threat to
shoot him.

"Go ahead and shoot, but you still won't have any cartridges. I
don't have any," the usually easy-going Trapp repeated. "I used the
last one last week."

Charlie and Allen stayed outside with the rancher. Charlie waved
a hunting knife around.

"This is the knife that killed Johnny Ussher," he informed Trapp, trying to claim the murder. "I'll fight any sonofabitch who comes after us."

Trapp said nothing.

"Do you think that old grey-haired sonofabitch Judge Begbie will

Tom Trapp

ever get the drop on me?" Charlie continued. "Not much."

Lowering the butt of the rifle he had been resting across the saddle horn and putting the muzzle to his cheek, Charlie added, "A shot from this would put him on the right hand side of Jesus Christ. Just like Ussher."

"Is that John Ussher's blood you've got all over you?" Trapp asked in disgust.

"That's right, and there'll soon be a lot of other people's."

Allen decided to go into the house and see how Archie and Alex were doing, and gestured to Trapp to go in ahead of him.

Trapp saw that Allen was carrying a pair of shackles, undoubtedly taken from Ussher.

"Get away from me," Hare told him. "I have blood on me."

"What blood is that?" Trapp asked him, knowing the answer as soon as the words were out of his mouth.

"That's Johnny Ussher's blood," said Hare.

Trapp now saw blood on Hare's left shoulder. So their claims of having killed Ussher were true.

"I'm sorry to hear about this, boys," said Trapp. "You've killed a good man."

Allen and Alex went into the bedroom. Hare asked for a powder flask and Trapp told him it was hanging on the wall. The boys took the powder, and went through the bed pillows to make sure Trapp hadn't hidden any money or ammunition there.

"We need some spurs," said Allen.

"There's a pair on the wall there but they aren't mine," the rancher said.

Allen grabbed Richie McDonald's spurs. When they had taken what they wanted, Hare produced a fifty-cent piece and told Trapp to take it.

"No thanks," Trapp said. "I don't want a dead man's money."

Hare insisted, looking as though insulting his generosity might be a big mistake.

Trapp reluctantly took the coin but laid it on a table.

Allen picked it up and pocketed it. "Let's go."

As they went back outside again Trapp noticed Hare was taking the satchel containing his money from the house.

While they had been inside, Charlie remained behind, whooping and dancing around, obviously drunk. The whole scene would have been comical if it weren't so frighteningly bizarre: a kid bragging about killing a man as though he'd bloodied some bully's nose in a schoolyard brawl, while his brother hopped around in the snow like a fruitcake.

"I'll kill any sonofabitch who comes after me!" Charlie was yelling at nobody in particular.

"That goes for all of us," said Allen. To Trapp, he said, "We've made a beginning and we'll make a clean sweep, but we won't bother you. Not if you don't betray us. Say nothing of seeing us today."

"Swear to that," Charlie added.

"I can't do that," Trapp told them.

"Swear to it if you like living," Charlie ordered, suddenly vexed.

"It's foolish to talk about killing a lot of people," said Trapp. "In the end, you're sure to be taken."

"I'll never be taken alive," Charlie snarled.

"They'll track us down the mountain," interjected Archie. "Say you saw us ride by and you saw six of us. Swear to that."

"Well," Trapp relented. He had little choice. "I might of seen a couple of fellows ride by awhile back. There are four of you here. Guess that makes six."

"That's more like it."

"Look boys, this isn't going to work out," Trapp said. "Allen, I've known you and Alex for a long time now. A lot of the half-breeds and Indians are my friends. Why, you had breakfast here with me just last June. We can talk straight to each other, right? You've got to give yourselves up or clear out of the country altogether."

"It's too late for that," Allen said. "If we went to the other side we'd only be brought back here."

"We can only die once," said Archie.

"Our father died in the face of cold lead and I'm ready to do the same," Charlie boasted.

"Goodbye, Mr. Trapp," said Allen. "Remember what we said about not telling about us and you'll have no worry. You've behaved like a man —you'll be the last one we'll kill. We'll return your weapons when we're finished."

They each shook hands with him as they prepared to mount up.

"Don't worry," Alex threw the words over his shoulder as they were leaving. "We won't harm you."

They rode off side by side in the direction of Nicola and Trapp watched them until they got to the edge of the flat and disappeared into the trees, going out along the wagon road. Then he went back to his work. But he had trouble keeping his mind off the gang and what had been said about Ussher.

He decided he'd better ride to Kamloops and raise the alarm.

# [28]

KAMLOOPS, British Columbia
Monday, December 8, 1879, early afternoon

When Shumway, Palmer and McLeod reached Kamloops with the news of what had happened, a predictable ripple of shock and fear swept through the town. The McLean boys, sometimes amusing, loud-mouthed young ruffians, suddenly were killers.

There was a curious mixture of sympathy, fear, fondness and hate associated with the four sons of Sophia McLean. There was, for one thing, an esteem for their dead father that endured in the hearts of those who had known him. People like Donald McAuley, John McIvor, Joseph Bourke, Michel Fallardeau, Fred Griffin, who had worked with Donald McLean for the Company, stayed at Kamloops to start their own farms and families, and who now remembered McLean for all of his best qualities, and for the way he died. It was they who reminded their neighbours, should they be tempted to call the name of McLean into question, of Donald McLean, and of his sons and daughters who now lived respectable and even profitable lives from the Bonaparte to Kamloops. Donald Jr., married to the fer-ryman François Savona's widow, Julienne St. Paul, with several children of his own. Duncan, a successful packer. Alex, a hotelier and rancher, likewise with a growing family. And Christina, married to hotelier and CPR man John Glassey. The younger ones, Sophia's sons, were wild, but little wonder.

Who, surely, would recount the story of Donald McLean's tragic death without telling how Harry Wilmot had personally ridden hard to Soda Creek and sent down a letter by express stage to Hat Creek with the terrible news? And how rumours had arrived there even ahead of the stage, Sophia refusing to believe them until the letter was opened and read to her, and the uncontrollable grief of the widow and her children.

Though the government, having tricked Klatassine into surrender and then hanged him and four of his followers, awarded Sophia a small pension, that didn't save their home. Despairing of being able to afford lawyers in far-away England to establish her right to Donald's Company back pay and shares, Sophia had tried to hang on at Hat Creek. But even that was to be denied them, because Donald had never gotten the pre-emption on which their farm and restaurant sat transferred from Neil McArthur to himself, so that legally they were nothing more than squatters. Within three years she and the family were forced out of their home and off the land, obtaining only a few dollars in "good-will" money from a freighter named George Dunne who bought McArthur's pre-emption.

The family broke up after that, Sophia moving back to Kamloops. The older boys were alright. John stayed in the Bonaparte area, though neither he nor any of his brothers hung on to the property pre-empted in their names. John and Hector wrangled at Ashcroft Manor for the Cornwalls. Donald Jr. lived at Savona's Ferry and then Kamloops, where he and his own son John became renowned as the best dance fiddlers around. Duncan ran his own packing outfit, while Alex married Margaret, the young half-breed daughter of Company labourer Caesar Vodreaux, a French-Canadian.

It was the younger boys who really suffered. Allen was soon old enough to go out and find work of his own on local ranches, but without the strong hand of their father, he and his brothers grew up without the sense of discipline that had been instilled in Donald McLean's first family. And there was the youngest McLean, Peter Arthur — better known as Archie — who had never even seen his father, because he was born a few days after Anukatlk ripped out Donald McLean's heart with a musket ball.

It was common at the time to assign the problems of breeds to their mixed parentage, as though they were homeless, unable to connect. But the truth of the matter was that in the 1870s there were more breeds than "pure" whites in Kamloops or anywhere else in the Upper Country. Their generation was the majority, they were the baby boomers of their time, for their fathers were the Hudson's Bay men who had pioneered the country and their mothers were the Indian women taken as wives. As the children grew up, they were faced with a choice between white society and Indian society and, in general, the daughters married white men and so "went white" while the sons "went Indian."

While these young breeds were anything but homeless, a class system had grown up that made any sort of advancement difficult. Their fathers, tough Scots frontiersmen-turned-farmers and -ranchers, played an important role in the economy and so occupied a place of moderate respect, but they weren't in positions of control. The politics and the commerce of Kamloops were controlled by Europeans who had arrived in the '60s during the gold rush, who were married to white women, and whose white children would be groomed to inherit the stores and sawmills and hotels where the good money could be made.

The half- and quarter-breed children, among whom were the McLean offspring, did the jobs the whites wouldn't dirty themselves with. So there was a lingering bitterness, a lack of guidance, and an inherited lifestyle that the older McLean boys could tolerate and even thrive upon, but which for the youngsters was a recipe for trouble.

There was one final ingredient that guaranteed the younger McLeans — Allen, Charlie, Hector and Archie — would seek revenge on society with a malevolence that only wronged youth could muster. While the so-called death list had grown to include many in the white community, it had started with John Andrew Mara, a wealthy and corrupt local merchant and MPP for Kamloops. It was a well-known local scandal, talked about by the matrons of Kamloops as they knitted in their sitting rooms and by the men of the town over cigars and shots of rum in the hotel billiard rooms, that Mara had good reason to worry about the McLean boys.

It was well-known that their sister Annie had given birth the previous August to an illegitimate baby girl, whom she named Mary-Ethel. And while, on the record of birth, the Oblate priest Charles Grandidier had made the notation "pere inconnu" — father unknown — it was known very well that the father was John Andrew Mara, who had simply abandoned Annie like a two-dollar whore after making her pregnant.

It was the sort of thing that made excellent gossip when writing to friends and family in other places. Charles Semlin of Cache Creek, reporting to Premier Walkem the activities of the brothers, wrote of it too. "It is talked here that the young McLeans, wild, reckless and lawless as they were, had never killed anyone until their sister Annie was seduced by Mara and bore a child to him." Then he asked Walkem not to reveal publicly the story about the affair. And noting the boys had sworn to kill both Mara and John Tait, Semlin re-

John T. Edwards

marked, "What a sad commentary on the magistracy."

It was certain that should the boys catch Mara now they would shoot him on sight. He might be dead already if Charlie had carried through with a mission he set for himself upon hearing of the dishonour Mara had brought upon his sister months ago. In a rage, he had ridden into Kamloops to gun Mara down, but his older sister Christina and her husband, John, talked him out of it.

Events seemed to conspire to set the boys on a fatal course. Archie, who now stood accused of pulling the trigger on Ussher, had always been quick-witted, full of life and good humour. Palmer himself had first hired Archie for herding four years ago, and had admired his and Charlie's horsemanship even then. But Archie had undergone a sudden and dramatic personality change, had become totally disillusioned with just about everybody, but especially people like the ones on their "list."

The murder of Ussher may have come as the greatest shock to the younger boys' half-brother Alex. He would have thought Archie, for all his recent bragging and activities, incapable of such an act. One day, after Archie had gotten into a fight, he rode up to the ranch of Alex and Margaret McLean on the North River, where he and his brothers sometimes sought refuge. Margaret told him to go back to town and get the matter straightened out. Archie stayed the night and, next morning, got his horse and rode back to Kamloops. Sophia was there, telling him to get out and fight like a man and die if need be, as his father had. Archie headed for the hills, with grub and supplies, and was soon joined by his brothers. Once he tasted the power of rebellion, he couldn't be turned back.

While at first it had been the running off of stock, they now stole small things but kept getting braver and braver, and, when Alex Hare made them four, the real trouble began.

And now John Andrew Mara, who had a greater personal stake in their capture than anyone, was helping John Edwards hastily round up twenty men for a new posse. By early afternoon they were ready to go. Shumway went along to show them the way, and Palmer, on a fresh horse, also went. A short distance outside Kamloops they met Roxborough on his way in.

## [29]

STUMP LAKE, Nicola Valley
Monday, December 8, 1879, early afternoon

Near the north end of Stump Lake, at the edge of a meadow, there was a large rock similar to many others characteristic of the valley, and on this rock, on this day, Jim Kelly sat watching his sheep. Huddled under his plaid —a heavy scarf-like cloak —he blew on his mouth organ as the sheep milled almost imperceptibly across the white sheet of snow. His vantage point was only a few yards off the Nicola Road.

He stopped blowing when the four riders came into view, two abreast, and headed straight for him.

His greeting was unfriendly, of the "what do you want?" variety. Kelly didn't like the McLean boys. The McLean boys, especially Allen, didn't like him.

The problem was Kelly's lousy hospitality. When Allen "stopped by" for breakfast at somebody's place, he was used to getting it, cheerfully. Sometimes he paid, sometimes he didn't. Sometimes he just took what he wanted, though he preferred a properly cooked meal. Not long ago he had asked Jim Kelly for some food. Kelly had not only refused, but had done so in a most rude manner, telling Allen he hardly had enough for himself without giving it to a freeloader. On that day Allen had let Kelly get away with it, content with robbing him sometime later.

"Don't tell anyone that we have passed here," Allen told him.

Apparently it didn't dawn on Kelly that facing four heavily armed bandits known for their mean treatment of people they disliked might call for just an ounce of discretion.

"I don't know anything about you," Kelly said in a way that did nothing to mask his disdain. "What would I want to say?"

The conversation turned to the refusal of food, where Kelly was clearly on dangerous ground. His unrepentant attitude toward his four antagonists that day made him a very brave, or a very foolish, man. It didn't take much to make Allen mad, but he especially couldn't stand rudeness. He especially couldn't stand rudeness when it came to food. It may have been that Kelly had awakened that morning and said to himself, "How can I get myself shot?" and answered, "Maybe I'll be rude to the McLean boys."

The sheepherder kept a small pistol in his clothing at all times. According to Allen McLean, Kelly drew on him. *He growled about some bread and presented a revolver at my head. I then raised my rifle and sent a ball through him.*

But Hare would claim Kelly never got a chance to draw. *Allen cocked his rifle and shot him in his stomach. After he fell down Charlie shot him in his right side some place. Archie also fired at him with his pistol; I do not know whether the ball struck him or not.*

Charlie's shot was the coup de grâce to the writhing Kelly, who abruptly lay still on the snow-covered road beneath the rock. After the explosion of the guns, loud as dynamite, there was a moment of silence. Then Archie leaped off his horse and ran to the fallen sheepherder to make sure he was dead. Kelly was, indeed, perfectly dead. Archie removed the shiny Waltham pocket watch with the fancy numerals and silver chain that stretched up around the man's neck and back to the vest pocket. Everyone who had ever met Jim Kelly knew it had been his proudest possession. Archie also took his mouth organ, and his pistol.

Allen dismounted, grabbed the body by the feet, and dragged it off to the side of the road.

All four of them went to Kelly's nearby cabin. Charlie kicked open the door and went in with Allen, while Archie and Alex waited outside. Charlie and Allen found some grub and handed it to the other two, then Charlie pulled the mattress off the bed and on to the floor. In an act of pointless vandalism, he cut open a sack of salt and scattered it all over the cabin.

That done, they remounted and moved on, leaving their second murder victim of the day lying in the snow.

NICOLA ROAD near Stump Lake, Nicola Valley
Monday, December 8, 1879, 4:00 PM

Just as sparing Tom Trapp had been no whim, so shooting Jim Kelly off the rock was no sudden impulse. The McLeans had nothing against Trapp; they, or at least Allen, had a grudge to settle with Kelly. So they relieved Trapp of what was useful to them and evened a score with Kelly. It wasn't to be an indiscriminant slaughter.

Their plan was relatively simple, and cold-blooded. They would ride south into the Nicola Valley taking weapons from settlers along the wagon road. This would accomplish two things: disarm the people who would likely be called upon to help catch them and arm the people from whom the McLeans intended to get help, namely the Nicola and Douglas Lake Indians. Allen expected little trouble inciting at least several dozen young bucks to join in a fight against any whites who opposed them. His plan didn't extend beyond that to long-term realities, but in his fantasy war he fully intended to take revenge on those he and his brothers believed had wronged them. Undoubtedly the names of Mara, Tait, Stevenson, Moore, Kennedy and, as of today, Palmer were constantly on his mind.

At the Stump Lake ranch of Robert Scott, the owner was killing pigs near the stable and had a big fire going as his young son watched. One can imagine the pig, the tendons of its hind legs slashed, hanging from a pole tripod over a big kettle of scalding water, damp wood under the kettle crackling and spewing glowing twigs, hissing as the red changed to charcoal, melting shallow depressions in the snow, flames licking upward around the pot, biting into the crisp air. And Scott thankful for the warm fire as he prepared to lower the beast into the water and scrape off the bristles.

He first saw he was about to have company when they were a mile away and coming fast. Fifty yards from him, the riders unslung rifles and shotguns from their shoulders and cradled them horizontally in their arms. It was three of the McLean boys and Alex Hare; their guns were pointed in the general direction of Scott. Charlie continued on a few paces and parked himself on the wagon road, turning his horse sideways and looking up and down as though he were waiting for someone.

Scott left the gory carcass of the pig, walked toward them and said tentatively, "Hello, boys. Cold day, isn't it?"

"Sure is," replied Charlie McLean, with a smirk on his face that was almost, but not quite, friendly. "And one hell of a lot colder ones coming."

"And a damn sight hotter times," Archie added.

Scott, not understanding the joke, said, "I guess last night was the coldest we've had this winter."

He looked at the youngster, not much older than his own boy, seated in his saddle looking for all the world like a kid playing Cowboys and Indians. When Scott had first arrived in the Upper Country, he'd met Archie McLean and ridden up the North Thompson with him. Archie, who was obviously an expert horseman and cowhand despite his youth, had told him then he'd been born a few days after his father was killed in the Chilcotin War.

Their conversation today was taking place eighteen miles from where Johnny Ussher had been killed, and about eleven miles from Trapp's. Scott was about to find out what the boys had been up to.

Archie, Allen and Alex swung their rifles back to their shoulders, dismounted, approached the fire and warmed their hands for a moment. The long guns were leaned against their horses and replaced with revolvers in their hands, fully cocked.

"Where's Johnston Stevenson?" enquired Allen. "We've got a score to settle with that sonofabitch."

"I haven't seen him since yesterday morning. Guess he's on his own place."

"Where's his place?" Allen asked.

"He bought William McCormick's."

"Where's that no-good Kennedy?" Allen asked. "We want him too. We'll see if he's any better at facing four men than three bears." There was a story about Jim Kennedy, one of the specials who had been hunting them, fighting three bears at once. "They'll all get what's coming. Is Kennedy still at Sullivan's?"

Kennedy had lately been working at a flour mill owned by Edward Sullivan where the Nicola River ran into Nicola Lake.

"I think so."

"This is the last night he'll have to live," remarked Charlie.

"What's bothering you, boys?" asked Scott, puzzled by the odd talk.

"We'd better hurry," Charlie said from his post on the road.

"Okay," said Allen. "We're expecting a crowd after us," he explained to Scott.

"From Kamloops?"

"Yes, we left a crowd on the mountain. I may just as well tell you we have killed Johnny Ussher."

"You didn't," said the stunned, disbelieving Scott. "You're only fooling! Allen, are you only fooling or did you really kill Johnny Ussher?"

"Upon my soul, we did."

"Here's the knife that killed him, if you don't believe us!" Alex Hare cried, pulling the weapon from its scabbard. "There's the blood!"

*I then saw the blood on his knife and some spots on his face and also on one of his hands, I think the right hand.*

"I've got his boots," Archie told Scott, holding up his left foot. "Look, pretty good boots for a government agent."

"I've got his hat and gloves and this is his overcoat," added Alex.

Scott saw there was blood on the light-grey coat Hare wore. It looked like the coat he'd seen Ussher wear. The gloves looked like his, too. Now that he was paying attention, he noticed that the over-shoes Allen McLean was wearing looked like Ussher's — they were distinctively embroidered on the front. Around Allen's neck was a bolo tie with a slide ring that Scott knew for sure belonged to Richie McDonald. And the rifle leaning against Archie's horse was undoubtedly the Henry from Trapp's and McDonald's. It was sinking in very quickly that they were serious about having killed Ussher. The clincher was when Allen McLean pointed to one of the horses and told him it was Ussher's. Indeed, it was a horse Scott had seen Ussher ride very often. It was mouse-coloured. Two of the others were black, one a bay.

"We have made a commencement and we'll make a clean sweep of every damned mean sonofabitch of a man that ever said or did anything against us," said Allen. He added, as an afterthought, "But any decent, respectable person we won't touch."

As Archie, Allen and Alex moved back to their horses to remount, Scott also noticed that Alex wavered slightly. As a matter of fact, they all seemed at least a little the worse for the whiskey taken to warm them against the bitter wind and to reinforce their courage in the new role of killers.

"Don't believe us still?" Allen asked. "Well, we killed another man today," and, with that, pointed at his own plaid garment. "I shot a sheepman, too."

"Allen, who was it?" Scott asked anxiously. "Was it Kelly?" Everybody knew everybody in the Nicola; it wasn't hard to figure out who Allen meant.

"I guess so," the older McLean replied laconically.

"I guess he won't howl anymore about a small piece of bread," said Archie.

Then the leader took out a pair of handcuffs. "Here's the hand-cuffs Ussher brought to put on me, but he didn't get them on. I'll keep them for Palmer, that damned sonofabitch."

Now Charlie spoke again. "Yes, the first time we run across Palmer we'll put them on him and we'll give him fifty lashes every day and fifty lashes every night before he goes to bed."

Allen and Charlie found this very funny.

"Surely you won't kill him!" It was Scott's boy, Sam, speaking for the first time.

"No, we'll keep them to torment him. We'll get Palmer and the Moores and the others," Charlie continued.

Allen asked for a chew of tobacco. Scott gave him a piece and Allen bit some off, handing the rest to Archie and Charlie.

"It will be a long time before we'll have a chew together again," Allen told his brothers. "Not till we meet again."

Archie handed what was left of the tobacco back to Scott.

"Anyone at Palmer's house?" Allen now asked.

Scott told him George Cavanaugh was there.

"Tom Cavanaugh's brother?" Archie wanted to know.

"That's him." Then, of Allen, Scott asked, "Have you seen anything of Palmer?"

"When Palmer came after us with Ussher, I raised a gun and I guess I gave him what he wanted because he went back to Kamloops. He left me with something, too," Allen said, showing where a ball had gone through his shirt.

Young Sam Scott asked if they were going to Sullivan's.

"I think so," said Allen. "I guess we will."

"Don't worry, Scott," Allen then assured the rancher. "We aren't going to kill you —we know you've got a big family. You're a brave man to talk to us that way . . . there's a lot of men who will regret treating us the way they have." He added, "If you see Palmer, tell him we're going to his house. How's your daughters, Bella and Elizabeth?"

"Fine."

Allen nodded. The two younger daughters were musically inclined, and occasionally favoured Allen with a song or two when he stopped by for breakfast. Suddenly, he dug his heels into the flanks of his horse and they all rode off into the murky late afternoon light.

As soon as they were gone, Scott sent one of his hands to try to beat them to the mill and warn the workers, and another, Bill Manning, to look for Kelly.

## [31]

### THE PALMER RANCH, Nicola Valley
### Monday, December 8, 1879, 4:30 PM

At the time Scott was sending out riders, Jane Palmer was at home two miles away fretting about her husband. Though she was a tough, self-centred woman, George Cavanaugh, who was visiting with her now, couldn't deny he liked her. He often worked for them carpentering or looking after their pigs and horses. He had, in fact, built the very house they were now sitting in, a job he was well proud of, having added twelve inches extra head-room to accommodate a staircase to the sec-

Jane Palmer *(KMA, 5874)*

ond floor. He had put in crown mouldings and beaded baseboards. Palmer himself was a cheapskate but then so was his wife.

William Palmer had sent a message that he was in Kamloops and would be going out after the McLeans and Hare with Ussher to get his horse. It was now a good twenty-four hours since Jane knew of her husband's last whereabouts.

Cavanaugh, sipping black coffee, was trying to reassure her that her husband could take care of himself, and that the McLeans were probably many miles away from there by now, anyway. But he checked Palmer's rifle to see if it was in good working order, finding to his disappointment it was inoperable.

When they heard horses outside, Cavanaugh stepped out onto the porch to see who it was. Light was already dim, but he could see three of the McLean brothers and young Alex Hare getting off their horses at the gate. Hare held the horses, which looked loaded for war, as the McLeans walked toward the front door, one by one. Cavanaugh heard their guns being cocked.

Jane Palmer had come to stand beside him, immediately frightened and trembling when she recognized the visitors.

"What shall we do?" she asked.

Without answering, Cavanaugh turned and they went back into the house to wait.

Archie McLean, with Allen and Charlie —both carrying rifles — close behind, walked in a few moments later. Allen had been there several times before, since he had taken up residence in the valley, and pointedly placed himself between Cavanaugh and Willie Palmer's gun, which was hanging on the wall. Archie stood beside him.

"Come and warm yourselves," Jane Palmer told them. "I'll get you coffee."

"Thanks," said Archie, moving over to the stove. "My feet are cold."

Allen and Charlie, who was standing by the door, then spoke in Chinook and Indian. The Chinook patois itself was an odd mixture of native Indian and French, and most white people didn't understand it.

Then Charlie spoke to Cavanaugh.

"Are you George Cavanaugh? Tom Cavanaugh's brother?"

"That's me," George Cavanaugh confirmed.

"Your brother," said Charlie in the oddly formal way he and the rest of the McLeans had of talking, "has been making some bad reports on us in Kamloops, injuring our character."

Since they'd stolen a saddle from Tom Cavanaugh's ranch at Cache Creek, it was little wonder he'd made a "bad report" on the McLeans, but the boys viewed friends and enemies in the most basic of terms. If they stole from somebody, and that person complained, he became an enemy. So it was with the cowardly Tom Cavanaugh and his arrest warrant for Charlie, Archie, Hector and Alex.

"I don't know anything about my brother," George Cavanaugh responded carefully. "I haven't seen him in six or seven years."

"Do you have any paper to arrest us?" Charlie asked next, referring to any of the warrants floating about the Upper Country.

Cavanaugh told him he didn't.

"Who told Palmer we had his horse?" Charlie demanded.

"I don't know," said Cavanaugh. "I didn't know anyone had told him."

"We've killed Johnny Ussher and we are thirsting for blood," Charlie suddenly announced. "And we will shoot your brother the first sight we get of him."

The boys waited for the familiar shocked response.

"Are you joking?" asked Cavanaugh.

Allen spoke for the first time, putting a foot forward. "These are his overshoes on my feet."

Cavanaugh saw spots on them that he took for blood.

"Archie has his boots on," Allen continued. "Alex has his overcoat.

Alex finished him off with a knife; he cut his throat."

Archie watched Palmer's wife pour out three cups of coffee from a fresh pot. Her hair was pulled back tightly and gathered together at the back in a ribbon, so that a long, thick tress fell down the front of her dress. She was feeling anything but aggressive at the moment. Instead she felt weak and powerless. But when Archie said, "We are thirsting for blood," she couldn't contain her anger.

"How can you talk that way? You're only a little boy." It was a characteristically undiplomatic thing to say, but it didn't seem to make the youngster mad.

"If I am, I am brave," he said. "I would as soon die with a bullet through me as my father did."

Jane Palmer handed Archie a cup of coffee and took the other two to Allen and Charlie.

"Where did it happen?" Cavanaugh asked woodenly.

"Ask no questions," said Allen, taking down Palmer's gun and asking if it was a good gun. Cavanaugh lied that it was.

"We need it. We'll take it with us."

Jane Palmer again broke her silence. "Allen, I thought you would be the last man who would take anything out of this house. You've often been fed here."

Allen looked at her. Had she aroused his quick temper?

"Your husband snapped a pistol in my face," he told her, "and I will take it in return. I gave him his life on your account and the children's. I told him to get away."

Given Allen's cold temperament and his reputation as the best shot around, what he said about purposely sparing Palmer's life might be true.

"But," Allen continued, "if I ever come across him again, I will kill him. I told him that. I hit young John McLeod, but I didn't kill him, as he didn't drop his gun. I might have missed him but I don't think so."

Allen then took a dagger from his belt and whet it on the stovepipe, felt the blade with his thumb, put it back in his belt. Keeping Palmer's gun in his left hand, he gave his own pistol to Archie to hold and reached for Cavanaugh's spurs where he'd hung them on a nail. He gave them to Archie, took Palmer's powder flask and put it in his own pocket.

"Any shot in the house?" he asked.

"Ask Mrs. Palmer. I'm a stranger here."

The boys kept up a constant volley of questions. Did they have any caps, any bullet moulders, any more guns? Where were Jamieson and Caughill, where was Kennedy, where was Stevenson, where was Reuben McDonald? When they asked about these men, the questions were usually accompanied with comments about the unpleasant fate that awaited them at the hands of the McLean Gang, about it being

John McLeod and Robert Scott

their last night on earth. Jane Palmer and George Cavanaugh responded as vaguely as possible. The special constables had stopped at Scott's the last time they'd been this way, Stevenson was probably at Alex Coutlie's store down past Nicola, they hadn't seen Reuben McDonald. And Allen told Jane Palmer not to be afraid, that they wouldn't hurt her or her children.

"We shot a sheepman on our way coming here," he said, almost as an after-thought.

"We'll shoot any sonofabitch white man that comes to arrest us!" said Charlie. "White men are a no-account bunch. As soon as Alex and Ussher clinched, Ussher's feet flew up in the air!"

With that, he raised his heels a few inches in the air and let them thunk back to the floor, then laughed and wandered off into the bedroom.

"There never was a bullet moulded to shoot me!" he added.

"Was it the sheepherder you shot?" Cavanaugh asked.

"Kelly won't growl anymore about a piece of bread," Charlie replied from the bedroom.

Archie and Charlie were in the bedroom staring into the dresser mirror. Charlie looked at his haggard face and the black mustache dropping over the upper lip.

"I look like the devil," he decided.

"You are the devil," retorted Archie.

Allen called them back into the parlour, telling them it was time to move on. They'd gathered up Palmer's spurs and broken gun, a few caps, tea, sugar and other articles to take with them.

"Let's warm up for a few more minutes," suggested Archie, standing by the stove once again. "My feet are still cold."

"Put them in the stove and they'll soon be warm," Charlie told him.

"I'm sorry to take your husband's gun," said Allen, but he wasn't. He was only sorry that Willie Palmer wasn't there right now, but he said, "Don't worry, we won't harm him."

"Speak for yourself," Charlie told his brother. "If I ever catch the bastard again, I won't go easy on him."

And then they were gone.

"George, take me home to Portland," Jane Palmer begged Cavanaugh.

Since heading for the border with another man's wife didn't strike Cavanaugh as the smartest thing to do, not to mention the fact there were three children napping upstairs, he said no.

"Take me to Peter Fraser's."

Cavanaugh said no to that, too.

"Take me to Robert Scott's."

That finally made sense, so Cavanaugh went out to get the horses ready.

# [32]

BRIGADE HILL, Nicola Valley
Monday, December 8, 1879, early evening

The posse arrived at the scene of the shootout shortly after nightfall. The camp fire still glowed, but the bootless, coatless body of Ussher, lying in trampled snow dark from blood, was frozen stiff. Among the ashes of the fire were burned saddles and blankets.

Some of the party stirred up the fire and moved the body nearer the flames.

Palmer wasn't anxious to relive the horror of that day and didn't look too closely at the body. *I saw a large gash in the cheek – I think the left one. There was a handkerchief tied on the head over his ears, thick with blood. There was a hole in his forehead and one in the back of his head where the ball had come out. There was a very large cut in his cheek.*

Those who checked more thoroughly saw the terrible extent of the damage done by the outlaws. The head was completely battered, and caked blood covered the face, or what was left of it. Most of the nose was missing. There was a deep wound in the left cheek. The hole in his forehead near the left eye showed where the bullet had entered and another near the jugular vein was evidence of where it exited, tearing the flesh to such an extent that it looked like a large knife gash. Hair was singed near where the bullet had entered but there were no powder marks on the face. Ussher's throat had been cut from ear to ear. The body was generally hacked and mutilated, and there were cuts on Ussher's arms and hands where he'd tried to fend off Hare's knife.

Looking around, Edwards found some pieces of paper. They were the torn-up warrant written by Cornwall against Allen McLean for beating up the Chinaman. There was no sign of the warrant Edwards himself had written for Ussher the previous day. There was various other camp junk, some saddles, a pair of worn-out boots, and a quarter of beef. The boys had evidently been using the spot for a campsite for some time.

The posse loaded its grisly package on a sleigh and returned to Kamloops.

## [33]

DUNBALLOCH, Napier Lake, Nicola Valley
Monday, December 8, 1879, 7:00 PM

Tom Trapp saddled up and rode out towards Peter Fraser's ranch to see what his neighbour had learned of the McLeans. After they'd left early that afternoon, he had started for Kamloops, then changed his mind and returned home, realizing that the alarm would already have been raised in Kamloops and that his ride would accomplish nothing.

The other reason for now heading to Fraser's was that Jim Kelly had been expected for supper and might have taken ill. Trapp followed the wagon road south, nervously aware this was the route the McLeans had taken. He was about halfway there when a dog came out of a swamp, barking. In the moonlight reflecting off the snow, Trapp made it out to be one of the sheep dogs owned by Kelly. He was near Kelly's cabin, about two and a half miles from his own spread. Carefully he guided his horse into the marsh for a look-see but after several minutes of searching he could find nothing. It was unlikely Kelly would be out so late anyway, but maybe he should stop by the herder's cabin to learn if he had seen or heard of the McLeans or knew of their boast to kill Ussher. Then he saw Kelly's other dog, a spunky little border collie, go off toward the other side of the swamp with the first. Nervous but determined to see what was going on, Trapp followed them.

Kelly's body lay on its back twenty-five yards from the wagon road. The two dogs stood over it, one of them licking the dead man's face. Kelly's crumpled brown fur hat rested half on his shoulder, with the brim on one side touching the snow.

Trapp dismounted and knelt beside the body. Touching the face, he found it stone cold, and clammy from the slobber of the dogs. Trapp didn't notice any blood. He placed the hat on the dead sheepherder's face, then quickly got back on his horse and rode toward Fraser's.

He had no way of knowing for sure, but if Kelly had been murdered, and the McLeans had done it, Trapp had no desire to meet up with them in the dark. He heard a loud rustling in the bush nearby. The thought came to mind that the McLeans had camped near here only a couple of days ago. The noise was just a few sheep, but it was enough to convince Trapp this wasn't a good place to be. Though his horse wasn't the fastest around, Trapp spurred him hard and got the hell out of there.

When he got to Fraser's there was no light. Everything was quiet. Fraser must be visiting with somebody else. There was nothing Trapp could do by himself except return home —by a round-about way — and wait until morning to get help. If there was still no one at Fraser's then, he could go north to Bartlett Newman's ranch.

During the night Trapp was awakened by a persistent pounding on the door about the same time he heard his dogs. He gathered himself up, managed to light a lamp, and stumbled out to answer the door. It was Peter Fraser and Bill McLeod, formerly one of Fraser's sheepherders who now had his own sheep ranch with his brother John. They had a sleigh with them and announced that Jim Kelly was dead.

Trapp was suddenly awake, explaining that he too had found the body, but couldn't move it without help.

Fraser and McLeod shook the snow from their clothes and boots and came in as Trapp closed the door behind them.

When Fraser had gotten home there was no sign of Kelly nor of the sheep, which should have been corralled for the night. Bill Manning from Scott's showed up, so they went looking for the sheepherder and found the body.

Other than the McLeans and Hare, McLeod was the last person to have seen Kelly alive. Not having seen Kelly since two o'clock that same day, he'd decided at about eight to ride over and check on his neighbour.

> I went up to Kelly's cabin, saw that he was not at home, and saw that the sheep had not been brought home and corralled as usual. I then went down to Mr. Fraser's house to inform him that Kelly was not home with the sheep. When I got to Fraser's house, I found out that he was away from home also. I then went back to the place where I had seen him last in the afternoon. There I found Mr. Fraser

and William Manning coming back from where Kelly was. They told me that they had seen Kelly and that he had been murdered.

Fraser added that Bill McLeod had received a message from his brother John about a shoot-up with the McLean boys earlier that day and that Johnny Ussher had been killed.

The news dumbfounded Trapp for a moment, though he'd heard it from the murderers themselves earlier in the day. Now it was official.

Fraser was even more incredulous than Trapp when he heard Trapp had received a visit from the boys and escaped alive.

Trapp said yes, they had been there around lunch time and had taken a few things.

He should consider himself lucky, Fraser told him. They had stopped by his own place, too, but he wasn't there, just his wife, and they don't bother women. They took some ammunition and food, but they didn't mention anything about Kelly.

After Trapp got dressed, they went to the swamp to pick up Kelly's body. Checking his cabin, they found that it had been ransacked. Kelly's corpse was loaded on the sleigh and hauled to Fraser's. It was 5:00 AM by the time they made it.

In the light, they found that a bullet had entered the sheepherder's body below the ribs, in the stomach. Another had slammed into his abdomen. His plaid, revolver, mouth organ and treasured watch were missing. Later in the morning, Bill McLeod headed for Kamloops with the body.

## [34]

VICTORIA, British Columbia
Tuesday, December 9, 1879

The panic started early in the day. Even before the sun was up, Superintendent Charles Todd of the B.C. Provincial Police was hustling to the offices of Premier and Attorney-General George Walkem, summoned by the news that the McLean boys had killed a constable, that they were terrorizing the entire Upper Country, and that an Indian massacre of the white settlers could be expected to begin at any moment.

Arrival of this startling intelligence less than eighteen hours after Ussher had been hacked and shot to death was made possible by a combination of pioneer fortitude and modern technology, such as it was in frontier British Columbia. At the time, British Columbia was not the envy of the world in transport and communications systems.

Where possible, ships operated on the coast and short distances inland by river. The Interior, or Upper Country, was served by steamers
going as far as Yale on the Fraser River. Stage coaches and pack trains
were a major means of transportation, especially from Yale up the
Fraser Canyon. There were, as yet, no trains, but a telegraph system
operated sporadically between the Upper Country and the coast, with
Spences Bridge and Cache Creek having the telegraph stations closest
to Kamloops. When a message had to be delivered from Kamloops to
New Westminster or Victoria quickly, the practice was to ride to Cache
Creek, send a telegram, and hope there were no breaks in the land lines
or underwater cables. So, when Mara and Edwards had gotten back to
Kamloops with Ussher's body about eleven the night before, they immediately sent a rider to Cache Creek with a desperate message to be
telegraphed to Walkem. In the dead of night, in twenty-five below
weather and through deep snow, the rider travelled fifty miles to deliver
the message. It's not recorded, but Mara probably ordered that his
company's sternwheeler, *Noisy Peggy*, be fired up to take the messenger
down the Kamloops Lake stretch of the trip to Savona's Ferry.

Walkem and his friend Todd now consulted on a strategy. They
were an odd couple, Walkem and Todd. Walkem was a brazen lawyer-
turned-politician, who never hesitated to speak his mind even if it didn't
make sense. Todd was a failed-lawyer-turned-policeman, who seldom
spoke in anything more articulate than a grunt. He was widely regarded as
owing his job more to his friendship with Walkem than anything else.
"Charles the Silent, surnamed the Todd . . . has dipped his spoon into the
Government pap-bowl and pulled out a plum," editorialized Victoria's
*Daily British Colonist* after the new superintendent was announced in
1875. "Mr. Todd alights on his feet in the snug billet of Superintendent of Police with $1,752 a year, a residence and pickings galore."

Running the B.C. Provincial Police, however, wasn't quite the plum
job the *Colonist* made it out to be. In the entire rural countryside, including Vancouver Island, Todd was allowed just twelve constables. One of
them had been John Ussher. In theory, special constables — who were
little more than glorified bounty hunters — could be added in emer-
gency situations, but the government was notoriously cheap about it.
Men like John Ussher literally went begging for more help and resources as Walkem counted his pennies. Things were going to get
worse before they got better. Within a few months, construction
would begin at long last on the railroad, and that would mean thousands of navvies sweating, drinking and whoring their way through
the mountains. The other problem was the Indians, who continued to
mutter dire warnings over the "generosity" of the whites in taking
over their land. From the time Walkem had handed Todd the job,
he'd had to worry about it. There were rumblings of a massive rebel-

lion in the interior. The Chilcotin uprising of many years ago had demonstrated the dangerous possibilities. Ranald McDonald had written from the Bonaparte of renewed fears:

> By the arrival of a special messenger from Kamloops that the Indians were massing and making warlike preparations, coupled with former rumers [sic] of Indian raisings [sic] also with an urgent request from Clinton to Govt for arms in anticipation of a Raid on the settlers from the combined tribes of Chilicotin [sic] and Indians of the Frazer [sic] River, has caused quite an excitement in our peaceful community. . . . They had their grievances about their lands & pastureage. . . .

That fortunately came to nothing, but there were even more recent stories from up country about new plans for an uprising. There were probably fewer than four dozen ranchers in the Nicola Valley, and it wouldn't take much of a rebellion to wipe them out. The settlers there believed as many as four hundred would answer the call to war. The explosion of violence by the McLeans and Hare might be the clarion that triggered it.

The first thing Walkem did was hike the government's reward for their capture to a thousand dollars, in addition to the HBC's $250. Todd's strategy consisted mainly of putting the entire province into a state of panic and getting together posses from everywhere possible. The citizens of the province would have to be made aware of the situation, but the outlaws' escape routes would also have to be cut off. Todd took a schooner the few miles across the Juan de Fuca Strait to Port Angeles in Washington, to telegraph a warning and description of the wanted men to police headquarters in Colville. American police would keep watch should the gang cross the border.

By courier, stagecoach, telegraph, newspapers and neighbours, the word spread quickly. The province that awoke so innocently that day was soon pre-occupied with only one thing — the events of the previous day in the Nicola Valley. From the parlours of Victoria to the ranch houses of the Cariboo, one word — McLeans — was on everybody's lips.

# [35]

UPPER COUNTRY, British Columbia
Tuesday, December 9, 1879

By the time Bill McLeod made it into Kamloops a little before daybreak with the body of Jim Kelly, ranchers and hands were already being organized into a posse to set out after the killers. They didn't

William Palmer *(KMA, 5873)*

have any idea where they were or where they were going, but that didn't stop Mara and Edwards. They were swearing in special constables as though they were handing out wedding invitations. Mara was sure the gang would head for the border via Osoyoos in the Okanagan Valley, so five special constables were sworn in and sent that way.

There would be no mistake like that made by the late Constable Ussher. Posses would be large, and they would have to be well armed. This presented a problem, because there were a lot more volunteers than weapons, and the three McLean brothers and Hare had much more weaponry among them than there seemed available in the whole of the Upper Country.

One man a little more anxious than most to join the posse and capture the McLean Gang was William Palmer. Not as anxious as Mara, perhaps, but anxious just the same. Firstly, he had seen Johnny Ussher hacked and shot to death and his friend John McLeod shot up, not to mention narrowly escaping with his own life. Secondly, as far as he knew, the McLeans still had his best horse. And thirdly, he knew they would gun him down the first chance they got.

As British Columbia was digesting the exciting news, and Mara and Edwards were getting organized, the half-breed Simpson was urging his horse along the Nicola Valley wagon road. He was seeking George Caughill, the special constable who had expressed an interest in capturing the McLeans, and was willing to back up his words with money. The breed had some valuable information for Caughill.

When Simpson found him, he first extracted a promise of a hundred dollars in payment for what he knew, which was the location of the McLeans. After playing hide-and-seek with the gang for months, Caughill wasn't about to refuse this usurious demand. Simpson revealed what every rancher in the Upper Country wanted to know. The outlaws, with their leader weakening from a wound received in a big gun battle with the now-dead Johnny Ussher, had spent the night at the Indian village and had since moved to a small log cabin near Douglas Lake.

Caughill sent for help to sheep rancher John Clapperton, the JP for Nicola, before starting for Douglas Lake. The messenger, Sam Connor, rode hard and made it to Clapperton's place that night. After giving Clapperton news both of the murders and the whereabouts of the gang, he continued down the valley to get men and arms. Another rider headed for Kamloops.

Clapperton was the immediate hope for hemming in the outlaws before they escaped. He had a personal interest —Jim Kelly had worked for him for two years. Fifteen years before, on his way to the Cariboo goldfields, Clapperton had stopped by Donald McLean's roadhouse at Hat Creek. Allen would have been only ten years old, Charlie a toddler, Archie still in the womb. He'd hoped to buy food, but Donald McLean had none to spare, so Clapperton had continued on to Bill "Scotty" Donaldson's for the night. It was less than three weeks before Donald McLean left on his ill-fated expedition against the Chilcotins.

Now it was Clapperton's job to capture the boys for the murder of his former employee and of a policeman. He realized the urgency of his mission in light of the McLeans' previous bragging about starting an Indian uprising. While the Douglas Lake chief, Chillihitzia, was intelligent and reasonable, there were quite a few malcontents living on the reserve. Clapperton sent a messenger to tell the chief to keep all band members away from the McLeans. He knew, though, that the settlers must put on a pretty good show of strength. The Nicola JP spread the news around his own area, and by midnight he had mustered up a handful of men, including his brother George, and some firearms and ammunition. At break of day they would start for Douglas Lake two dozen miles away.

## [36]

### SPAHOMIN VILLAGE, Douglas Lake, British Columbia
### Tuesday, December 9, 1879

It wasn't yet known in New Westminster or Kamloops, or even Victoria, but the Indian uprising so feared by the whites had already been dealt a fatal blow. In a small cabin of cottonwood logs a hundred yards from the Nicola River, the McLeans and Hare were trying to figure out their next move. The support from the Indians Allen had been so confident of was evaporating, thanks to the refusal of his father-in-law, Chillihitzia, to rise up against the whites.

Chillihitzia had been the key to Allen McLean's plan, Allen having lived among his people and married his daughter Angele. After riding through to Nicola in the south end of the valley, where the gang bought ammunition from some Indians with their stolen money, then cutting east to Douglas Lake, they had sought out old Chillihitzia, and called for a meeting with him and others in the band.

If Allen had known Chillihitzia's mind better, he would never have expected help of the kind he was asking. Two years before, the Okanagans were pressing land grievances and wanted to join up with the Shuswap and Nicola Indians to attack the whites. It would have gone ahead but for Chillihitzia, who refused at the last moment to take part. Now he didn't entertain for a moment throwing in with the McLeans.

Allen cajoled him, flattered him, appealed to his ancestry, and insulted his masculinity, even threatened him, but Chillihitzia was resolute. The unspoken bottom line was this: he feared the wrath of the whites even more than the whites feared the Indians. From the time that William Cox — the same man who led the expedition against the Chilcotins with Donald McLean — had created the first reserves back in the early 1860s, Chillihitzia had been a willing collaborator. He went along with, even encouraged, the changes effected by the white men. In the wake of the Cariboo gold rush, many who had failed to strike it rich now looked for land, and they found it in the Nicola and other places. Suddenly a whole new system of trading for goods was introduced. Cattle and horses became part of the new economy. Chillihitzia saw the intrusion on Indian land, the interruption of traditional hunting and fishing rights, as an acceptable condition of the new kind of prosperity offered by the whites. Part of the change was Christianity, which gained solid footing among the Indian tribes as a result of the unremitting work of the Oblate missionaries. The Oblates had much influence with the Nicolas and other Indians of the Interior, and further entrenched the new ways by converting them to a Christian system of values. Little by little the Indians saw their power ebb. Eventually the whites would outnumber the Indians. In 1876 the final insult had been perpetrated in the form of the Indian Act, which established two distinct classes: white people, and Indians. The latter had no rights to buy or sell what had been their land for centuries. Some, like Chillihitzia, knew that acceptance meant survival; others wanted to try one more time to recapture pride and the old ways.

Thus, after a big meeting at Head of the Lake, Okanagan, in 1877 had resolved to start a war, Chillihitzia betrayed the cause despite the strength of the Indians, who had ample weapons and horses. It had scared the hell out of the whites, who had expected the entire country from Kamloops to the American border to erupt in bloodshed, especially since a number of chiefs from the American side had been urging the Okanagans on. Having sided so clearly with the whites in this case, it would have been impossible for Chillihitzia now to throw in with the McLeans, despite the urging of many of his young men and visitors from the U.S. still smarting from the defeat of Chief Joseph and his Nez Perces by the American cavalry. Wondrous tales were told of the magnificent failure of Joseph and White Bird in their 1877 bid to outrun the cavalry to the Canadian border, of how Joseph had fought one of the most brilliant military campaigns in history. His defeat made him a martyr, a model of courage, a hero to be revenged. So while Allen McLean had good reason to think the war he dreamed of was a real possibility, he hadn't taken into proper account the one man who could, and would, stop it.

While it apparently escaped the McLeans, the irony of their situation could not have escaped Chillihitzia. Their father had been killed by Indians as he tried to hunt them down. Although the boys idolized Donald McLean for his bravery, they placed themselves on the opposite side, urging the destruction of the whites.

Chillihitzia didn't just turn down Allen McLean and his partners; he threw them out, ordering his people not to help them. Any man caught helping them, he said, would be shot.

After that Allen had gone into one of his nutty tantrums, deciding they must now destroy evidence. He returned to the stable near the Nicola River where they had tethered their horses. But instead of getting rid of Ussher's clothes, or the stolen weapons, he somehow figured that the saddles had to go. Alex Hare didn't want to go along with this stupid move, but Allen was the boss.

> Allen took out his knife and cut up the rigging of Mr. Ussher's saddle. One of the other boys went and cut up another saddle belonging to George Caughill, and then turned out two of our horses. Then Allen told me to cut up my saddle and turn my horse out also. I did not consent at first. Then he, Allen, told me again to do so, then I cut my saddle and threw it off the horse, but did not turn my horse out. Then Allen took an axe and cut up the trees of the three saddles, then we left the stable and went into the cabin.

Now, in the cabin near the stable, they awaited events while Allen nursed his wound. The cabin, which had been there as long as any-

one could remember, had often been home to Allen during the past
year. Basil Chillihitzia, his brother-in-law, owned it, but had let Angele
and Allen use it. Allen didn't take Angele or his son George with them
into the cabin, wouldn't endanger them. The boys still had friends
among the Indians, who were willing to supply them with food and to
keep them informed of activities around them, despite Chillihitzia's
warning. The McLeans were told that at least a half dozen whites
were now looking for them.

## [37]

SPAHOMIN VILLAGE, Douglas Lake
Wednesday, December 10, 1879

All through the morning there was no sign of life in the cabin, except
for smoke rising from the chimney. The men who waited outside, a
safe one thousand yards away, had been told the McLeans and Hare
were in there, and, though the horses in the small corral outside the
cabin seemed to support the theory, they didn't yet know for sure.

And inside the cabin, the McLeans and Hare waited and watched,
growing more certain that there was somebody out there waiting and
watching too. The cabin had only one small window on the river side,
so they knocked chinking out from the logs and squinted through,
jamming gun barrels into the cracks. They didn't know how many
there were, and they clung to the hope some of the breeds and Indians might still join them, so the thought of a few settlers who couldn't
shoot straight didn't much concern them. The one thing that did was
the lack of water. They had whiskey, but only a half-bucket of water.

The morning turned into afternoon. The sun hung sluggishly in
the sky, casting bright reflections off the fresh cloth of snow that had
fallen the previous night. The horses in the corral were restive because they too now sensed there was somebody, somebody with
horses, out there.

Out there was John Clapperton, who stood in a cluster of trees
watching the cabin through a pair of binoculars, as an Arctic wind
played a dirge through the cottonwoods. The cabin looked lonely and
lifeless down there under the snow. Behind it was the Nicola River, and
behind that a treeless white mountain, brooding in the cold like a cur.

Beside Clapperton was George Caughill. Clapperton's dozen-man
posse had arrived about 1:00 PM to find Caughill and his partner, Jim
Jamieson of Kamloops, and some Nicola men, waiting for them. Jim
Kennedy, one of the men the McLeans were so anxious to kill, was

there, too. The early arrivals were taking caution to extremes. The immediate advantage went to the boys. The cabin was warm, and its huge logs made it a virtual fortress. The shivering settlers were so far away that even if a bullet reached its target it would probably bump off the building and fall in the snow.

The good news for the good guys was that Chillihitzia would not help the McLeans, and that he might even help the settlers. The bad news was that the men who had arrived so far were poorly armed. And when Clapperton asked Caughill about the chances of the gang surrendering, the special constable just laughed.

A teamster named Tom 'Pike' Richardson claimed he'd already talked briefly with the McLeans, and when Richardson suggested surrender the gang vowed death before arrest. Since Richardson's conversation was held through the good offices of a couple of Indians friendly to the boys, Clapperton decided no one should be allowed to talk to them except with permission.

Clapperton and Caughill moved to an old cabin three hundred yards from the gang's and heated some coffee. The Nicola JP ordered the place patched up as headquarters and a warming-up place for posse members.

Chillihitzia arrived later that day with more than a dozen braves and agreed not to let any of them, or the Indians who had been around earlier, talk with the outlaws. The chief gave the posse his blessing to shoot the boys if they got a chance. His assistance afforded the whites considerable relief.

Clapperton reasoned that if he could keep the McLeans and Hare penned up, sooner or later they would have to come out. Their food and water wouldn't last forever. The job now was to assess his own strength and put up an effective barrier around the cabin. The bench mark distance would be three hundred yards, the same as the posse's headquarters, still safe but close enough to keep a more effective watch. He found no arrangement had been made for night watches, so he called for a muster of posse members. Albert Elgin Howse, a Nicola storekeeper, acted as clerk of the roll call, and counted twenty-two whites and fifteen Indians.

Eighteen men at a time were put on duty at points around the besieged cabin. Every two hours, three of them were relieved. Those who had kept watch the night before were given first rest, and the first watch of the evening was scheduled for 5:00 PM. The password was agreed upon as "Chillihitzia" and anyone, Indian or white, going to or coming from the McLeans' cabin, who did not give the word, was to be shot.

NEW WESTMINSTER, VICTORIA & the UPPER COUNTRY
Wednesday, December 10, 1879

As the first watch was going on duty at Douglas Lake, Police Superintendent Todd was on the steamer *Maude* heading for New Westminster. With him were two Victoria city police officers and nine special constables, one of them a Maori War volunteer, another a veteran of the expedition under Colonel Garnet Wolsely that had kicked the Métis rebel Louis Riel out of Fort Garry. The whole party, described as "lusty and fearless fellows," took with them eighty Snyder rifles, several revolvers, and eighty-four hundred rounds of ammunition. Todd intended to get more volunteers in New Westminster.

News that the McLeans and Hare had been harboured overnight at the Indian village offered no cheer to Kamloops residents. That night a messenger from John Andrew Mara reached the Cache Creek telegraph station. A telegram was sent off to Walkem noting that the outlaws were now guilty of two murders "and have cleaned Upper Nicola out of firearms the Indians have given them protection and we are afraid they will join them we are short of firearms send a party immediately and extra rifles and pistols if not put down at once we may have an Indian war." In New Westminster, government agent J.C. Hughes intercepted Mara's telegram and forwarded it to Walkem, adding a telegram of his own that said he was short of rifles and pistols himself. Hughes belatedly recommended that a special steamer and a posse be sent from Victoria.

About the time Hughes was sending that plea, another special messenger was arriving at Spences Bridge with news of Kelly's death. The messenger said the McLeans were in a log house and that the Indians would not assist the settlers. There was still fear that the Indians would rally to the cause of the McLean Gang and attempt to dislodge white settlers from the country they, the Indians, had so recently owned. This information was forwarded by telegram to Walkem.

From Kamloops yet another messenger was riding to the Okanagan to bring back the five specials and have them go to Douglas Lake.

When Cache Creek JP Charles Semlin received a letter from Mara asking for men and arms, he immediately called a meeting at Bonaparte House, a hotel on the Bonaparte River he'd owned several years earlier. Several men from Cache Creek were joined by another group from Clinton. Senator Clement Cornwall left Ashcroft Manor to attend and was elected captain of the posse by acclamation. The men began making preparations to head for Savona's Ferry on Kamloops Lake,

John Andrew Mara *(BCARS, 3518)*

where a steamer would take them to Kamloops. They, like the other assembling posses, were still unaware of the relatively safe situation with the Nicola Indians and were acting on the assumption that there could be a full-scale Indian war. Yet they could produce only a couple of rifles and some revolvers. Based on the same fears, a similar need for arms was expressed on behalf of Clinton settlers, who likewise telegraphed to Walkem.

## [39]

SPAHOMIN VILLAGE, Douglas Lake
Thursday, December 11, 1879, 12:00 noon

John Clapperton was beginning to wonder if he'd been fooled. From the time he'd reached Douglas Lake the day before until now, he saw nothing that would indicate anybody was in the cabin. There was somebody watching it through binoculars pretty well all the time, but there was no obvious activity behind those log walls. He began to suspect that if they were in there, they'd committed suicide.

John Edwards arrived from Kamloops with at least two dozen

men, including ten Indians from the Kamloops reserve. They had travelled all night, with Edwards and about nine men catching up to a
group that had left earlier. Mara decided not to come after all. Better,
perhaps, to stay in Kamloops sending off desperate messages to
Walkem, begging for men and arms, than to stand around in the cold
where a man could get shot.

Clapperton suggested they try sending a message to the cabin before deciding whether to burn it down or storm it, just in case there
really was nobody inside. The two posse leaders found Chillihitzia
and asked him if his son Saliesta, or Johnny, would act as messenger.
Johnny was reluctant to expose himself to such danger until Edwards
promised him a hundred dollars from the government. It was the
same amount promised Simpson by Caughill and the same amount
John Ussher had once said would make the Kamloops jail secure.

Clapperton took out a piece of paper and wrote:

*McLean Bros & Alex Hare will you surrender quietly? If so send in
your arms, and I guarantee you [sic] personal safety. No surrender,
and we burn the house over your heads.*

*Jno. Clapperton, J.P.*

The Indian was given a piece of paper and a pencil so the
McLeans could answer. Johnny mounted up and rode out into the
clearing in front of the cabin, vigorously waving a white flag. About
one hundred yards from the tiny house he reined up and continued
waving his flag. He sat there on his horse for at least fifteen minutes,
waving away. Clapperton, watching through his binoculars, could see
no sign of activity from inside the old cabin. *I began to think my
conjecture right, but no; I see a tiny piece of rag protrude through the
joints of the door, and flutter in the cold west wind, our brave courier,
sees it, and dashes forward to within speaking distance of the besieged.
For half an hour the conversation lasts although he rides up, hands in his
papers and retreats some distance.* Clapperton and Edwards can't hear
anything that's being said, but what's happening is that Johnny, after
spotting a grubby handkerchief tied on the end of a stick, has ventured closer. Shouts of Klahowya! are exchanged, and Johnny says he
wants to make wawa. He walks his horse carefully toward the cabin
door and, without dismounting, leans down and holds out the paper
upon which Clapperton has written the message. Allen McLean sticks
a hand through the space where the flag has been and snatches the
paper and pencil offered by Johnny, then orders his brother-in-law to
back off. Though Archie can read a little and sign his name, Alex is
the only one of the four who can both read and write, so he reads the
note out loud to the other three. Allen and Johnny resume their con-

Undated picture of cabin at Douglas Lake where the McLean brothers and Alex Hare were captured in December 1879 (KMA)

versation. Who else is out there besides Clapperton? Johnny says John Edwards and maybe more than sixty, maybe a hundred. *Klonas taghum tahtlum pe ikt, hiyoo big bonch. Koonas tuk-a-mo'nuk.* More will come. They will not go away. Allen demands to know why Johnny is helping the whites. The whites will win, says Johnny. But if Allen wins, he hopes they will still be friends. Resisting the temptation to shoot the double-dealing sonofabitch off his horse, Allen dictates a note to Alex, then calls Johnny back to the door. The poetic Clapperton is still watching anxiously through his glass. *The Indian returns to the door, bends low in his saddle and reaching for the answer whirls and furrors the flanks of his steed as he races from the habitation of infuriated demons. I advance to meet him but he stops not till he reaches the rear of the headquarters when he handed me the following reply which I read aloud.*

> Mr. Clapperton,
> Sir: –
>
> *The boys say they will not surrender, and so you can burn the house a thousand times over.*
>
> Alexr. J. Hare
>
> *I wish to know what you all have against me. If you have anything, please let me know what it is.*
>
> A.H.

The postscript undoubtedly struck Clapperton as being a bit funny, but the other part, about burning the cabin down, might eventually become necessary. Johnny Chillihitzia said that if they wanted to send more messages, they could find somebody else. Risking his neck twice in one day was quite enough.

More white men from Nicola arrived with supplies for the posse. Douglas Lake Ranch women sent unsolicited food, as did those from the Moore ranch. Other food came from a Chinese restaurant at

Nicola. The waiting game settled down in earnest — but not for long.

Archie McLean was sighting down the long barrel of Trapp's heavy Henry rifle when into range came a man struggling to retrieve a horse that had gotten away and wandered out in front of the cabin. It was none other than Johnston Stevenson, who had come out from his ranch near Douglas Lake to join the posse. Archie couldn't believe his luck. He squeezed off a shot and Stevenson piled into the snow, while the horse squealed in fright and took off. Suddenly there was a loud crackling like that of a giant string of fire crackers, and the cabin veritably shook with bullets pounding into the wood. After a minute the shooting died down, and the four outlaws ventured a peek through the wall again. Stevenson was gone; a couple of the posse members had crawled out and dragged him back to cover during the fireworks.

And at the posse's headquarters, Stevenson lay grimacing in the snow, grasping the shoulder where Archie's bullet had hit. He was the first official member of the boys' death list to get shot, and he would live.

## [40]

NEW WESTMINSTER
Thursday, December 11, 1879

Hughes had been scrounging up arms to send into the Interior. He was able to send the following telegram to Walkem: "Will dispatch today seven Henry rifles to Mara Kamloops and one thousand rounds ammunition which is all the arms and ammunition to be had here."

Unfortunately, the message didn't get to the premier very quickly. There was a break in the cable. So Hughes telegraphed to Burrard Inlet to charter the nearest steamer, the *Leonora*, to go to Nanaimo with that message and others that had come in. But it was found that the line between Nanaimo and Victoria was down. The government agent decided to telegraph to Matsqui, thirty miles up the Fraser River, for the steamer *Gem* to come down to New Westminster and proceed back up to Yale with the arms and ammunition.

Meanwhile, in Cache Creek, Clement Cornwall and his posse left for their journey to Kamloops. More men were ready to follow, but without adequate ammunition and arms there was no point in them going with Cornwall. Before he left, Cornwall telegraphed John Murray in Spences Bridge to move all canoes and boats to the far side of the river and to watch roads and bridges in case the gang should escape from Douglas Lake.

While Hughes was waiting for the *Gem* to reach New Westminster, four more Winchester rifles were donated to the cause, and he bought two more Winchesters and a thousand cartridges. He felt that because there were many Winchesters in the Upper Country, the extra ammunition would come in handy. From the New Westminster Jail came four Colt revolvers and six hundred bullets — all that could be spared.

These were all loaded on board the *Gem* when it arrived, along with instructions to transfer them to land transportation at Yale as quickly as possible and get them to Kamloops. Hughes figured it would take until about Sunday the 14th to make it.

## [41]

SPAHOMIN VILLAGE, Douglas Lake
Thursday, December 11, 1879, early evening

Living in a hundred-square-foot dirt-floor log cabin for several days presents problems. For one thing, there's the matter of sanitation. If you can't go outside, you can't go to the outhouse, so you have to dig out a hole in the floor to do your business. Even among friends, the results can become a sensitive issue.

One time, after one of their patented escapes from the Kamloops jail, a couple of the boys holed up in a cave on the east side of the Bonaparte River about seventeen miles north of Cornwalls'. It was a pretty good hiding place, secure from siege and well-stocked with everything they needed. That cave was better accommodation than this cabin.

Aside from matters of comfort, there was the water problem. The McLeans and Hare had lots of food in the cabin, but they were running out of water. Archie decided he wasn't going to stay cooped up in the cabin and die of thirst. Less than a hundred yards north of the cabin was the Nicola River, with all the water they could ever need, and he was going to get some of it. So he grabbed a bucket, heaved himself through the doorway and made a dash toward the creek accompanied by cover fire. He hadn't gone a third of the distance before realizing it was hopeless. Fortunately the poor shooting of the settlers allowed him to make it back to the cabin, tired but unhurt.

Now they developed another plan. Allen, seeing that it was starting to snow again, believed they could make a break. Despite his wound, there was no percentage in staying where they were; the numbers against them would only increase, and it was obvious they weren't going to get any help from the people they had hoped to get help from. So they would run for their horses and ride away.

It might seem, to a sane person, that running out of a cabin, trying to catch a bunch of scared horses, getting on them, and blazing your way through seventy some-odd guys with guns of their own isn't much of a plan, but it wasn't entirely goofy considering Allen's skill with a gun and his younger brothers' expertise with horses.

Archie and Charlie were so good they'd ridden in races all over the Upper Country for years, that is, until they got into so much trouble they didn't have the time or opportunity. An old geezer named Archie McConnell was the most successful race breeder around and used to hire Charlie and Archie to ride for him, at Clinton, at the annual Cornwall brothers' derby at Ashcroft Manor, at Grande Prairie, down at Keremeos and up in the Cariboo. Archie started riding for McConnell when he was barely ten or eleven years old, and weighed in at a hundred pounds. Even in those days, Archie knew how to make a dishonest dollar. At a race at Williams Lake, he was supposed to ride for Doc English, a well-known Cariboo rancher. He cut a deal with Doc's opposing horseman, Tom McDougall, to throw the race. But English found out about it and pulled him off the horse at the starting post. Archie pulled a gun and was about to shoot English when somebody else grabbed him.

Horses weren't all the boys rode. Two men, Henry Ingram and Frank Laumeister, had imported camels to the Upper Country for packing. They figured the desert animals would be good, because of their strength and ability to travel long distances without water, but their body odour caused a rodeo every time they got near mules or horses, so they were turned loose. The McLeans learned to ride them, and one evening their black sense of humour came into play. A group of ranchers was out rounding up stray cattle. Without warning, the McLeans crashed out of the bush on the camels, stampeding the horses and scattering the steers in every direction.

The boys were so good they could probably have ridden a bunch of camels through the eye of the posse. Charlie would have settled for Willie Palmer's black gelding; he was wishing they hadn't turned him loose after their encounter with Palmer at Long Lake.

The snow increased considerably in the next while, big, flat flakes floating leisurely through the raw air to the ground. The boys ate some canned meat and biscuits, then stuffed a few things into their coats, including extra guns and ammunition. Then they kicked open the door.

During the next few minutes there was a lot of noise, a lot of running around, a lot of confusion. The posse responded quickly with everything they could muster. With a roar, revolvers, rifles and shotguns opened up on the four outlaws. The boys were in a thick, moving soup as bullets whizzed by them. They fired back with their own pistols, their rifles, their shotguns. If they saw movement in the grey evening light, they fired at it; if they didn't they fired anywhere they thought a posseman might lurk.

A couple of them got to the stable, knocked down the gate poles, grabbed some reins, leaped on, started galloping on panicked horses that were screaming in fright, the riders themselves howling like wounded steers. Along with the gunfire, there was a whole lot of shouting, the McLeans and Hare shouting at each other and daring the posse, the posse shouting back and at other posse members. A horse bellowed, a horse lurched around here, a man ran there, a hail of bullets met each try. And the result of all this running and lurching and shouting was that all four of them ended up in front of the cabin, shooting to get back in instead of shooting their way out. None of the boys was hit, not once, but two Indian possemen fell wounded and the McLeans yelled in glee.

After they all got back inside, the firing from the posse, as if on cue, died down once again, except for a few sporadic shots from some of the greenhorns. The boys all slumped on the floor, puffing away, no doubt amazed at the suddenness of their failure, perhaps in awe at the same time that they were still alive. But they had, at least, got two of the black, traitorous bastards. On the other hand, they had lost three more horses. Maybe they'd have done better with camels.

Exhausted and thirsty, their next plan was probably to sleep, for quite awhile. Soon it was quite black outside, though the moon's reflections bouncing off the snow provided a smudgy outline of the trees behind which the posse waited.

# [42]

## SPAHOMIN VILLAGE, Douglas Lake
### Friday, December 12, 1879, very early morning

All that work would serve to increase a man's thirst, and Archie decided to make another try for the creek. First he smeared his face with soot from the stove, then woke up Charlie, telling him to provide cover.

No hat, no coat, no gun, Archie opened the door as little as possible and slithered out. He moved a little at a time, staying flat on the snow. Inch by inch he crawled toward the creek, his arm through the bucket handle, waiting for the inevitable crack of a rifle. He made it to some trees and it still hadn't come.

Archie got to his hands and knees and moved more quickly, pausing behind each tree to carefully check things out. There were campfires in a wide swath around the cabin, and an occasional dark figure seated on a stump or standing with a bigger dark figure, a four-legged one. He worked his way to the water's edge and plunged his face in. It must have seemed as though he could stay there with his face in the river forever, gulping his fill, not minding the numbing cold of the water. But then, the snap of a branch on the ground, and he must tug his head up. He could see nothing, and the sound was not repeated. He filled the bucket and headed back. It was hard work, shoving the bucket along in front of him as he crawled towards the trees' edge and started across the snow.

"Hey, there, what's the password?" came a distant voice.

Password?

The question was repeated, and when there was no answer a rifle exploded in the darkness.

"They're trying to break out again!" came a yell from the alert rifleman.

This was followed by indiscriminate firing in the general direction of the cabin. Flashes from the weapons blinked around the edges of the forest. Archie was now up and running, water sloshing over the top of the bucket as it bounced around.

The boys, now wide awake thank-you very much, were returning the fire as Archie entered. For his efforts, there was about an inch of water left in the bucket.

The posse was jittery for the rest of the night. Among them, one young man marched slowly back and forth in the snow, trying to be ready for any possible movement anywhere near him. After the attempted escape and the later sighting of one of the outlaws outside the cabin, he was as nervous as the rest of the posse.

This fellow was Joe Coutlie, the half-breed son of Alex Coutlie who ran a hotel-store near Nicola. The youth had considered Alex Hare a friend. And Hare considered Joe Coutlie to be his real best friend other than the McLeans.

Joe and his father had played a role in the McLean Gang story only a couple of weeks ago. When the McLeans and Hare fled after using the Chinaman for a punching bag, the brothers separated from Hare, planning to meet later. The three McLeans, with some of the fast horses they'd stolen from Johnny Wilson's stables, took the direct road through Savona while Hare went around through the Nicola Valley.

The story goes that on the same morning that a stage driver brought news of the robbery to Coutlie's, Joe discovered Hare in a hayloft, drunk. Joe woke him up.

"Leave me alone," Hare mumbled. "I'm going to Hell to ride bucking broncos for the Devil."

Joe managed to sober Hare up in a few minutes, however, and the outlaw was ready for breakfast. He was warned that Wheeler, the stage driver, was an ex-lawman and had bragged he'd get the stolen goods back if he ever came across the gang.

Hare, unworried, entered the hotel. The proprietor and Wheeler had sat down to breakfast. The look on Wheeler's face, the story-tellers said, was something to see. Hare and Wheeler greeted each other casually as Hare seated himself. He didn't take off his thick woollen pea jacket, under which he had a pistol strapped to his side. He calmly started on his meal, always keeping an eye on Wheeler, who left fifteen minutes later with no attempt to make good his boast.

Knowing that Wheeler would set a trap for him if he took the route on the wagon road through Quilchena on Nicola Lake, Hare went on a detour near Hamilton Mountain to the east, finding the McLeans without trouble.

Now Joe Coutlie found himself on the opposite side, part of a posse that intended to capture Hare and the McLeans. He was responsible for patrolling a portion of the wide circle around the cabin during the night shift. It was now 4:00 AM and he was cold and tired. Near him was an old Indian underground shelter, called a kickwilly, that had been tempting him. Finally, he crawled down into the depression and took out his cigarette makings, peeling out a paper and attempting to fix the tobacco with his cold-stiffened fingers. He got it made, lit it and was puffing contentedly when he heard a blast rumble through the night. The young man jumped up and looked out – a fellow posse member had pulled off a shot from his 10-gauge shotgun.

Were the McLeans and his friend Hare making another break for freedom? This wooded sector might offer them a chance to make it. Joe Coutlie grabbed his own gun and crawled back out of the shelter – then saw a horse swallowed up by the darkness. He could see the man who had fired the shot.

"What's wrong?" he shouted anxiously to the man.

"Hell, the way that pinto was coming on I could have sworn it was a man, or at least somebody was riding him. I filled his hide full of buckshot for nothing."

Thus the night went, a settler occasionally being spooked at an imaginary adversary and firing a shot. But the gang made no more attempts to escape or get water.

## [43]

NEW WESTMINSTER
Friday, December 12, 1879

Back on the coast, the *Maude* was still being awaited. Todd's posse would be increased to fifteen men and maybe more when it reached

British Columbia Telegraph.

The following Message is received in compliance with the rules and conditions of this company, as endorsed on form No. 1 of this Company, which have been agreed to by the sender.

R. B. McMICKING, General Superintendent.

Ferry — Kamloops Dec 10 Cache CK Dec 11 1879.

Received at Victoria Dec 12 187 12.15 P.M.

To Honl G. A. Walkem

Check 60 Colleck

The outlaws have killed Kelly at Stump Lake and have cleaned Upper Nicola out of fire arms the Indians have given them protection and we are afraid they will join them We are short of fire arms Send a party immediately and extra rifles and pistols if not put down at once we may have an indian war

J. A. Mara

Telegram from John Andrew Mara urging help in catching the McLeans (BCARS, K/J/M22)

there. Meanwhile still more weapons were being found, and it was decided to forward twenty-two rifles to Yale via the steamer *Royal City*. It would leave that night, and its cargo of arms would include seven Henry rifles with a thousand rounds of ammunition and fifteen Snyder rifles with three thousand rounds. The *Maude*, carrying breech-loading rifles and eighty-four hundred rounds of ball cartridges, would follow the *Gem* and the *Royal City* to Yale.

A half-dozen men were waiting in Cache Creek for the arrival of arms from New Westminster. Seven other volunteers left Spences Bridge that morning for Douglas Lake. The distance from Cache Creek to the "seat of war," as one posse organizer called it, was estimated at ninety-five miles, while from Spences Bridge it was seventy.

The telegraph lines, now repaired, were buzzing hotter than ever. James Newland at Cache Creek sent down to Walkem the news that the Edwards posse and the Kamloops Indians had arrived at Douglas Lake, though the situation regarding the part the Nicola Indians would play still wasn't clear. Newland also noted that Cornwall expected to leave Kamloops for Douglas Lake the next day and, in a second telegram to Hughes, revealed that Stevenson had been wounded.

There were more pleas to the premier to get arms to the settlers quickly. Walkem telegraphed Constable George Lindsay at Barkerville to meet Constable George Tunstall at Cache Creek, from there to go to the aid of the settlers at Douglas Lake. "Bring down any good firearms and handcuffs. Don't fail," Walkem added.

Hughes wired Newland to establish relays of messengers, at least four of them, with good horses, between Cache Creek and Kamloops, so that news could be sent to New Westminster and Victoria with as little delay as possible. Newland replied that he would send a man to Kamloops that evening and that three more would station themselves along the way the following day.

Provincial Secretary Thomas Humphrey arrived in New Westminster and decided he would go up to Yale. He also decided to take a doctor up-country with him to care for Stevenson and any other wounded. Humphrey suggested to Hughes that he get the clergymen of the Interior to do what they could to discourage the Indians from rebelling. So Hughes called upon Roman Catholic Bishop Louis D'Herbomez, who composed a telegram and sent copies to the Oblate clergymen in charge of three missions: Father James McGuckin at Williams Lake, Father Charles Grandidier in Kamloops, and Father Pierre Richard in the Okanagan. It instructed each one to "use your influence" to deter the Indians of his area from aiding or joining the McLeans and Hare.

Government agent Hughes also wrote a letter to Walkem, explaining the situation as he knew it, and asking that at least a hundred more rifles and five thousand cartridges be sent to New Westminster to be held there in case of need.

Meanwhile, the press was having a field day with the whole incident, and advice on how to handle things was flying freely.

The *Daily British Colonist* had the following suggestion to offer:

> There are at the dockyard a number of Hale's war rocket batteries and we have no doubt that one or two could be obtained for this service on application. The discharge tube is so light that it may be carried, with a stand and elevation scale, on a mule's back. Each shell weighs 26 pounds. A mule can pack 10 shells. Three mules would pack a battery and apparatus and 20 shells. Supposing the outlaws to be entrenched in a log cabin, a shell or two would dislodge or kill them. The shells were used in Abyssinia and Zululand with great success. We would also suggest that the force sent from Victoria be uniformed if possible, as the Indians hold uniforms in great awe.

When not offering advice, the newspapers of the province were issuing headlines such as these: "THE KAMLOOPS OUTLAWS! THEY ARE STILL IN THE LOG HOUSE! Attacked by the Settlers! THEY SHOOT AND MORTALLY WOUND ONE!" (referring to Johnston Stevenson, who in fact was to recover), in the *Colonist*; "THE KAMLOOPS MURDERS, Men and Arms to the Front, Another Man Shot, The Vigorous Measures of the Government, INDIANS ALL QUIET," in the *Daily Standard* of Victoria. For the *Dominion Pacific Herald* and the *Mainland Guardian* in New Westminster, the gang would also provide news material for many coming editions. Even in the East, the *Toronto Mail* carried accounts under such headlines as "LAWLESSNESS IN BRITISH COLUMBIA."

## [44]

SPAHOMIN VILLAGE, Douglas Lake
Friday, December 12, 1879

Clapperton and Edwards had other things to worry about than the kind of press they were getting. The siege was in its fourth day and the posse members were impatient — it was a rough winter and they would rather be back tending to their ranches than risking their lives. These weren't professional man-hunters but ordinary citizens protecting their property. As yet there were no representatives of the provincial police force. If the settlers had waited for the official system of law and order to handle everything, the McLeans could have gone anywhere they pleased and carried out their threats. As it was, though the total posse was now a good size, only half its members had weapons.

The McLeans and Hare were getting thirsty. The last of their water was long gone. They were out of wood, but they had to eat, and when they ate the canned food, it made them thirstier. Allen sulked about not having anyone to cook his meals for him. The whiskey was of no help and the boys didn't touch it.

They were now completely pinned down. Any obvious movement was met with a volley of fire. They could not even grab snow from outside the door. Instead, they tried poking sticks through a chink hole near the ground and scraping up snow but this was spotted and a burst of gunfire discouraged them. Then they tried sucking up what little moisture they could by putting straws through the lower holes but this, too, was discovered and prevented.

Tom Richardson was an excellent rider and had the idea of galloping past the cabin, lassoing the chimney and pulling it down. That would cause the McLeans some discomfort and maybe cause other damage to the cabin. The man did as he said he could do, riding in from the side and arching the lariat up over the chimney before the outlaws knew what was going on. Only problem was the chimney wouldn't give, and Richardson had to abandon his rope and run for it as the slightly amazed McLeans caught on and sent some bullets his way. Richardson made it back safely.

The posse, though, wasn't out of tricks. Some of the members, under direction of Edwards and Clapperton, were working on making good the threat to burn down the house around the outlaws. Hay bales were brought in and piled on top of a wagon, then soaked with coal oil. The idea was to light the hay and push the wagon down onto the cabin. Two hours later, all was ready, but the hay was wet and would only smoulder. The men tried it anyway. Hiding behind the bales and the wagon, they pushed it toward the cabin. Those providing the horsepower barely escaped with their hides. The McLeans kept up a withering fire and the hay bales provided no protection whatsoever. The determined but hapless posse members tried several times but it was no use. It was decided to soak the wagon itself with oil and try again in the morning.

That night, the McLeans and their partner must have started to realize that their options were running out. Their alternatives had been reduced to simplicity. They could surrender and be lynched, or found guilty and hanged, or at least be slapped in jail for the rest of their lives with escape their only hope. Or they could make a run for it in the dark, and likely be shot down. The other choice was suicide, and they apparently considered it despite having been raised as Catholics.

By now, an estrangement had formed between Hare and the three McLean brothers. Hare had come to the conclusion, as he contemplated the possible outcomes of their venture, none of which looked good at this point, that all of his troubles were due to the McLeans. If it hadn't been for them, he believed, he would not have ended up in this predicament. If Archie hadn't blown Ussher's brains out they would have been alright. He convinced himself that there had been no choice but to go along with them.

"I have only one friend left," he'd said to Charlie McLean one day, "and that is Joe Coutlie."

"There are no friends," Charlie had answered. "They're all the same to me."

And that was the way the McLeans thought, that they were alone and that they could trust no one. Allen certainly believed that now more than ever. He and his brothers were as angry with their older brother Hector as they were with the Indians. Hector hadn't helped them the way he should, and he wasn't here now. None of them, of course, had any way of knowing that Hector was at this moment enjoying the hospitality, under guard, of the Kamloops jail.

Though Hector's supposed defection ate at all of them, Allen was the one the two younger brothers looked to for leadership. In this, he was in some ways a strange choice. Despite all his strong qualities, including a certain violent charisma, he was erratic. The horse-stab-bing incident was a good example of his sometimes irrational behaviour. He was riding the brown mare, which they'd stolen from Jim Eard, from Douglas Lake to the mountain-trail camp one day. Most people would sell a horse that was too slow, but Allen pulled out his knife and stabbed her in the neck, then turned her loose. It served no purpose except a misdirected means for Allen to vent his spleen. Towards the end of November, they'd sold a grey mare they'd stolen from Johnny Wilson at Cache Creek to a one-name fellow called Pablo. Instead of cash, Pablo gave Hare a rifle. But that same evening Pablo couldn't find a pair of spurs he'd left in his cabin, and went looking for the boys. The accusation was barely out of his mouth when Allen smashed him in the chest with a rifle, yelling at the others to take out their pistols. Charlie and Archie instantly drew, but Hare hesitated. Another man named Basilio Mucado was there, and stepped between Allen and Pablo. Allen, in a rage, ordered the boys to shoot them both. *Allen told us that whoever did not obey his orders and fire whenever he told us to do so, he would blow our brains out.* The standoff ended with Pablo keeping Wilson's horse and the boys keeping the rifle, but it showed how dangerous Allen's temper could be, and how absolute he expected loyalty to him to be.

Yet, in a warped sort of way, he wasn't totally without honour. He would never shoot anybody, or beat him up, unless he felt he had cause. Not passively standing by and saying thank-you to being robbed was enough for Allen to get mad. Then all his real and im-agined grievances against the whites would come to a boil. No wonder he hated so many people.

Hare, though, had his own reasons to be bitter against the white settlers and merchants. He was in love. Like a puppy, he adored Annie McLean, and because he adored her, he hated John Andrew Mara. It was an unrequited love. She was older, and very pretty, and there's no evidence whatsoever that she had any feelings for Alex Hare. Yet it's known that he carried a serious torch for her and fanta-sized about marrying her and having their own ranch. The brothers may have found this a bit of a joke. For their part, they were coming to think Alex Hare was trying to use them as a scapegoat. Archie had probably saved his life by shooting Ussher, yet Hare now resented them. It was Hare who had pulled a knife on Ussher in the first place. They began to distrust him, with good reason, for if the posse had given him the choice at this moment of walking away from the cabin and leaving the brothers there to starve, he would have done it.

SPAHOMIN VILLAGE, Douglas Lake
Saturday, December 13, 1879

This day was the same as the entire winter had been: cold and snowy and miserable. For the posse surrounding the cabin, the day was also the same: another day of waiting for the banditti (as they were being called in the telegrams flying back and forth) to make another get-away attempt or to surrender. Another day of frustration in trying to hurry them up. The burning wagon idea was abandoned. Instead, as the day progressed and there seemed little prospect of any change in the situation, it was decided to fortify the wagon and use it as a breastwork to charge the cabin and ram into it. A group of possemen set to putting together a kind of fort on wheels, using logs to build protection for the men who would charge.

In the cabin the banditti languished, their tongues swollen, their energy drained. They could stomach no more salty canned food. They were out of firewood, and the cabin was almost as cold inside as the weather was outside. Even worse, their ammunition was all but gone. They had only a few revolver bullets left. No water, no fire, and no bullets. Lots of food. Not a good equation.

Allen, though, wasn't finished coming up with ideas. He wanted to propose that the posse give them a five hundred-yard head start to get to Kamloops and shoot the sonofabitch Mara. He would have liked to get that bastard before he went down.

As if the posse could hear them talking, a few minutes later a Métis named John Leonard rode up in front of the cabin, waving a white flag.

Allen immediately poked his own makeshift flag of truce out the door and waggled it up and down. Leonard came in closer.

"McLeans and Hare!" Leonard yelled. "Mr. Edwards wants to know what do you want?"

Allen told him about the head start. Leonard rode back to the waiting posse leaders but returned to the cabin almost immediately.

"They say they're sorry but they can make no deals!"

"Then tell the bastards they can damn well wait, because we aren't coming out! We'll see them in hell first!"

Leonard returned with the message. There was no further response from the posse. It looked like another day would end in stalemate.

Edwards and Clapperton ordered the wagon to be pulled out where the McLeans could observe the work but kept it at what was considered a safe distance from the cabin. They were confident the logs on the wagon would withstand any fire the gang might put up. When the wagon hit the cabin, coal oil would be tossed on it and lit. That would get them out, though more men might get shot up, too. They could not, however, afford the safe and sure siege business forever. Besides the anxiety about getting back to their jobs and ranches, it was too cold to stay there long. One of the posse members, Tom Ombie, had already gotten his feet frozen.

A few Spences Bridge men came in. Another posse arrived from Kamloops, bringing the strength of the entire force at the cabin to some seventy-five men, including Kamloops and Nicola Indians, and Kamloops and Nicola ranchers and hands. Some estimates ran up to two hundred men, but that was undoubtedly high since there were barely that many whites in the whole region.

Edwards, watching the cabin through his binoculars from near where the work was proceeding on the wagon, saw the McLeans' flag poked through the door again.

When Leonard rode up in front of the cabin, he was ordered to dismount and approach the door. He did so cautiously.

What, Allen wanted to know, were those men doing with the wagon.

They were planning on burning the cabin down, Leonard explained. They had six cases of coal oil and were going to push the wagon down and light the place up.

Allen told him to wait, and moved away from the door. Leonard could hear mumbled conversation. Then the outlaw came back and told him, "Go tell the bastards to burn the place and be damned."

Work continued on the wagon, and it was almost completed when Clapperton and Edwards wrote out yet another message and both signed it. It was sent to the outlaws: "Surrender by coming outside and laying down your arms. We will protect you."

The answer came back: "Give us one hour to consider."

There was little to discuss in that hour. They knew they were beaten. They could stay in the cabin and freeze and dehydrate until they were so weak the posse could walk in and drag them out. If they surrendered now, they might somehow be able to retain a little dignity, and the hope of escape. The minute hand moved slowly around the dial of the silver Waltham watch taken from the sheepherder Kelly, the quiet but sharp ticking taking them closer and closer to capture. They weren't unanimous about surrender. Charlie was all for sitting right there and letting the posse burn the place down on them. But Allen, as cold as ever, in a flash of logic reasoned there was no longer any chance of escape or making a deal. Besides everything else, his wound was festering. There was a noise outside.

"Your hour is past," Leonard said from his horse. "Mr. Clapperton and Mr. Edwards want to know your decision."

Allen asked for a piece of paper and Leonard had one ready. He dictated a message while Alex wrote using the stubby pencil given them previously:

*Please come with Frederick Rush and we will speak together.*

The reply came back from Edwards: there would be no parleying with the posse leaders until they sent out their arms.

They sent back another message:

*Go back to Kamloops and we will go there to surrender, which we cannot do here.*

*Alexdr. Hare*

The boys, apparently, still had a sense of humour. The wagon-fortress was moved into position.

Again the flag of truce from the cabin. This time rancher Fred Rush, also known as Oscar, went to talk. He returned with a request for only Edwards to come up.

Again this was rejected.

Finally it came: "We will surrender if not ironed, and supplied with horses to go to Kamloops."

Edwards and Clapperton knew the almost fanatical value the gang placed on freedom. They wanted to retain at least some face by going in unshackled; no doubt they would also take the opportunity to seek some means of escape on the way. But this might be the farthest they'd go in terms; if this provision were also rejected, they might decide to refuse surrender once more. Edwards later claimed he made no promises, but in his reply he must have given the boys the impression their condition would be met.

The McLeans had one other proposition. If Edwards would come out with Rush and meet them halfway, they would come out one by one and allow Rush to search them. Edwards agreed. As he and Rush walked forward, every posse member's eyes drilled into the cabin door, every gun was cocked.

As the boys watched Edwards and Rush approach, their hearts must have been like lead, their spirit evaporating along with their dream. The pair stopped, waiting.

Allen got up and slowly pushed open the door. Alex walked out first, followed by Archie, Charlie and then Allen. They walked a few paces. Edwards and Rush were startled as the boys suddenly raised their arms straight up — they had pistols in them. Then they emptied their guns into the air. When Indians surrendered they fired off their unexpended ammunition, so that they did not give up until the last shot was gone. The four youths had put off doing this until the last possible moment. Then they tossed their weapons to the ground. They were no longer free men. From every direction guns were trained on the weaponless outlaws as they walked toward the two posse members.

Allen greeted Edwards; Edwards ordered him to hold his hands high and told Rush to search them. As this was going on, Edwards asked Hare, "What possessed you to kill poor Johnny, Alex?"

"There's no use talking about it now," said Hare. "It's too late."

In Hare's coat Rush found a pocket book with the messages Edwards and Clapperton had been sending them.

Among the rest of the possemen, rancher William Palmer watched Rush carefully search the McLeans and Hare. And quietly breathed a deep sigh of relief.

Edwards waited until they were closer to where the entire posse was now gathering around. Then he gave the signal, and several men quickly approached, grabbed them, started shackling them. The boys cursed and fumed. Sonsofbitches. More men ran up. Charlie fought them off well enough to momentarily get free, but after several minutes they were all subdued and tied.

"This was not a condition of surrender!" an angry Alex Hare yelled at Edwards.

"We can't let you go in unbound," said Edwards. "You have to be ironed as prisoners." Then he ordered his men to give them some water, tie them onto mules, and to search the cabin.

In total they found six revolvers, four single-barrel shotguns, two double-barrel shot guns, and Trapp's Henry rifle. There were no shells in the Henry. Among the pistols were Kelly's and one with a broken handle initialled A.J.H. The cabin was littered with accumulated junk and garbage. And there was a large hole dug in the ground.

They found one other thing — a silver Waltham watch and chain.

Edwards was worried, at first, that some of the posse might want to lynch the gang right there rather than wait to get them back to town, but that fear quickly vanished.

"My feet are going to get damn cold," complained Archie, whose boots had been taken away.

"You've had enough hot times to last you, McLean," one of the posse members said, as preparations were made to decamp and start back toward Kamloops.

Archie grinned. "Damn right we did, and we aren't finished yet."

"The only hot time you'll have from now on will be in hell," came the reply.

Some of the posse members guffawed loudly but the boys had regained some of their composure.

"Hey, Scotty," Alex called to a one-eyed man he knew. "The man says we're going to hell; maybe we are. Before I go you come and help yourself to an eye!"

This time the settlers laughed with Alex and Archie. Allen managed only a slight grin, and Charlie looked grouchy.

Chillihitzia and his men, and the ranchers from farther south, departed, leaving most of the posse to take the gang to Kamloops. The posse leaders agreed to recommend that at least three-quarters of the government's thousand-dollar reward be distributed among the Indians who had helped in the siege, and there would also be requisitions for damage done to reserve land.

Before leaving for Spences Bridge to telegraph the good news to Walkem in Victoria via New Westminster, Clapperton spoke to Allen.

"Could be a bad reception for you boys in Kamloops. People aren't happy about what you've done. If they lynch you I won't be surprised, but Edwards will do his best to have you protected."

"Why did you shoot Kelly, Archie?" the youngest outlaw was asked by a posse member as they rode.

"Just to watch him fall off the rock."

Charlie and Palmer exchanged a few words. "If I had kept your horse I would have broken through and killed five or six more of you and all the Nicola couldn't have gotten me," Charlie said, talking about their attempted breakout from the cabin. "But there's no use of crying over spilled milk. A man has only got to die once and I would as soon die now as any other time. All I care about is to see Kamloops once more."

One of the posse noticed Alex Hare was wearing a pair of gloves and told Edwards he thought they were Ussher's. When Edwards asked him, Hare confirmed it, so the JP took them away.

They stopped at Palmer's for the night, where the prisoners were manacled in irons. What different circumstances from the last time they'd visited this place a few days before. Then they were killers on the loose, feared by everyone. Now they were feared but humbled, and anything but free. When another search was done, considerable blood was noticed on the coat worn by Hare. When Edwards asked whether the coat was Ussher's, Hare replied he guessed it was. It was taken from him. Allen was relieved of Kelly's plaid, and they were left to shiver in the barn with twelve guards for company through the night.

## [46]

**KAMLOOPS**
Sunday, December 14, 1879

Kamloops —white, establishment Kamloops —awaited the arrival of the infamous McLeans and Hare with anticipation, relief, and anger.

In the morning Edwards and his men loaded their prisoners into a sleigh provided by Palmer for the rest of the trip back to town. When they reached Fraser's sheep ranch at Stump Lake they were met by Clement Cornwall and his nine men, and Bill Livingstone from Clinton with six. They turned back to Kamloops, disappointed they'd missed out on the capture.

The parade of possemen and prisoners arrived in town just after two o'clock. The general feeling against the prisoners among the whites was, as Clapperton predicted, running high. There were many who could have been persuaded to take part in a lynching, "some saying they would shoot them as quick as a coyote and others saying that they would hang them to the first tree handy," as Shumway and Palmer described the mood. Indeed, a group of vigilantes led by A.E. Howse of Nicola was on its way to Kamloops. With Howse, who had been at the Douglas Lake siege, were Trapp's partner Richie McDonald, Ed Rutledge, Jim Leigh, and Ben and Joe Moore. Their intention: "to hang the McLeans at Kamloops, lynch them is the proper term no doubt."

However, those in favour of instant "justice" weren't given the chance. The jail from which the McLeans had escaped so easily was heavily guarded, with eight men on duty day and night, and the prisoners were closely watched. There would be no lynching, nor any rescues by the Indians and breeds who still sided with the McLeans.

The rest of the province was winding down from the excitement of the hunt, titillated anew by the capture. Down in New Westminster, officialdom was still plodding along a full week after the murders, still having sent no men nor arms of its own to help the settlers, when word came from Clapperton of the surrender. Todd and his motley, but now larger, posse went home. The Victoria newspaper's suggestion to blow the cabin and the outlaws to smithereens with cannons would not be needed.

Two funerals were held this Sunday at the cemetery on Lorne Street in Kamloops. There, Constable John Ussher and James Kelly were buried. The service for Ussher was read by Senator Cornwall, for Kelly by Reverend Father Martin. Ussher's epitaph stated simply, "John Tannatt Ussher, Departed this life Dec. 8, 1879. Aged 40 years."

Meanwhile, as her husband stayed in town for the preliminary hearing set for the next day, Jane Palmer returned home from the ranch of Robert and Mary Ann Scott, where she had fled for safety, with her three children, after the gang's visit.

In preparation for the hearing, the task of collecting depositions, complaints, statements of the accused, recognizance to prosecute and evidence forms was begun. That job went to Cornwall, who talked to the main witnesses and to the McLeans and Hare. All the gang members were charged with killing Ussher and Kelly, and with shooting at Roxborough.

Charlie stupidly confessed to putting a bullet in Kelly after Allen shot him, but the others would admit nothing.

"I killed no man," stated Allen.

"I never shot Ussher," said Archie. "I fired one shot at Palmer. I know nothing about that shepherd. That's all I have to say."

Hector McLean, on the basis of information sworn by Tom Cavanaugh and John Veasey of Bonaparte that he had "aided and abetted" his brothers and Hare "in certain murderous and felonious plans," was charged with being an accessory before the fact. Veasey's willingness to side against Hector was a cruel blow; he and his family had known all the boys for ten years and they had always been friendly.

Hector denied knowing anything about his brothers' plans. "I did not know what the boys were going to do. I never aided or abetted them."

The hearing would be no problem, but when it came to a trial, jury selection was going to be difficult. There were 116 people on the Kamloops voters' list. Four of them were living elsewhere. Another was a Roman Catholic priest. Three were Justices of the Peace involved with committing the gang to trial. Four were relatives of the McLeans. Another was the brother-in-law of John Ussher. One was a witness for the prosecution. Thirty-three more had been special constables at the Douglas Lake siege. Some of those were still employed to guard the gang. Still others were away from the area. Almost half the entire list of potential jurors were automatically ineligible.

That night Hare asked to see Edwards, and gave a lengthy statement admitting to a number of thefts, but laying all the blame on the McLeans and claiming innocence in the deaths of Ussher and Kelly. "I was obliged to go with them and obey their orders," he stated.

[47]

KAMLOOPS
Monday, December 15, 1879

The hearing was held in the Kamloops Court House. Presiding were Clement Cornwall, John Tait, John Edwards and John Andrew Mara, JPs for the District of Yale. The panel was an illustration of how difficult it was even to find objective upholders of the law. Cornwall was the only one of the four who had not been directly embroiled in the McLeans' feud with the white community. Mara and Tait had been among the most guilty in their treatment of the McLeans, and Edwards had been the most involved in their capture.

The first witness was Palmer. He related his initial encounter with the McLeans and Hare after they had stolen his horse; his report to Edwards and Ussher; the first posse's tracking down of the prisoners; the murder, and the bringing in of the constable's body.

Scott told of his conversation with the prisoners on Monday the 8th, of how they'd claimed the killings of Ussher and Kelly.

Then Roxborough, Shumway and John McLeod gave their accounts of how the murder of Ussher had transpired.

On the basis of their testimony, Cornwall committed the prisoners to trial.

Trapp then testified as to his own conversation with the McLeans and Hare, and his discovery of the body of Kelly. Cornwall now formally committed them for trial on a charge of murdering Kelly, also.

Because of the dual problem of high emotions and a poor selection of jurors in Kamloops, Cornwall ordered them all — including Hector — transported to the jail in New Westminster, where they were to be held in the "said common jail" until delivered by due course of law. The trial venue could be set later.

## [48]

CACHE CREEK, British Columbia
Wednesday, December 17, 1879

The weather was, if anything, worse than it had been in previous weeks. The prisoners arrived from the Kamloops jail on the first leg of their journey to New Westminster, and when Charles Semlin saw them he was shocked at the way they had been treated. *The weather was very severe and the prisoners almost naked, especially Hare. I was surprised to see the condition in which the authorities at Kamloops sent them out. One of them was frost bitten and the whole party half perished, being heavily ironed.* Alex Hare was apparently now being made to pay for the fact he'd worn Ussher's coat.

Semlin bought a hat and coat for Hare, and a pair of blankets, and warned Caughill, who had accompanied the prisoners from Kamloops, and Bill Livingstone, the Clinton constable, that those guarding the prisoners would be held responsible by the government for their safety.

Livingstone would go along as far as Chilliwack with the prisoners and special constables Solomon Schuler, Frank Crotty and Joseph Burr.

The winter had been playing havoc with communications. Telegraph lines were down, stage service was interrupted, and steamers were stalled at the Coast because of ice on the river. Nevertheless, the first part of their journey from Cache Creek, by stage, went well and took them through the snow-covered Interior hills to the Fraser Canyon. From there they progressed slowly on horseback along the Cariboo Road, made treacherous by the winter snow and ice. At each stopping place people came out to view the prisoners, many already familiar with them.

They would continue down to Yale, then to Chilliwack and on to New Westminster.

## [49]

NEW WESTMINSTER
Thursday, December 25, 1879, 11:00 AM

The telegraph below the Fraser Canyon was working, and word reached town that the wild McLean brothers and Alex Hare, escorted by several guards, were approaching the river opposite New Westminster. At noon a message was received that the prisoners would be brought over the river after lunch. Forty people gathered on the bank, teeth chattering and arms flailing to warm themselves, to await the famous outlaws — a Christmas Day outing.

It had been an eventful trip down the canyon from Cache Creek and then along the Fraser. At Yale, Provincial Secretary Thomas Humphrey had met the party and taken charge. Here the group transferred to two small open boats and all went well until they reached a point on the river called Tinker's Bend. The ice hemmed them in and they found themselves trapped out on the river. The only thing to do was try and make it to shore. Even for the guards and Humphrey it was dangerous, but for the manacled prisoners it was almost impossible. Cold, hungry, weak and restricted in movement by the irons, the four McLeans and Hare were forced ahead of the guards and it appeared that if the cold didn't claim them, drowning would. But the strength and endurance of the boys saved them. They would jump from one piece of ice to another; then, resting for a moment, again summon their strength and leap to another ice floe. In some places, even their strength wasn't enough to get them over the heaved-up ice, but, rather than unchain them, the constables carried or dragged them.

They made it to a point near Agassiz at Cheam, where two steamers were ice-bound. There they were able to rest for the night, but the next day the entire party set off by road for Chilliwack, in company with about ten of the passengers and crew of the steamers. Here the snow all but ended and the prisoners were bound and laid in a straw-covered wagon for a rough, bouncing ride. The prisoners spoke little, and when they did it was usually in Chinook, so the constables had no inkling of what they said. At one point in the journey, as the wagon approached the Harrison River, Allen broke into shouts and curses, kicking and shaking his fist at Hector. It took some time to get things under control. Only Alex Hare did not take part in the disturbance. The constables didn't realize it, but the outburst was over Hector's failure to be of any help to the others. Allen and his two younger brothers still blamed him for not joining them before the shootout.

After four days of this hard travelling, the men reached Chilliwack where Livingstone took his leave. He put Burr in charge of the constables, under Humphrey. Superintendent Todd had started on his way to Kamloops to begin investigations; meeting the party on the way, he went with Livingstone.

Continuing by stage, the prisoners, their guards, Humphrey, and the party from the steamers stopped over at Langley Prairie and Sumas. Three days from Chilliwack they arrived across the river from New Westminster.

At 3:00 PM the party was seen working its way slowly across the ice, the prisoners being herded along in front. A few disparaging and cruel jokes were exchanged among those waiting on the bank. As the group came closer, the crowd saw that the outlaws were heavily bound, the four who had been captured in the cabin being fastened together in pairs. Shackled hand and foot, they occasionally stumbled.

When they reached shore, they hobbled as they walked to the sleigh that would convey them to the New Westminster prison. They looked haggard and exhausted, but their physiques nevertheless impressed the onlookers. They walked proudly and upright, using all the power of their strong bodies to drag the manacles and chains. The appearance of Archie caused a particular stir. He looked like the young lad he was; he also looked innocent and utterly incapable of blowing somebody's brains out with a .44 Colt.

It was nearing four o'clock when they arrived at the New Westminster Jail to be locked up.

The state of the jail was open to debate. It was almost twenty years old. While those in charge liked to remind people that no one had ever escaped from it, others claimed that anyone with half a mind to could get out simply by kicking down the cell doors — one door was said to have been so rotten it had fallen off the hinges. The first point was the more relevant.

The jail consisted of sixteen cells, eight on each side of a narrow passage from one end of the building to the other. The cells themselves were nine feet high and nine by seven feet square, lighted by a small window nine by eighteen inches, eight feet from the floor, with perpendicular bars. They were devoid of furniture except for the beds. The nine-inch thick walls were white-washed and the skirting coal-tarred. The *Daily British Colonist*, years ago, had described the cells as "entirely too small . . . illy ventilated, untreated, and an offensive effluvia arising from beneath them, the result of no proper system of drainage having been adopted to carry off the impure deposits that accumulate. . . . "

Since British Columbia had no insane asylum, lunatics were kept in the jail along with thieves and murderers. Prisoners in the cell block to be used for confining the four McLean brothers and Hare were removed to other quarters.

The new prisoners were put in alternate cells on one side of the building, except for Hector, who was placed in a cell on the opposite side. This would be home for Allen, Charlie, Archie and Alex for the next thirteen months.

The prisoners, ushered into their cells and locked up, appeared depressed to the jailers — especially when they found they would be separated in order to keep communication to a minimum.

From the start, their behaviour was extremely disruptive. There was much loud and heated conversation between them, as they shouted to be heard by each other down the passage-way, and swearing and banging on bars. They attacked anyone who came near them and threw their food at the cell doors. Warden William C. Moresby ordered them chained to the walls.

## [50]

NEW WESTMINSTER JAIL
Friday, February 27, 1880

*To The Hon. G.A. Walkem,*
*Premier,*
*British Columbia*

*Sir:*

*We the undersigned at present awaiting trial on certain charges of wilful murder and which are to be tried on 13th March beg most respectfully to ask that you may be pleased to provide us with Council to defend us at our approaching trial. Immediately after our arrest and imprisonment we retained Mr. Bole to defend us which retainer was conditional upon our being able to pay his fee a reasonable time before trial, and altho we have used every effort in our power we have failed to procure any funds we therefore can no longer expect Mr. Bole to act for us, and therefore we humbly request you will make arrangements to*

*employ Counsel to defend us as without Counsel duly instructed it is*
*nearly impossible that we can have a fair trial more especially as we*
*know nothing of the jurors so as to be in a position to exercise our*
*power of challenge. We feel assured you only desire to have the issues*
*fairly tried and on these grounds and these alone we most respectfully*
*appeal to your aid and sympathy.*

*We are, Sir,*
*Your most obedient servants*
*Archie McLean*
*Charlie (X) McLean*
*Allen (X) McLean*

Archie scratched in his name with the quill while Charlie and Allen, who couldn't write, added their X's. The letter was written when it became apparent they weren't going to be able to produce any money to pay the fees of their lawyer, W. Norman Bole, who agreed to continue on the case anyway.

Bole was a thirty-four-year-old Irishman who had emigrated to the United States, then gone to Quebec and then to New Westminster, where he'd arrived a little more than two years before. Bole had the distinction — after being admitted to the British Columbia bar — of being the first lawyer to locate permanently on the mainland, but he had more to recommend him than that. He had started his career in British Columbia by successfully defending almost every prisoner on trial at the assizes that year, and his practice and reputation had been growing rapidly since then. Still a bachelor, he led an energetic and varied community life. In the courtroom he tenaciously picked at the credibility of Crown witness testimony and had a stubborn way of discounting all but the most unimpeachable evidence of the other side.

From the day the prisoners arrived in New Westminster, Alex Hare's first and most frequent request was for a good lawyer; he would say nothing, grant no interviews, until he'd gotten one. He got his wish. Theodore Davie was a bearded, slightly balding, knock-kneed young man of twenty-seven who had been a barrister only four years but was quickly becoming known in British Columbia as a determined, energetic and resourceful man of law. A native of Surrey, England, he had left home at fifteen and was now practising law in Victoria. It was said that he was prime legislative material. Like Bole, Davie was a bachelor.

The evidence in the case was overwhelming but the strategy of the two lawyers found common ground on only one major point. They both felt it would do no good to call witnesses; there would be no sympathetic eye-witnesses, and even reputable character witnesses would be impossible to find. Under the existing law, the accused were not allowed to testify under oath. Neither was there any provision for appeal should they lose.

While Davie fully believed his client was guilty along with the

Sir Henry Pering Pellew Crease, B.C. Supreme Court judge, who presided over the trials of the McLeans and Hare (BCARS, 29626)

McLeans, he would defend a "not guilty" plea, basically on grounds of mercy, when it came court time.

Bole would kow-tow to nobody. He would challenge everything the Crown threw at the McLeans, in hopes of putting "a reasonable doubt" in the mind of at least one out of the twelve jurors. He would choose his jury carefully.

Meanwhile, both lawyers would challenge the Crown's right to change the venue of the trial from Kamloops to New Westminster, without an order from the Court.

While their lawyers were getting the legal machinery for the defence honed into shape and under way, the boys lived impatiently in confinement. They were still kept in their separated cells, were heavily ironed and for the most part could not communicate with one another. Under care of the prison surgeon, Allen's wound had soon healed. (In the Nicola, John McLeod spent five weeks in bed after a gunsmith extracted the bullet from his knee cap. A wet cloth had to be placed on the wound every few minutes, and neighbouring ranchers helped out in his care. His other wounds healed well, but, even after he got up and around, the knee bothered him, and would for a year.)

To those who asked, Archie said he was fourteen. "My father was killed when I was three days old," he would tell an inevitably wonder-struck listener, ignoring the arithmetic that made him fifteen, and charming them with his boyish manner. (The Crown, fearing that his youth might become an issue, was scrambling to get evidence of his age, and got affidavits from his mother Sophia and oldest half-brother Donald Jr. confirming his birth at the time of his father's death. A baptism record was also unearthed that further proved his age.) But he could cause a ruckus when he wanted to, along with his brothers, and the cell block rang with their shouts and insults.

Hector would be tried at a separate assize, so did not look for-

ward to the March trial with the same apprehension as the others. But
he wished he would be walking into the courtroom with them to get
it over with, instead of being kept in suspense for more weeks. He
was cooler than his brothers and calmly informed one reporter that,
"The shoes worn in this jail are made by prisoners and cost $1.35 per
pair against $2.16 contract price." And that was about as much infor-
mation as he gave out that day.

The issue of venue had been causing considerable inconvenience
for the witnesses. Issued summonses by Chief Justice Matthew Begbie to
appear in New Westminster, they were then told to go to Victoria to wait
for the fixing of the place of trial. It was proving to be a long wait.

Counsel for the Crown applied to the Supreme Court of the province February 16 — over a month and a half after the prisoners had
arrived in New Westminster — for an order setting New Westminster
as the place of trial. The judges — Begbie, Judge John Hamilton Gray
and Judge Henry Pering Pellew Crease — asked for the commitments
by which the prisoners were being held for trial, but they weren't
produced. So, the change of venue was denied.

But the fact the Court wasn't officially sitting in a case didn't rule
out an extra-judicial opinion, and the judges gave one: that subject to
any objections by the prisoners, New Westminster appeared to be the
most proper place of trial "under all the circumstances." The opinion
also stated that the time and place of holding assizes were always
appointed by the government. The Crown dropped its application, so
the change of venue was now accepted without an official document.

Bole's agreement to continue as counsel for the McLeans, fees or
not, guaranteed them of a competent defence.

## [51]

VICTORIA
Wednesday, March 11, 1880

The much-vaunted British justice system was moving slowly. Waiting
in Victoria for a decision on when and where the trial was to be held,
the witnesses were being boarded at great expense in hotels, chafing
every minute as they imagined more and more of their stock freezing
and starving to death back in the winter-ravaged Nicola. But the system
was about to mess up in an even bigger way. The implications of what
started with a letter from Provincial Secretary Humphrey to the three judges
wouldn't be appreciated for several months, but, when it was, it would
throw everything for a loop. A commission — the document that officially

Premier George Anthony Walkem
(BCARS, 4431)

authorizes a trial or set of trials — had been issued three days before
by the lieutenant-governor's office in Victoria. The deputy provincial
secretary was Thomas Elwyn, who had served as second in command
of the New Westminster Expedition in the Chilcotin War. On instructions from Humphrey, he had forwarded the commission to Crease. It
gave authority for the trial, but when Begbie saw it, he pointed out to
Humphrey that it was made returnable to Victoria instead of Ottawa.
He called it a "novelty," adding, "It may invalidate the commission."
He told the provincial secretary, "All the expense of the assize will be
thrown away and the prisoners would have to be tried over again."

In response Humphrey's letter now stated that no commission
was necessary to entitle a judge of the Supreme Court to try prisoners
at New Westminster, so the lieutenant-governor was cancelling the
commission of March 8.

Walkem was out of the province at the time the commission was
issued and professed surprise that this had been done, since he
thought it unnecessary. Crown advisors Alexander Rocke Robertson,
QC, a thirty-nine-year-old former Victoria mayor and former provincial secretary, and John Foster McCreight, QC, a fifty-three-year-old
controversial figure who had been B.C.'s first premier, agreed. They
felt that the general commission of November 19 the previous year
was an expansive enough document to include the coming trial.

So the commission was cancelled. On the same day, and the day before
Crease was to head for New Westminster, the *Colonist* of Victoria editorialized:

The deadlock in the matter of the Kamloops murderers continued yesterday and there is no certainty that Mr. Justice Crease will proceed to New Westminster on Friday to try the cases. From the Attorney General's office we learn it is claimed that no change of venue is necessary, inasmuch as there are no judicial districts defined in the Province. The Crown therefore claims that it has a right to try the prisoners anywhere it may please, but in opposition to this contention we have the action of the Crown itself, a fortnight or three weeks ago in applying to the Chief Justice for authority to change the venue. If there exists no necessity for an order why was one applied for? Again, it is stated that the prisoners were not legally served with a notice of the intention of the Crown to apply for a change of venue; and that, finally, in the warrant of commitment no venue was named, and the whole proceedings must be done over de novo. But another and still more serious obstacle has arisen. It appears that the Gov't has issued a commission to Judge Crease to hold the Special Assize at New Westminster and have the Commission returnable to the Gov't House at Victoria; while the Judge's instructions require them to return the royal Commission to the Government House at Ottawa. The wording of the Commission is therefore irregular if not illegal.

Crease, however, made a last-minute decision to go ahead with the trial, making it clear that if any failure of justice took place he wouldn't be held responsible for it. He prepared to take the same steamer as the long-suffering witnesses to New Westminster.

As the *Colonist* would claim, "The affair seems to have been a miserable bungle for which the Gov't are entirely responsible."

Bole would act for the McLeans. Davie, in defending Hare, would be assisted by Charles James Leggatt.

McCreight would work with Deputy Attorney-General Eli Harrison, Jr. Of the five lawyers in the case, McCreight was the only senior law practitioner. Harrison, like Bole, Davie and Leggatt, was a young bachelor, new in the practice of his profession.

## [52]

### NEW WESTMINSTER COURTHOUSE
### Monday, March 15, 1880, 10:00 AM

The courtroom in which Regina vs. McLeans and Hare would be heard, besides being small and inconvenient, was poorly ventilated and even in the nippy days of early spring it could be steamy with a large number of people in the public gallery. In those seats were Upper Country ranchers and New Westminster merchants, politicians and the curious hoi polloi. One can imagine the Nicola settlers slouched in their seats, their worn boots propped on the floor by the heels, or legs crossed, arms folded or hands stuffed in pockets, wide-brimmed hats on the floor in front of them, in contrast to the relatively spruced-up city folks, the coat-and-vest men and primly dressed women. On the floor, strategically placed spittoons for the convenience of those, city or country, who felt the need to chew.

In front of them were the lawyers, the clerks, and the judge. The prisoners' dock was empty today, for this was an assize, called especially for the McLeans and Hare, but which would include a number of other trials as well. So, the judge would talk to the grand jury, mostly about the outlaws, which was the reason the public gallery was so full. On Saturday, it had been full, too, though little had happened. A seventeen-man grand jury had been empanelled, Crease referred briefly to Regina vs. the McLeans and Hare, saying great care must be taken in such serious cases. And he'd adjourned the court.

But today, though the outlaws still weren't there, the people were there to listen to Crease talk about the four young men they all wanted to see given a fair trial and then hanged.

"The occasion which has called us together is of grave import," Crease began. "Not only is the calendar we have to clear a large one, but the crimes charged are the highest known to the law, and committed under circumstances which attracted serious attention, not only of the whole province, but of places far beyond its boundaries."

He continued: "This is one of the considerations which, in addition to affording opportunities for the prisoners to prepare their defence that all they have to say may be heard, induced me to adjourn our enquiries till today — to begin our investigations with the commencement of a new week.

"The work before us is too heavy for me to occupy much of your time with preliminary observations; but there are certain reflections which are necessarily suggested by the occasion. We are brought face to face with the condition of our numerous and growing half-breed population through the country. What is their future? Sons of the hardy pioneers, who pierced the Rocky Mountains and freely flung themselves into the heart of the wilds and forests of the Interior and up to the Arctic Ocean in search of furs, often to save their lives, allied themselves to the native tribes who surrounded them.

"So long as civilization kept away from them, or they from civilization, all was well. They fell into many of the habits of the natives among whom they lived and many a trapper and trader owes his life to the fidelity and sagacity and courage of his Indian wife. The off-spring of these marriages, a tall, strong, handsome race combined in one the hardihood and quick perceptions of the men of the woods, with the intelligence and some of the training and endurance of the white man which raised them into a grade above their mother's but not yet up to the father's grade.

"Quick shots, unrivalled horsemen, hardy boatmen and hunters, they knew no other life than that of the forest. They never went to school or had the semblance of an education, and when the wave of civilization, without hurry, without delay, but without rest, approached, it met a restless, roving, half-breed population, who, far from imitating, did not even understand the resistless agency which was approaching them.

"So long as the white father lived, the children were held in some sort of subjection, but the moment he was gone they gravitated towards their mother's friends and fell back into nature's ways.

"Is it any wonder then that, remaining unchecked and uncared for, they should at last adopt the predatory Arab life which in a scattered country is fraught with such danger to the state?

"The cases before us give a terrible illustration of my observations. Three young men in the opening prime of life, scarcely beyond the stage of youth, sons of a gallant man who was shot while serving the country in the Chilcotin expedition, are now arraigned before you for the murder of a constable and another white man and several other crimes of equal grade. No one becomes bad all of a sudden. There usually are years of gradual change for the worse before matters culminate in the highest crime.

"We may investigate, and if proved against them punish the wrongdoers in this case, and if proved, it must be done; but we must go further than mere repression. Prevention is better than cure. We must go below the surface and see if other causes do not combine to produce the ill-results.

"Ask yourselves, is it a magistrate the less or a constable the less at Kamloops that has caused or could have prevented these murders? Look deeper. What care, what education, have they had whether from state or parent?

"There is no effect without a cause. Is there not little by little growing up among even our educated youth a spirit of misrule, an impatience of wholesome discipline and restraints of society and home?"

Then Crease instructed the grand jury.

"You have to enquire whether in any of the cases about to be submitted to you there is a *prima facie* case for enquiry before a petty jury. In every case in which you, or rather any twelve of your number, come to that conclusion, you will return a true bill; if the contrary, no true bill."

"Judging from the depositions, which are very meagre in some of the cases, I think you will probably find no difficulty in returning a true bill in every case. You will have witnesses before you, and if they say such and such a crime has been committed and by such a person, that will be sufficient *prima facie* case for enquiry before a petty jury."

What the judge was saying was that all that was necessary to bring an accused man to trial was for someone to say he committed a crime. *Prima facie* meant at first view, or without contradiction, so that it was not necessary for the Crown prosecutors to prove evidence against the accused that could stand up under challenge. While in the trial, an accused got the benefit of the doubt, it was the other way around in a hearing to determine if that trial should take place. A "true bill" was a true finding, a decision by the grand jury that there was enough evidence on which to try a case. Some witnesses couldn't or wouldn't appear in court, and in such cases statements of evidence, or depositions, could be obtained from them.

The other cases that would come up at the assize, all relatively minor (assault, theft of a small amount of money, etc.) were briefly reviewed.

Broken down into individual charges, there were several indictments against the McLeans and Hare. All of them were charged with the murders of John Ussher and James Kelly. Others included commitments of Alex Hare and Archie for using deadly weapons with intent to kill John Roxborough and John Ussher, and all for shooting at William Palmer with intent to murder. The first trial would be for the murder of Ussher; if they were found guilty, the other charges would become irrelevant. Hector's later trial would be for being an accessory before the fact, meaning he helped or encouraged the commission of the crime, but wasn't there when it took place.

Crease suggested the indictment for the murder of Kelly be withdrawn for a minor amendment, and meanwhile carefully examined each document placed before him. He repeated his earlier warning that any failure of justice would not be the fault of the Court.

Twenty minutes later, the indictment in the Kelly case was handed up in its amended form and placed in the hands of the grand jurors. The cases against the outlaws were placed last and would come up the next day.

[53]

NEW WESTMINSTER COURTHOUSE
Tuesday, March 16, 1880, 10:45 AM

"Not guilty."

One after another, "Not guilty." Not guilty of the murder of John Ussher. "Not guilty," said Allen, and "Not guilty," said Archie, standing beside him, and the same was mumbled by Charlie then Alex.

In the dock, under heavy guard, the prisoners, expressionless, appeared to the spectators to be unconcerned, as though they were on trial for cheating at cards.

But it wasn't for card cheating, nor stealing a saddle, nor beating somebody up that the boys were here. The court, on behalf of "our Lady the Queen," was charging that "Charles McLean, Allen McLean, Archibald [sic] McLean and Alexander Hare on the eighth day of December in the year of our Lord one thousand eight hundred and seventy-nine did feloniously, wilfully and of their malice aforethought kill and murder one John Ussher."

What some in the public gallery took to be a lack of concern was as much exhaustion as nonchalance. Their long confinement had taken its toll on the boys, and they weren't in a mood for causing a disturbance today.

The grand jury having returned a true bill, the judge explained that although Archie might be the only one who fired the fatal shot, the others, in aiding and abetting (directly helping and encouraging him to commit the crime) would be equally guilty.

In regard to Archie's youth, even if the defence showed he was still of the age of infancy when he committed the crime, he would be held responsible, if it was found he knew the consequences of his actions. A plea of infancy was to be expected from Bole on behalf of Archie, for the outlaw was young enough that his age could be doubted, and the judge wanted to make sure it was clear to everyone what the law was. No person up to the age of seven could be found guilty of a crime. Between seven and fourteen, a person was deemed able to commit a crime, but it was up to the Crown to prove the person knew the difference between right and wrong when he committed the crime, and that he knew the consequences of the crime.

A panel of potential jurors was now to be called, but Davie claimed that since they were not selected from the neighbourhood of Kamloops they had no right to try his client. On behalf of Hare, he handed in a written challenge against the entire jury array —all those citizens who had been called to appear as potential jurors —on the grounds that the prisoners were not going to be tried "in the vicinage, neighbourhood or district of the crime, nor is the said array composed of men from the said vicinage." McCreight formally opposed the challenge.

"The plain point is: Can a man who has committed a crime at Kamloops be tried at New Westminster?" countered Crease, allowing Davie and McCreight to open discussion briefly on the subject, after which Davie insisted, "The prisoners had no voice in changing the venue to New Westminster, My Lord."

John Foster McCreight, former premier of British Columbia, who acted for the Crown in prosecuting the McLeans and Hare (BCARS, 3369)

"The Court made no order changing the venue," interjected Crease.

"That I know, and I contend the Crown had no right to change it."

"Perhaps you were not aware that a petition had been presented to me — and among the names was that of Mr. Hare himself — that the case might not be tried in Kamloops where the feelings of the people are so strong against him, and danger of their being executed by lynch law," Crease interrupted again.

But Davie would not be put off. Citing various authorities, and dragging out precedents, he said the test of venue was the county, the lines of which were defined by legislation. The jury must be summoned from the vicinage, and a change of venue could not be obtained by the Crown.

"Is there no authority which states that the trial may take place within the jurisdiction of the Court?" asked the judge.

"I raise an objection to the jury, not to the jurisdiction of the Court, which extends all over the province," replied Davie. "Does the omission of the legislature to define judicial districts take away from the prisoner his constitutional rights? The notice served on the prisoner on the 12th of February last of the intention of the Crown to apply for a change of venue shows that the Crown then entertained the same opinion that I do now."

McCreight contended that two local Acts gave the Supreme Court jurisdiction over the whole province. If a crime was committed in the Peace River district how could a jury be empanelled there?

"My Lord," he said, "I applied for a change of venue but did not deem such an order necessary and got what I wanted — an opinion of the Court that an order was not required."

"I think the prisoners would have had short shrift if they'd been left to the Kamloops people," observed the judge. "They couldn't get a fairer trial than in New Westminster, as the recollections of their father whose history is still quite fresh in the minds of many people here is the guarantee."

"I did not mean to insinuate they won't get a fair trial in New Westminster," Davie assured him.

But Crease overruled Davie, so the jury array stood and the defence lawyer could not use vicinage as grounds for challenging any potential juror. But he and Bole would still have plenty of opportunity to challenge. In addition to being allowed a fixed number of peremptory challenges, for which no reason had to be given, they could challenge as many jurors as they wished on grounds that the jurors would not be objective.

Of forty-eight potential jurors called, only eight were accepted. One man was challenged by McCreight because he opposed capital punishment. The panel exhausted, McCreight requested that "the usual mode provided by statute" be adopted to select the remaining necessary number of jurors.

"Close the doors," Crease directed. "Let no one be allowed to leave the room."

This done, the sheriff started selecting jurors from the audience. One refused to appear and was fined ten dollars (but this was later refunded when he showed good cause for not being able to serve).

Forty-two more people were called, and finally the twelfth juror was found. A man named William Turnbull was selected foreman by fellow jurors S.A. Spilsbury, A. Couttes, Joseph Maynard, F. Christopher, F.L. Budlong, F. McLennan, F. Sparling, W.M. Bues, M. Grey, F. Forrester, and L.E. Braden.

Eli Harrison stood to open the case for the Crown. The young, grim-faced deputy attorney-general, the son of a well-to-do and respected pioneer Victoria family, had been raised and educated to the law within the province. Not quite nine years ago, he had been made a solicitor in the attorney-general's department, and had been admitted to the bar along with Charles Leggatt in 1875 by Judges Crease and Gray. He had a habit of doodling on his note papers while defence lawyers were speaking.

He now reviewed the alleged facts that the prosecution intended to prove, explaining the charges. Reiterating the judge's earlier mention of infancy, he said a boy of fourteen was responsible for his acts in the eyes of the law, if he realized fully what he was doing.

For his first witness, Harrison called William Palmer to the stand. After taking the oath, Palmer explained how he had found his horse in the possession of the McLeans and ridden to Kamloops that same day to lay a complaint. He was explaining how Edwards had issued a warrant and handed it to Ussher, when Crease called an adjournment.

The work of choosing a jury had taken up almost the whole day.

NEW WESTMINSTER COURTHOUSE
Wednesday, March 17, 1880, 10:00 AM

When Palmer resumed testimony he described the search for the outlaws, and Ussher's sanguine lack of concern. Then the ensuing battle
and the few stunned moments of watching helplessly as Ussher was
killed. Then the ride to town, the panic caused by the news, and the
return to retrieve the dead constable's body.

"Can you identify this coat?" asked Harrison, showing the witness
a light-coloured garment.

"I believe this to be Ussher's overcoat."

"This overcoat was taken from the prisoners after their capture, as
were these boots and gloves," explained Harrison to the jury.

Under further questioning by Harrison, Palmer said he had first
seen Archie in 1868 when he was already a good-sized child. Seven
years later the youngest McLean had herded cattle for him, when he
must have been about twelve years old, or looked like it, and "could
drive cattle then as well as I could."

"No more questions," said Harrison.

Bole got up to cross-examine. How long had he known the other
McLeans, and Hare? How old did he think they were? To these questions the answers were vague.

What condition were they in?

When he overtook them the first time they did not seem very
drunk. He had heard they liked their booze but he had never seen
them in a drunken condition.

What kind of men were they?

He did not think them to be excitable men.

What was their relationship with Ussher?

Hare should have been an excellent friend of Ussher's because the
constable had always treated him well.

How did he know that? Was he certain of this friendship? Had
not Ussher done something against them?

No, Ussher was a friend of nearly everyone who knew him.

What were the feelings of the posse when they went after the
outlaws?

There was no hesitation or forlorn feeling about going after them
but they felt a need for haste.

Wouldn't he think a posse that felt concerned about danger in
seeking four young men would be better armed?

The firearms of the posse were poor, but he could only speak for himself, and his gun was the best he could get.

At 7:00 PM Palmer had been on the stand the full day. Court adjourned until 10:00 AM Thursday.

## [55]

NEW WESTMINSTER COURTHOUSE
Thursday, March 18, 1880, 10:00 AM

Harrison called as his next witness, Amni Shumway. Again the confrontation between the outlaws and the posse was described. He had previously seen Ussher arrest Allen on one occasion. In the incident at the mountain camp, when the posse went after the boys trying to get Palmer's horse back, Ussher left his horse and advanced on Hare. The constable's pistol was apparently on his horse. The constable wore a light-coloured overcoat that day.

A pair of gloves and an overcoat were produced.

"Those look like Ussher's," said Shumway.

Bole cross-examined to little avail.

John McLeod took the stand next and supported the previous evidence. This time both Davie and Bole cross-examined, but without profit, except to bring out the fact that McLeod, like Shumway, had not actually heard Archie's gun go off when he shot Ussher.

Next was Tom Trapp, and a description of his meeting with the McLeans and Alex Hare, and his discovery of Kelly's body.

Through leading questions and by slipping in information of his own, Davie, in cross-examination, brought out the facts that charges had been pending against the outlaws for months, that at least eighteen months ago Charlie had escaped, that the Kamloops jail was insecure, that the outlaws had stolen horses and killed cattle to make a living, and that Judge Begbie had made promises to get the matter fixed up if possible by the provincial government.

"These questions seem irrelevant," Crease finally said.

"I wish to show who is to blame for these men being at large at the time of the murder," Davie stated. "No harm to society or to the prisoners can be done by this course."

"Then proceed," Crease relented.

Trapp continued in testimony that a grand jury had noted their lawless acts, and that they had broken jail and special constables had been unable to capture them. Trapp's testimony was finished.

Edwards told of the warrants issued, and sketched the background of the gang's career, and the capture.

"My Lord, I submit under exhibits a pistol, the one used by Alexander Hare to strike Constable Ussher," said Harrison, producing a broken pistol and taking it to the judge. "You'll see the initials 'A.J.H.' are on the handle, and if you examine it closely under microscope you will see hair on the handle as well."

The gun was examined, then Harrison also produced the pocket-book found in the overcoat.

Davie was first to cross-examine Edwards, asking details of the warrants and having the witness describe the circumstances of Charlie's imprisonment and escape. Always Davie tried to show up the slackness of law enforcement in Kamloops.

Under questioning by Bole, Edwards said he had known the McLean boys for seven years, and they were fond of drinking and fighting. He said Ussher's whiskers were scorched about the throat when the body was recovered.

Davie asked him why special constables could not be enticed to complete the job of capturing the McLeans while they were still only horse thieves and cattle rustlers.

"I believe I had a circular to the effect that special constables, whilst travelling on duty, were not allowed their travelling expenses," said Edwards.

How long was it after Charlie McLean escaped before efforts were made to capture him?

"Charlie and the other prisoner who escaped from jail were about three months in the district before anyone attempted to arrest them."

A Kamloops resident named William Thornhill was called to testify about Archie's age.

"I've been told he was born about the time his father was killed. That was in 1864."

That would mean he was about fifteen now. For Archie to be fourteen, his father would have had to be killed shortly after Archie was conceived. Davie asked when Thornhill first met him.

"I'd known of him before I met him . . . known of his reputation as a good rider because he'd ridden races. I first saw him ride in 1874, I think it was. He rode pretty well, just a youngster. He didn't seem an excitable type, usually pretty calm and collected."

Next was Preston Bennett, MPP for Yale and the lover of Christine Selpa McLean, a daughter of Donald McLean, Jr., the boys' half-brother. He testified he'd first seen Archie in 1866 when his mother had said he was two years old. "I've been in Kamloops or the neighbourhood since 1864 and have seen the prisoners frequently since 1874," he said.

There were no more questions.

"The Crown rests its case," said Harrison.

Bole rose. "My Lord, as the defence proposes to call no witnesses, I appeal to the Crown *ad misrecordian* to allow counsel for the defence to address the jury last."

"There's the law," answered McCreight. "We make no promises."

Bole sat down and Davie got to his feet to address the jury first.

"I will address you on behalf of my client, Alexander Hare, but what I say will bear generally upon the accusations made against all the prisoners," he began.

"His Lordship, in his charge to the grand jury, stated truly that crime progresses by stages. A man is not born a criminal, neither does he suddenly become a criminal. The first phase in criminal life of the prisoners before you now appears to have been an assault of a trifling character by one of them upon an Indian, his consequent sentence to three months imprisonment and escape from jail. Then the whole of the prisoners appear to have banded together and to have been the perpetrators of several outrages against society, such as stealing horses and killing cattle — serious enough, it is true, yet of a venial character in comparison with the present charge. Upon these acts being commenced we find that warrant after warrant was issued for the apprehension of the prisoners, but strange to say during a period of eighteen months and upwards, through all of which time rapine and robbery were going on, no one was found to execute the warrants.

"Ussher, the deceased, who was constable, had numerous duties to attend to and had no full-time assistants. Two successive presentments by grand juries as to the conduct of the prisoners were made and represented to the government. Appeals were made to them to render aid for the capture of the men who now had become outlaws; but during the entire period, covering the space of nearly two years, not the slightest attempt was made by the government to supplement Mr. Ussher's authority. Had the government performed its duty at the outset and caused the arrest of the prisoners they would have been brought to justice and have had punishment commensurate with the offence meted out to them. Such punishment would, in all probability, have had the effect for which it would have been inflicted. The prisoners would have been taught that further crime would receive adequate punishment and probably by this time would be law-abiding, peaceable citizens instead of men in the terrible position they now are; the lives of an invaluable officer and a good settler would have been saved and the expense to which the country has been put, avoided.

"The government, although fully apprised of the situation, from the first refused to augment the civil staff and it appears, refused to allow expenses for special constables. The government, therefore, is responsible for the bloodshed and expense which ensured consequent upon the lack of authority."

Davie paused. "There is no question that all the prisoners deserve some type of punishment, but the question before the jury to decide is, shall the death penalty be meted out to them all? Are they truly guilty of murder? They have pleaded not guilty and it has been shown clearly where the true guilt lies for the crimes of which they are accused by the government. I did not cross-examine any of the witnesses at length because the defence is satisfied they said substantially the truth.

"As far as the actual cause of death of Constable Ussher is concerned, look at the facts: It has been argued that Alexander Hare participated and is therefore as responsible for the death as any, but it is obvious the death was not caused by any wound inflicted by Mr. Hare."

Here Davie produced more precedent cases to try to show that his client was not guilty simply because he was present when the alleged crime took place. He took out a heavy volume. "Roscoe's Criminal Evidence, page 600 . . . although several go out with a common unlawful object yet if one of the party do an act as, for instance, murder, beyond the common intent, his companions are not liable.

"The original intention of the prisoners was to steal horses, and Hare, not actually having caused it, is not responsible for a murder not contemplated by him. Certainly, he may have assaulted the constable, but he did not contemplate his death." His bragging about "this is the knife that went through Ussher" was merely the bravado of a frightened young man.

If Hare was to be punished, let it be a just punishment that would give him a chance — a chance the government had failed so miserably and irresponsibly to provide — to become a better man. Davie asked that, if the jury could not release his client from custody, to put him in a penitentiary where he could be rehabilitated.

Bole would take another tack.

"It is my hope," he said, "you will return a verdict not of murder, but of homicide, commonly known as manslaughter.

"Testimony has shown that the constables forced the fighting on the prisoners that day, in a fashion entirely not in keeping with the normal conduct of peace officers.

"The constables met more than they bargained for, and were lucky to escape, most of them, with their lives. Lucky because if my clients had meant murder that cold day, they could have killed them all. It's true. But they meant merely to intimidate the posse, and Constable Ussher knew this better than anybody. Feeling their firing not seriously meant, he dismounted his horse to talk with them. He did not draw his revolver. Up to this time no damage had been done except to McLeod.

"There is not enough evidence to prove they actually purposely murdered Constable Ussher. While Ussher was down with Hare hitting at him with a pistol, Archie McLean is said to have come out and shot him with a pistol. Only one witness, William Palmer, testified he actually heard Archie McLean's gun go off. Only one. Yet all the members of the special force were nearby and had the same privilege of seeing the proceedings! Shumway and McLeod did not hear Archie's pistol go off and there were no powder marks on Ussher's face."

Why the discrepancies? Because William Palmer could easily be mistaken. They did not know that Ussher was on the ground when he was shot, nor that Archie McLean shot him. They did not know, in fact, really what happened that day, but there was no question of murder. The only evidence against the youngest prisoner was that someone thought he might have seen him snap a pistol at Ussher's head.

"I deplore the absolute lack of medical testimony available as to the cause of death. Just as unfortunately, I have no proper medical testimony to show the state of mind of my clients at the time of Mr. Ussher's death, but I submit that any actions under the stress and shock of being suddenly attacked by an armed band of peace officers could not result in sane actions under those circumstances. Certainly, Ussher's death was not the result of sane action. There are many, many doubts."

Bole was ready to conclude. "The father of my three clients was a strong and brave man who fell in the service of his country. You have watched the prisoners during this trial; they have caused no disturbance, they are young men thrown into tragedy by fate."

If the jurors had any doubt — any doubt whatsoever — as to their guilt, they must return a verdict of "not guilty."

McCreight undertook the summary for the prosecution, and first sketched the proceeding of the case and of the activities of the prisoners.

"The prisoners were the terror of the Upper Country for a long time."

The jurors had heard testimony from Palmer that they threatened to kill anyone who came after them.

"They carried out that threat. The law has been quoted as to responsibility for a crime, but the law is capable of being misapplied and misquoted. Common sense should tell you that this crime was an atrocious murder.

"Constable Ussher had been very kind to Alex Hare and could not believe Hare would kill him," McCreight continued. "As for the youngest prisoner . . . Hare attacks Ussher, Archie McLean fires into his head, and the two hammer his brains out. Every act of the prisoners shows that they had entered on a course of systematic opposition to authority. Each is as guilty as the other. Allen and Charlie McLean are just as guilty of Ussher's murder as the actual perpetrators.

"When they had completed their grisly task, they all stripped the body. Not one objected to the other; all were involved. They rode away and boasted of their murder and robbed various settlers of their firearms. They then fortified themselves and had anyone approached them they would have committed more murder. When they surrendered it was for want of water.

"There is absolutely nothing here to permit reducing the charge down to manslaughter. By this terrible crime of murder they have forfeited their lives, they deserve no mercy, and the best interests of society demand that they should be so dealt with."

McCreight kept stressing how terrible the crime was. Over and over he tried to impress this upon the jury. "There is no excuse, no palliation, no justification for this awful crime. It was a shocking murder. The evidence is distinct, there is no contradiction. They all intended to commit murder. The whole transaction shows a systematic design.

"A more important case could not be brought before a jury. It is a painful duty, but divine and human laws must be carried out. The most sorrowful part of all this, of course, is their youthfulness, particularly that of Archie McLean. But the law makes a boy of fourteen as responsible for his acts as a man of twenty-one if he knows the difference between right and wrong, and the boy in this instance was clearly one of the worst of the four. Furthermore, it has been shown in all likelihood he was already past the age of infancy.

"If there are failures in this case I have only to remind the jury of what has taken place in other communities where justice has failed. Your duty is a painful one but it nevertheless must be discharged."

Judge Crease told the Court: "Owing to the lateness of the hour, and the fatigue of all of us, I suspect, I will adjourn the Court until eleven o'clock tomorrow morning before I address the jury."

The New Westminster Jail held four restless young prisoners that evening. Tomorrow the judge would instruct the jury, and that jury would retire to decide their fate. They ate their supper, voraciously but nervously, each in his separate cell, and they intermittently paced their cells or sat staring. Visitors were received quietly. When sleep finally came, it was deep but not restful.

NEW WESTMINSTER
Friday, March 19, 1880

*To the Grand Jury empanelled at New Westminster at the Assizes held there in March 1880.*

*Gentlemen:*

*The undersigned witnesses in the case of Regina vs. McLeans and Hare, feeling that in consequence of their testimony they have probably incurred the resentment of relatives or friends of the prisoners; and knowing that certain firearms belonging to the Government were sent to Kamloops at the time of the late outbreak, and still remain there, beg to suggest that you will be pleased to make a presentment to the judge of the Supreme Court now sitting at New Westminster to the effect that a breech-loading, repeating rifle or carbine of those now at Kamloops, be supplied to every such witness who may apply for the same, on his giving a guarantee that said firearms will be kept clean and in proper order and that it shall be returned to the Government Agent on demand, or paid for by the person receiving it.*

*We are, Gentlemen*
*Your Obedient Servants*

*Wm Palmer*
*Robert Scott*
*John McLeod*
*A Shumway*
*Preston Bennett*
*Thomas Jn Trapp*
*John T. Edwards*

*The Grand Jury recommend this petition.*

*W.D. Ferris, foreman*
*for self and fellows*

Crease began his instructions to the jury at exactly 11:00 AM, telling them to dismiss any preconceived notions about the prisoners and all consideration of what the effect of their verdict might be. They must give their attention with calm, impartial care, to the issues before them. The prisoners had been skilfully defended and no point or argument that could assist them had been omitted, Crease said. Did the facts sworn to in this case come up to what the law required to constitute the crime against them or any lesser crime?

The public gallery listened attentively as the judge spoke on, for two hours, clearly defining the duties of the jury. They were all interested in one thing that morning — hearing a verdict of guilty brought down on the McLean Gang.

"They are charged in the first count with the wilful murder of John Ussher. The second count charges two of the prisoners with the actual deed which deprived Ussher of his life and the rest of the prisoners with aiding and abetting in the murder. The effect of the two last counts is the same as the first count, but you will find it simpler to confine yourselves to the first count and ask yourselves, did all of these young men participate in the murder of Ussher?

"The killing of Ussher by some one or more of the prisoners is not denied and that all the prisoners were there together is not denied. Consequently it rested with the prisoners to show that the killing of Ussher was not done with malice before they could be entitled to ask that the verdict be reduced from murder to manslaughter. Malice makes the difference between homicide and murder. All present during the crime are guilty of aiding and abetting and equally as guilty of the crime itself. If one is guilty, all are guilty. In all matters of a criminal nature, the intention qualifies the act.

"Constable Ussher was cruelly battered senseless and then shot in the head with no chance to defend himself. . . . "

As the description of Ussher's death continued, Alex broke from the expressionless appearance he had presented during the trial and hid his face briefly behind his left hand, finally dropping his face to his chest. He was seen to shake noticeably. Charlie, seeing the reaction of Alex, also bent his head briefly, then raised it again to watch the judge. Allen looked at Crease intently, affecting an audible yawn and vigorously chewing tobacco. Archie, meanwhile, was trying to look unconcerned.

"The only way in which they could rebut the presumption of malice arising from the fact itself of their having killed Ussher would be by showing either that it was justifiable or excusable or that at most it amounted to manslaughter only and not to murder. Now, murder is only justifiable in three ways: 1) Where the proper officer executes a criminal in strict conformity with his sentence; 2) Where an officer of justice or other person, acting in his aid in the legal exercise of a particular duty, kills a person who resists or prevents him from executing it; 3) Where the homicide is committed in prevention of a forcible and atrocious crime, as for instance if a man should attempt to rob or murder another and be killed in the attempt, the slayer shall be acquitted and discharged.

"No such justification has been set up in this case."

Here, Crease cited cases to show that in a riot where a constable was killed, all present were held guilty of the death although they did not actually strike him or any of the constables.

"All who were present aiding and abetting in concert when Ussher was killed are equally guilty of his death with those who actually delivered the fatal blow. The contention that Archie McLean was an infant does not lessen his culpability. The law holds that the capacity of an infant to commit a capital crime commences at the age of seven and from that up to fourteen years. There is evidence that he is over fourteen. Insanity has been mentioned, but if the accused was conscious that the act was one that he ought not to do, and if that act was at the same time contrary to the law of the land, he is punishable."

Crease continued.

"There is no evidence that the prisoners are or were insane, or that any of them has ever shown an insane tendency. Every one of the prisoners knew that Ussher was a constable and that the killing of a constable is at all times a heinous offence. It is especially so in this country where the enforcement of the law depends entirely upon the moral effect which the power of an officer of the law has throughout the country to enforce the law's mandates. If there were not the moral force to rely on for instant and implicit obedience to the law, a whole regiment of constables would be ineffective to produce that result. That is partly why I said in my address to the grand jury, 'Ask yourselves is it a magistrate the less or a constable the less at Kamloops which has caused or could have prevented these murders?'

"It rests with the jury to re-establish the moral effect of the law in the Interior. There has never been so serious, so open, so flagrant a defiance of the law as this, and should the jury fail in its duty the consequences would be almost irreparable."

Crease was saying, it seemed, that the jury should make an example of the gang.

"British Columbia has ever been a respecter of law and order and it is so now, thanks to the gallant conduct of her magistrates, and the settlers in the Interior who underwent the rigors of a severe winter frost and snow and gave their time and imperilled their lives to give irrefragable evidence that the country on the subject of law and order is sound to the core. Palmer, Shumway and McLeod showed a courage beyond all praise. Thanks to these the jury now has an opportunity of redeeming the good name of that portion of the province, and enforcing the lesson that even in the most isolated places the law must be implicitly obeyed. A failure to do that would be an encouragement of bowie knife, revolver, and lynch-law reign."

The judge then read over the principal portion of Palmer's evidence and said the evidence was direct and conclusive.

"The prisoners were the terror of the whole of that part of the country; neither life nor property was safe so long as these men were at large. You are now called upon to pass upon their fate.

"I have great pity for the prisoners, great pity for their youth, but the force of the law must be carried out. You must give your verdict without fear, favour or affection."

The jury was out only twenty-two minutes when it was ready with a verdict. At 2:00 PM the court was reconvened and the jury filed in.

"Mr. Foreman," the registrar asked William Turnbull, "have you agreed?"

"We find the prisoners guilty of the wilful murder of John Ussher."

Alex Hare closed his eyes for several seconds, raising his left hand to his face again. Charlie's head sank to his chest, as it had before.

"I entirely concur in your verdict," stated Crease.

"I ask your lordship to pass sentence," said McCreight.

"I shall pass sentence at 11 o'clock tomorrow." Then he added, "Ample time will be given the accused to prepare for death."

For all that was left to do was to state the death sentence.

## [57]

### NEW WESTMINSTER COURTHOUSE
### Saturday, March 20, 1880, 11:00 AM

The courtroom was as crowded as ever the next morning as the four outlaws were led in and placed in the dock for sentencing. Everyone stood as Crease entered, and they remained standing until he seated himself at his desk.

While the four prisoners betrayed no emotion, as if they didn't realize what was coming, Crease looked like a man who did not easily send men to death.

"Allen McLean, do you have anything to say why judgment should not be passed upon you for the murder of John Ussher, of which you have been found guilty?" the judge asked.

It was the first time since the trial had started that any of them had been asked to say anything.

"Some of the witnesses said what is not true. Palmer said we cocked our guns at him; that is not true. While he was there, I was drinking at a little creek. Archie did not have a gun."

"Have you any reason to state why I should not pass sentence of death upon you for the death of John Ussher?" Crease asked again.

But Allen wanted to explain. "I was stopping at Nicola, and the boys said we had better go to Kamloops for grub."

"You have said nothing about the death of Ussher."

Allen said he tried to stop Hare from killing Ussher, yelled at him to stop, but Hare kept swinging at the constable with his knife. Then it was over, and they left.

"Anything further to say?"

"No, that's all."

"Archie McLean, what have you got to say why the sentence of death should not be passed upon you?"

This mere boy, standing convicted of murder, who had so readily bragged about killing a man, now denied it in a vain hope, perhaps, that they would be more willing to believe in the innocence of a child than in reality. He didn't kill Ussher, he said. He had pointed his gun, but it had misfired.

"What else have you to say?" It didn't really matter one bit what he had to say. It was only a courtesy being shown to condemned men.

"I have got nothing further to say."

"Charles McLean, what have you to say why the sentence of the court should not be passed upon you for the murder of John Ussher?"

"I don't know which of us fired first," said Charlie. "We all fired, and I fired too, I fired twice. The first shot was with a gun, the other with a pistol."

"Anything further?"

"We then started down to Trapp's. Alex said there was a Henry rifle and double-barrelled shotgun there. We got them and left. Allen and Archie were ahead. We met a sheepherder. Alex fired and struck him here," said Charlie, pointing to the left side of his chest.

"Then I fired at him. Alex jumped off his horse and I held the horse, and by this time the others had come up. Hare took Kelly's watch with a silver chain. At first I had no firearms. Alex stole a five-shooter from Bartlett Newman. It was an English pistol. I took it. When near Ussher I threw the pistol away. If I was alone I would never have done anything to Mr. Ussher."

"Anything further to say?"

"No, sir."

"Alexander Hare, what have you to say why the sentence of this court should not be passed upon you for the murder of John Ussher, as stated by the verdict of the jury?"

"If I was not with the crowd, I would not be here a prisoner."

"What have you to say why you should not be sentenced for the death of John Ussher?" Alex hesitated and Crease repeated the question.

"Mr. Ussher's life was not taken by my hands. What is more, some of these boys have made statements that are false. I killed nobody," Alex said angrily.

"The witnesses testified that you were there, and he was murdered by one of you or both," Crease reminded him.

"I have nothing further to say," Alex mumbled. He was no more willing to drag Annie into it than her brothers were, though, if it had not been for their intense desire to get Mara, they would not have been so desperate to stay out of jail.

Crease stood up to pronounce sentence.

"Allen, Archibald and Charles McLean and Alexander Hare, after a long and patient trial, in which you had the benefit of able counsel and after you had eighty challenges, you have been found guilty of the murder of John Ussher. You have caused great terror throughout the whole country, and by a system of robbery and outlawry have disgraced British Columbia. I have carefully looked over the evidence to see if I could discover a single point in your favour. Not one such point could I find in your defence. You, Allen, were not content with forfeiting your own life by your wayward course, but you led your younger brothers into crime. Seldom have such cases as the present occurred in any civilized country. You have disgraced the name you bear, instead of honouring it. You have had to be hunted around the country like wild beasts, and all good men desired your capture. You may now expiate with your lives — for no hope can be held out — and receive that mercy beyond the grave you refused to give here. Your Saviour may be more merciful, but here you need not expect it. Therefore I hope you will sincerely repent. The sentence of this court is that you be taken to the place from whence you came, and from thence to the place of execution, and be there hanged by the neck until you are dead. Sentence to be carried out within a period of not less than two months' time. May God have mercy upon your souls."

"It's a well-deserved sentence, Your Lordship," commented Alex.

Crease wrapped things up quickly. "The jury is dismissed with thanks, and this court is adjourned. The prisoners will be kept in custody until such time that the sentence is carried out." Allen and Archie, and Charlie and Alex, chained together in pairs, rose and the four of them were led toward the side exit of the courtroom to be taken back to their cells. Palmer stood near the doorway. Suddenly Allen's fury, pent-up during the trial, unleashed itself and as he walked by Palmer he let fly a kick at the rancher's leg, hitting him on the left thigh.

Palmer let out a yelp and a few of the women screamed and the guards closed in.

Allen swore at Palmer, who was shielded by the guards, one of whom landed a whack on Allen's back with a billy club. Archie slugged the guard a couple of times and there was a confused melee as they were shoved out the door toward their cells.

BRITISH COLUMBIA
Spring, 1880

Break-up was the most beautiful time of year in the Interior of British Columbia. The chilled winds weakened and the air began to warm. The ice on the rivers fractured and gradually disappeared as the spring came on, snow melted and patches of green and yellow began appearing on the landscape like a beautiful disease. Soon flowers would blossom, birds would chirp. In the Nicola ranchers impatiently began emerging from one of the worst winters they could remember, a winter that ruined many a cattleman of the country. With no hay put up for the stock, the weakened animals had died by the hundreds from the cold or from starvation. After this the change in weather was a relief. As signs of the new season breathed over the rolling, thick-grassed hills, it was a time to open up and meet life again.

For those who had been witnesses at the trial, the winter had been even tougher to take. At the Coast for a month and a half, they'd had to hire men and horses to look after their stock until they returned. Even after the trial was over, they were stranded in New Westminster for another five days before getting transportation home. For their trouble, they were told by Todd of the provincial police that he had no authority to allow them expenses during the time they had been awaiting the trial, testifying at it, or waiting to go back to the Upper Country.

Tom Trapp, on behalf of the witnesses, went to Victoria and appealed to Walkem. "We think it would be both unfair and unjust to expect us, in addition to the loss of our stock, to be losers in other respects." Expense estimates were submitted and reluctantly approved by the government.

The Trapp-McDonald ranch had fared poorly through the tough winter, and the McLean episode soured Trapp's enthusiasm for the country. He decided to sell out his share of the spread to Richie McDonald and move down to New Westminster permanently, in favour of the less strenuous and less worrisome tasks of a small business — he opened a hardware store. Though Semlin recommended Trapp for the job of constable and government agent to replace Ussher, George Tunstall, a Montrealer and one of the gold-seeking Overlanders party that had arrived from Fort Garry in 1862, was given the job.

Meanwhile Kamloops residents were pushing the government for speedy processing of a pension for Annie Clara Ussher.

Down in New Westminster, the boys saw the arrival of spring

mostly from the insides of their cells. Charlie moped in his confinement, feeling miserable, wanting to strike back. Archie was rebellious as ever, with Allen egging him on. Alex alternately brooded and displayed sullen anger. Sometimes they passed the day quietly, sometimes they danced and sang in their cells in a mood of bravado to show contempt for their fate.

Allen dictated a letter to Bole to send to his wife Angele in the Nicola: "How is the boy?" he asked about his son George. Not realizing that Angele hadn't yet given birth, he asked, "Was the last child a boy or a girl? I send you my love. Write soon or I shall not get your letter alive. I die in two months. Goodbye."

Alex had his own special way of reminding himself of his fate, and of letting any who might later occupy his cell know the same thing. On the cell wall, he scratched "A. HARE" and under his name, the single word "Death."

There was little to break the monotony of what they had left of their lives. Each day the work gangs now confined in the jail with them left for their day's labour and each evening they came back. The boys, especially Allen, got to know a few of them in an off-handed sort of way and a tenuous camaraderie developed. They never did get friendly with the guards.

A few days after the trial, a photographer named John Uren came to visit the boys. Uren, who had toured the gold-rush country a few years before, then worked in Victoria, now had a studio on Front Street in New Westminster. He had photographed some of the witnesses and wanted to take pictures of the condemned prisoners, so they stood proudly outside the jail in the prison yard while he worked away diligently under his black cloth. He took their pictures one at a time standing near a prop stair rail and post with a drape hung over it. They looked uncomfortable in their irons, a big leather belt wrapped around their waists with support straps holding up the heavy metal for walking.

Allen put on his go-to-town suit coat that had long ago become grubby from rough wear, along with a vest and kerchief, stuck his thumbs defiantly in his pant pockets and stared grimly at the photographer.

Archie, in a prison shirt much too big for him, struck a Napoleonic pose with half a right hand poked through the opening in the front.

Outside the walls of the jail, the legal system was grinding onward. Not a member of the jury, not a person who had sat in the public gallery at the trial, not even Theo Davie nor Norman Bole doubted the justness of the verdict. The three McLeans and Hare were guilty. But British justice did not end with a conviction. The British Columbia Supreme Court, headed by Chief Justice Begbie and membered by Judge Gray and Judge Crease, sent a report of the proceedings back to the State Department in Ottawa. Crease warned Walkem that in the report he must touch on the validity of the trial, and that all opportunity must be given for both sides to argue the matter so it could be settled.

At issue was the fact that the government hadn't issued a commission for the trial. Commissions were a throwback to thirteenth-century England, when they were used to appoint judges for trials. In modern-day British Columbia, with its full-time judges, commissions weren't sensible, but plans to enact legislation making them obsolete hadn't been carried through. As Crease saw it, he technically had no authority to preside over the trial that had condemned the boys. Yet Crease had made the decision to go ahead with the trial despite the government's unwillingness to issue a commission the way he'd asked.

Why hadn't Crease simply refused to let the trial begin until everything was prepared the way he liked it? Only Crease knew the answer to that, but one thing is clear: he was a pig-headed judge and George Walkem was a pig-headed premier. They took such matters of law personally. Crease and Begbie both disliked Walkem and thought he was a poor lawyer. Walkem particularly disliked Begbie. As far as the premier was concerned, the Supreme Court judges were constipated old fogies, intent on stifling judicial reform and afraid of losing their independence to democratically chosen legislators. With this as a backdrop, a legal battle was shaping up over an obscure technicality that neither the public nor, certainly, the four men whose lives depended on it, much understood.

Walkem resisted. He told Crease that since it was the government's opinion that the lieutenant-governor wasn't empowered to issue a commission, it became a question for the judges. They were responsible for any problems because the government put no pressure on them to have the case tried without a commission (if they had objected the government would have gone along with it, he said). It's hard to imagine the judges taking Walkem's rebuke calmly. By telling them that if the lack of commission made the trial illegal it was their fault, Walkem virtually guaranteed that the judges would lean toward overturning the trial.

Crease's reply to Walkem was that the premier was changing his tune. He said, "I cannot admit the accuracy of your recollection of facts and entirely fail to perceive the cogency of your argument."

He would have expected Walkem's objections, but Crease got a surprisingly unenthusiastic response from the two defence lawyers. In early May, several days after Crease had informed him of his intention to revisit the commission issue, Davie replied laconically, "I am not instructed to take any proceedings on behalf of any of the prisoners. Apart from this consideration I cannot see that any practical good could result in event of success in the suggested application." Bole reluctantly indicated he would show up in court to discuss the question. Their willingness was bolstered when the federal minister of justice ordered they be paid to continue representing the boys in an argument before the Supreme Court to test the validity of the trial and sentence.

"Not less than two months." That sentence had given the boys at least until May 19 before execution. With the appeal hearing scheduled for June 1, Crease ordered a reprieve until June 2.

On May 16, back in Kamloops, Father Pierre Richard conducted a baptism in pretty little St. Joseph's Church on the Indian reserve. It was one of dozens of baptisms the Oblate missionaries did every month. On this day the children were five-year-old George Allen McLean and his new brother, John Donald McLean, just four weeks old. Their mother, Angele, was there, but their father, Mathias Allen McLean, was otherwise occupied, in a jail cell in New Westminster. The godmother to little George was an aunt, Christina Glassey. For the baby, it was another aunt, Annie McLean, who only a few weeks before had attended this same church for the baptism of her own baby, Mary-Ethel. Fred Griffin and the children's uncle Alex McLean were officially named as the godfathers to George and John Donald. A family friend, Selina McIntosh, was there, too. After the ceremony, Angele McLean returned to Douglas Lake with her two children, not knowing what would become of her or her children, or of her husband, the now-famous outlaw, Allen McLean.

Davie wrote to Crease in Victoria asking for clarification regarding the non-issuance of a commission. If the judge had presided at the New Westminster trial without a commission, then by what authority? Davie requested copies of correspondence between the government and judges on the matter of issuing commissions. Without waiting for a written reply, Davie and Bole, on May 26, moved for a *rule nisi* or a writ of *habeas corpus* on grounds that no commission had been issued by the Crown. This was the route earlier recommended by Crease. An order would be issued for another trial by a specified time unless it was shown why it shouldn't be done. Crease laboured for several hours to make copies of the correspondence Davie asked for and forwarded them in a May 29 letter.

The task for Davie and Bole, now, was to show that a commission was actually required. The Crown, in technical phraseology, was called upon to show cause why "a rule directing the issue of a writ of *habeas corpus* should not be made absolute."

When June 2 came, and technicalities had delayed the hearing, the latest reprieve was ordered, this one good until Thursday, June 17.

## 59

VICTORIA, Supreme Court
Friday, June 4, 1880, 11:30 AM

Chief Justice Matthew Baillie Begbie, Justice Henry Pering Pellew Crease and Justice John Hamilton Gray sat as an Appellant Division of the Supreme Court to hear argument in the case. The prisoners weren't present, but it was a distinguished group of legal minds that assembled for this hostile battle of wits.

The three judges sat with their black robes hanging around their shoulders met by long, knotted white wigs. There was the elderly Gray, examining documents with the aid of a pair of shaftless, round-rimmed eyeglasses that, when not in use, dangled from his neck by a cord. A receding chin was over-shadowed by a heavy, curling mustache and shaggy sideburns. It seemed almost impossible that any one man could have packed so much public service into a career. Born in Bermuda, he was raised and educated in Nova Scotia, where he served in the army before becoming speaker of the House of Assembly, attorney-general, premier, a talented international diplomat, and a Father of Confederation. He had been on the B.C. Supreme Court eight years.

There was Crease, who had tried the McLeans and Hare in New Westminster. A native of England and a member of the English bar, he had become the first barrister of what was to be the province of British Columbia, and later a member of the Legislative Assembly of Vancouver Island and attorney-general of the colony of B.C., before being appointed to the Supreme Court bench in 1870. As a circuit judge, he had refused to carry a gun with him while making his rounds of the colony, and made sure the Union Jack flew outside his courtroom whenever a case was in session. Crease spoke several languages and was a pretty good sketch artist and a good athlete. He sported a frothy beard under a thick mustache, above which peered round, kindly eyes.

But neither Gray nor Crease boasted a more adventurous or controversial career than Begbie. More than any other man, he had been responsible for establishing and enforcing British justice on the West Coast. Like Crease, he was a native of England. He was a Cambridge graduate and member of the English bar for fifteen years before coming to Canada. On November 15, 1858, he had been sworn in as the first judge for the Court of British Columbia. For the next eight years he travelled throughout the Interior, almost single-handedly upholding the law in the face of hordes of American prospectors who invaded in the mad search for gold. He earned himself the nickname "The Hang-

Judge John Hamilton Gray
(BCARS, 22873)

ing Judge," though there was nobody who would say he ever hung anyone without good reason. Among those he'd sentenced to die were Klatassine and his followers after the Chilcotin War of 1864. In 1870 Begbie became chief justice. He was strong and wilful, and he encountered his share of controversies and criticisms, but in private life he was a man of considerable grace — a scholar, athlete and musician, popular in Victoria society. He let his greying hair grow just over his ears; with black mustache and grey goatee, he was a handsome man.

The talented young lawyers, Davie and Bole, acting for the prisoners from the beginning of the year, both appeared at the hearing. For the Crown were Walkem along with legal advisors McCreight and Robertson.

Walkem peered grouchily from behind a drooping white mustache; propped on his nose, little round metal-framed spectacles accented the natural roundness of his face. His Irish temper, when directed to the right purpose, could be an advantage. He had served throughout the most important political changes in British Columbia's history. A long-time member of the Legislative Council, chief commissioner of lands and works under McCreight, attorney-general under Premier Amor de Cosmos — these were the results of his political ambitions before he became premier in 1874. After once being put out of office, he was again premier. He was known as a difficult man, stubborn and defiant, but he kept British Columbia in confederation during the important first years and ensured the building of a railway to B.C.

With Walkem was McCreight, who had himself served a stormy

Hon. Alex Rocke Robertson
(BCARS, 4531)

year as B.C.'s first premier. His stringy beard was almost a perfect match for his short-cropped barrister's wig, but he looked uncomfortable under the hairpiece. McCreight hailed from the Irish bar, ending up on Vancouver Island in 1860. Even in middle age, McCreight was hot-headed and as likely to throw a punch as use words to settle a private argument. Like Walkem, he had been heavily involved in the debate on whether British Columbia should join the confederation. Politics were new to him at the time he became first premier, and his term was predictably short. He was a failure at political manipulation, but as a lawyer he worked hard, doing thorough research on which to put his aggressive and biting courtroom manner to work. Better than almost any other person in British Columbia, he knew his law.

Robertson, in contrast to the background of his two confederates in this case, was a native Canadian, born in Ontario thirty-nine years before. Following legal training there he came west in 1864, where he not only carved a reputation as an excellent practitioner of law but became involved in politics – he was a former mayor of Victoria and former provincial secretary. As was stylish for the day, he wore a thick beard and mustache. In common with McCreight and Walkem, he had been among those in the thick of the confederation and railway debates.

The other thing the three Crown representatives shared would not be an advantage: all of them at one time or another had been on the wrong side of Begbie. McCreight, particularly, over a span of eighteen years, had had his differences with him, which sometimes culminated in courtroom shouting matches. The case at hand gave no indication this animosity was at an end.

Now Walkem opened the proceedings and submitted that there could be no possibility of discharging the McLeans and Hare, even if the court sustained the defence lawyers' argument that a commission should have been issued and that therefore the first trial was invalid.

Davie replied that when the application for the rule was made there was no submission that the prisoners be discharged, but that the validity of the first trial was what was being questioned.

Walkem proceeded to explain the contentions of the Crown. If such a commission were necessary, the lieutenant-governor could not issue it legally, that being exclusively the right of the sovereign's or of the sovereign's direct representative in Canada, the governor-general. If the commission of November 1879 was valid, the trial and conviction of the prisoners was valid. But he stated:

"The Supreme Court, by the acts constituting it, has full jurisdiction in all pleas, and a court presided over by one of the judges is fully empowered without any supplementary power of commission of nisi prius or oyer and terminer. If the contention in this respect is good it follows that the convictions now under consideration are also good."

He submitted that if it was decided commissions issued by the lieutenant-governor were necessary, then the commission of November 19, 1879, was valid. He cited several cases of previous trials that he said did not require special commissions.

"The contention of the other side is that a judge cannot sit in such cases without a commission," Walkem stated. "My contention is that he can — that a commission may or may not be issued at convenience."

Crease remarked that if the commissions under which past assizes had been held were not valid then the disturbing fact existed that men convicted and hanged by them had been murdered.

"No doubt about it," said Walkem.

"A very awkward position for the crown prosecutors," observed Begbie.

"Fortunately I did not pass sentence on them, My Lord."

It was an inauspicious first day, these government men exchanging accusations of judicial murder with the triumvirate on the bench. But it would get much worse during the days to come.

## 60

VICTORIA, British Columbia
June, 1880

Hector McLean was the forgotten man in the McLean Gang drama. In the days following the murders of Ussher and Kelly, while his three brothers and Alex Hare were holed up in their cabin at Douglas Lake trying to fend off the settlers, Hector had stewed in the decrepit old jail in Kamloops, keeping company with his guards. While the other boys were on trial Hector remained in his cell at the New Westminster jail. As Walkem and McCreight sparred with the judges, Hector seemed virtually forgotten in jail in Victoria. It was as though he didn't belong, an uninvited guest to the party, the fifth wheel. As the British Columbia legal system focused all its energies on the boys, twenty-six-year-old Hector waited impatiently for his own day in court.

Finally, when it became obvious he wasn't going to be dealt with quickly, he'd been given the courtesy of removal to a different jail. Hector had behaved himself in New Westminster but was subject to the same restrictive confinement as the boys, which proved doubly uncomfortable because of Allen's hate-on for him. So in May, Hector had been taken by two constables in a steamer across the strait to Victoria. He gave no trouble on the way, and was giving no trouble now.

Hector's was a strange and somewhat pitiful case. Like his younger brothers, he had drifted aimlessly through life, not overly anxious to make much of himself. Sometimes, when a man got out of sorts, a person might say he was acting like he'd been kicked in the head by a horse. In Hector's case, it was true. The charges against him, brought with the aid of a couple of extremely vague depositions claiming he must have had something to do with the murders, resulted indirectly from an unfortunate accident he'd had as a kid.

He was the oldest of the children of Donald and Sophia McLean, born in Fort Alexandria shortly before his parents were officially married. He wasn't even ten years old when his father was killed. After that, he stayed at Hat Creek with the rest of the family while Sophia tried unsuccessfully to keep the ranch and stopping house going.

In the fall of 1866, two years after the death of their father, Hector and Donald Jr., helped by an Indian boy, were rounding up horses and breaking them at Hat Creek. As Donald told it, Hector "picked a pretty wild horse. The horse commenced to buck and throwed him down. He laid there for awhile."

On the way down, Hector's head connected with a flying hoof and he was out. They carried him into the house, and Neil McArthur came over to help look at him. Two or three days later he was up and around again. Getting bashed in the head didn't seem to affect Hector except for one strange thing — he couldn't tolerate liquor. Whenever he drank, he would get drunk quickly, and when he got drunk he would talk stupid. This would prove to be his undoing.

After the ranch was lost, the family split up, but Hector stayed in the area along with his half-brother John. He broke horses for the Cornwall brothers at Ashcroft Manor from time to time but they fired him when he "made such a fuss" about riding a particularly rebellious brown colt. Later he moved to Kamloops and was living with a woman and was engaged in various pursuits, wrangling, packing, prospecting and bootlegging whiskey to the Indians on the Kamloops reserve. Hector somehow managed to stay out of trouble with the law other than an occasional arrest for bootlegging, but Ussher and others knew he helped the boys, hiding them and keeping them supplied with food.

Late in November 1879, just before things really went to hell, Hector was sitting around the stove at the Dominion Hotel in Clinton, drinking and exchanging stories with some of the locals. The bar itself was in an alcove at one end of the room; the stove was out in the middle near a billiard table. Besides Hector, there was Will Smith, Bill Burger, George Runyan and Pete Calder. It was about three in the afternoon.

They were joined by Tom Cavanaugh, who didn't sit down, and didn't add much to the conversation. Two days before, on November 22, Cavanaugh had sworn out a complaint against Hector, Charlie and Archie McLean, and Alex Hare for theft. Besides having lost a saddle of his own, Cavanaugh knew they were suspected of stealing a saddle and three horses from Johnny Wilson. Cavanaugh eventually worked up the fortitude to tell Hector there was a warrant for his arrest.

"Don't care if there is," said Hector.

"Ain't you afraid of them taking you in?" asked Calder. That set Hector off.

"I haven't done nothing to be taken in for!" he exclaimed. "That damned John Ussher is a damned sonofabitch, always bothering my brothers! I told Charlie to shoot the sonofabitch or I'll shoot Charlie. Archie's braver than Charlie; he's the bravest of the lot. They'll make it warm for anyone who tries to take them. I told them after they kill Ussher they can have my horse to leave the country with! They're going to New Mexico."

Cavanaugh soon moved away from the stove and went over to the bar, but Hector was talking so loud everyone in the room could hear him. It was the liquor talking, but there it was, the threat against Ussher.

It was the only time anyone heard Hector talk that way. He did get food for the boys from time to time, and was supposed to have given Charlie a rifle. And, once or twice, after Charlie had escaped from jail, Hector had carried messages to him from Ussher urging him to give himself up.

For his troubles, Hector sat in a cell month after month, imprisoned without trial, waiting for the incredibly slow, incredibly fastidious justice system to take its course.

## [61]

VICTORIA, Supreme Court
Friday, June 26, 1880

The Supreme Court issued its judgment. It had taken a week of convoluted, petty and often hostile argument for the Crown and the defence to present their cases to the three judges, then another two weeks for them to decide. After the opening salvos between Walkem and Begbie over the validity of commissions, and sly accusations of judicial murder, things had gone downhill. When McCreight tried to support Walkem on the contention that many assizes had been held without commissions, there was a major blowup.

It started innocently enough, McCreight beginning that commissions were unnecessary and that the Supreme Court had the power to hear, try and determine all indictable offenses.

"Indeed, it has been shown by the affidavit of the provincial secretary that no less than ninety-six assizes have been held in the province without any commission at all."

Begbie, who had already told Walkem that the affidavit proved nothing, that commissions were often issued without being recorded, and that at least one commission the Crown said didn't exist was in a tin box in his office, exploded.

"What?! That statement is utterly untrue! The affidavits merely show an absence of record of the commissions issued, and no person can be brought forward to say the affidavits are true."

"Well, I will concede for the sake of argument," said McCreight, "that the statement is incorrect, but I must ask to be allowed to proceed with my argument without interruption. Pray let's have no angry words, or we shall not get on."

"I have a right to be angry, sir," retorted Begbie. "There is not one word of truth in the assertion you have made."

"I will sit down until you have finished."

"Your language casts an imputation on the judges and the statement you have just made you must have known to be untrue," pressed Begbie.

McCreight jumped back to his feet. "I deny —."

"You have sat down, sir, and you shall sit down. I will hear Mr. Robertson."

"In accusing me of wilfully making a false statement you have said what is quite untrue and you had no right to make such an assertion," McCreight stated.

"Take your seat, sir," Begbie demanded. "I will not hear you further."

"Indeed I shall not," McCreight told the chief justice.

"You must apologize before I hear you again," insisted Begbie, rising to his feet.

But McCreight wouldn't apologize, so Begbie adjourned to the following day, saying he would listen to Robertson but not to McCreight. But McCreight wouldn't apologize that day, either, so Begbie refused to listen to him. Robertson intervened, asking Begbie to relent, since McCreight was better versed in the Crown's case.

The proceedings were now completely derailed. Walkem, Gray and Crease compared notes on exactly what had gone on the day before to bring about the fracas, and got into lengthy discussions about previous cases to determine if what McCreight had said was actually true or not.

Walkem threatened to walk out with McCreight and Robertson if Begbie insisted on an apology. That made Begbie even madder.

But Walkem went on the attack. "I have suffered some of this same experience myself at the hands of the chief justice. It is the duty of counsel to act to the best of their ability in the interests entrusted to them, and to do this in Court they must preserve their independence of character — not course, offensive independence, but the independence of a gentleman. I myself have been treated badly time and again by the chief justice and his overbearing and tyrannical conduct has kept me out of my profession, for I would not be in politics today if I could have been at all sure of being treated with common respect by the chief justice. The treatment of Mr. McCreight was unbearable. No man of spirit would sit still for a moment and not resent to the last an insult such as that offered to Mr. McCreight. Mr. Justice Crease and Mr. Justice Gray have always treated me with courtesy and respect but such is not the case with the chief justice."

The argument droned on. "Have I ever treated you as these two gentlemen allege they have been treated?" Begbie asked in frustration. "Have I not always treated you with courtesy?"

He received no reply.

"I appeal to members of the bar present if I have not treated them with courtesy?"

Still no reply.

"In fact practitioners coming to my chambers have always left them with a smile."

"Yes, a sarcastic smile," said an unrelenting Walkem.

Finally, realizing he wasn't going to get his apology and that they would never get through this hearing, Begbie backed down. "Well, from what has transpired I think a misunderstanding has occurred and the matter should be dropped as if it had not occurred and I propose that the Court should be adjourned if counsel wishes it, to enable everyone to cool off."

Somehow they stumbled through. Walkem and McCreight backed up their arguments with a number of precedents and legal opinions. They debated the fine points of whether a commission should be made out to Victoria or Ottawa, whether a commission issued last November 19 was good enough to cover the McLeans' trial, the question of why that same commission wasn't read at the trial. Bole and Davie claimed a commission was necessary, that there was no proper commission, so the trial was invalid. "A criminal is entitled to have the benefit of any flaw that may occur," said Davie as he effectively tore apart the Crown counsels' arguments.

"I felt much embarrassed in dealing with this in consequence of the inconsistent positions taken by the Crown." In the first place, he said, they claimed no commission of any kind was necessary and required Crease to hold the assizes without one which, protesting, he did. "Their second position is that if a commission were necessary Mr. Justice Crease was responsible for having held the assizes without one and, thirdly, their most recent contention is that an old and valid commission existed all the time."

At the end of it, Davie said, "My learned friend Mr. Bole and I thank the court for its patience."

"On behalf of the Crown," said Robertson, "I apply that the prisoners might be further reprieved."

Crease gave them two more weeks.

The two weeks being up, the judges were now back to announce their decision. In court for reading of the document were McCreight for the Crown and Davie for the prisoners.

Begbie summed up the arguments for the McLeans and Hare: "The prisoner says, 'I am to be tried by a court of oyer and terminer. You, not I, selected that court. You might have selected another court. That court cannot be held without a commission. You say that the lieutenant-governor cannot issue the proper commission. You must find somebody else, then, who can. If you cannot find anybody able to issue a commission, that only shows that you have summoned me before a non-existing, impossible court. With that I have nothing to do. You shall not send me to another tribunal than that you have announced. I insist on being tried before a legal judge."

Gray opined that, "All the law and learning in British Columbia on this subject has been gathered to the feast." He said the matter was a pure question of law, and hinged mainly on the construction of the British North America Act. "So far as the facts are before the Court, no sympathy can be felt, or ought to be felt, for the prisoners."

Begbie, Crease and Gray were unanimous in the opinion that a commission was necessary, and that none had been issued.

The prisoners were given their new trial.

## [62]

Mary Anne Moresby often sat outside the cells and read to the boys from the most recent editions of the newspapers. No doubt, she read them the *Colonist*'s account of the judges' decision.

> The decision of the Supreme Court on Saturday [sic] draws the pen through the proceedings instituted against the Kamloops outlaws. The men now stand in the eyes of the law as if they had never been tried. The Westminster special assize court was irregularly convened — in fact, legally speaking, was not convened at all — and the provincial exchequer will be drawn upon to foot the bills incurred in consequence of the meanness, stupidity, obstinacy and ignorance of the legal department of the Crown. No decent excuse can be framed that will palliate the conduct of the Government. The English language does not contain words in which to frame an explanation that will be deemed satisfactory. The most devoted friends of the Government stand aghast at the astounding record. Their organ has been struck deaf, dumb and blind.... To make a good budget showing, provincial constables were cut off, and the costs incurred by magistrates and special constables in arresting criminals disallowed. Probably $3,000 per annum was saved by this course; but alarms were frequent. The opposition press called attention to the want of security for life and property. Their warnings were unheeded. And when 'the wolf' came, where were 'the reapers'? Economy would have dictated that the trials be held in the district where the crime was committed.... A strange fatality would seem to dog the footsteps of this Government. They appear utterly incapable of doing anything as it ought to be done.... The officials responsible for the state of affairs which cul-

minated on Saturday last should perform political hari kari and save the country the trouble and expense of doing it for them. It is the least they could do to show their appreciation of the forbearance with which they have been treated.

That was what the *Colonist* had to say in an editorial called, "The Beginning of the End." It was the latest edition to reach New Westminster, printed three days after the judges made their decision. The papers were always arguing. It didn't matter what the government did, the *Colonist* would say it was wrong.

For the boys, it didn't matter what the newspapers thought, nor what the strange legal reasons were for the judges' decision. They weren't going to hang. They didn't have to sit around waiting to hear whether or not they had gotten another reprieve. They were starting over.

They must have felt immense relief, not only from the prospect of hanging, but from the pressures of trying to escape. They weren't finding it easy, dreaming up ways and means of breaking out. Only a few days before the judges' decision, Moresby and the guards made a routine check of the cells, their contents, and the irons of the four prisoners. As Allen watched them vigorously searching the cell, he shrugged and gave in. "You'll find it anyway," he said, directing them to a crack in one corner of the wall. Moresby looked in the spot and came up with a small file. Moresby thanked him and asked him where he'd gotten the file. But Allen wasn't offering any more help that day. Moresby found out, though. He knew his prisoners, and some of them talked more than others. The culprit was Fred Guaymas, a prisoner who had been convicted of a minor offence at the same assizes at which the McLeans and Hare had been tried. He'd smuggled the file into the cell block and gotten it in to Allen. Guaymas was put on bread and water and forced to wear double irons for a week.

Mary Anne Moresby had become the messenger between the boys and the outside world. She liked them, sympathized with them. It was Archie who had first heard her singing and asked her to come into the cell block and sing for them. The living quarters for the warden or "governor" of the jail were close enough to the cell block that when it was quiet one day the young Mrs. Moresby's melodious voice filtered into the dim confinement area. She had consented gladly to come and sing for them in the cell-block corridor, and she did so often, in addition to reading to them. They would listen intently and appreciatively as she sang:

"Would God I were the tender April blossom,
That floats and falls from the twisted bough."

And when once they would have cracked a joke, they were quiet and unsmirking at:

"To lie and fain within your silken bosom,
Within your silken bosom as that does now. . . . "

Mary Anne Moresby was a kind, happy and compassionate young woman of twenty-three, who felt pity and even friendship for the four prisoners. And they felt friendship and admiration in return, for she was not only sympathetic, talented and pretty but she was of their age and they talked easily to her. She seemed to understand them, though she had spent her entire life, from the age of six months, in the relative security of New Westminster.

She brought them news of the outside world — gave them a mental picture of what was happening beyond the jail walls. They didn't even mind when she talked about the silly social goings on of New Westminster society, or about her husband.

William Moresby, governor of the provincial jail, was quite a fellow. He'd been warden only two years, but already he was known for his slyness and efficiency not only in managing the jail but in his detective work. He'd married Mary Anne Edwards five years ago, while he was turnkey at the jail. Before that he had been a lumber yard foreman. Mrs. Moresby said he was born in London but had lived in China for two years before coming to the Cariboo, then to the Coast. He was ten years older than his wife. Apparently, they made quite the charming couple socially.

The boys liked Mrs. Moresby a lot more than they liked her husband.

## [63]

KAMLOOPS, British Columbia
Monday, October 19, 1880, late afternoon

For two days Hector McLean had been on trial in the whitewashed log courthouse at the west end of town. While the community was divided in its opinions about his fate — some thought he was unjustly accused, others wanted to hang him along with his brothers — it had been deemed safe to send him back up to Kamloops from Victoria for trial on the aiding and abetting charge. On October 1 Hector had been shackled up once more and taken back across the strait to New Westminster and up to Kamloops.

The legal heavies were all there for it: Theodore Davie defending; Alexander Robertson, instead of advising the Crown, now assisted Davie;

Eli Harrison Jr. *(BCARS, 5836)*

Eli "Young Putty" Harrison was there, too, prosecuting; and, sitting on the case, the ever-present Henry Crease.

Crease took his wife, Sarah, with him, and it turned into a pleasant holiday foray into the Upper Country. While there was now a chill in the evening air, the days were still sunny and pleasant. The distinguished couple was the toast of Kamloops, with its most respected citizens competing to entertain them. Sarah barely had time to poke her head into the courthouse during the day to see how the trial was progressing; she was too busy receiving guests. The aging Oblate father, Charles Grandidier, came to pay his respects ("very pleasant, and great favourite with all," in Sarah's estimation). So did A.W. Sillitoe, the Anglican bishop for New Westminster and the Southern Interior, on a trip through Kamloops with his wife. There was Mary Ann Scott and her daughter Matilda and Matilda's lover Walter Clarke, and daughter Margaret Maria, now married to John Edwards, with their baby. And John Tait's wife Emma and Arthur Pemberton's wife. Sarah visited Mrs. William Roper and Annie Ussher ("nice, pretty house"), still very much in mourning over the death of Johnny. There was dining at the Cosmopolitan Hotel and pleasant conversation. Always there was much interest in the McLeans, though of course Henry couldn't take part in these chats ("ladies expressed much interest in the cases, especially in young Hare, and Hector McLean, who they hope will be hanged!"). Sometimes, in the evenings, there was piano playing and singing, and even Henry joined in.

The interest of the "ladies" in the trial was shared by all of Kamloops, and by some from other places, too. Crease noticed among the spectators a stately old Indian — Chillihitzia had come to observe the proceedings.

The witnesses were lined up in large number to testify against Hector McLean. There was William Palmer, John Tait, John Veasey, Tom Cavanaugh, and the boys from the Dominion Hotel: George Runyan, Pete Calder, Bill Burger. Harrison even called Hector's sister-in-law, Margaret McLean, to tell about a visit to her house by Hector and Charlie in September, 1879. Charlie was still on the run over his jail escape, and had come to say goodbye, to say he was leaving by himself for Red River. Hector had told Charlie then, "Don't let nobody catch you."

After she, Cavanaugh and the boys from the bar testified, it was John Veasey's turn. Since he was on trial at these same assizes for cattle rustling, he wasn't a sterling witness; Crease believed it was Veasey — "the father of cattle stealing in that district" — who had given the McLean boys early lessons in rustling. Veasey testified that Hector, his brother Archie and Alex Hare had come to Tom Morgan's cabin in the Bonaparte last fall to borrow a sack of flour. Hector, like Veasey, was working for Morgan at the time. He had claimed they were going hunting for deer in the mountains, so Veasey gave him part of a sack and some cooking utensils. On cross-examination, Veasey said he had seen no weapons.

At that point, Robertson asked Crease to stop the proceedings and acquit Hector for lack of evidence, but Crease refused, so Harrison called Tait, Palmer and Edwards. Then it was Robertson's turn.

Fred Rush, the Jacko Lake rancher who had played a role in the gang's surrender at Douglas Lake, testified that Hector had worked for him. By coincidence, Rush was suing his wife Julia for divorce in the same assizes, for running off and having two children with Antoine Lamprone, Charlie McLean's friend. Rush had never known Hector to ride with his brothers. In fact, Rush said, Hector had tried to get Charlie to give himself up, carrying messages from Ussher. "I can give Hector McLean a good character (reference). Trustworthy — always has been so far as I be aware."

Tom Morgan said he'd once heard Hector tell Archie to stay away from Alex Hare and Charlie. Archie was "a little fool" for having anything to do with them, Hector said. That made Archie mad, and Archie had cried. Another time, Hector and Charlie had an argument over a horse. Charlie wanted it; Hector wouldn't give it to him. Morgan also said drinking sometimes made Hector "crazy." He'd known Hector since the year his father was killed. "He behaved himself with me very well. I have nothing against him in that respect."

Then Ed Grant testified about Hector's willingness to accompany Ussher's posse, and said Hector was "a peaceable man." He added that everybody called Ussher "Johnny." "I don't mean everybody but

Theodore Davie, lawyer (and future premier of British Columbia), who defended Alex Hare at his first trial (*BCARS, 2615*)

people who were intimate with him. Charlie and Allen were also on good terms with Ussher and always in the habit of calling him Johnny."

After Donald Jr. testified, the jury recalled Tom Cavanaugh for some more questions. Robertson summed up: Hector McLean was a man of good character. The only evidence against him was some joking talk in a bar about going after Ussher.

Harrison, though, said the charge against Hector was that he had "incited, moved, hired or commanded to incite to the murder of John Ussher," and his threats and actions showed he had done just that.

The jury agreed with the defence: Hector was involved in no conspiracy to commit murder. When the "not guilty" verdict was announced, Crease agreed with it. And shook Hector's hand.

Part of the town was shocked ("terror and amazement at hearing of his being found not guilty and consequently liberated," according to Sarah Crease). Others — his relatives, his friends on the reserve, and a few white families like the Urens at Savona's Ferry (even though the McLeans had broken into their store room and stolen provisions), and the McQueens, up the North Thompson — were happy for him. He was free.

The grand jury having found true bills in the indictments, the new trial for the murder of Constable John Ussher got underway.

The boys were heartened by Hector's acquittal. It could indicate hope for their own trial. The government, though, wasn't about to mess things up again. New legislation allowed assizes to be held with or without commissions.

This time, there would be two trials consecutively, one for the murder of Ussher, one for the murder of Kelly. It seemed like a replay of the first one as court opened that day, except there were some changes to the cast. A few of the witnesses would differ, and the defence and Crown counsels were altered.

Davie wasn't in court along with Bole this time. Hare had decided to let the court-appointed Bole defend him, also.

"Who cares for the prisoners?" inquired Crease.

"I have been by the Court assigned to the McLeans," replied Bole.

"To your care I will leave all the prisoners," the judge officially instructed.

Bole immediately entered an objection that his clients had already been tried and convicted.

"And should be hanged?" retorted Crease.

There would be no double-jeopardy protection for the McLeans and Hare. Though a person could not be rightfully tried twice for the same crime, he was not counted to have been tried at all if his first trial was nullified. Thus the four boys were, in effect, on trial for the first time.

So Bole objected that the lieutenant-governor had no authority to issue a commission. That had been a Crown argument in the appeal hearing on the first trial, but Bole figured on tossing in as many doubts as possible. His objection was overruled.

Now the jury panel was challenged because they were not from the vicinage or district where the crime was committed. The prosecution — McCreight and Harrison — pleaded that there were no judicial districts in B.C. The demurrer, or objection, was overruled by the Court, as it had been in the first trial.

Thirty-four jurors were challenged by the defence, and one by the Crown, the latter because he didn't believe in capital punishment. The petty jurors were finally chosen and sworn, with a man named William Holmes elected foreman. Other jury members were James Colbeck, William Powers, William Innes, Daniel Emerson, William

Letser, John McIvor, J. William Draper, and H.G. Anderkink.

Crease addressed the jury, explaining the nature of the alleged crimes. (He had remarked to the grand jury: "The youth of the country, who have no proper guardians, should be placed in reformatories. Also those who are guilty of misdemeanours, so that by preventing them from coming into close contact with hardened criminals, they might be taught trades and become useful members of society.") Then Palmer, Shumway, John McLeod, Scott and Trapp were sworn.

Harrison, for whom the sombre business of the murder trial contrasted with the cheering fact that he was to be married later in the month, opened the case for the prosecution. It was 4:00 PM by the time Palmer, the first witness, was put on the stand. He was still there when Crease adjourned for the day.

## [65]

NEW WESTMINSTER
Friday, November 12, 1880, 10:00 AM

Palmer continued his testimony. He, Scott, Shumway, McLeod and Trapp told their stories as they had eight months before — the threats, the fight, the bravado.

George Cavanaugh was almost the only new witness called. He testified that the prisoners had taken arms from Palmer's house the day Ussher was killed. They did no harm to himself or Mrs. Palmer, he said.

John Bennett of Osoyoos swore that Archie was now sixteen, judging from a remark made by his mother when he was supposedly two.

Edwards was sworn in and described his part in the posse that captured the boys.

It all went very smoothly, like a well-rehearsed play, and it seemed over quickly. The boys were perplexed that there were no new twists, no dramatic changes from the first trial. When the prosecution was finished, the defence lawyer said there would be no defence witnesses. And when Bole even declined to address the jury, McCreight shot him a surprised look.

"My duty is doubly painful to me as this is an undefended case," said Crease in instructing the jury. He referred to the McLean boys' father, and reviewed the alleged facts of Ussher's murder.

At 3:45 PM, fifteen minutes after retiring, the jury returned with a verdict of guilty of the wilful murder of John Ussher.

As the trial for the murder of James Kelly got under way, there was another challenge from the defence on vicinage grounds. Though Crease affirmed the jury array, Bole — as previously — could liberally challenge prospective jurors. He asked, in the meantime, that Crown witnesses not be allowed to enter the courtroom until they were required to testify.

It took until noon to select the jury. The array was exhausted three times. At one point the sheriff had to leave to obtain another supply of jurors. While Crease waited impatiently, Bole challenged juror after juror — seventy-nine of them. The prosecution challenged six. The judge remarked that Bole was making somewhat more use of the right to challenge than was probably necessary. What he meant was that the defence lawyer was abusing that right.

Jurors finally chosen were William Kent (the foreman), William Hancock, A.C. Fraser, J. Shaw, a Mr. Bourassa, H. Eikoff, William Jenkins, James McKee, Neil McColl, J. Turnbull, Robert Johnson and James Reid.

Trapp testified to searching for Kelly and finding his body, then later finding Kelly's cabin ransacked, with the sheepherder's watch and revolver missing.

"How far did you say the body was from the wagon road?" asked Bole.

"A couple of dozen yards."

"You've indicated that it took some time for you to find the body after arriving in the area of Mr. Kelly's cabin, is that right?"

"Yes."

"You didn't see the body from the wagon road?"

"No."

"So anybody riding on that wagon road could easily have passed by without even seeing Mr. Kelly," concluded Bole. In response to a question from jury foreman Kent, Trapp said there was dim moonlight at the time he found the body.

Now Harrison: "What time was it, again, that you left your home to go to Mr. Fraser's?"

"After supper — about 7 o'clock."

"This was December, so it would have been quite dark?"

"Oh, yes, although there was a moon."

"And the four defendants left your home shortly after or around lunch time, so it would have still been light for some time, perhaps three and a half or four more hours?"

"That's right. At least that long."

"How long did it take you to ride to Mr. Kelly's cabin that night?" continued Harrison.

"About forty-five minutes. I couldn't go too fast by moonlight, in the snow."

"It would have been faster by day?"

"Sure."

"Have you before or since passed by Mr. Kelly's cabin during the day, on that wagon road, and been able to see the rock on which Mr. Kelly sometimes sat to watch his sheep?"

"Yes, I've seen it from the road."

Scott testified about his own run-in with the boys. Here Bole fought against their admission to him of killing Kelly being received as evidence. But the boys had done too much bragging, and it was impossible to convince the jury that they had been lying to make themselves look tough.

William Palmer's wife Jane was sworn in and she described their visit to her house and their inquiries about the whereabouts of various people.

Trapp was recalled to describe in more detail for Judge Crease the relationship of the wagon road to the spot where the body was found, and also to say he saw no blood on Kelly when first examining him. Next Cavanaugh was called to the stand, and he told essentially the same story that he had for the indictment on the murder of Ussher.

Then came Bennett with his claim that Archie was sixteen, the purpose of this testimony being to discredit any claim that might be made about Archie's infancy. Of course, if Bole could have shown beyond doubt that Archie was not over fourteen at the time of the alleged crimes, his chances would be dramatically increased. Even though the Crown prosecutors had succeeded in discounting any such claim in the first trial, they were guarding against it again.

Edwards related some background about Ussher, then again recounted the capture and the condition of Kelly's body when it was brought into town. He had stripped and examined the body of Kelly and found the bullet wound in the stomach, with the bullet lodged under the skin at the back in a horizontal direction from where it had entered. The second bullet had hit the abdomen and passed through the body in a slanting direction. Either bullet would have killed him. Kelly's clothes had been destroyed.

"It's unfortunate that this was done," remarked the judge. "It so often happens that important evidence is carelessly disposed of like this. You would have been wise to keep the clothing."

"My Lord, the people of Kamloops had no expectations at that time that the murderers of sheepherder Kelly and Constable Ussher would be given a regular trial."

Palmer testified that on his way to Kamloops that day he'd seen Kelly.

At this point Harrison attempted to introduce a statutory statement made by Charlie to JP Clement Cornwall after the capture, but a vigorous objection by Bole resulted in its withdrawal.

Basil Chillihitzia was sworn in and, through an interpreter, Tilman Herrington, said he knew the prisoners and knew that the initials "A.J.H." on the pistol on exhibit stood for Alexander Joseph Hare. He also told them he owned the cabin in which the outlaws had been besieged by the posse. After the capture, he had entered the cabin to find it a shambles, with the hole dug in the ground, and had seen the watch chain, Hare's pistol, and a bowie knife.

The Crown ended its case with McLeod, who said he had known Kelly since April 15, 1877, had known him in Ireland, and that they had been fellow passengers to New York. He said the silver Waltham watch taken from the McLeans after capture had belonged to Kelly.

Again the defence offered no evidence, though Bole this time gave a dramatic and forceful address, emphasizing the doubts raised by Crown witness testimony.

McCreight gave a lengthy summation, after which Crease gave an even lengthier summation and charge to the jury.

## [67]

NEW WESTMINSTER
Tuesday, November 16, 1880, 11:00 AM

The boys were placed in the dock for sentencing. The jury had retired at 9:30 PM the previous night. Everybody, except Crease, waited in the courtroom expecting a fast verdict. The boys, too, remained in the dock, occasionally muttering among themselves and letting out a brave guffaw to show they couldn't care less about the result. The jury was gone a surprisingly long hour and a quarter before returning with the verdict.

"After a very careful but painful consideration of all the evidence placed before us, we find the prisoners at the bar, Allen McLean, Charlie McLean, Archie McLean and Alexander Hare, each and all, equally guilty of the wilful murder of James Kelly."

The foreman then thanked the judge for providing the jury with comfortable quarters during the trial.

Now, the boys awaited Crease and the inevitable sentence. Alex

Hare had changed places and stood second in the dock —he had previously stood at the lower stand at one end. He now stood between Allen and Archie. They waited patiently and sombrely —some took it as an air of unconcern —as the judge looked down at them.

"Do you have anything to say why the judgment of the court should not be pronounced upon you for the murders of Constable John Ussher and James Kelly?"

He was greeted with a silence that lasted several seconds.

"Allen, I presume you are mute by intention."

Allen looked angrily at Crease. "I have nothing to say."

The sentence: "That you be taken from this place to whence you came, and from thence to a place of execution and there to be hanged by the neck until dead. . . . May God have mercy on your souls. . . . You have had benefit of able and warmhearted counsel."

The courtroom remained hushed while Crease paused before adding, "Sentence will not be carried out before Monday, January 17, 1881, so that there will be ample opportunity for the exercising of the pardoning power by the governor-general, if he should deem it just."

As they were removed from the courtroom, Allen looked at Crease again, nodded and said, "Thank you."

## [68]

NEW WESTMINSTER
December, 1880

In legal circles, there was a faction that supported Bole's argument that the second trial represented a violation of double jeopardy. The possibility of such an opinion being upheld made many people shiver. The McLeans and Hare might still go free, despite twice being convicted and sentenced to death.

Bole, indeed, pressed his point to the State Department in Ottawa. As a matter of fact, though, chances of upsetting the second trial were slim.

The only sure way out for the boys was to escape. In their anger and rebellion against confinement, they kept the guards hopping. They made a point of giving the jailers a rough time and took every chance to initiate something that might develop into an escape. Archie continually threatened the guards and one day wielded a bucket at one of them before being subdued by several others. Allen's determination had been demonstrated long ago. His mind was always working on new schemes. Through his contact with the chain gangs lodged in the jail with them, he got hold of a knife and figured, when the time was right, to sink it in whichever guard happened to be unlucky enough.

When Moresby came by himself one day to let the boys out to exercise, Allen's chance came. He concealed the knife up his shirt sleeve. Unfortunately, Moresby let Allen out of his cell first. Allen could have used some help but after he had finished with Moresby he would take the keys and let the others out. Moresby was crafty; he always made sure the boys had no advantage in numbers when out of the cells.

As the warden stood by the cell door, Allen shuffled out as if to go past him. Suddenly he fell backwards against Moresby, starting to whip around as he did so. But the warden was too quick. Before Allen could even draw the knife, Moresby gave him a violent shove forward, pushing him several feet out of slashing distance. The warden pulled his revolver and levelled it at Allen.

"Get back in your cell, Allen," he ordered.

"I won't!" Allen screamed in frustration. "Shoot! Shoot, you sonofabitch, shoot!"

They stood staring at each other. Any false move would bring a shot from Moresby's pistol. Prisoners in the cell block watched through the doors in silent amazement.

"Get the bastard, Allen!" Archie shouted. Though he could not clearly see the activity from his position, he knew what was going on. "You can do it!"

For a moment, Allen teetered on the edge of making a desperate lunge at Moresby. The weight of the irons would make it almost suicide. His jaws clenched and his eyes narrowed as Moresby looked at him steadily, gun ready.

Allen straightened up and walked back into his cell, resisting the urge to try something as he went by. Moresby backed away until Allen was inside the little confinement room, then slammed the door shut and locked it.

But Allen by no means gave up after that, and neither did Charlie, Archie or Alex. They wanted to live. And they wanted to get back to Kamloops and settle a few scores. They had a common dream of riding back up through the Nicola, maybe with a dozen or so other breeds (not those cowardly black Siwashes) and putting the whole country into a panic. Think of the looks on their faces when they heard the words: "The McLeans have escaped! They're coming!" Nobody would stop them.

They had a lot of free time in their cells, and didn't spend it idly. They sharpened up the ends of nails, flattened out the handles of tin cups and honed the edges, and made storage places for their weapons. But the chain gangs, who went out to work on roads and sidewalks, remained the real hope —they had access to the outside world. Allen, after the unsuccessful effort with Guaymas and with the knife against Moresby, befriended a couple of the other prisoners enough so that they smuggled in knives and another file that could be used for getting rid of the irons.

December 8 passed without incident, but the province remembered the violence that had marked those same days a year ago. When Christmas came, it had been a year since these four desperate youths had been locked up in those same small cells.

Despite the boys' continuing attempts to escape and their frequent bad conduct, William and Mary Anne Moresby's small son Willy was sometimes allowed to visit with the condemned men. Archie, in particular, took to the lad and would chat with him like an older brother.

Bole continued to work diligently to stave off execution and, if possible, to have the death sentence commuted. Crease, though, was making it as difficult as he could. In his formal report to Ottawa, Crease wrote, "There only remains the references to His Excellency to pass upon the Case in exercise of the blessed gift of Mercy, and deeply pained and grieved I feel to be unable, conscientiously, to pray for the shedding of one scintilla of its rays upon the heads of any one of these unhappy hardened men." Ottawa was nervous about executing a boy of Archie's age, but Crease was insistent that an example must be made. As 1880 ended, the boys began to feel an urgency to carry out their escape. It had to be soon if it was to be.

The schemes kept coming – and failing. John Henry Makai was a Kanaka (a Scotch-Hawaiian half-breed) serving a two-month sentence for selling liquor to the Indians. If Makai was not particularly interested in getting back at the white man, he was interested in money. For a hundred head of cattle and forty horses, he would try almost anything.

It was a surprised Moresby who received a request from Makai that he be allowed to be the executioner when the three McLeans and Hare had run out of reprieves.

Makai was told a regular executioner would probably be employed but the warden would think about it. The guards kept a close ear and a watchful eye on conversation and activities in the cell block for the next few days. Finally a stoolie explained Makai's request.

If the bootlegger had been appointed executioner, he would have cut the ropes almost through when pinioning the condemned men prior to their being led to the scaffold. As they entered the courtyard, they would have shucked their bonds and made a run for it, depending on the element of surprise. If that chance didn't come, the hanging ropes themselves would be cut almost through as they were positioned around their necks. When the traps dropped, the ropes would break, the prisoners would drop to the ground and shake loose the bonds tying their hands. Makai would toss them what weapons he could have obtained, and they would all escape. Nobody would have the presence of mind to be able to stop them in a situation like that. For this, Makai would get his one hundred head of cattle and forty horses from Hector McLean (a chance, perhaps, for Hector to redeem himself). When confronted with the story Makai confessed. A search of Makai's cell resulted in the discovery of two knives.

Frequent searches of the cells of Hare and the McLeans continued. Often knives or weapons they had fashioned were found.

## [69]

NEW WESTMINSTER JAIL
Thursday, January 20, 1881

Bole ran out of appeals and challenges. A reprieve to January 31 had been granted to allow communication with Ottawa, but the governor-general confirmed the death sentences. Father Edward Horris, assigned to minister to the condemned men, wrote Crease asking if it was true.

"You would oblige me very much if you could inform me as to what you think will be the fate of the three McLeans and Hare. Some say they will be sent to the Penitentiary, some or rather others say not. As I am at present charged with the onus of preparing them for their fate, and the time named for their execution is drawing near you would confer a great favour if you can comply with my request."

On January 19, Crease replied. "I cannot conceive a more painful thing than to hold out hope where, I believe, there is none whatever. Now, I have received express information from Ottawa that those murderers 'are to be executed'.... You asked me and I promised to tell you their fate. That is their fate."

He underlined the last sentence. There would be no more reprieves.

On this day, a day later, Allen was led to the office of the sheriff.

"Good morning, Allen," Moresby greeted him from behind his desk. "Time for a change of clothes. Take off the irons and strip him," he told the two guards.

The rigging and leather straps were unfastened from the irons to allow the change.

"I think I can undress myself, jailer," said Allen. He was mad because Moresby wouldn't even allow them knives to eat with anymore. "Don't worry about us trying to kill ourselves. We'll meet our fate like men. If I wanted to commit suicide I could easily tear my shirt up and hang myself."

When the change of clothing had been made and the irons were back on, Moresby asked Allen to sit down.

"Your day of execution has been fixed for the 31st of January, Monday week, at eight o'clock in the morning."

That was eleven days, a week and a half.

"Have you any word to send to your friends and relatives?" Moresby asked.

Allen's voice was subdued, but steady. "I knew it must come some time. You will write to Hector and tell him not to take revenge on Palmer or anyone else for our death. It can't be helped now. Tell him to do nothing, as we died perfectly resigned to our fate."

As Allen was talking, Archie was brought in.

Telling a man when he would die was a tough thing to do. Telling a child was even tougher. Moresby took the most humane route, simple and direct.

"No, I've nothing to say or send my friends," was Archie's angry reply to a question about letter writing. His chest heaved at the news of his execution date, but his was not the reaction of a boy in his mid-teens. "They've done nothing for me and I wouldn't care if all my friends got hung." And he turned and stalked out heavily in his irons, the guards following him closely.

Charlie's face paled when he received the news, but he said nothing. Alex Hare, like Archie, acted almost as though he didn't realize what was being said. But he had no comment on it, and left quietly.

On his way back to his cell, Allen was downcast and quiet, saying nothing to the guards until they approached his cell door once again. Then he thought of something.

"Green, ask Moresby to please write to my wife in the Upper Country and tell her it is my dying wish that she should take good care of the children."

Then he walked into the cell that had been his home – his last home – for over a year.

Later, he told Horris that he was thinking of suicide rather than letting his life be taken on the gallows. He believed the other boys felt the same.

Horris and Father Eugene Casimir Chireuse had visited the condemned men frequently, trying to bring them peace before they met their end, and to show them the way to repentance. Horris, a fifty-one-year-old Irishman, had already been in B.C. for fifteen years and was well-known for his religious work. Chireuse, his clean-shaven young companion, had been ordained an oblate priest in his native France only a year and a half before. He'd left for B.C. a short time later, by way of the Isthmus of Panama, in company with Father Jean-Marie LeJeune of Kamloops. Father Chireuse was twenty-six.

The New Westminster Jail (*BCARS, HP9355*)

They had a difficult job. The boys didn't accept their fate easily — they so desperately wanted their freedom to carry out revenge on those they felt had done them wrong. One evening, the guards heard a great deal of excited conversation going on among the four of them but, of course, when they entered the cell block to check, all was quiet. But Horris, when he came to see the four the following day, was asked to find out their intentions, a search of the cells having produced nothing unusual. The priest emerged from his visits with more of the knives, sharpened nails and tin-cup handles. The boys would defy their jailers and anyone else they thought responsible for their predicament, but they would not defy a priest of their own Catholic religion.

Horris was appalled at Allen's suggestion of suicide. It required a stern lecture about the gift of life, a gift that no one has the right to take away, even from himself. To do so would be to deny oneself the glory of being with Him in Heaven, and to be punished with eternal damnation and suffering in Hell. They must have faith, and repent. That was the only answer.

Allen was reluctant to give up even the option of choosing when to die. The priest had learned much about him in the few weeks he'd come to counsel the outlaws. Allen was a brave but illusion-harbour-ing and stubborn man who forever dreamed of becoming someone important. He wanted to be a person everyone knew about, and a person people listened to.

That was really true of all the boys, though perhaps in varying degrees and for varying reasons. Certainly, the unkind treatment of the McLeans' sister was part of the reason for their rebellion, and this and other grievances — some legitimate, some not — made them hate easily and transform their emotions into a general hostility to the organized world around them. All the Nicola ranchers were bad, and anyone who had anything to do with the trials — except their own lawyers — were bad. Poor Allen was suffocating from a desire to revenge himself on those who had prevented him from attaining his dreams. What was Scottish and what was Indian in his makeup could equally have conspired to produce his downfall.

Alex was a different sort. Through his limited education and own natural intelligence he more clearly realized the distinction between right and wrong than did the McLeans. But he didn't care. When not trying to blame his troubles on the McLeans, he, at times, liked to flaunt his committing of obviously wrongful acts. He was moody, shifting from periods of reason and consideration to flashes of rage and cruelty. If it was a sin to take a life he supposed there was no hope for him anyway, he told Horris matter-of-factly. And maybe he didn't want to repent. No doubt at the time he very much meant it, partly because he didn't feel like admitting a mistake.

Charlie, as usual, was quiet, and on the edge of deep despair. Now that there no longer seemed any hope, he tried hard to reconcile himself to death. Near to tears, he told the priest to have patience. He wanted to feel sorrow for what he'd done, but he couldn't. When he was thrown in jail in Kamloops without even a trial, Tait had felt no sorrow. When his sister had been wronged and made pregnant, who felt sorrow? When his father died and they had had to feed themselves from the time they could walk, nobody had cared. It was hard to repent when no one had repented back.

Archie would never quit believing he could get out of it. He'd brag about being brave, even though he was just a kid, still using talk the other three had long ago abandoned. Then he'd insist he was only fourteen at the time of the killings.

## [70]

NEW WESTMINSTER
Friday, January 28, 1881

None of the McLeans did much letter writing. Since Allen and Charlie couldn't write themselves, they had to get in an amanuensis to do it for them. Allen did have a letter written to Moresby's wife, thanking her for her kindness in singing and reading to them in their cells. And, on this day, three days before they were to be hanged, Allen dictated a letter to a friend serving time in the provincial penitentiary.

*When you get out of prison don't go into bad company. If you happen to
see some poor devil drunk when you are round, think of your poor
friend Allen, and say a prayer and go about your own business.*

*Look round, my dear friend, and see what we have brought on
ourselves. But what is done is done. If the past is bad, we can make
the future good; so now let yourself commence and do the will of
God. It is never too early to commence.*

*Do remember me in your prayers. I am sure I will not forget you
when I am in Heaven. We part for a while, but will meet again, and
I hope it will be in a better place than this earth.*

*When you get out keep an eye on my children and always think of
your friend Allen; and let God's will be done – for what He does is
always the best.*

Nick Hare must have been surprised to receive a letter from his
condemned son. Since Alex had been thrown off the ranch at Cherry
Creek, he hadn't gone near his father. But this was a time to say what
needed to be said.

*Dear Father,*

*I have a favour to ask of you, and I am sure you will not scorn a
truly penitent son. I ask you to pardon me for all the evil that I have
done you, whether directly or indirectly. Now my dear father, I am
sure you will grant me this favour.*

Father Horris had reason to be encouraged, for as the fatal day
approached the boys seemed finally to be seeing the error of their ways.
If they had been set free at this moment, they might well have immediately returned to their path of vengeance, but, now that they saw
there was no escape, they began accepting the teaching of religion and
hoping for forgiveness. The voice of God was making itself heard.

Allen was making definite efforts to overcome his hatreds and
passions for revenge so that he might meet his fate calmly and man-
fully. His drive for revenge was now being overcome by a drive to die
with honour. He listened carefully to all that Father Horris had to say.

Peace finally seemed to come to Charlie. In these final days, he
became resigned to his death, accepting it as repayment of a debt,
and seeming happier for it.

For Archie it was still hard, but he too tried. Only now did he begin
to realize he was going to die, and started preparing himself mentally.

But the greatest change of all came in Alex Hare. He had been the
most stubborn of the four. He was also the most sarcastic and cynical.
His grudges died hard. He still blamed Hector McLean for not helping

them escape the law and harboured dislike of Allen for misleading them. He changed his feelings over the weekend before the thirty-first; he was smart enough to realize the futility of his prejudices. He was going to another judgment and might as well quit fighting the battles of life. Thus his stubborn rebelliousness waned, his actions became more controlled and steady.

All of them were determined to stand on the gallows with courage.

## [71]

NEW WESTMINSTER JAIL
Sunday, January 30, 1881, noon

Since early morning, passers-by outside the jail walls, as well as prisoners, had heard the noise of construction as timbers were sawed and assembled. Charlie wanted no part of seeing the scaffold, but Allen asked Moresby if he could look at it, and he, Archie and Alex were led out into the jail yard. There in the northeast corner was the gallows. This walk toward it was the same they would take tomorrow morning; it was both eternal and frighteningly short.

The scaffold was a formidable structure, towering above them as they stopped in front for a moment. Nine feet off the ground was the platform where they would spend the last seconds of life. A heavy iron bar ran under the long trap, so that a lever pressed by the hangman would drop the prisoners simultaneously.

Allen went up on the platform and looked up at the overhead beams and the bolts from which the ropes would suspend. Then he bowed his head, closed his eyes, and prayed silently: "Oh, Lord, I have sinned terribly. Please help me and give me strength tomorrow."

Moresby was standing beside him.

"Mr. Moresby," said Allen, "That's a fair piece of work and well put together."

Archie and Alex stood underneath the platform where the traps would be sprung.

Alex stuck out a hand to Archie, and as his friend took it to shake, he said, "Arch, under here we'll meet again and bid a last goodbye to one another."

That afternoon Allen spent his time washing and grooming himself and sitting patiently while a guard shaved him. He directed the "barber," who methodically trimmed the beard around the edges and evened it out. After washing he dressed in his suit, vest and best shirt, polished his boots and slicked back his thick, curly black hair.

Father Horris, Father Chireuse and two Sisters of St. Ann visited all of them to listen and to offer strength and consolation, but there wasn't much talking to do.

Mary Anne Moresby came to pay them a surprise visit. She sang for them once more and read a little poetry. When she left, reluctantly, her eyes were brimming with tears, tears for four outlaws.

In the evening they were allowed to visit together and have dinner. All of them, especially Allen, dug into the steak and potatoes as if they'd just put in a hard day's work on the ranch. The tension whetted their appetites, as with a man who chain smokes out of nervousness. They were allowed a bit of wine with the meal and this accented the taste.

Afterwards they sat back and relaxed for the few minutes allowed them. It was the first time they'd all sat down as a group alone for a long while. They probably talked about the good times, and about the need to be brave, and to die with honour, not the way Johnny Ussher had died, begging for his life. Perhaps the McLeans and Hare called off their feud, for grudges were of no purpose now. Perhaps they shook hands and resolved to die friends.

No one can know what went through the minds of these four condemned young men that night, each alone once more in his cell. Alex Hare probably thought about Annie McLean and, no doubt, about John Andrew Mara. Probably about his father, too, and about the strange circumstances that had brought him to this fate, about how, but for timing, he might have been somewhere else that day instead of at the campfire on Brigade Hill, when Ussher arrived with his posse. Would Ussher have lived, or would Archie and his brothers have killed him anyway? Who could say what might have been. Had he and Archie not happened to go to the Cache Creek boarding school at the same time, they might never even have met. The big, two-storey school was a crazy place, less important as an educational institution for the four dozen ranchers' children who boarded there than as a heavy consumer of local farm produce and merchants' wares. The children, mostly teenagers, broke up the furniture and smashed the dishes just as fast as they could be replaced. The principal had foolishly thought strict moral conduct could be upheld by bolting the inside of the girls' dormitory doors; when the board of trustees found out the girls were removing the bolt every night all hell broke loose. It was quite a scandal. But the school was where Alex had learned to read and write. Archie wasn't as good a pupil, but he'd enjoyed dime novels about Jesse James and his exploits robbing banks, stage coaches and trains. Maybe that's where Archie got some of his crazy ideas. In real life, of course, Jesse James was being constantly hounded by the law now, his best years past. He wasn't everything the dime novelists pretended he was, but he wasn't in jail waiting to be hung.

Archie's concern was to die like a man. Everyone had talked about his youth, had argued about whether he was fourteen or fifteen on the day they'd killed Ussher and Kelly. But now his age didn't matter. He was going to be hanged like the rest. He'd acted like a man when they'd killed Ussher. Neither he nor Alex had expected anything like what had happened. Both were excited and scared at the same time — here was Ussher, the law, and there was Alex sitting on him like he was butchering a calf. Archie comes out to help and doesn't know anything but that Ussher and Palmer have betrayed them. And that Allen is yelling to shoot. And then Ussher is dead.

There were people who were sleeping well tonight, content in knowing the McLeans would be dead in the morning. But there were others, like Margaret McLean, who wouldn't be sleeping at all. Though she had a brood of her own (her sixth child was born back in November) she'd always treated Archie as though he were one of her favourites. There were times when Ussher or the special constables would come around Alex's and Margaret's place on the North Thompson looking for Archie. Margaret would shove him under her bed and look innocent, brew the law a coffee and feed them a little cake and send them on their way, and they'd be happy just to have visited her. And they'd forget all about even looking to see if Archie's horse was there. There were days of just lazing around the ranch, away from his mother and all her talk about standing up to everybody and his dog. Just sitting out on the steps or laying on the grass feeling the heat of the sun beat down on his face, looking up at the sky. There were good times with Annie, and Charlie, and Allen, and Hector and Alex and even the half-brothers like Donald Jr. with his fiddle. Archie was not going to cry in the morning.

## [72]

NEW WESTMINSTER JAIL
Monday, January 31, 1881, 5:30 AM

Moresby awoke them one by one, clanking open each cell door and telling them it was time to get up. They had all slept well, and were slow to rouse, though Charlie was already awake.

A blacksmith came in and took the iron bracelets off their wrists and ankles.

Horris and Chireuse arrived, dressed in their many-buttoned black robes. Each had a large, ornate cross hanging around his neck.

The priests spoke first with Allen, saying good morning, assuring him of their support, and of God's, and asking if there was anything he wanted to say to them. No, said Allen, he and the boys would say what they had to say on the scaffold.

The doomed men were given a breakfast of buttered toast and coffee, which was wolfed down quickly. They were then brought together for pinioning, and, at a few minutes to eight, the hangman came in to do his job. He clumsily went about the job of fastening their hands in front, and binding their arms to their sides by means of leather straps passing around their bodies above the elbows. It took longer than he had expected.

"What's your name?" Allen asked him, as the man fumbled with the elbow and hand straps, which had been specially made and were supposed to be strong and easy to place.

"Ed O'Brien," the executioner replied.

"How much they paying you for this?"

O'Brien directed a questioning look at Moresby, who kind of shrugged.

"Two hundred dollars," O'Brien told Allen.

"Well, you'll earn it, even with the poor job you're doing so far. I just hope you hang people better than you tie them up."

When O'Brien had finally finished, and there was nothing left to do but to lead the prisoners to the scaffold and have done with it, Allen asked Moresby, "What time is it now?"

Moresby took out his watch and looked at it. "Just after eight o'clock."

A little behind schedule. Allen thanked O'Brien for his incompetence.

They lined up as if in a parade. As they were doing so, Charlie remarked to Chireuse, "I'm afraid, Father, but I can do what is expected of me."

Chireuse assured him the Lord would give him courage.

The procession was formed with the executioner in front, followed by New Westminster Sheriff James Morrison and prison surgeon Dr. Charles Trew side by side. Behind them were Superintendent Todd, and Moresby, then Fathers Horris and Chireuse. Following the two priests were Allen and Archie, with a policeman on each side, then Charlie and Alex, each flanked also by a policeman.

A small group of spectators had been gathered at the gallows since 7:30. They included Inspector of Penitentiaries Dr. William Walker, Dr. L.R. McInnes, Deputy Attorney-General Eli Harrison, members of the press, the scaffold contractors, and a few leading citizens.

It was a cold, blustery morning. Though it was after eight o'clock, a grey light was just beginning to flood the city. The ground was almost clear of snow; a light but cold wind blew against the faces of the prisoners as they walked steadily and calmly toward the gallows.

The pungent smell of chimney smoke was in the air.

As the procession approached the scaffold, the eyes of all those assembled were upon the four boys. They said goodbye to those near them as they passed. Todd and some of the others stopped in front of the gallows, but Allen, with Archie beside him, led the way unhesitatingly up the steps to the platform. They were shown where to stand on the scaffold, over the trap door. Alex was placed on the west end, with Charlie and Allen in the middle, then Archie. They appeared resigned and unconfused. They understood what was about to happen.

"Remember all we have talked about," Father Horris told them. "God loves you and needs you with Him."

Moresby asked them if they had any final words.

Alex, his face slack and lifeless, could not stop the tears from coming to his eyes, and he tried to wipe them away now with his shoulder. He looked down at the stoney faces of those watching below, seemingly looking for anyone he might recognize.

"I wish to ask forgiveness for my sins," he heard himself say. His throat was probably tight and aching, and he trembled. He raised his voice, "And I wish to forgive those who have wronged me. I forgive everyone and thank everyone for their kindness. I am guilty of the crimes laid to my charge, and justly deserve the impending punishment. I hope . . ." He paused to control his voice. "I ask Our Lord to forgive me and to accept me into His Kingdom."

He stilled and stared down at the trap under his feet.

Charlie spoke quietly with ashen lips, heavy beads of sweat forming on his sheet-white face despite the coldness of the air.

"I truly and sincerely ask forgiveness for my sins. I want to die a good soldier of God. I have tried my damnedest to repent for my sins, like Father Horris and Father Chireuse say I should, and I'm sorry. I'd like to thank Father Horris and Father Chireuse for their unselfish help which they gave me and my brothers and Alex these past weeks. They have been a big help." He said Norman Bole was a good lawyer, even if he'd lost.

Then he recited the prayer of forgiveness he had chosen and memorized: "Oh, Jesus Christ, thou lovest me so much! I love thee all I can! I am sorry, for all the sins I have made. I will not sin any more. Do have mercy on me!"

It was Allen's turn. "For the honour and glory of God I acknowledge my guilt," he said, speaking rapidly. "I forgive everyone from my heart, even my executioner, and I humbly beg of Almighty God to forgive me. May our friends and relatives attempt no revenge on our behalf. Thank you to those who have helped us. I am prepared to die. May everyone know that we died like McLeans, realizing our sins and content in the knowledge that Jesus Christ is our Saviour."

Archie, meanwhile, had appeared his natural self. He stood steady and untrembling on the trap, but he spoke quietly.

"I am here today to die, and I accept my fate willingly. There are others who should be dying, but I have been convicted by the courts and by God, so I'll go along with it. It'd be best if we all parted on good terms. So Lord," he added, "here I am, at Your mercy. Take me and I hope You know what You're getting, and that I can do better for You than things turned out down here."

Horris summarized Archie's comments for those standing below who had not been able to hear, then stepped forward with a cross and held it up for each of the four to kiss. They shook hands with the priests, with Moresby and with Morrison.

"Remember me to little Willy," Archie asked of Moresby.

O'Brien now secured the nooses around their necks, the feel of the coarse, thick rope no doubt adding yet another new sensation to the strange mixture of fear and resignation that must be sweeping through their bodies. When O'Brien approached Allen, the executioner hesitated and averted his eyes.

"Do your work, hangman, I forgive you," Allen told him. And, for a reason he might not even have understood himself, except that he wanted to show that his previous words had been sincere and that he remained unafraid, Allen held out a hand.

O'Brien reluctantly took it and moved it limply, though they couldn't grasp in a true handshake because of the straps holding Allen's arms tight to his side. Alex Hare also offered a hand when his own noose was being adjusted.

"Warden Moresby, please forgive me for all the trouble I've caused you," Allen added as the officials were preparing to leave the scaffold.

O'Brien took out the white hoods and quickly pulled one down over Alex's face. The gesture surprised Alex, and he turned his head beseechingly.

"Goodbye," he said to the others, through the cloth. "*Nika nanitch mika alto.* I'll see you soon."

Charlie looked neither left nor right as O'Brien placed the hood over his face, but stared straight ahead over the heads of the people below.

Archie looked at Allen. Archie still wasn't crying. Allen looked back at his kid brother, smiling a smile that said, "You're brave, Archie, I'm proud to be your brother."

Then Allen's own face was covered with a hood, then Archie's.

O'Brien moved past them toward the other end of the scaffold. There was a ringing in the distance.

"What is that?" The hood muffled Allen's voice.

"What is it?" he shouted. "What is that noise?"

Father Horris had approached the scaffold below Allen and

strained to hear. "What do you say, Allen?"

"That noise."

"Those are the bells of the Roman Catholic Church."

Moresby looked at his watch. It was 8:30. O'Brien positioned himself at the hand lever.

From the foot of the steps, Chireuse cried out, "*Courage, mes enfants, courage!*"

Sheriff Morrison nodded at O'Brien. The executioner pulled the lever and the trap dropped.

Only Charlie struggled for a moment, then was still. The bodies were left to hang for an hour, as was customary, so that there could be no doubt. They were then removed and autopsies were performed. A jury was empanelled for an inquest, and the verdict was delivered.

The bodies were then coffined and transported out of the jail to the cemetery on Douglas Street for burial. The execution cost the taxpayers $533 in labour and materials.

# Part 4

SHOOTOUT ON THE RESERVE

KAMLOOPS INDIAN RESERVE
Saturday, October 29, 1887, 10:30 PM

Hector McLean heard hoofbeats in his sleep, heavy hoofbeats of a horse being ridden hard and fast. Then there were voices, excited talk, and yelling. And then gunshots. It wasn't a dream.

He was lying there in Boney's house after visiting and smoking with old Louis, the chief. Though Hector didn't live on the reserve, he often visited there. The reserve was huge, but the village was tiny. It consisted of a row of log cabins strung like beads along a road on either side of St. Joseph's Church, built on the spot once used by Jean Baptiste Lolo, the famous man they called St. Paul. On this particular day, Hector was breaking a colt for a rancher on this side of the river and so stopped by Louis' house on his way back, and they'd sat there for awhile, smoking and passing the time, Louis with his long grey hair, thin mustache and goatee, talking in Shuswap. To his own people, the chief was known as Hlihlehkan, but to the whites he was Petit Louis, or just Louis. After awhile Hector had decided to go stay at Boney's, near the chief's house.

When the sound of the horses and the shouting interrupted his sleep, Hector went outside. There was quite a racket going on. Louis was in front of his house, hollering at one of his Indian constables, who spurred his horse and took off down the road. A second constable galloped by a few seconds later.

Hector asked Louis, in Shuswap, what was happening. It was Alex, said Louis — he was drunk and shooting up the place. Hector should go to town and bring help.

Alex was Hector's nephew, one of Donald Jr.'s boys. His full name was Alexander Patsa McLean, the middle name after the chief who preceded Louis. He was in his twenties, lived on the reserve with his wife Maggie and three children — the youngest not even a year old — and was something of a wild man. When he got drunk, he got mean. Hector wasn't a model citizen either, but he too was married, having tied the knot with Annie McIvor just three and a half months after his three brothers and Alex Hare were hanged. Annie was the daughter of John McIvor, a long-time Hudson's Bay Company employee, friend of the late Donald McLean, one-time neighbour of Nick Hare, and now a rancher on the North River. Annie and Hector had a six-year-old son of their own, Archie, named of course, in honour of the youngest McLean who had died on the gallows.

Hector knew he'd better hurry. When Alex got drunk, and when he started shooting, he could get himself and everybody else in a lot of trouble.

KAMLOOPS INDIAN RESERVE
Saturday, October 29, 1887, 10:40 PM

It had been a long day for Alexander Patsa McLean. That morning he and another Indian from the reserve, Philip Tomah, had tied their horses up at the river and crossed over into Kamloops on the little ferryboat owned by Chief Louis. Alex was returning a blanket he'd borrowed from a Chinaman named John Lee. On the way they stopped at a bootlegger's house just on the other side of the river and ordered some whiskey. When they got back from John Lee's the bottle was there. Alex and Philip drank it down and Alex paid the bootlegger, Ah Loy, another dollar for another bottle. That was soon gone, too. Then, another dollar, and another bottle. Finally they headed for home, having made a serious dent in the bootlegger's whiskey supply, and feeling good. When they got back across the river, Philip's horse was missing, so they both got on Alex's horse and rode to the village. Alex galloped around and started firing off his pistol to let people know he was having a good time. That's when Louis sent the constables after them, and that's when Hector started for Kamloops to get the B.C. provincial policeman, Bill Dodd.

It was awkward riding double, so Alex and Philip decided they would borrow a horse from Lazar Sikes. While Philip was in Sikes' house, Alex stayed outside squeezing off a few more shots. Petris, a young reserve resident, came up and said he'd been sent by Louis to tell them to quieten down, and that the constables, William and Oxime, were on their way.

"Let's go home and turn our horses loose," said Alex. "We'll run away from the watchmen."

But when they got to Alex's house, Oxime was there waiting for them, so the drunken celebrants spurred their horses into the bush. Alex managed to drop his watch. Considering the watch more important than eluding the Indian constable, he reined up and got off to look for it. For a reason known only to him, it seemed like a good idea to take off all his clothes, which is what he did.

As Philip stopped to see what Alex was doing, Oxime grabbed the bridle of his horse and started walking toward the village. Seeing this, Alex jumped back on his own horse and caught up.

"Let go of that horse or I'll blow your brains out," Alex McLean told the constable as he raced by and turned around for another pass. Oxime ignored him.

"Oxime," Alex said again, "let that horse go or I'll blow your brains out."

Kamloops Indian Reserve village, shown during Passion Play in 1901 (*KMA, 758*)

Again Oxime ignored him, determinedly pulling the stuporous Philip toward the village, intending to present him to the chief for a lecture. It must have been quite a sight, a naked, drunken Indian cowboy on a prancing horse, waving a gun in the air while the subject of his threats totally ignored him. Deciding that words weren't having the desired effect, Alex stopped waving his pistol and fired it at Oxime instead. He missed once, warned him again, missed again; Oxime kept walking. "I've had this in my heart a long time and I am going to do it tonight. This is my last night!" Alex announced grandly. Finally, on the third shot, Oxime dropped like a stone, a bullet in his head about two inches above the left ear.

Petris, who had been watching the strange scene, couldn't believe it. *When I saw Oxime drop I was alone. Alex made for me and I ran. He fired at me and missed me. I thought I was a gone man and ran for the village. Alex shot at me again and just grazed my neck. I ran for home.*

Sikes ran up. Seeing Oxime on the ground he yelled, "Oh, no, Alex, you've hurt that man!" and grabbed at McLean's horse.

"Let go of my horse or I'll shoot you, too!" Alex told him.

Sikes took him at his word and ran for the bushes. McLean took a shot at him.

There's nothing like seeing somebody get shot to sober you up. Philip Tomah was ready to call it a night and go sleep it off and hope by morning it would all turn out to be a hallucination. When Alex told him to come with him, Philip refused. This vexed Alex even

Chief Louis *(KMA, 6304)*

more, and he told Philip he'd have shot him first if he'd known Philip wasn't going to go with him.

"This is the last night for you and the last night for me," said Alex McLean. "I'm going to shoot you and then shoot myself!"

Philip, following Sikes' wise example, didn't wait for Alex to prove he meant it. He whipped his horse and got out of there.

Petris, meanwhile, was still on foot, exiting the general vicinity as quickly as possible. Alex decided on the easier prey and spurred his horse after Petris. As Petris got close to his house, William, the other constable, hurried past him on foot toward McLean. Petris didn't stop.

"Is that you, William?" Alex asked when they came close.

"Yes."

Alex shot him through the heart, and William fell down grunting.

Petris and Philip reached the house about the same time. Both ran inside just as Alex McLean rode up to the door. "Philip, I know you're in that house now! It's because of you I'm going to die tonight. This is my last night. I've shot two of them already."

Those inside the house listened to the sound of Alex's horse galloping away, then went back outside. Lazar Sikes showed up with a bullet wound in his wrist, and his wife Mary took him inside to tend to it. William's body lay where he'd fallen. A little further away, Oxime's wife was cradling him in her arms. And just about every man who had a gun had loaded it up with the intention of blasting Alex McLean from his horse.

Louis somewhat belatedly showed up, having walked down the street toward the sound of the shots. He passed the mortally wounded Oxime and the stone-dead William, and called some of the boys together.

Before they could figure out a plan of attack, and before they could see him, they heard Alex returning like a midnight phantom — without clothes.

"This is the last night for me," he was shouting again. "I'm going to kill the first one I come to. I'm going to shoot all of you!"

Then, on the moonlit road, there was Alex, coming on at full speed.

"Watch him," Louis told his boys. "I don't want any of you to get killed."

Alex fired at Louis and missed as he tore past.

"What are we going to do?" asked one of the men.

There was only one thing to do. "Shoot his horse," Louis answered.

A few seconds later, there was a whole lot of shooting, then silence, then someone running towards him.

"Alex is hurt," an Indian reported. "He's shot."

## [75]

KAMLOOPS INDIAN RESERVE
Saturday, October 29, 1887, 11:45 PM

Louis was sitting on a horse, rifle across the saddle, waiting on the riverbank as Hector, Bill Dodd, Allan Walker and James McMillan pulled up in the boat. Dodd had a pair of handcuffs, a pistol and a rifle. From Kamloops, and as they came across the river, they had heard the shooting.

"Who is it?" Louis asked.

Hector identified himself.

"Come on then, it's me," the chief told them. "But keep quiet." As they got out on shore, he explained, "We've got Philip, but Alex is dropped. He fell off his horse. I don't know if he was hit or not."

They hurried to the village. In Oxime's cabin, the Indian constable lay trying to cope with his terrible head wound. The bullet seemed to have ended up somewhere in his neck.

At Louis' house, several Indians were clustered outside, acting very excited. Inside, there were a few more, including Philip Tomah. Two pairs of feet, one of them without boots, were sticking out from under a blanket.

Underneath, side by side, lay the bodies of William and Alex. There were three wounds in Alex McLean's body, one in the arm from a pistol, the other two in the body from a single rifle bullet. From the angle the bullet entered and left the body, it appeared the shooter had been above him; the fatal bullet was fired into Alex McLean after his horse had been shot out from under him.

William's face was contorted, frozen in his last earthly sensation — pain. Alex McLean was smiling.

## [76]

KAMLOOPS
Monday, October 31, 1887, 10:00 AM

An inquest into the deaths of Alex McLean and William convened with twenty-four "good men of this district." Jury members went over to the reserve to look at the bodies and walked the quarter of a mile out onto the plain where most of the shooting took place. Then they went back to the courthouse, where several witnesses, including old Louis, described the events of the previous Saturday night as best they could. The *Inland Sentinel* reporter noted that "the courtroom presented quite a picture when half a hundred Siwashes and Klootchmans seated or squatted themselves at the end of the hall, eagre [sic] to watch the proceedings."

Though everyone was certain that Alex McLean had shot Oxime and William, nobody admitted shooting Alex McLean. As far as anybody knew, he had ridden off and been gunned down, along with his horse, by men without names. One jury concluded, "that the said Alexander McLean was shot by the Indian constables in the discharge of their duty." The other jury returned a verdict "that the same William came to his death by a wound from a pistol in the hands of one Alexander McLean, who did wilfully and maliciously shoot the said William with intent; the said Alexander McLean now being dead."

The said Alexander McLean's body was claimed by his sister, Christine, who had it placed in a wagon and taken to her husband's ranch east of Kamloops. Christine, a year younger than her dead brother, had led a hard, but not uninteresting, life. She worked for a time as a cook on the ranch of Victor Guillaume, a French Canadian known generally as The Frog, who was even richer than John Andrew Mara. She was married for a short time to a man from the Kamloops Indian Reserve, Jacques Kotlinhiehlieh. Then, for several years, she lived with Preston "Bunchgrass" Bennett, a former HBC employee elected as a local member of the provincial legislature. It had not, apparently, been a totally happy relationship. Bennett, in a letter to his friend Henry Crease, the Supreme Court judge, referred to her after they split up as the "wickedest woman." When Bennett died a short time later, Christine received nothing from the estate. But she went back to Guillaume, at least twenty-five years older than she was, and married him.

Alex's children presented a problem. His widow, Maggie, had no way of looking after all of them with Alex gone. So two-year-old Cecilia was taken home with Christine. Taking in relatives was a common thing with the McLeans. Sophia, Donald McLean's widow, always had someone's youngster in her house. Earlier that year, almost twenty-three years after her husband's death, and after a four-year legal battle carried on in England, Sophia had received her inheritance. Settlement of Donald Sr.'s estate caused almost as much turmoil as his life. After his murder, when Sophia could find no will, Judge Matthew Begbie had appointed Neil McLean McArthur administrator to settle the estate, and the Hudson's Bay Company supported Sophia as beneficiary. But London wine merchant John Maclean, husband of Donald's only surviving sister Anna (John Maclean was also her and Donald's first cousin), claimed the entire estate on his wife's behalf. He contended that Donald had never been legally married and that any family he left was illegitimate. The situation was further muddied by the question of the rights of Donald McLean's first family by Ali; his son Alex (uncle of the Alex now being hauled to the Guillaume ranch for burial) sought advice on that issue but decided not to pursue it. McArthur obtained a marriage certificate to support Sophia's claim, but, convinced she could never afford the cost of proving her right to the money owed Donald by the HBC, she dropped it until 1883, finally hiring Theo Davie to resume her claim. Davie in turn hired a London law firm, and Anna Maclean renewed her own claim. At long last Sophia was granted letters of administration and became the legal beneficiary. At the last minute, in a "friendly" arrangement, she decided to give the recently widowed Anna some of the money. Anna received four hundred pounds, Sophia 1,604. It was enough to support Sophia, and her new ward, for some time.

The wagon carrying Alex McLean's body bumped its way along the road and onto the Vic Ranch. There on a hillside overlooking the South Thompson River, within sight of the place he'd been shot, another McLean was laid to rest.

# Part 5

THE COWBOY AND THE OUTLAW

LITTLE FORT, British Columbia
Wednesday, November 5, 1907, early evening

There was quite a crowd standing around at the ferry dock, watching two men. A stranger riding toward the dock might have thought the two men were engaged in some sort of primitive dance. From time to time, those in the crowd joined in. Most of them were Indians, who just happened to be there. One of the men doing the dancing was Bob Williams, a rancher and trader who ran the ferry across the North Thompson River. The other was named Stout, an American who had brought sixteen horses from North Dakota, across the line and up to Edmonton, and sold them for a nice profit. Stout, who called himself H. Stout, perhaps for Harry, or Henry, then decided to save a little more money by stealing an Indian's horse to ride home on. He headed west and south along the North River Trail, intending to pass through Kamloops, then probably on through the Okanagan and past Osoyoos into Washington. But when he stayed at Allingham's road-side house in Peavine, or Vavenby, he was recognized as the subject of an arrest notice. The proprietor, George Fennell, sent word on to Williams. So, when Stout reached Little Fort, Williams refused to take him across the river and told Stout he was under arrest.

That was the point they were now at, with Stout and Williams circling each other like wrestlers, the Indians doing their best to stay out of the way, since Stout had a gun he was trying to point at Williams, and Williams had a gun he was trying to point at Stout. They had drawn on each other at the same instant, but, with everybody milling about, it was a few seconds before either could get a clear shot. Williams was shouting at the Indians to grab Stout; the Indians were too busy trying to stay out of the line of fire to listen to him.

Stout fired first, but the kick from the pistol knocked him off balance just a bit. Being on the edge of a cutbank, he lost his footing and tumbled over. The embarrassed bandit picked himself up, crawled back up the embankment and threatened to shoot everyone there if they didn't clear out.

As one, including Williams, they backed up several paces. Suddenly Williams' hands shot out as if he were offering Stout an embrace, but, instead, he fell on his face. Stout's bullet had sliced through the aorta, and with Williams' last heartbeat Stout became a murderer.

BLACK PINES, North Thompson River, British Columbia
Monday, November 10, 1907, evening

It was dark by the time Charlie and Duncan McLean and Donald Gordon reached the ranch at Black Pines. For several days, after being sworn in as special constables, they'd tracked Stout in the area around Little Fort, back up to Peavine and Mosquito Flat, but the American was always just ahead of them. It was cold work; the first snowfall of the winter was expected any day now. Then, at Mosquito Flat that morning, they found out Stout had doubled back, stealing a canoe and heading downriver. So the trio rushed down to Black Pines to get ahead of him.

The ranch house, a big two-and-a-half-storey building with a single gable, a covered front porch and a picket fence, was on a high bank at a wide, sweeping bend in the powerful North Thompson River — still called the North Branch or North River by some. The house belonged to Alex and Margaret McLean, the parents of Charlie and Duncan. Alex, brother of Donald Jr. and half-brother to the McLean Gang, had built up the ranch during the 1890s, after getting out of the hotel business in Kamloops. There was a barn, ice house, chicken coop, other buildings, and corrals. The house itself was sturdily constructed of logs, with clapboard siding. It was a pretty spot: hayfields stretched from the house along the river bank for about three miles, and west toward the tree line. A short distance from the house, Margaret nurtured an orchard of fruit trees, watered by an irrigation system Alex had built down from the hills.

Catching criminals was not new to Charlie McLean, who was in charge of the posse. He was the opposite, in many ways, of his brooding namesake uncle, who had met such a sad end twisting on the end of a rope at the New Westminster Jail. Born only two and a half months before the other Charlie was hanged, he had grown up around Kamloops, and on the ranch at Black Pines twenty miles north of town. He was an outgoing man who found it easy to laugh, fearless like so many other McLeans, and almost too handsome for his own good. He learned to ride and rope, and to quick draw, and, though he wrangled and ran a string of pack horses and sometimes worked at the Bauman sawmill, he was often in demand for dangerous situations. When Charlie was only nineteen, there was a murder in town. The killer was a thug named Baptiste Casimir, who had terrorized people for years. Many years before, he had threatened the life of Hector McLean, who complained to justice of the peace John Edwards,

Charlie McLean, the outlaw catcher (*Nora Rothenburger*)

who, in turn sent a constable to arrest Casimir. Instead, Casimir shot at the constable, who prudently retired. In 1899 Casimir was drinking with some of his friends on the Kamloops Indian Reserve, who bet him he didn't have the courage to kill a white man. Casimir accepted the bet, rode into town, and shot down the first man he saw, who happened to be a well-known resident named Phil Walker. Charlie McLean was hired to bring in Casimir, who holed up in a cabin on the reserve. Charlie walked up to the cabin cool as a cucumber, looked into the barrel of Casimir's gun, ignored the Indian's threats, and talked him into surrendering. They hung Casimir outside the Kamloops courthouse a few weeks later.

There was even more excitement in store for Charlie and his older brother Alfred. War broke out between Britain and the Boers in 1899, and the call went out to the colonies for volunteers. When a new regiment called the South Africa Constabulary was formed, Charlie and Alfred enlisted. Alfred was taller than Charlie, almost six feet, and, though an excellent shot and not a bad rider, his ambition was to be an actor. Charlie, though, was well-suited to the situation. They spent two years in that pointless, greedy imperialist war, galloping across the veld after the Boers, fighting one bloody battle after another, learning to detest places with names like Modderfontein, Krugersdorp, and Bloemfontein. The fighting would usually begin with an exchange of heavy ordnance, but before the day was out there was almost always a close-in, desperate struggle with rifles, pistols,

Alfred McLean in his Boer War
uniform (*Pat Spiers*)

and bayonets, where you got so close to the enemy you could see the colour of his eyes, and have time to play, in the instant before one of you killed the other, guessing games about wives and children and jobs. On one such occasion, Charlie killed a young Boer when he hadn't even wanted to. It just happened, and probably he really had no choice, but the thought that he had needlessly taken a man's life haunted him ever after, waking him in a cold sweat in the middle of the night.

Alf took to the bottle whenever an opportunity presented itself, being disciplined on a number of occasions for getting drunk, for "highly irregular conduct," and for swearing at a superior officer. Despite his less-than-perfect record, he was promoted from trooper to corporal (though later demoted back to trooper). When the war ended, Alf went to Europe to join a travelling wild west show, and Charlie went home. Only a few months ago, Alf had finally come home, too, broken down with consumption.

When Bill Fernie, the police constable, heard about the murder of Bob Williams the day after it happened, he immediately hired Charlie McLean to hunt down the killer. Fernie, who also had a ranch on the North Thompson, obtained a degree of local fame himself, the year before, when he'd tracked down the "Gentleman Bandit," Bill Miner. The old train robber and two accomplices, Shorty Dunn and Louis Colquhoun, had stopped a CPR freight at Ducks, east of Kamloops, in hopes of getting a big haul. But instead of a carload of relief funds for victims of the San Francisco earthquake, they found a train with only $15.50 and a bottle of catarrh pills. Fernie tracked them to their camp not far from where the McLean Gang were captured at Douglas Lake, went for help and returned with several Mounties. After a shootout, the trio of outlaws were captured. At this moment they were guests at the New Westminster penitentiary.

After the posse's hasty ride from Mosquito Flat to Black Pines, they found only Margaret, Alf, and the younger children at the ranch. Their father was away. Alf would be of no help in the quest; he was ravaged by his mortal disease, his body weakened by chills and fatigue. His constant anguished cough was heart-breaking to hear.

There was no time for rest. Charlie, Dunc and Donald resigned themselves to watching the road and the river through the night. They didn't want Stout slipping away again.

## [79]

BLACK PINES, North Thompson River
Tuesday, November 11, 1907

There was no sign of Stout through the night. Margaret made the boys breakfast in the big ranch house while they planned their next move. Charlie decided Donald Gordon should ride north along the wagon road a few miles to look for sign, while Dunc and William Spalding Wilkie kept watch closer to the ranch. The forty-eight-year-old Wilkie was a native of Dublin who came to B.C. at age twenty, and had worked as a labourer on government public-works projects and as a cowboy for ranchers — including Victor Guillaume — all over the Interior before starting his own place on the North Thompson. Dunc McLean was married to his adopted daughter, Edith.

Charlie would help them for awhile keeping a look out for Stout; if they found nothing, he'd ride south to get Fernie, who was supposed to be coming up from Kamloops.

Alex McLean still hadn't come home. Once in awhile he would go on a bender that would last several days, and Margaret would be left to keep the ranch and farm going. Alex had led a varied life, from the days of working as an interpreter and packer with his father in the Hudson's Bay Company to ranching, then owning the Colonial Hotel in Kamloops, then back to full-time ranching. He had a sense of frontier adventure in him. He'd once kept a wild bear chained up behind the hotel for the interest of customers. One day it broke its chain but Alex lassoed him. It was a bad idea. The bear rushed him and knocked him over, mauling his foot and knee. Jim McArthur, who ran a general store, ran to help out, so the bear left Alex McLean and charged McArthur instead. As the merchant tried to get away he tripped and fell and would have been mauled as well, but J.E. Saucier, a jeweller and recent arrival from Quebec, leaped over a fence, picked up a large stick, and hit the bear on the nose. According to the *Sentinel* account, the bear was knocked unconscious, and the men quickly cut its throat. "Mr. McLean," reported the paper, "is confined to his house by his injuries."

Three years later Alex McLean, McArthur, and a couple of others —Frank Savona and Fred Griffin—embarked on an expedition three hundred miles up the North Thompson River in search of mineral deposits. They left Kamloops on horses the evening of July 30, 1890, and reached Tête Jaune Cache twenty-nine days later. Alex had travelled the route during a trip from the Cariboo to Montana seventeen years earlier, but the trails were in disuse and overgrown, making it a tough trip. While climbing a mountain for a view of the country near Tête Jaune Cache, Alex was nearly killed when he fell down a deep two-and-a-half-foot-wide fissure, but managed to grab onto a piece of rock and jam his rifle in the cleft for support; he then was able to climb out. After staking out several mica claims, the group started back on August 28, in an unseasonable, raging snowstorm, with only fifteen pounds of flour and little other food. Alex shot a grizzly bear, and the party also ate grouse, pork, porcupine, and ground hog. Two days after leaving for home, the horses of McArthur and Griffin couldn't carry them any further, so they started walking, thirty miles a day for six days. With food running low, they caught a dozen salmon at Raft River by beating them with sticks. Two hundred miles from Kamloops, McArthur and Griffin almost drowned crossing the North Thompson. Alex bought a canoe from an Indian at Clearwater and took McArthur with him the rest of the way by water, with Savona and Griffin following with the horses. Their mica finds were expected to make them all a great deal of money, but they apparently never followed up the claims.

The Colonial Hotel had been a success, boasting "an experienced whiteman cook in charge of the culinary department," the best billiard room in town, and, of course, a bar supplied "with choice liquors and best brands of cigars." But town living and hotel keeping didn't suit people used to life in the country, so Alex and Margaret rented out the Colonial, then sold it to Victor Guillaume and took over the A.J. Venn Ranch on the North Thompson, adjacent to a pre-emption they already had. It wasn't the most convenient choice: there wasn't yet a bridge between the north and south shores in Kamloops, so Alex had to hire men and drive his horses and cattle down to the west end of Kamloops Lake, cross them at Savona's Ferry, then drive them back along the north side of the lake and up the valley. What would have

Alex McLean of Black Pines
(*Pat Spiers*)

taken half an hour with a bridge took three days.

They built up an excellent ranch and farm, raising pigs and chickens in addition to the livestock, and continuing to add acreage through homesteading applications. Margaret was a sturdy, kind woman who readily fed any hungry stranger who happened by. A half-breed like Alex, she was born in Fort Kamloops, the daughter of a French-Canadian HBC labourer named Caesar Vodreaux and an Indian woman. Alex and Margaret had, all told, fourteen children. They were very much the new patriarch and matriarch of the McLean family, having succeeded Donald and Sophia in that role by virtue of their own industry and proliferation and, at least to some extent, by default. Sophia had lived her last years in a small, one-storey frame house in the west end of town, on Main Street across from the Queen's Hotel. She died there in 1902. Donald Jr., now stooped and white-haired, in his eighties, never did have much ambition, having stuck mainly to packing and guiding, and some bootlegging. His main love had always been fiddling, which he did with considerable skill, being the first choice along with his son Johnny whenever there was a dance, but he was getting too old for that now. John Allen was the only one of Donald Sr.'s sons still on the Bonaparte. He alone had stubbornly remained, working his own small ranch, marrying a woman from the Bonaparte Band and raising a small family. Hector, the last of the McLean Gang, was gone. In his later years, he had become increasingly focused on prospecting, making some significant

Margaret Vodreaux McLean

finds but, like Donald Jr., still up to his old habit of bootlegging to the local Indians to raise a little ready cash when he needed it. He and Annie divorced; she was now married to Donald Manson, the grandson of the old fur trader. Hector had also remarried, to a woman named Nancy Whycott, and they had a son George, now being raised at the huge Gang Ranch in the Chilcotin. But Hector had died this past February at the age of fifty-three.

Sadly, Alex and Margaret's children had a tendency to die young. Minnie, their first-born, was twenty when she died. Alexander died before he reached two. The first Duncan lived barely a year. Within a few short years, the second Alex Jr. would be dead of typhoid fever at thirty-two, and young Angus would cry out to his mother from his sick bed, "I don't want to die!" and she would put her arms around him, and he would be dead at just twenty-two years of age. Alf was already dying from galloping consumption. Even sister Rose, who was running a brothel in the Yukon, would die suddenly. No one could tell the future, of course, and for now, Alex Jr., Angus and Dunc had the beginnings of their own farms at Black Pines, and the younger surviving children — the second Minnie, Hugh, Cliff and Lena — were still at home. Alf had been staying at the ranch since his return from Europe. Tillie was married to George Brown, a stepson of Alex Gordon, and also lived nearby. And Charlie, though he stayed mainly in town, visited often. "Hell, kid," he'd say to a friend, "I've got to go and see Mother." He called all his friends "kid."

The morning spent waiting for Stout proved to be tedious and tiring, and unsuccessful. They found no trace of him, and at two o'clock Charlie decided to go look for Fernie. Maybe the man who had caught the famous Bill Miner would have some ideas about how to catch an unknown American killer named Stout.

## [80]

BLACK PINES, North Thompson River
Thursday, November 14, 1907, after 6:00 PM

William Spalding Wilkie managed to cut around the man on the wagon road without being seen and galloped down to the McLean Ranch, finding first Donald Gordon and then Dunc McLean. He didn't know who the man was, but he was a stranger, and he was on foot, so he was worth checking out. Donald and Dunc took a short cut through a neighbouring rancher's hayfield.

Neither of them had the rough-and-ready experience of a Bill Fernie or a Charlie McLean, but by the actions that followed you'd never know it. Donald Gordon was twenty-five, the son of Alex and Margaret Gordon, long-time friends and neighbours of the Alex McLean family. Donald was a packer and a wrangler and a pretty good cook. Dunc, twenty-one, was the comedian of the McLean family, always kidding around, always ready with a joke to suit any occasion. Everybody who met Duncan McLean took an instant liking to him.

It was getting quite dark when they came up a little behind the stranger, who was plodding along the wagon road, carrying a rifle. Donald Gordon shouted at him to stop. The stranger ignored them, carrying on down the road. Again Gordon shouted, and again. Finally, the man stopped, turned around, and came back a few steps toward them.

"Hello," said the man. "What the hell do you want?"

Gordon asked him who he was and where he was coming from. The stranger gave his name as Anderson, and said he had been working at a logging camp.

Duncan McLean covered the man with his pistol while Gordon went closer. The stranger was a small man, perhaps five feet five inches tall, only about 130 pounds. Explaining that he needed to see what he looked like, Gordon lit a match and held it to the man's face. The stranger didn't have the beard and mustache the killer was supposed to have, and instead of heavy boots he wore moccasins, but his dark red hair and a lazy eye, together with his small frame, answered the description given them of H. Stout.

The McLean Ranch at Black Pines

"I'll have to hold you till morning," said Gordon, telling Stout to hand over his weapons.

Stout surrendered the .22 rifle.

"Do you have anything else?" Gordon asked him.

"No."

But Duncan McLean, watching him closely, saw Stout start to make a move. "Throw up your hands!" he demanded.

Stout ignored him, crouched, pulled out a .44 Colt with the words, "I have another gun here!" and fired point blank at McLean.

Dunc McLean, at the same instant, was pulling the trigger of his own gun. *I fired almost as soon as the flash came. I was only a second later. I shot for his arm but missed. Donald shot almost at the same instant and I fired a second time. It was all very quickly done, only a second or two. I think my second shot struck him in the breast.*

Charlie McLean heard the shots from a little more than two hundred yards away. After going as far south as the 14 Mile House, looking for Fernie, he'd given up and ridden back to the ranch. Before he dismounted, Margaret came out and told him about the man Wilkie had spotted on the road. Charlie headed straight for them. When he got to them, he saw two men standing on the road in the dusk.

"Is anybody hurt?" he yelled anxiously as he rode up.

"We're all right, but this man is dead," Dunc answered.

The shots from Duncan McLean and Donald Gordon had hit Stout almost at the same instant, Duncan's bullet getting him in the chest, Gordon's in the neck. Stout's shot had grazed Dunc McLean's cheek, leaving a powder burn. Searching the body, they found a notebook and other papers. In a canvas money belt around Stout's waist were twelve twenty-dollar gold coins and, in one of the pockets, some bills, $330 in all. Charlie went back to the ranch for a wagon and they loaded the body into it for the trip to town.

There was a small irony in the fact that Charlie, who had so much experience with dangerous situations, wasn't in at the finish. But his brother Dunc, and Donald Gordon, had handled it with cool courage. Dunc McLean, in particular, showed amazing calm literally under fire. At almost point blank range, with a known killer shooting at him, he had the presence of mind to attempt a wounding shot to the arm. Failing in that, before Stout could get off a second shot, he instantly fired again, making no mistake. It was typical McLean mettle, but by no means ordinary, and thus a new McLean legend was born — about the day a cowboy faced an outlaw and won. This time, the McLean was on the right side of the law.

# Part 6

FAMILY HONOUR

CANADIAN FRONT LINE, Vimy Ridge, France
Easter Monday, April 9, 1917, 5:29 AM

Twenty thousand Canadian soldiers sat silently in their rat-infested, urine-soaked trenches, stretched out for four miles along the so-called Vimy Sector. Across No Man's Land, a cratered sea of mud and bones, were the Germans, behind rows of barbed wire, in their ditches, tunnels and pillboxes, facing the Canadians with rifles, machine guns, and heavy artillery. Behind them lay the dark escarpment of Vimy Ridge. For two and a half years, the German army had held it against every Allied attempt — at great cost — to take it. The French had failed, then the British. Today, after five months of preparation, the Canadian Corps would try what the French and British had failed to do.

On the left flank of the Canadian front line, the men of the Fifty-fourth Battalion, Fourth Division, awaited the signal to fix bayonets. On this northern end of the front, the first Canadian line was only seven hundred yards from the crest of Vimy Ridge. As the line extended to the south, it veered further away from the ridge, but here the Canadians and Germans were almost within talking range. Directly in front of the Fifty-fourth was the Germans' own front-line trench, and behind that the second line. Looming behind both was Hill 145, the highest point on the ridge, towering 470 feet above the trenches in which the Canadians huddled in their heavy greatcoats, trying to keep warm in the driving sleet. Hill 145 was the toughest obstacle facing the Canadian Corps, impregnated with machine-gun nests that meant quick death to any Allied soldier trying to scale it. Beyond the Hill were yet more German lines of defence. Hill 145 was assigned to the Fifty-fourth Battalion, nicknamed the Kootenays.

Waiting in the trench with the other soldiers of the Fifty-fourth was Private George McLean, loaded down with his rifle, ammunition, rations, gas mask, water bottle, shovel, and Mills hand grenades. He'd been sitting there in the muck for hours, the shots of rum being doled out by the officers, helping to stave off the cold only a little. This was a much different sort of war from the one against the Boers. In that one, George McLean had enlisted in the Canadian Mounted Rifles; though he hadn't seen much excitement, riding a horse on the open veld easily beat waiting in a stinking trench to see whether a sniper, mustard gas or trench mouth got you first. Since October, 1916, when he'd joined the 172d Battalion being recruited in the Okanagan and then being transferred to the Fifty-fourth in France, he'd been just another foot soldier in the great European stalemate between Fritz and the Allies.

All along the trenches the order finally came to fix bayonets.

## [82]

The train station, a big stone and brick building proudly pointed out by residents as proving Kamloops was no longer "a one-horse town," was unusually busy. A crowd of 250 milled around inside the wainscotted passenger terminal and outside on the platform, where the Kamloops Band blared away with peppy tunes, and a dozen Red Cross girls clutched packs of cigarettes, all waiting for the Canadian Pacific Railway steam engine to arrive.

When it finally came chugging into the station, belching great puffs of steam from its stack, the crowd quieted in anticipation. The train scraped to a stop and sat there rumbling away. A step was placed in front of a passenger car and the crowd spotted the object of its attention, a diminutive but powerfully built middle-aged man, dressed in the uniform of the Canadian Overseas Expeditionary Force. He was one of fifty-eight soldiers on the train, including three others from Kamloops, but no one was interested in them, only in George McLean. As he jumped down onto the platform, the waiting citizens of Kamloops erupted into a cheer.

George McLean was an unlikely hero. At forty-four years of age, he was also an unlikely soldier. He was barely five feet, seven inches tall, just over 150 pounds, with dark skin, jet-black hair, and soft brown eyes. Age and physical stature had had nothing to do with heroism the previous Easter Monday, when Canadian soldiers had won a glorious victory (some said the country had won more than that, had at long last achieved a true sense of nationhood). On that day George McLean won the Distinguished Conduct Medal for his actions.

> For conspicuous gallantry and devotion when dealing with enemy snipers. Single-handed, he captured nineteen prisoners, and later, when attacked by five more prisoners, who attempted to reach a machine gun, he was able, although wounded, to dispose of them unaided, thus saving a large number of casualties.

George McLean, son of
Allen, and hero at Vimy
Ridge, standing at right
(*KMA, 930*)

The official *London Gazette* citation told in clinical form what had
happened, but could not approach the horror and confusion that had
reigned during the assault on Vimy.

Those who survived the battle have used any number of compari-
sons to try to describe the sound and sight of the barrage that opened
up on the German lines at precisely 5:30 AM. A monstrous, deafening
roar, like a thousand planes and trains, dozens of volcanoes, the
Devil's fireworks, the wrath of God, a canopy of flaming steel, a scene
from Hell, the detonation of Earth itself. None of these does justice to
what faced George McLean and the thousands of other Canadian soldiers going over the top and heading into No Man's Land behind the
rolling artillery barrage coming from behind their own lines. And the
Germans, suddenly shaken out of their complacency, were answering
back. The Canadians advanced from objective to objective, from shell
hole to shell hole, as men were sliced to ribbons with machine gun
fire or blown to bits by mortars and heavy guns. All along the front,
the Canadians were bowling through first one German line, then the
next, then the next.

But not the Fifty-fourth. The German machine guns on Hill 145 continued to prattle on against the advancing Canadians, mowing down the Forty-second — or Black Watch — Battalion far to the right of the Kootenays, over in the Third Division. Fifty of them lay dead or wounded in the mud; the rest dispersed and became lost in the confusion. Immediately to the right of the Kootenays, in their own Eleventh Brigade, half the Grenadier Guards — the Eighty-seventh of Montreal — were hit. And to the left, Mississauga's Jolly Seventy-fifth remained stuck in its own assembly trenches, unable to move because the battalions in front of them were stalled. The Ottawa Thirty-eighth in the Division's centre, having swept past the Hill, found itself virtually surrounded as the German defences caved in everywhere but on the Hill. Near them the Seaforth Highlanders were pinned down between fire from Hill 145 and from a lower slope called The Pimple. The Winnipeg Grenadiers in the Division's left wing suffered heavy losses. On the Hill itself, Warden's Warriors, a B.C. battalion like the Kootenays, made it halfway up but lost every officer doing it. And the Kootenays themselves, who were supposed to relieve the Warriors and make the final assault to take the Hill, found themselves pinned down, all of their officers killed or wounded.

Within this broad stage upon which the Fourth Division struggled, many individual scenes of suffering and courage were played out, as men died and corpses piled up. One of these involved George McLean, and for his role he would be given the nickname "The German Killer." Standing on the platform of the CPR station in Kamloops while admiring citizens listened, he described what had happened next:

> There were two machine guns playing on us and one of our officers got hit. I pulled him out of the mess, and at the time I was close to the Germans' dugouts. I knew there were about sixty of the enemy there and I got hold of my bombs and just as I was in the act of pulling the pin my partner, who was close to me, got it in the head. Then I bombed them. And I bombed them again and again. I used nine bombs altogether and they ran like rabbits into their dugouts. After they ran into the dugout I kept bombing them until their sergeant-major threw up his hands shouting, "Don't throw the bomb," and I didn't. He came out of the hole and handed me his automatic pistol and asked me how many there were of us and I said there were 150.

The Mills bombs spoken of by George McLean were the size and shape of large eggs. To use one, a soldier pulled out a pin and held a lever down until he threw it. Four seconds after the lever released, the grenade exploded shrapnel all around. After the sergeant-major's surrender, the Germans came out with their hands up, shouting surrender, and McLean escorted them back to the Canadian lines.

Among the prisoners was an officer who had learned excellent English in North Dakota and was home in Germany for a visit when he was conscripted.

But McLean's day wasn't over yet. Returning to the battle, he was shot twice in the left arm, but captured five more Germans and started back to the Canadian lines with them too. When they bolted and tried to get to a machine gun nest, he killed them all. His nickname was well-earned.

At last fresh troops from the Eighty-fifth Battalion, the Nova Scotia Highlanders, were brought into the fray, Hill 145 taken, and the Canadian juggernaut rolled on. Beyond, on the Douai Plain, the German Army retreated in panic.

The ceremony at the Kamloops train station was only a brief welcome home, for the train was carrying on to the Coast, and George McLean and the other soldiers travelling with him had to be on it to report. But, designated unfit for further duty because of his bullet wounds, George McLean's army days were over. He wanted nothing more than to be a cowboy again on the Douglas Lake Ranch.

George McLean didn't go into the Great War intending to be a hero. But heroes aren't created by intent; they materialize in the worst of circumstances, when instant decisions in the face of danger save or cost lives. There were many who said McLean should have received the Victoria Cross; several were awarded for actions that day that were much less heroic.

After handshakes, words of congratulation, and more cheers, George McLean climbed back on the train clutching a pack of cigarettes and carrying with him the admiration of a community with a new hero of its own.

## [83]

MERRITT, Nicola Valley, British Columbia
Friday, September 7, 1934, morning

Sometime during the night, George McLean curled up in the bush behind a local farmer's barn to sleep. They found him there in the morning, after someone had spotted his horse tethered nearby and started looking for him. He'd spent the previous evening around town, as he often did, getting drunk. Since it wasn't yet very cold outside, even overnight, it wasn't exposure that killed him. Probably he'd passed out, thrown up and suffocated on his own vomit.

Since the war George McLean had done exactly what he wanted

to do, wrangling at Douglas Lake and other ranches in the Nicola, living in a small cabin. He was "a likeable type," and for a few beers in one of the local watering holes, he'd tell any who wanted to listen about Vimy. He might even pull out his medal for people to admire. The legend of George McLean tended to get enhanced. It became an accepted part of the story that when he'd captured the German soldiers, they'd thrown up their hands in surrender and shouted, "Me go England," and George had supposedly shouted, "You go Kingdom Come," and bayonetted all of them.

Dying there on the ground, pointlessly, alone, was a sad end for a war hero. The Canadian Legion offered to arrange a funeral service, but some Indian friends claimed the body and took it to Douglas Lake for burial instead. George McLean had never again achieved the incredible strength of character that emerged from nowhere during those few hours at Vimy, for that was impossible, and maybe he'd lived in the past ever since, but the bravery of his actions on the slopes of an ignominious ridge near the coast of France would never be forgotten. The exploit at Vimy vindicated the name of McLean, at least in the minds of those who had lived under the dark memory of that bleak winter's day when Allen McLean, George's father, had helped kill Johnny Ussher and ruthlessly murdered a sheepherder named Jim Kelly.

## [Epilogue]

KAMLOOPS, British Columbia
Saturday, May 16, 1992, 1:15 PM

"He was a good man."

Those words, spoken by George Brown, a nephew of "Uncle Cliff" McLean, were a simple but flattering eulogy for a man who had lived a simple but productive life. About two dozen people were in Schoening's Funeral Chapel that day to pay their respects to Uncle Cliff, who had died two days before at the age of ninety-eight. George spoke of Uncle Cliff's generosity, his shyness, and his gently kidding sense of humour. But, spoken from the heart, to say "he was a good man" seemed to me the highest form of compliment that could be paid to anyone in summing up a lifetime.

Afterward, as we drove home, my mother said with sadness, "He was the last of the McLeans."

I thought that was an odd thing to say, since she and several of her brothers and sisters, and their children and grand-children, and even great-grandchildren, were evidence that the McLeans of British Columbia would be around for quite some time yet. Gradually, though, what she meant sank in.

Clifford McLean was the last of the old-time McLeans in that he was the last surviving child of Alex and Margaret McLean. Those who have followed are a generation and more removed from the wild old family that pioneered the province. Those who bear the name today can't possibly comprehend what the McLeans of old experienced. My mom and her brothers and sisters certainly didn't have an easy life, but they represent a transition, born into the automobile age, and into a new century. Mom spent several years of her childhood at the Black Pines ranch, so she has an appreciation for that period of change, hearing stories of the "old days" and growing up in the "new." When Uncle Cliff was born, the stagecoach was still the major means of public transportation — no one could have imagined daily travel without benefit of a horse. When law and order needed to be served, a posse of citizens was sworn in to help do the job. Children were raised on a rum bottle full of goat's milk with a piece of rag tied around the neck, which was how Margaret McLean did it. Leisure time was precious, but when there was any, a game of cards, a few drinks with friends, or a Saturday night dance served for entertainment. The advent of modern law enforcement, daycare, and invention of television were decades away.

The more recent McLeans had their moments. My second cousin Pat Spiers tells of an incident in which her mother, Adeline "Lena" Benson, was accused of murder. "Lena" McLean, one of the daughters of Alex and Margaret, was a beautiful woman, with high cheek bones and big black eyes. She married and divorced Herman Benson, a man her brother Charlie had disliked intensely. A few years later she broke up with a fellow who then asked her to come to his rooming-house room to talk things over. Foolishly she did, and when she got there he locked the door, pulled out a gun and shot her, then killed himself. Though badly wounded, she was suspected of killing the ex-boyfriend, but was exonerated.

And there was the sad case of Aunt Minnie, another daughter of Alex and Margaret. Minnie McLean married Art Connine, and they ranched for many years in the North Thompson. My mom's memories of Aunt Minnie are all fond ones, of a kind, gentle woman who loved the outdoors. On November 23, 1950, she was found dead with a bullet in her head. Though it was ruled a suicide, family members strongly suspected her husband had shot her in a mercy killing to relieve her suffering from a painful thyroid condition. Less than two years later, Connine killed himself with a shot to the head.

But it's the adventures of Alex McLean of Red River, Donald of the Hudson's Bay Company, the infamous McLean Boys, the ubiquitous Hector, Margaret and Alex of Black Pines, Alf and Charlie, my grandfather Duncan, and George at Vimy Ridge that write themselves across my mind like the pages of a novel being turned by the hand of time. Only a few days before Uncle Cliff died, Pat Spiers and I had talked of going to visit him at Ponderosa Lodge, the long-term care facility in Kamloops. I had never met him and had long wanted to. Though I was always told by family members that he was withdrawn and didn't enjoy the company of people he'd never met, and that he no longer talked of times past or of much at all, I wanted to at least see him. It's to my great regret that Pat and I did not go to Ponderosa that day, for I never got to meet "the last of the McLeans."

During the funeral service I felt neglectful and a little ashamed, not because Uncle Cliff's last days would have been in any way brightened by my visit, but because had I discovered Cliff McLean ten or twenty years ago, who knows what additional treasures of information he might have revealed to me, what stories I might have been able to record for the interest and benefit of the generations that will follow. Sadly, it seems all too often that we let the living history of our immediate forbears escape us.

Such was the case with Uncle Cliff McLean, but we still have people like my mom and Pat Spiers to recount the stories they heard from Uncle Cliff and Margaret "Granny" McLean, who in turn retold tales of the earlier McLeans. To at least some extent, a tradition of oral history remains strong within the family. And, fortunately, because the early McLeans played such prominent parts in history, they were well documented, waiting in archives to be discovered.

I regret that my father, Ben Rothenburger, did not live to read this book, as he had an enduring interest in both sides of the family. One day I hope to tell the story of the Rothenburgers, because that family has an exciting pioneering history of its own.

The story of the McLeans doesn't end with this book. Generations to come will make their own contributions to family lore, and I hope they will also take the time to look back at the past, perhaps discovering even more about Donald, Allen, Charlie, Archie, and all the other McLeans. I know that, for me, the thirst for knowledge about this wild old family will never be fully quenched.

# CHAPTER NOTES

## ABBREVIATIONS

BCARS: B.C. Archives and Records Service
HBCA: Hudson's Bay Company Archives
HCRA: Hat Creek Ranch Archives
KMA: Kamloops Museum and Archives
PAM: Public Archives of Manitoba
NAC: National Archives of Canada
NVA: Nicola Valley Archives
SACA: South Africa Constabulary Archives

## PART 1 – DEATH AT RED RIVER

### Chapter 1

p. 3. " . . . not so much with a view to his personal services . . . ": Earl of Selkirk to Alexander McDonald of Dalilia, 6 January 1813, Selkirk Papers, NAC, vol. 79: 70.
p. 3. " . . . of fair and honourable character . . . ": Selkirk to Miles Macdonell, 20 June 1812, Selkirk Papers, NAC, vol. 2: 715.
p. 5 . . . .an example of "ingratitude" and "infamy": William Auld, York Factory, to Macdonell, Fort Daer, 9 July 1813, Selkirk Papers, PAM, MG19 EL Series 2: 171.
p. 6. " . . . appear to be condemned on vague evidence . . . ": Macdonell, Fort Daer, to Auld, York Factory, 1 December 1813, Selkirk Papers, PAM, MG 19 EL Series 2: 174.

### Chapter 2

p. 6. "They are making for the settlers . . . ": John Pritchard's narrative, in *Statement Respecting The Early Days of Selkirk's Settlement Upon the Red River*, 82.
p. 6. "We must go out and meet these people . . . ": Ibid.
p. 8. " . . . an independent situation": Deposition of Alexander McLean to Archibald McDonald, 5 August 1815, ibid, xxiv.
p. 8. "That family occasioned me a great deal of trouble": Macdonell, York Factory, to Selkirk, 9 September 1814, Selkirk Papers, NAC, vol. 63: 17,098.
p. 8. McLean sent him one back calling him and his ilk "barbarians": Alexander McLean to Duncan Cameron, April, 1815, Selkirk Papers, NAC, vol. 49: 13,312.

### Chapter 3

p. 11. Those fleeing for Fort Douglas were unarmed, some carrying children, and they continued past Semple's men, shouting about "the half-breeds . . . ": Pritchard, *Statement Respecting*, 82.
p. 12. "They should be erased from off the Earth . . . ": Alexander McLean to Selkirk, October, 1816, Selkirk Papers, NAC, vol. 77: 20,265.
p. 12. "I'm too fond of revenge . . . ": Christina McLean, Fort Douglas, to Selkirk, 15 October 1815, Selkirk Papers, NAC, vol. 77: 20,259.
p. 12. "If she had been my wife . . . ": Robert Semple to Selkirk, October, 1816, Selkirk Papers, NAC, vol. 50: 13,458.
p. 12. " . . . a fickle unsteady man . . . ": Semple to Selkirk, n.d., Selkirk Papers, NAC, vol. 77: 20,210.

### Chapter 4

p. 13. "Gentlemen," he said, "we had better go on": Selkirk quoted in Pritchard's narrative, in *The Romantic Settlement of Lord Selkirk's Colonists*, George Bryce, 123.
p. 13. "Their faces painted in the most hideous manner . . . ": Pritchard, *Statement Respecting*, 82.
p. 14. Grant waved his own men forward . . . : Among those in Grant's party were Lacerte, Alexander Fraser, Antoine Hoole, Thomas McKay, Pangman Bostonois, Francois Deschamps, Francois Deschamps Jr., Ka-tee-tea-goose, Wa-ge-tan-me, La Grosse Tete, Coutonahais, Lavigne, Baptiste Morralle, La Certe, Joseph Truttier, J. Baptiste Latour, Duplicis, J. Baptiste Parisien, Toussaint Voudre, Francois Gardupie, Bourassin, Louison Valle, Ignace McKay, Cha-ma-tan, Ne-de-goose-ojeb-wan, Baudry, De Lorme.
p. 14. "What do you want?": Pritchard, *Statement Respecting*, 83; Michael Heden's statement, Selkirk Papers, NAC, vol. 50: 13,825.
p. 14. "We were within about a gunshot . . . ": Ibid, NAC, vol. 50: 13,826.
p. 14. "Do what you can to take care of yourselves!": Ibid, 13,829.
p. 15. "Rogers, for God's sake, give yourself up! Give yourself up!": This and following exchanges involving Pritchard from Pritchard's narrative, *Statement Respecting*, 83.
p. 15. "You dog, you have been the cause of all this . . . ": *A Narrative of Occurrences in the Indian Countries of North America*, 55.

### Chapter 5

p. 16. "I hope the unfortunate situation I am placed in will plead my excuse for addressing your Lordship . . . ": Christina McLean to Selkirk, 12 March 1817, Selkirk Papers, PAM, MG2A1: 3262.
p. 16. "Joseph Lorain, after imbruing his hands in the barbarous murder of Mr. McLean . . . ": HBCA, E.10/1, vol. 6, f. 385, in E. E. Rich, ed., Colin Robertson's Correspondence Book, September, 1817–September, 1882, Hudson's Bay Record Society, vol. 2: 1939:55.
p. 17. "On my arrival at the fort, what a scene of distress . . . ": Pritchard, *Statement Respecting*, 88.
p. 17. To Alexander McDonell, left in charge of the fort by Semple, went the sad job of reclaiming the mutilated bodies: Colonists killed were Alexander McLean, Robert Semple, James Bruin, Daniel Donovan, James Gardiner, Brian Gilligan, Reginald Green, Ener Holte, Pat Maroony, James Moore, Sr., James Moore, Jr., Duncan McDonell, George Mackenzie, Duncan McNaughton, John Mihier, John Rogers, Henry Sinclair, Adam Sutherland, Donald Sutherland, James White, Laurence C. Wilkinson.

## PART 2 – THE COMPANY MAN

### Chapter 6

p. 20. Kuschte te'Kukkpe – the Fierce Chief: R. C. L. Brown, *Klatsassan*, 69.
p. 20. . . . nany a time they starved and froze . . . : Donald McLean to James Douglas, 23 February 1859, BCARS, M-107, notes, "The Indian are suffering from starvatiion . . . "

McLean's correspondence and journals refer often to the plight of the Indians. This particular letter continues, "God only knows what will eventually be the fate of the poor Aborigines if there should be no salmon again this year. This winter has caused them to eat up nearly all the horses they had and many are reduced to eat any offals chance may throw their way indeed I am afraid of poisoning bates for the wolves fearing that the starving Indians might be induced to the eating of them the baits."

p. 21. "I wish the glib-tongued speakers . . . ": Donald McLean, quoted by Adrien Gabriel Morice, *History of the Northern Interior of British Columbia*, 271.

p. 21. Donald McLean's house wasn't much of a house.: This building was constructed at the confluence of the Bonaparte River with Hat Creek, but now sits behind the main roadhouse building several hundred yards away, where it was moved by a subsequent owner and used for storing meat. A tree-ring study established the year of construction as 1863, meaning it was built later than the original roadhouse itself. Results of the study are reported in "Tree-Ring Dating of the Cabin Behind Hat Creek House," Marion L. Parker, March, 1984, Contract Report to British Columbia Heritage Trust.

p. 22. McLean's Restaurant: The original log building for the stopping house has been shown by tree-ring dating to have been erected in 1861, the first full year Donald McLean spent at Hat Creek. Subsequent owners made several wood-frame additions — including a second floor — to the building and sheathed it with wood siding. Today it is operated as a tourist attraction by B.C. Heritage Trust.

p. 22. His years with the Company hadn't made Donald McLean a rich man . . . : Although McLean had a good stock of cattle and horses, and built his ranch and roadhouse business up in a very short time, there are indications that finances were tight. A hint of McLean's financial status came when Lytton gold commissioner Henry M. Ball wrote to Judge H.P.P. Crease, Lytton, 28 July 1864 (Colonial Correspondence, BCARS, F97/29) that McLean "was much in debt." McLean's estate, when it was finally settled many years after his death, amounted to 2,104.89 pounds.

p. 22. Sophia: The most exact source of Sophia Grant's date of birth is the 1901 Canada Census, which says she was born in 1831. That would make her thirty-three in 1864. However, there is no consistency among sources. Based on the age given on her death certificate, Sophia was about forty-two in 1864. If the age recorded in the 1881 census is correct, she would have been only thirty-one. A different age was also given in the 1891 census – she would have been thirty-eight in 1864.

p. 23. . . . Donald, his son Duncan, and his friend Oregon Jack mounted up . . . : There is some reason to believe that John D.B. Ogilvy brought the message to McLean at Hat Creek about the uprising, and rode with him from there to Soda Creek.

## Chapter 7

p. 26. "My God, I'm shot!": *Colonist*, 14 October 1864.

p. 27. "I'll give them all I have, first . . . ": Ibid.

## Chapter 8

p. 27. Only to men like Donald McLean and Oregon Jack Dowling . . . : John Dowling was an American who ranched and ran a roadhouse on the Cariboo Road south of Cache Creek. Oregon Jack Creek was named after him.

p. 29. On one such trip, on the brigade trail between Tulameen and Fort Hope in October, 1858, he'd lost almost seventy horses: Explorer Henry Spencer Palmer of the Royal Engineers described a trip up the treacherous Manson's Mountain on the brigade trail east of Hope and said, "Mr. Donald McLean of the Hudson [sic] Bay Company who crosssed in 1857 or 1858, on the 16th October had a very disastrous trip and lost 60 or 70 horses. Traces of their deaths are still visible, and in riding over the mountain, and more particularly on its eastern slope, my horse frequently shied at the whitened bones of some of the poor animals, who had broken down in the sharp struggle with fatigue and hunger, and been left to perish." Lieutenant H. Spencer Palmer, R.E., "Report on the Country between Fort Hope on the Fraser and Fort Colville on the Columbia River," 1860, Cmd. 2724, 1st Series, 3: 81-82, cited 127, *A Pioneer Gentlewoman in British Columbia, The Recollections of Susan Allison*, ed. Margaret A. Ormsby.

p. 29. . . . island of Mull: The only direct clue to Donald McLean's origins is his contract with the Hudson's Bay Company, which does not state a parish, but refers to him as being "of Mull in the County of Argyle in Scotland." HBCA, Reel 407, A32/42, f. 117. While it doesn't guarantee he was born there, it's probable, since the practice was to give the place of birth. However, the journal of John Brough, one of the volunteers on the Chilcotin Expedition, says he was born in Red River. That appears highly unlikely given Donald McLean's probable age and the dates of his residence at Red River as a child. It's of interest to note that John Maclean, Donald's first cousin, who married Donald's sister Anna, was from the island of Coll, another stronghold of the McLean clan. 1871 census, RG10/22 f. 20v.

p. 29. . . . he sailed the seas on a man-of-war . . . : John Tod, *History of New Caledonia and the North West Coast*, wrote, "McLean in his youth having served on board of a man of war, he was not very scrupulous in his idea of justice and was therefore a likely man for the work." Tod was referring to the reason McLean was chosen to lead the hunt for Samuel Black's murderer. BCARS, E/A/T56: 14. McLean's Royal Navy dagger is in the Kamloops Museum.

p. 29. Preston: Correspondence between Donald McLean and the Hudson's Bay Company in 1832 and 1833 shows his address as 8 Garden Street, Preston, Lancashire. The date his mother remarried Rev. William Robert Browne isn't known, but since Browne's name is given as the officiating clergyman at the marriage of Anna McLean to John Maclean, which took place October 1, 1831 (Lancashire

Record Office, MF 2/119, Marriage licence, "John Maclean of London, County of Middlesex, Bachelor, to Anna Maclean of this Parish"), it seems likely the mother had remarried to Browne by then Browne was born about 1790. Donald's mother, Christina, was born about 1782.

p. 29. Recommendation of Colin Robertson: By the time Donald McLean was applying for a position with the HBC Robertson's health was failing and he was in disfavour with Sir George Simpson. Unfortunately, neither Donald McLean's original letter of application nor the letter he enclosed from Robertson have survived.

p. 29. Donald wrote the Governor and Committee of the Company in London: Secretary William Smith's answer to McLean on behalf of the Company was dated 2 January 1833, and said, in part, " . . . You will inform me of your Age . . . the Voyages you have made . . . the Capacity in which you made them, and on board what Ships you have served . . . and whether you are inclined to be apprenticed to the Sea Service on the North West Coast of America for a term of five years . . . ." (HBCA, A.1/58, f. 25; A.5/10: 56). McLean answered 5 January 1833, but this letter hasn't survived, either, leaving the question of his earlier experiences a mystery. On 9 January 1833, Smith wrote to McLean offering him a position as apprentice clerk on the North West Coast of America on a three-year contract. McLean wrote back 14 March 1833 to remind the Company of his availability and was told a ship had been commissioned and was scheduled to sail the following month (HBCA, A.5/10: 61-62; A.5/10: 87-88, Smith to McLean dated London, 16 March 1833). He was later informed, on 6 April 1833, that the Nereide would sail 20 April (A.5/10: 96; A.32, f. 172). Most of the above dates, as well as those of McLean's subsequent postings with the HBC, were originally researched in a paper commissioned by Pat Spiers from the Company, Beaver House, Great Trinity Lane, London, and forwarded 3 December 1970 under the title "Donald McLean 'C'." This paper has since been used by a number of writers as the basis of stories about McLean.

p. 29. " . . . either afloat or on shore": Smith to McLean, 9 January 1833, HBCA, A,5/10: 61-62.

p. 30. " . . . faithfully serve the said Company as their hired servant in the capacity of Apprentice . . . ": HBCA, Servants' Contracts, Donald McLean, 1833, A.32/42, f. 172.

p. 30. " . . . leaking because nails not properly driven . . . caulkers busy caulking . . . crew busy pumping ship": HBCA, Ships logs − Nereide 1833-1834, Reel IM241, c/1/609.

p. 30. Columbia River: A good description of the scenery on the trip up the Columbia can be found in the journals of William Fraser Tolmie, who arrived at Fort Vancouver via the barque Ganymede 4 May 1833, a day after Donald McLean and the Nereide left London. William Fraser Tolmie, Physician and Fur Trader. Journal entries from arrival off Fort George to landing at Fort Vancouver are on pp. 165-170.

p. 31. Fort Vancouver: Description based on that in The History of Fort Vancouver and Its Physical Structure, John A. Hussey, 44.

p. 31. John Maclean: It is not known whether

Donald McLean was related to John Maclean. However, John Maclean was the uncle of Neil McLean McArthur, who was also from Mull. McArthur was a fellow HBC employee and close friend of Donald's, and became executor of Donald's estate upon the latter's death. The excerpt of John Maclean is taken from Notes On A Twenty-Five Years' Service in the Hudson's Bay Territory.

## Chapter 9

p. 32. "We learn that the British Columbia expedition . . . ": Colonist, 4 June 1864.

p. 32. "I had the honour to receive . . . ": Seymour to Kennedy, 4 June 1864, Colonial Correspondence, BCARS, F1588/3a.

p. 34. "The Chilcoaten Indians are a dirty, lazy set . . . .": Colonist, 9 May 1864.

p. 35. "His was a striking face . . . ": Brown, Klatsassan, 5.

p. 38. "There is something almost fiendish . . . ": Colonist, 12 May 1864.

## Chapter 10

p. 39. "An enlightened Indian is good for nothing": George Simpson to Andrew Colville, 20 May 1822, in Fur Trade and Empire, ed. Frederick Merk. Simpson was objecting to establishment of schools for Indian children in Rupert's Land, saying they would benefit only greedy missionaries.

p. 41. Pelkamu'lox: The first Pelkamu'lox, a chief of the Upper Spokane (often spelled Spokan by early writers), lived in the late 1600s and early 1700s. His son, also named Pelkamu'lox, was a chief of the same tribe and was born about 1705-1710. He left his tribe and lived among the Sanpoil, Okanogan and Shuswap. The third Pelkamu'lox was engaged for several years in wars in the area of the junction of the Similkameen and Okanagan Rivers. Kwolila convinced him to take over Shuswap territory in the upper Nicola Valley. Ali was descended from the first Pelkamulox and his Spokane wife.

p. 41. . . . Nicola, whose native name was Hwistesmetxe'qEn, or Walking Grizzly Bear . . . : Also known as Shiwelean, was the most important chief among the Okanagans in the first half of the 19th century. He was a good friend of Chief Trader Samuel Black and other HBC men. Nicola died in 1859.

p. 41. He served at Fort Hall, then at Fort Colville . . . : McLean was at Fort Colville during Outfit 1839-40.

p. 41. . . . he scouted the wild rivers, shot buffalo on the vast plains, guided for explorers . . . : Some flavour for McLean's life during these years can be obtained from the Correspondence of Archibald McDonald relating to Fort Colville, 1838-1842, BCARS, A/B/20/C72M1. "I hope you will be able to furnish us for our trade here a few Buffalo Robes − an article greatly in demand" (McDonald to McLean, 2 November 1840); a request by McDonald to McLean to teach him the Indian language on a trip to Flatheads (18 February 1841); and re: the United States Exploring Expedition, " . . . And at the Flatheads Mr. McLean will be able to supply you with all you may require in the tough and humble way of the country until you get to Buffalo" (19 June 1841).

p. 41. " ... A cold-blooded fellow who could be guilty of any cruelty ... ": George Simpson's Character Book, *Hudsons' Bay Miscellany*, 1670-1870, ed. Glyndwr Williams, 192-193.

p. 42. ... to Thompson's River Post and eventually to Alexandria ... : Tod, at Thompson's River Post, was not happy to see Donald McLean. "I had scarcely finished taking the inventory, when a party from Colville arrived headed by a Mr. McLean, who had received instructions from his chief factor, a Mr. McDonald, to abandon the place and save all the furs. McLean brought me these orders but I held a commission, while he was but a clerk in the Co. service. I replied, 'Mr. McLean, I have no authority over you, but I am determined the place shall not be abandoned.'" McLean was to hunt down Black's killer. "He was used to making raids upon Indians. He would dash upon a band of savages and in case a murderer was not found, he would take their horses, break their canoes and commit such like depredations. The hunt continued for months until the Indians all were hostile to these men. The murder was but the act of one Indian and the Indians themselves regretted it as much as the whitemen. It was a great mistake ...." Tod, at the first opportunity, "at once returned all the horses taken from the Indians by McLean." Tod, 13-15. Brown, 68-69, says McLean was successful in capturing the murderer. " ... He seems to have made it his business to be among them (Indians) a kind of incarnation of wild justice, and to avenge, by swift and summary retribution, crimes which had otherwise gone unpunished, and bred fresh deeds of violence. For instance, he it was who slew the treacherous knave who murdered Black, the Hudson Bay agent at Fort Kamloops; the Indian also who, in cold blood, did to death a Canadian at that river of doom, known in consequence as Deadman's Creek (*Rivière des Defunts*), fell by his hand."

## Chapter 11

p. 42. "In moral character the Bella Coolas ... ": Henry Spencer Palmer, *Report of a Journey of Survey from Victoria to Fort Alexander via Bentinck Arm*, 7.

p. 43. The frightened and angry Wallace had run into a back room and returned with a long sword, charging at the invaders, "who incontinently left": *Colonist*, 28 June 1864.

## Chapter 12

p. 45. "During my stay here this disease ... ": Palmer, *Report of a Journey of Survey*, 7-8.

p. 46. "We followed, and saw in many of the houses, corpses ... ": In Cliff Kopas, *Bella Coola*, 81-82.

p. 47. " ... in my humble opinion a dead loss ...": HBCA, B5/A/5. On 4 October 1842, McLean wrote at Alexandria, "the news from that post (Chilcotin) is by no means favourable. The Indians of the Grand Lac stole one of the Co.'s horses, and one and all of them appear inclined to mischief. The keeping up such a paltry Establishment is in my humble opinion a dead loss to the H.H.B. Co. and risking the lives of people placed at it — who are little better than slaves to the Indians, being unable to keep them in check ...."

p. 47. "God help me ... ": In Morice, 221.

p. 48. "It is really too bad ... ": Donald McLean, Fort Alexandria Journal, Thursday, 18 October 1849, HBCA, B/5/a/7.

p. 49. "Worthless scamp ... ": Peter Skene Ogden, Fort St. James, to John McIntosh, Babine, 13 June 1839, in Morice, 261.

p. 49. "Where be Tlhelh?": In Morice, 269, 274. While other parts of his account of the expedition to Quesnel River do not jibe with HBC journal records of the time, including McLean's, Morice claimed a contemporary source for McLean's exchange with Nadetnoerh.

p. 50. ... the son-in-law was also cut down ... : Morice claims this man was shot on purpose by other members of McLean's party, as was the daughter-in-law and baby, but McLean's notes in the Alexandria Journal say stray bullets fired by him at Nadetnoerh were responsible.

p. 50. "News has arrived from above ... ": Donald McLean, Fort Alexandria Journal, Monday, 12 February 1849, HBCA, B/5/a/7.

p. 50. "Tlhelh tatqa?": Morice, 274.

p. 50. "Messrs. McLean and McGillivray ... ": Donald Manson to Sir George Simpson and Council, 26 February 1849, cited in Morice, 270.

p. 51. "If my will was only concerned ... ": Donald McLean, March, 1850, in Morice, 271.

p. 51. "Begged for peace ... ": Donald McLean, ibid, Thursday, 1 March 1849.

p. 51. " ... good proof of the scoundrel being dead ... ": Donald McLean, Fort Alexandria Journal, Thursday, 28 March 1850, HBCA, B/5/a/7. Morice gives quite another version. He says McLean threatened another of the Indian's uncles, Neztel, with death if he didn't kill Tlhelh. Three other Indians received the same advice, says Morice. In this version, handing Neztel a gun, McLean offered him the one hundred skins for the scalp of Tlhelh. The alternative, for failure, was death. "Look at this gun," he told the Indians. "Its contents will find your heart if I see you come back empty-handed." Neztel, says Morice, had no choice but to obey. With his three companions, he travelled to Tlhelh's hiding place beside the Cottonwood River, walked up to him, and shot him to death. Tlhelh's body fell into the river but was pulled out and his scalp taken. The enormity of his act hit Neztel, who first tried to kill his companions, then himself, but was finally calmed down. Tlhelh's corpse was cremated on the spot. When Neztel returned to Alexandria he supposedly threw the scalp of his nephew at McLean. I have chosen to use the version of events as described by McLean at the time rather than Morice's version written decades later, but mention the Morice account as it is the one that has been repeated in many stories about McLean's alleged brutality.

p. 51. "By virtue of the Charter to us ... ": Archibald Barclay to Donald McLean, 30 March 1853, Donald McLean Papers, BCARS, E/B/M221.9.

p. 52. "We hear that McLean and Odgen [sic] ... ": George Simpson to Donald Manson, dated Norway House, 19 June 1853, HBCA, D.4/46, f. 67d-68.

p. 52. "It is to your kindness ... ": Donald McLean to Donald Manson, 6 February 1854, in Morice, 109.

p. 52. ....his widow ... : Donald McLean's Alexandria journal, 25 October 1849, notes,

"Peter Grant's widow laid up." HBCA, B/5/a/7. For more on Sophia Grant, see Index.

p. 52. "Oh, what is it, late yester night . . . ": Donald McLean Papers, BCARS, E/B/M221.9. Three poems by Donald McLean, including this one, were found in the papers of Peter Skene Ogden. Since there is no date or name on the poem, it's not known which son it was, and there is no other record of a son dying. It's possible it was written about John, who disappeared in the mountains in October, 1860, but was found alive a few days later after a search by his father.

p. 53. The next day Manson . . . put Donald McLean in charge of Kamloops: An extract from Chief Trader Donald Manson's letter to Chief Factor James Douglas, dated "Campment de Chiv," 29 July 1855, states, "I have this moment (1 p.m.) arrived here from the Quaquyalla where I left Mr. McLean, at 6 a.m. this morning, with our Brigade — I am very very sorry to inform you of the death of our old and worthy friend Mr. C. Trader Paul Fraser, poor Gentleman he only survived the blow about an hour, and during that time he never spoke. I shall see the body interred and arranged as well as our means admit, and bring the Kamloops Brigade on with me to that place where I shall leave Mr. C. Trader McLean in charge until further instructions from the Board. On reaching Kamloops I shall have his papers collected and sealed up immediately . . . . N.B. He died yesterday about 6 p.m." HBCA, A.11/56.

# Chapter 13

p. 53. "Mr. Moss, who has just arrived . . . ": *Colonist*, 9 June 1864.

p. 57. . . . enticed by . . . forty dollars to sixty dollars monthly wages: That was the top rate for expedition members, and was paid to packers. Duncan McLean was assigned this rate, entered on record as one hundred dollars per month, effective 1 June 1864. Guides received eighty-five dollars per month, cooks seventy-five dollars, and regulars sixty-five dollars. It is not known what Donald McLean was to be paid, but it would have been substantially more. He drew an advance of $150, which may have been a month's pay, 4 June 1864. Sources are William Henry Fitzgerald's Daybook and Diary, Chilcotin Expedition (BCARS, Add MSS 690), and Cox papers (BCARS, C2229, f. 74-A-653), invoices relating to Alexandria expedition.

p. 57. John D.B. Ogilvy: Reference to the baptism is found in the 8 July 1859 entry in "Notes from the Diary of the Reverend Ebenezer Robson," BCARS, H/D/R57/R57.2A, 13. Ogilvy served as a constable at Bella Coola and was shot to death by a whiskey peddlar he tried to arrest on a ship there in 1865.

p. 58. William Robert Browne: Donald's stepfather died 21 June 1856, at the Union Workhouse, 6 Victoria Terrace, Landport, Portsea. His mother, Christina Brown, died at the same address 9 August 1856. General Register Office, Register of Deaths, Portsea Island, Landport, Southampton, Nos. 74 and 91, 1856. Donald had been sending her twenty pounds annually, and in 1858 asked the Company to send Anna one hundred pounds. In a letter to James

Douglas 26 September 1858, he wrote, "Not knowing to whom to address myself, in London, might I beg of you to empower Mrs. Anna MacLean of No. 5 Scarsdale Villas, Kensington, to receive from the H.B.C. the sum of one hundred pounds sterling on my account — by so doing you will render me great service." Donald McLean, Fort Hope, to Douglas, BCARS, F1062B/1.

p. 58 . . . . by 1857 the search for gold had spread . . . : Early in 1857, Douglas wrote to McLean, "I have . . . received your letter of the 19th January, enclosing a specimen of Gold received from the Indians of Thompson River," and told him to "collect a large party of Indians, and proceeding to the Gold district make them search and wash for the precious metal, buying it from them as fast as they collect it." Douglas to McLean, February 10, 1857, Fort Victoria Correspondence Outward, BCARS, A/C/20/Vi4A, cited in "Re-examining The Origins of the Fraser River Gold Rush," Lindsay E. Smith, Canadian West, January-March, 1993: 6. "We shall make a point of detaining the homeward bound ship till the 5th of March next, in expectation of your sending out the whole quantity (of gold) collected up to about the 20th of February." Douglas to McLean, 23 November 1857, ibid.

p. 59. Elizabeth: The poem about her death was written by Donald McLean in December, 1857, in all likelihood immediately after she died. Her son, Donald Manson, was born 12 September 1857.

p. 59. John Houston: A sailor and soldier of fortune who was attacked by Indians on his way from California to Fort Colville in search of gold in 1856. He decided to go north through the Okanagan Valley and across the mountains to Fort Hope but was again attacked near the border. By the time he reached Thompson's River Post he was broke and starving. Donald McLean at first thought he was an HBC deserter but decided to help him out with a loan of supplies. Houston repaid him with earnings from his gold-panning on Tranquille Creek. Houston died in Langley 7 April 1902. VCA, clipping file.

p. 60 . . . . Mayne was so impressed . . . : Mayne was also impressed with McLean. "A finer or more handsome man I think I never saw." R.C. Mayne, *Four years in British Columbia and Vancouver Island: an account of their forests, rivers, coasts, gold fields, and resources for colonisation* (London, 1862), 115-121, cited in *Dictionary of Canadian Biography*, vol. IX, 1861-1870, University of Toronto Press, 1976: 513.

p. 61. " . . . my own private opinion . . . ": Douglas to Col. Moody, R.E., Chief Commissioner Lands and Works, 12 April 1860, Colonial Correspondence, BCARS, F44856/3. Other correspondence on the St. Paul land claim includes Donald McLean to H.M. Ball, 12 March 1860, F920/40, and Ball to Moody, 24 March 1860, F920/40.

p. 61 . . . . He was well-acquainted with potential farming and ranching sites . . . : Mayne discussed agricultural potential of several areas with Donald McLean. For example, Mayne asked about the presence of nitrate of soda along the Nicola River. "Mr. McLean, the officer of the Hudson Bay Company, in charge of Fort Kamloops, told me that where it is in large quantities it destroys wheat, but that it has very little effect on vegetables." *Report on a Journey in British Columbia in the Districts bordering on the Thompson, Fraser, and Harrison rivers*, Communicated by the Admiralty, 12 December 1859: 215. Along the North, or North Thompson, River: "Mr. McLean considers the soil here as good, though not so fine as at the head waters of the Thompson, about 22 miles east of this, or in the Semilkamen Valley, which he considers the best place in the colony for an agricultural settlement. The land about Fort Alexandria where he resided for several years, he also considers better than this, though more subject to frost ....At Kamloops vegetables of all kinds thrive very well. An acre of wheat there yields on an average 15 bushels. Mr. McLean says that at Alexandria he has known it to yield 40" (216).

## Chapter 14

p. 62 ....Cox was to "at once proceed to the headquarters of Alexis ... ": Seymour to Duke of Carlisle, 20 May 1864, Governor-General's Office, Records, Governor to Colonial Office, 1864-1867. NAC, RG7/G8/C, vol. 23.

p. 62. "Alexis was not to be found, he having with his family fled to the mountains ... ": Cox, "Puntzeen Lake," to Seymour, 19 June 1864, in *British Columbian*, 2 July 1864.

## Chapter 15

p. 65 ....There was "no prospect of profitable employment ... ": Dallas to McLean, 14 March 1861, HBCA, B.226/b/19: 204.

p. 65. One summer almost the entire crop of barley and vegetables was lost ... : George Blair, travelling on his way to the goldfields, wrote in 1862, " ... Here there is a Ranch owned by an old Hudson Bay Man McClain who has about forty head of cattle. This was on the thirty-first of May. They ware in splendid condition yet they had nothing but what was picked up all Winter themselfs. He informed us that there was over fifteen hundred head of horses and mules wintered on the Bonaparte within a distance of twelve miles, which appeared incredible as the ravine in which the river runs is not more than eighty rods wide at the widest part, narrowing down to a canyon in some places but whare the ground is damp it is covered with bunch grass and as there is no rain to bleach it the sap or nutriment dries into it and makes excellent feed all Winter. The animal(s) are allowed to run out all Winter with(out) any shelter as there scarcely any snow falls. Mr. McLain had a large garden of vegetables and some barley but they looked very poor and yellow for the want of rain. He had been at a good deal of expence to fetch watter to irrigate it but the water was so cold that everything he let it run perished it being Snow water from the tops of the mountains which ware melting by the heat of the sun." Diary of George Blair, 17 February 1862–29 December 1863, BCARS, Add MSS 186: 40-41.

p. 65. Bonaparte Gold and Silver Mining Company: the *Colonist* reported 4 November 1863: "The Bonaparte Gold and Silver Mining

Co. is in course of formation to work a large vein of gold and silver bearing quartz in the Bonaparte Valley near the Wagon Road. The lead is ten feet wide on the surface, and specimens from the croppings assayed some five weeks ago, when the lead was first discovered, gave about $100 to the ton, in equal quantities of gold and silver. Since then the enterprising discoverers have sunk a shaft to the depth of twelve feet, and yesterday arrived at Victoria with a specimen from the lead at that depth. The rock, which we have seen, looks very good." On 11 November 1863, the *Colonist* announced formation of a board of directors to promote the new company.

p. 65. One of the boys built a roadhouse up the canyon at Pavilion ... : The son was likely Duncan, Donald Jr. or Alex. The diary of Richard Henry Alexander refers to this in the 30 October 1862 entry: "The (Pavilion) mountain is level on the top ....There is a house on top kept by McLean, brother of owner of Ploughboy ...." BCARS, E/B/Ac3.1A.

p. 65. " ... Although it is not my wish to throw the slightest impediment in your way ... ": McLain, Hat Creek, to Sergeant Money, 26 May 1863, BCARS, Colonial Correspondence, F935/35.

p. 66. Donald McLean and his family had well over a thousand acres under pre-emption ... : The McLean pre-emptions are described in Laing's *Colonial Settlers*, 351-358.

## Chapter 16

p. 67. "Who says these Chinese are not to land?": W.W. Walkem, *Stories of Early British Columbia*, 123-124.

p. 69. "A good brainy Scotchman he was ... .": Andrew Jackson Splawn, *Kamiakin*, 170.

p. 69. " ... provided him with a horse ... ": The encounter between Charles Grandidier and Donald McLean is described in *A Cross in the Wilderness*, Kay Cronin, 91.

p. 69. Ebenezer Robson: His description of his stay at McLeans' is found in the 28 July 1863 entry in "An Old Timer's Diary – Ebenezer Robson," ed. William Lashley Hall, BCARS, H/D/R57H/v.1: 176. Robson (1835-1911) was a Methodist converted from Presbyterianism, who served as missionary at Fort Hope between 1859 and 1864. Robson wrote: "Ten mi. further lived Hector [sic] McLean, a retired trader of the H.B. Co. wayside house, in the Bonaparte Valley, that night. But when I arrived at the sprawling group of cabins, I felt disappointed. Such a bunch of men, women, children, cattle, horses, dogs and insects I had not often come in contact with. My horse was turned out to grass, and I waited long for my supper, which was being prepared by a Chinaman, who was said to have graduated in the employ of the Shuswap Chief, St. Paul. The meal, when served, was not inviting, but I felt that I must fortify myself against the coming day's work, and so sat down to eat somewhat disagreeable, the cook taking his place on the opposite side of the table to entertain me, when the following dialogue took place: 'Where you come?': 'Yale'. 'What you do, you mine gold?' 'No'. 'You keep one store?' 'No'. 'You got one whiskey house?' 'No.' 'What you do?' 'I preach'. 'You keep one klootchman?'

'Yes'. 'One English klootchman, one Siwash klootchman?' 'One English klootchman.' 'You got one papoose?' 'Yes'. 'Ha!Ha!Ha! Bully for you! Where you go?' 'Clinton'. 'Well, s'pose you see one Chinaman cook, stop one old house, Clinton, you tell him I say How'd you do'. That conversation no doubt, saved me from an attack of dyspepsia. I did not take a bed, for the bunks were hard as a board; the pillows seemed to be flour sacks filled with grass, and the dark looking blankets had enwrapped too many sweaty, dusty travellers since last washed, if indeed, they had ever been washed. So placing my Mexican saddle against the wall and spreading the saddle cloth in front of it, I pulled off my shoes, said my prayers, and using my coat for a covering, slept the sleep of the weary."

p. 69. " . . . wild as colts": Bishop George Hills, Diary, BCARS, Add MSS 1526, vols. 1-12 (copy from the Archives of the Anglican Provincial Synod of B.C. and the Yukon, Vancouver). His entry for 19 June 1862 describes the Bonaparte Valley and Donald McLean's prize bull. On 20 June 1862, Hills wrote: "All of the children of Mr. McLean are from Indian mothers. The young boys are fine children but wild as colts. I saw one six years old lassoing an unbroken raging horse & then mounting it. One of them last year was but for 6 says he was sent out to search for two horses & could not find the way back. At length he did so but had no food. Mr. McLean said he should be glad if visits from a clergyman could be provided & he wd see all things made comfortable for them." On 22 June 1862 Hills noted passing "Mr. McLean's cabin" as he continued on his journey.

p. 71. " . . . the best farm in the colony": William Champness, *To Cariboo and Back In 1862*: 86.

## Chapter 17

p. 72. "It is needless to say . . . ": *Colonist*, 6 June 1864.

## Chapter 18

p. 72. "I have the honor to report . . . ": Cox to Seymour, 19 June 1864, BCARS, Colonial Correspondence, N355.

## Chapter 19

p. 75. " . . . the whole business is botched . . . ": *Colonist*, 14 October 1864.

p. 75. " . . . a comparatively trifling loss": Seymour to Duke of Carlisle, 9 September 1864. Despatches from Governor Seymour and Administrator Birch to the Colonial Office, 26 April 1864–20 December 1864: 10 (67), NAC, G series, no. 353-358.

## Chapter 20

p. 76. Cox's men – "virtually besieged by an invisible enemy . . . ": Ibid, 8 (65).

p. 76. Brew decided to send another party back some 150 miles to Bella Coola . . . : Among the names (compiled from various records) of those who served on the Chilcotin Expedition, mainly from the Alexandria contingent, were A.E. Atkins, William H. Adams (engaged 24 June 1864, arrived Puntzi 2 July 1864), John Allen (24 June), Baptiste (Indian, engaged at Alexandria 21 August), Frank Bennett, J. Berry, L.E. Brackenridge, Chartres Brew (in

command New Westminster expedition), Newton Briggs, John Brough, Charles Brown, Ward Bryans, Noah Buckley (24 June), Philip Buckley (24 June), Thomas Burrell (24 June), Capotblen (Indian engaged at Alexandria 21 August), Martin Castles, I.H. Conklin (went to Nancootlem with Ogilvy), T.W. Cook, William Cooper, Lieut. Cowper, Coushla (Indian, 21 August), William George Cox (in comman Alexandria expedition), T.N. Davis, Paulo Di Martini (to Nancootlem, a guide paid eighty-five dollars per month), George Dingmans (24 June), James Dougan, John "Oregon Jack" Dowling (packer), Dupuis (21 August), Herman Eberwine (to Nancootlem with Ogilvy), W.J. Ellis, Thomas Elwyn (second in command New Westminster expedition), Thomas Erwin (Alexandria 21 August), Evans, William Henry Fitzgerald (in charge of provisions), William Fox or Fuchs (to Nancootlem with Ogilvy), John W. Fulp (24 June), John Gibson (24 June), George Gregory, Harry Grover (24 June), Gillespie, T. Harrison, Hesslewood, Joe Hilton (a packer), I. Hoffman (cook, paid seventy-five dollars per month), Ignace (Alexandria, 21 August), Jack (Indian engaged 23 June), Johnny (Indian scout), J. Johnston, Jones, Michael Kaufman or Kaupman, Richard Keefe, John M. Kemple, John Kent, John Kirnick or Kernick (to Nancootlem with Ogilvy, a packer paid one hundred dollars per month effective 1 June), Iam Keyes (to Nancootlem, guide paid eighty-five dollars per month), La-Houz (Indian, Alexandria, 21 August), Little George, John Linton (24 June), Thomas Lloyd (20 August), McIvor, E.R. McLaughlin, Donald McLean, Donald McLean Jr. (engaged at Alexandria 18 August), Duncan McLean, McLeod, Alfred March, John Mole (to Nancootlem), Murdock (Indian engaged 23 June), John Myers, John D.B. Ogilvy (third in command Alexandria expedition), G. Onslow (to Nancootlem), Page, Andrew Patton, Andrew Poujade (24 June), Usibius Peters, H. Peters, John Ryder (a packer), A. Smith, W.D. Spears, P.H. Stacke or Stark, Lieut. Stewart, Arthur Taylor, Charles Trueworthy (24 June), Vicato, W.H. Weller, Charles Wheeler, G. White, John Wildman (or Wilkenson), N. Willer (to Nancootlem), T. Willis, Harry Wilmot, Yah-anna (Indian). Smith and Ladner's pack train joined the expedition on 6 August at $2.50 per man per day.

p. 77. "The few hours that the two parties had passed together . . . ": Seymour to Duke of Carlisle, 9 September 1864, Despatches, 14 (74), NAC, G series, no. 353-358.

## Chapter 21

p. 80. "Death," he wrote, "is a creditor that must be paid": Donald McLean, Fort Alexandria Journal, 28 November 1849, HBCA, B.5/a/7.

p. 80. Anukatlk, Shililika, Sachayel and Hatish: Anukatlk is identified by Morice (319) as the man who shot McLean. "He died scarcely three years ago." According to R.C. Lundin Brown in *Klatsassan*, 74, it was Shililika. Terry Glavin, in *Nemiah The Unconquered Country*, identifies the killer as either Sachayel or Hatish (50, 52). Hatish was probably the same man as Hachis, listed by Cox as among those who surrendered with Klatassine (*Colonist*, 24 August 1864).

Anukatlk may have been In-ne-qualth, identified by Cox as another who surrendered with Klatassine. Expedition volunteer A.E. Atkins refers to three Chilcotins – including Klatassine and Tellot – surrendering, and that the third was said to be McLean's killer (BCARS, F/56/At5A, 6). That man was Tapitt or Tahpitt, who murdered William Manning, and was also one of those who surrendered with Klatassine. He was one of the men executed.

p. 80. "Indians near . . . ": Jack, also known as Johnny, was said to have worked for Charles Waldron of Soda Creek, as well as being around Alexandria. After the death of Donald McLean, he continued on with the expedition for several weeks, and returned at one point to Alexandria to recruit five more Indian volunteers.

p. 81."They're behind us!": Brown, *Klatsassan*, 72.

p. 82. He wore a special breastplate . . . : William Shannon describes it as being of mail. "He wore a coat of mail which he had had prepared and sent out to him from England, and which would turn any ordinary musket bullet. The Indians had often fired at him and thought he possessed a charmed existence because they could not harm him" (Shannon, "The Chilcotin Massacre of 1865," BCARS, F/57/Sh1: 11). Shannon may have been writing from good authority, as he notes also, "After McLean's death his property on the Bonaparte River was sold and the writer had the privilege of looking over his beautiful and well selected library. He had a room in his house devoted for that purpose" (ibid, 13).

## Chapter 22

p. 82. "I have the honour to acknowledge the receipt of your letter announcing to me, that you had bestowed on me a pension . . . ": Sophia Grant McLean to Frederick Seymour, 1 June 1865, BCARS, Colonial Correspondence, F1063, f. 948/65.

p. 83. "We meant war, not murder": Klatassine quoted in *Klatsassan*, Brown, 100.

p. 83: "The ruggedness of the coast range, aided by the absence of all means of transport . . . ": Speech of His Excellency the Governor at the Opening of the Legislative Council, 12th December, 1864, in the *British Columbian*, 14 December 1864.

p. 83: "That Europeans should thus run down wild Indians . . . ": Seymour to Duke of Carlisle, 9 September 1864, Despatches, 16 (79), NAC, G series, no. 353-358.

## PART 3 – THE BOYS

## Chapter 23

p. 86. The winter of 1879-80 was one of the bad ones . . . : This was the first really harsh winter experienced by Nicola Valley ranchers. The first snow fell 7 November, and by January most ranchers were using up their hay to feed stock. Temperatures hit forty degrees below zero F. By March many had exhausted their supplies, and were forced to kill their cattle and sheep. The devastation caused by this winter is described on 28-29 of *Cattle Ranch, The Story of the Douglas Lake Cattle Company*, Nina G. Wooliams, as well as on 45-46 in *Three Bar – The Story of Douglas Lake*, Campbell Carroll.

p. 88. Allen McLean: The spelling of Allen's first name has been given over the years variously

as Allan and Allen. The latter is correct; his full given name was Mathias Allen McLean. Baptism record of George Allen McLean and John Donald McLean, sons of Mathias Allen McLean and Angele. Baptisms 1867-1882, Catholic Mission Records, Oblates of Mary Immaculate, KMA.

p. 89. Dane English: Alex Hare's alias appears in only one reference, the Statement of the Accused signed by Allen McLean in Kamloops 13 December 1879. British Columbia. Attorney-General Documents, BCARS, GR 419, vol. 18, f. 59.

p. 90 . . . .big black gelding . . . : Popularly, the horse has been referred to as a stallion, but Crease recorded Palmer as testifying at the first trial that "He was a gelding," fifteen and three-quarter hands high, and branded LC. Palmer also said he had ridden the horse in a race in Kamloops the previous July. Crease Bench Book, BCARS, GR 1727, vol. 698: 47.

p. 91. . . . it had a white face and a little white on the left eye: This description shows up in only one account of the entire horse-stealing incident. Palmer uses it in one of his depositions. Together with Alex Hare's deposition after capture, and descriptions of other horses by various witnesses, it explains what happened to the black horse.

p. 92. "Don't shoot, boys!": Conversation as described in testimony of William Palmer reported in the *Colonist*, 17 March 1880; Palmer deposition, AG Documents, BCARS, GR 419, vol. 18, f. 59; Judge H.P.P. Crease Bench Book, 15 March–6 July 1880: 50, BCARS, GR 1727, vol. 698.

p. 92 . . . .they were bad neighbours: Jane Palmer, in a letter to Attorney-General and Premier G.A. Walkem, 19 December 1879 (BCARS, GR 429, vol. 1, f. 8, 239/79), complained about Clapperton's handling of the dispute with the Moores, calling him "a danger to society." Clapperton defended himself, writing Walkem 16 January 1880 (BCARS, GR 429, vol. 1, f. 9, 7/80) that the Palmers' house had, indeed, been built on the Moores' land, and that a jury had found the brothers not guilty of assault. The Palmers, said Clapperton, abused him "in foulest epithets."

p. 92. "I dare not recognize my horse": Same sources as "Don't shoot, boys!"

## Chapter 24

p. 94. Others believed him to be the worst of the bunch: John Freemont Smith, a respected Kamloops merchant, noted that, "I became acquainted with Hector, the second brother (who was considered the bad man of the brothers), in 1876. He, in company with the late Johnny O'Brien, drove a bunch of beef cattle across the mountains in the Cassiar country, in that year. The cattle were the property of Victor Guillaume." *Sentinel*, 22 January 1926. Guillaume, a wealthy rancher, was Hector's future brother-in-law.

p. 94. "They say they'll shoot . . . ": H.P.P. Crease, Bench Book, Cariboo Circuit, 19 October–5 November 1880, BCARS, GR 1727, vol. 710: 124.

p. 96. Peter O'Reilly: He was appointed one of six colonial gold commissioners by Governor James Douglas in 1959. As was the case with all the gold commissioners, O'Reilly simultaneously acted in a number of other roles: Indian reserve commissioner, stipendiary magistrate and Justice of the Peace. In 1868 he became a county court judge, travelling throughout the interior of the province from his home in Yale.

p. 97. "If he cannot come up with them in the mountains . . . ": Charles A. Semlin, Cache Creek, to G. A. Walkem, Victoria, 30 November 1879, BCARS, K/J/M22.

p. 97. Caughill . . . now vowed to "proceed on their . . . ": George A. Caughill, Kamloops, to G.A. Walkem, Premier, Victoria, 4 December 1879, BCARS, K/J/M22. Caughill's exact spelling was, "I Shell Prosede on their Capture as long as My time and money will hold out."

p. 97. " . . . one horse of the goods and chattels . . . ": Crease, Legal Papers, BCARS, Add MSS 54, vol. 5: 3260-3261. The charge was "larceny of a horse" as well as receiving stolen goods because "at the time they so received the said horse as aforesaid they well knowing the same to have been feloniously stolen . . . ." Ibid.

p. 97. Ussher, with Shumway showing him the way, very soon cut the McLeans' trail: Tracking by the posse was described by Shumway in his Information and Complaint, 9 December 1879, BCARS, AG Documents, GR 419, vol. 18, f. 59.

p. 98. "I think we'd better get more help . . . ": John McLeod's deposition, n.d., AG Documents, BCARS, GR 419, vol. 18, f. 59.

## Chapter 25

p. 99. George Cavanaugh . . . knew the Palmers well . . . : Information contained in notes by George Cavanaugh in the papers of James Buie Leighton, KMA.

p. 100. "Meet you up the trail . . . " : Events and dialogue as they occurred during the encounter between the McLeans/Hare and the posse are based on testimony by the posse members at their first trial as reported in the *Colonist*, 18 March 1880, as well as on statements by the McLeans and Hare as reported in the *Colonist*, 19 March 1880, and on testimony notes, depositions and affidavits of the posse members, BCARS, AG Documents, GR 419, vol. 18, f. 59; vol. 22.

p. 100 . . . .near a ravine: Contemporary descriptions of the campsite, including notes taken by Clement Cornwall during an interview with William Palmer, and by Crease during the trial, suggest it was located a short distance from the cairn erected in this century in honour of Ussher. The cairn is at a spot higher up on the plateau than where the actual campsite probably was.

p. 100. "Should we leave?": Conversation according to Charlie McLean in statement to Crease, *Colonist*, 19 March 1880.

p. 101. Ussher told them, "They'll never fire a shot": This and other dialogue during the confrontation from testimony as reported in the *Colonist*, 18 March 1880; various depositions BCARS, AG Documents, GR 419, vol. 18, f. 59; Crease Bench Book, New Westminster Circuit, 10 November–19 November 1880, BCARS, GR 1727, vol. 533; Crease, Legal Papers, BCARS, vols. 5, 6.

p. 102. When Ussher was shot . . . : John Edwards deposition, n.d., BCARS, AG Documents, GR

419, vol. 18, f. 59.

p. 104. "Poor Johnny": This exchange according to Statement of Alexander Hare 14 December 1879. "After Ussher was dead I said poor Johnny. Charley [sic] said to me don't call him poor. He would not call you poor if he had you." Ibid.

p. 104. "Let's go down to Trapp's": Conversation according to Allen McLean in statement to Crease, *Colonist*, 19 March 1880; BCARS, AG Documents, GR 149, vol. 18, f. 59; Crease Bench Book, BCARS, GR 1727, vol. 698.

## Chapter 26

p. 104. Shumway was of the firm opinion . . . : Shumway's deposition, BCARS, AG Documents, GR 419, vol. 18, f. 59.

p. 105. His horse, in no better shape, laboured along: T. Alex Bulman, in *Kamloops Cattlemen*, says McLeod's horse gave out before the posse got back to town. "One story had it that McLeod's horse was hit several times but despite these wounds, carried him to the very edge of Kamloops before falling dead. John's handwritten diary mentions the episode in a very modest way and makes more of the fact that the bullet was removed from his kneecap by a gunsmith. There were no doctors in Kamloops in the year 1879 (43)."

p. 106 . . . .carried with them news . . . : A Kamloops resident foretold tragedy in a letter to a friend, written 28 November 1879. "We have our little excitement about here; no shooting affray as yet, but going to be. The McLean boys . . . have taken to the mountains . . . .This is a fine state of things to be terrorized over by four brats, who have threatened to burn the jail in order to destroy the records of their deeds. If these vagabonds are not either arrested or driven to American territory it may become pretty hot for us . . . .I'm afraid it will end in something more serious, for the boys are armed to the teeth . . . ." *Colonist*, 13 December 1879.

## Chapter 27

p. 107. Thomas John Trapp: It's of interest to note that in 1876 Trapp was hired to take charge of a pack train from Kamloops to Tête Jaune Cache, which was being used as a depot for Canadian Pacific Railway survey crews. His party included Louis Fallardeau, who had worked for the Hudson's Bay Company along with his father Michel, an old acquaintance of Donald McLean. In his journal of the trip up the North Thompson River, Trapp notes that Donald McLean Jr. "came along in a raft" 3 July 1876, and left for Kamloops 4 July. Trapp also knew John Glassey (Christina Pauline McLean's husband) who was in charge of that section of the CPR survey, and William Roxborough, the CPR employee who later rode with Ussher's posse. Thomas Trapp Journals, 4 October 1872–28 January 1877 (KMA). After the harsh winter of 1879-80, Trapp sold out to his partner Richie McDonald and moved to New Westminster, where he became a successful merchant.

p. 107. Banjo: This was the dog's real name. Banjo was a faithful companion to Trapp for many years.

p. 107. "Sorry to see you boys out in this weather": Conversation between Trapp and the McLean Gang extracted from Thomas J. Trapp deposition, December, 1879, AG Documents, BCARS, GR 419, vol. 18, f. 59.

## Chapter 28

p. 111. Harry Wilmot had personally ridden hard to Soda Creek . . . : The news of McLean's death didn't reach Alexandria until 22 July, when William Fitzgerald and Jones arrived to arrange for more supplies. Fort Alexandria Journal, 22 July 1864, HBCA, B/5/a/10.

p. 111 . . . she and the family were forced out of their home . . . : George Dunne acquired several pre-emptions, including the 160-acre parcel from McArthur described as "situated on the Bonaparte River at the point where Hat Creek falls into the Bonaparte." This was clearly the land on which McLean's Restaurant was situated. He also bought pre-emption rights to 160 acres between 125 and 127 Mile posts, and pre-empted 160 acres himself at 19 Mile post on the Bonaparte. On 22 November 1867, he applied to purchase fifty acres "situated on the south side of the pre-emption known as McLean's ranch and on the west side of the Bonaparte and lying level with the wagon road and bounded on the north by McLean's ranch. This piece of land was claimed by Sophie McLean, wife of the deceased McLean. I bought her good will to it a few days ago." This would seem to be the land pre-empted by Donald Sr. for either his son John or Allen. Laing, *Colonial Settlers*, 354.

p. 111 . . . . Neither he nor any of his brothers hung on to the property pre-empted in their names: On 15 October 1862, pre-emptions were entered for John McLean, Allen McLean, Charles McLean, and Duncan McLean. None was held. Neither was that of Alexander McLean, taken out the same date but abandoned and taken over by Thomas Morgan in 1867. A pre-emption by Donald McLean, Jr. 21 Decmber 1861 was also abandoned and taken over by James Campbell. Ibid, 357-358, 360.

p. 111. Caesar Vodreaux: A French-Canadian fur trader working for the Hudson's Bay Company. Little else is known about him.

p. 111. Peter Arthur: His name appears as Pierre Arthur McLean in the Oblate baptismal record (Baptisms 1864-1879, St. Andrew's Cathedral, Victoria), which is written in French, but he was probably named by Sophia after her father, Peter Grant. The Oblates often translated English names into the French version.

p. 112 . . . . an illegitimate baby girl, whom she named Mary-Ethel: Baptisms 1867-1882, Catholic Mission Records, Oblates of Mary Immaculate, KMA.

p. 112. "It is talked here . . . ": Charles Semlin, Cache Creek, to George Anthony Walkem, Victoria, 11 December 1879, BCARS, K/J/M22.

## Chapter 29

p. 114. "Don't tell anyone that we have passed here . . . ": Statement of Alexander Hare, 14 December 1879, AG Documents, BCARS, GR 419, vol. 18, f. 59..

p. 115. "I don't know anything about you . . . ": Similar wording of Kelly's comment comes from Judge H.P.P. Crease, who wrote, "I had from one of the convicts themselves, that Kelly only said, 'I

have nothing to do with you fellows.' When they shot him down like a wild beast, dragged his body into the bush – stole his watch, chain and pistol . . . ." Crease, Legal Papers, BCARS, Add MSS 54, vol. 5: 3,221.

p. 115. "He growled about some bread . . . ": This was told by Allen McLean to Robert Scott, the next rancher the gang visited. Deposition of Robert Scott, Victoria, 12 February 1880, AG Documents, BCARS, GR 419, vol. 18, f. 59.

p. 115. "Allen cocked his rifle . . . ": Statement of Alexander Hare, 14 December 1879, ibid. Description of ransacking Kelly's cabin is also taken from Hare's statement.

## Chapter 30

p. 116. They would ride south into the Nicola Valley . . . : Susan Allison, in *A Pioneer Gentlewoman in British Columbia* (edited by Margaret A. Ormsby) tells an interesting anecdote. "It was after they had killed Ussher that I was expecting my husband to return from one of his drives. I looked out of my window and saw six Indians passing. Frosty Nose was with them so I ran out to the fence with little Edgar following me to ask if they had seen him coming. They stopped, and one put up his gun pointing at an object behind me. Frosty Nose rode up to him, threw up his arms, and said something to him. I turned to see what he had aimed at – it was my son, little Edgar! When I turned again they had all ridden on except Frosty Nose, who, never at a loss for a lying excuse, said that the man had seen one of our pet deer in the distance and would have shot it had he not intervened. Times were very risky so I did not argue. I was afterwards told that it was one of the McLean boys on his way to the head of the lake and that he thought I had gone out to take off their attention to [from] those who would arrest him. His sister, a fair girl wearing a sunbonnet, passed riding a side saddle and carrying an infant. Poor girl, she was going to her mother's people! The Indians are good to those of kin to them. My husband returned from his drive next day and looking over the cattle found a three year old steer not long killed, with one hind quarter cut off. The Indians said the McLeans had done it. He hurried to the harbour to give information but our boat was gone. Afterwards an Indian brought it back and said that he had found it across the lake" (47). While the story is undoubtedly based on a true incident, it could not possibly have happened when she said it did, since she was living at Sunnyside, near present-day Westbank on Okanagan Lake, at the time. Susan Allison did not begin her memoirs until the late 1920s, when she was in her eighties, and Ormsby acknowledges that her memory for dates was poor.

p. 116. "Hello, boys. Cold day, isn't it?": The conversation between Robert Scott and the McLeans is based on testimony and depositions of Scott, mainly depositions in Kamloops, 8 December 1879, and Victoria, 12 February 1880, BCARS, AG Documents, GR 419, vol. 18, f. 59. The Colonist erroneously reported in its coverage of the trial that a man named John Roberts testified. In fact, the man the reporter thought was John Roberts was actually Robert Scott.

p. 117. "I then saw the blood . . . ": Scott's deposition, Kamloops, 8 December 1879, ibid.

## Chapter 31

p. 119. She was a tough, self-centred woman . . . : Cavanaugh wrote, "I enquired why you should not go to the sochial, she said I considder myself above them - - - man of Nicolavally their was a Misanick 100 cards their and the Mainigers told me that I was the prettes lady and the best figur at the ball I had my card 6 dances ahead And no paint on when other ladies had the paint streming down their face is that so I said is no wonder you think yourself above them . . . ." Notes by George Cavanaugh in James Buie Leighton Papers, KMA.

p. 121. "What shall we do?" she asked: George Cavanaugh deposition, n.d., AG Documents, BCARS, GR 419, vol. 18, f. 59. The rest of the conversation with the McLeans is extracted from the depositions and testimony of Cavanaugh and Jane Palmer, n.d. (ibid).

## Chapter 32

p. 124. "I saw a large gash in the cheek . . . ": Palmer's deposition, n.d., BCARS, AG Documents, GR 419, vol. 18, f. 59.

p. 125. They were the torn-up warrant . . . : John T. Edwards deposition, n.d., BCARS, AG Documents, GR 419, vol. 18, f. 59.

## Chapter 33

p. 126. "I went up to Kelly's cabin, saw that he was not at home . . . ": William McLeod deposition, Kamloops, 10 December 1879, AG Documents, BCARS, GR 419, vol. 18, f. 59.

## Chapter 34

p. 128. *Noisy Peggy*: That was a nickname for the Spallumcheen, a fifty-four-ton sternwheeler operated on Kamloops Lake by the Kamloops Steam Navigation Company, in which John Andrew Mara was a partner with Frank J. Barnard of Barnard's Express fame, T.L. Briggs, and John Wilson.

p. 128. "Charles the Silent . . . ": *Colonist*, 1 May 1875, cited in Lynne Stonier-Newman, *Policing a Pioneer Province*, 34.

p. 129. "By the arrival of a special messenger . . . ": Ranald Mcdonald from Hat Creek to his brother Benjamin, 14 January 1874, HCRA. They were sons of Archibald Mcdonald, an HBC trader at Fort Colville and Fort George. Ranald faked his way into Japan, which at that time was closed to foreigners, in 1848. He and brother Allan arrived in B.C. in 1858. In 1861-62 Ranald and George Barnston, who were related by marriage, explored the Bentinck Arm route to the Cariboo mining district. This was the competing route to Alfred Waddington's Bute Inlet road. Ranald later settled for a time in the Bonaparte and worked for Frank J. Barnard of Barnard's Express.

## Chapter 35

p. 131. Clapperton had stopped . . . : "Wed. May 11th, 1864. Walked to McLean's, Bonaparte River; expecting to get food to purchase; had none to sell; were obliged to go to Scotty's, 18 miles from Cornwall's. Stopped all night." John Clapperton, "Jottings from our first four years in

British Columbia (1862-66)," BCARS, E/C/C533.

## Chapter 36

p. 132. Chillihitzia: Albert Elgin Howse described him as "a fine old Indian, tall and dignified, who always had interpreted for Sir James Douglas," and as "a big Indian and a fine-looking figure as he sat upon his horse.": Howse said Chillihitzia had two wives. Howse interview, typescript, n.d., NVA, Add MSS 42, f. 2: 1. It is also of interest to note that Donald McLean apparently had known Chillihitzia. "D. McLean had a Conference with Indians of this place and Silakeepsah of the Ouckanaagans relative to the disputes and feuds amongst them in which it was attempted to be amicably settled to the satisfaction of all concerned." Kamloops Journal, 12 January 1859, KMA.

p. 133. "Allen took out his knife . . . ": Statement of Alex Hare, Kamloops, 14 December 1879, AG Documents, BCARS, GR 419, vol. 18, f. 59.

## Chapter 37

p. 134. The cabin: The cabin in which the McLean Gang were besieged still stands. It is used for equipment and meat storage.

p. 135. Chillihitzia arrived later that day . . . : Crease was not of the opinion that Chillihitzia was anxious to help the whites. "It was not until 3 p.m. of the first day of the siege of these outlaws that the chief . . . consented to let the law take its course against the outlaws." Crease, Legal Papers, BCARS, Add MSS 54, vol. 5: 3,223.

## Chapter 38

p. 136. The whole party, described as "lusty and fearless fellows . . . ": The Todd posse was so described by the *Colonist* of Victoria 14 December 1879. Officer Richard Quain was a volunteer in the Maori war "in wich he gained considerable distinction." Officer Henry Roycraft, in addition to serving in the Wolseley expedition, was said to have joined the French army during the Franco-Mexican war "and has frequently been in action." Members of the posse, besides Roycraft and Quain, included special constables F. Martin, L.B. Lewis, J. Graham, J.D. McDonald, J. Dowdall, V. Cooke, J. Hough, E. Hooson and A. Boggs.

p. 136. The outlaws were now guilty of two murders "and have cleaned Upper Nicola out of firearms': British Columbia Telegraph, J.A. Mara, Kamloops, to G.A. Walkem, Victoria, 10 December 1879, BCARS, K/J/M22.

## Chapter 39

p. 138. Johnny Chillihitzia, or Saliesta: Later became chief.

p. 138. "McLean Bros & Alex Hare will you surrender quietly . . . ": John Clapperton, Nicola, to G.A. Walkem, Victoria, 15 December 1879, BCARS, K/J/M22.

p. 138. "I began to think my conjecture right . . . ": Ibid. The wordings of the messages back and forth to the McLeans' cabin are also taken from this source, collaborated by J.T. Edwards' deposition/testimony, n.d., BCARS, GR 419, vol. 18, f. 59.

p. 139. "The Indian returns to the door . . . ": Ibid.

p. 139. "The boys say they will not surrender . . . ": Ibid.

## Chapter 40

p. 140. "Will dispatch today . . . ": British Columbia Telegraph, J.C. Hughes, New Westminster, to G.A. Walkem, Victoria, 11 December 1879, BCARS, K/J/M22.

## Chapter 41

p. 141. . . .A couple of the boys holed up in a cave: Ashcroft Journal, n.d. (Clipping file, Ashcroft Museum). "About 17 miles north of Ashcroft on the east side of the Bonaparte river, up a deep gulch, there is a natural curve running into the mountain. Tradition tells us that in this cave the McLean outlaws hid themselves when pursued by officers of the law after they had escaped from the Kamloops jail. They had an abundance of food stored there and were prepared to endure a siege of long duration. Tradition also tells us the same boys began their career of crime owing to a loss of the Hat Creek property which had been technically stolen from them."

p. 142. At a race in Williams Lake . . . : Anecdote recounted in *Cariboo Chronicles*, John Roberts.

p. 142. Camels: Henry Ingram, Frank Laumeister and Adam Heffley imported twenty-one camels from the U.S. for packing. After the venture failed, the camels were dispersed, some in the Lac La Hache area, others at Grande Prairie where Ingram took up ranching. The last one died at Grande Prairie around the turn of the century.

## Chapter 42

p. 143. Archie decided to make another try for the creek: William Ward Spinks, "The McLean Boys," *Tales of the British Columbia Frontier*, 58.

p. 144. "Hey, there, what's the password?" came a distant voice: Ibid.

p. 144. Joe and his father had played a role . . . : This story is recounted in various sources, including "The Last Stand of the McLeans" by Walter Deccar in the *Vancouver Sun*, 16 November 1935. John Murray also refers to the incident in a letter to G.A. Walkem. "Young Hare was at Coutlies along about ten days ago but it was not known there then that a warrant was out for his arrest he had a peajacket on and a revolver straped [sic] to his side underneath it. Allen Charlie and Archie were at Hugh Murrays houseat Douglas Lake about the same time and they told Murray that they would not be taken alive." Murray, Spences Bridge, to Walkem, Victoria, 13 December 1879, BCARS, K/J/M22.

p. 145. Now Joe Coutlie found himself on the opposite side . . . : Deccar, "The Last Stand of the McLeans." Joe Coutlie described the event in an interview with Deccar. Joe Coutlie later worked for the Douglas Lake Cattle Company, where he became foreman. He died 18 October 1945 at St. Paul's Hospital, Vancouver.

## Chapter 43

p. 146. The distance from Cache Creek to the "seat of war . . . ": John Murray, Spences Bridge, to G.A. Walkem, New Westminster, British Columbia Telegraph, 12 December 1879, BCARS, K/J/M22.

p. 147. "Bring down any good firearms and handcuffs": Walkem, New Westminster, to

George Lindsay, Barkerville, British Columbia Telegraph, 12 December 1879, ibid.

p. 147. "Use your influence . . . ": D'Herbomez to Grandidier, McGuckin, and Richard, British Columbia Telegraph, 12 December 1879, ibid.

p. 147. "There are at the dockyard . . . ": *Colonist*, 13 December 1879.

## Chapter 44

p. 148. . . .the posse members were impatient: Among those known to have been at the siege at Douglas Lake were George Caughill, Chief Chillihitzia, Johnny Chillihitzia (Saliesta), John Clapperton, Joe Coutlie, William Croft, John T. Edwards, A.E. Howse, James Jamieson, James Kennedy, John Leonard, Thomas Ombie, Thomas "Pike" Richardson, Frederick Rush, Johnston Stevenson, Thomas Trotter, William Palmer.

p. 149. Hay bales were brought in and piled on top of a wagon . . . : The fortified wagon remained at the scene for several decades after the siege but eventually arrived at such a state of disrepair that the owners, not realizing the significance of it, destroyed it.

p. 149. "I have only one friend left": Statement of Alexander Hare, Kamloops, 14 December 1879, BCARS, GR 419, vol. 18., f. 59.

p. 150. Allen told us that whoever did not obey our orders . . . : Ibid.

## Chapter 45

p. 151. John Leonard: Son of Jean Baptiste Leonard, who settled at San Poel Creek east of Kamloops in the 1860s. Louis Campbell, who settled near the Leonards, married Jean Leonard's daughter. San Poel Creek is now called Campbell Creek.

p. 152. "Surrender by coming outside . . . ": Communications between the posse and the gang, as well as the circumstances of surrender and dialogue in this chapter, are taken from John Clapperton's official report to Walkem, and John Edwards' deposition/testimony. Exceptions are noted in following chapter notes.

p. 154. "My feet are going to get damn cold . . . ": Deccar, "The Last Stand of the McLeans." Joe Coutlie was a witness to this conversation.

p. 155. "If I had kept your horse . . . ": This conversation related in Palmer deposition, n.d., AG Documents, BCARS, GR 419, vol. 18, f. 59.

## Chapter 46

p. 156. "Some saying they would shoot them . . . ": Shumway and Palmer deposition, New Westminster, March, 1880, BCARS, GR 419, vol. 18, f. 59.

p. 156. " . . . to hang the McLeans . . . ": Howse wrote, "We were going over to hang the McLeans at Kamloops, lynch them is the proper term no doubt, but the Kamloops fellows that were to be participants in the affair funked and so it did not come off . . . . That murder, the unprovoked and brutal killing of Johnny Usher [sic] and the sheepherder Kelly, had so thoroughly aroused this whole community that no one would have blamed us if we had carried out our plans and lynched the gang. I never knew any crime create the same public feeling that Usher's [sic] murder did . . . .It was just as well, however, that we did not take the law into our own hands. If we had Judge Begbie would have been down on us like a thousand of bricks, and I suppose we would have been tried for murder, but just as sure as the sun shines, not a jury in British Columbia but would have acquitted us without leaving the box." Howse, NVMA, E/E/84, 14-15.

p. 156. "John Tannatt Ussher": Markers were removed from gravesites and collected in a corner of Pioneer Cemetery in a misdirected "clean-up" many years later. However, a replacement plaque marks Ussher's original burial site. It reads, "In memory of John T. Ussher, 1844-1879, killed by the McLean Bros." Ussher is also remembered with a stone cairn erected and unveiled in August 1967 about twelve miles south of Kamloops near where he was killed. The bronze plaque on the cairn reads: "John Tannatt Ussher. In December 1879 Provincial Police Constable John Tannatt Ussher was killed near this spot by the notorious McLean gang. With deputies W. Palmer, A. Shumway and J. McLeod, the unarmed but fearless officer tracked and attempted to arrest these known horse thieves, and gave his life while attempting to secure peace and order in our growing West." The cairn is on private property but can be freely visited. Not far from it is a small lake called Ussher Lake. Elsewhere in the region are other geographical features honouring those citizens of the day either directly or indirectly involved: McLeod Lake, Trapp Lake, Shumway Lake, Shumway Hill.

p. 157. Charlie stupidly confessed to putting a bullet in Kelly . . . : Charlie's Statement of the Accused, Kamloops, 13 December 1879, BCARS, GR 419, vol. 18, f. 59.

p. 157. "I killed no man": Allen's Statement of the Accused, same date, ibid.

p. 157. "I never shot Ussher": Archie's Statement of the Accused, same date, ibid.

p. 157. Veasey's willingness to side against Hector . . . : The Veasey family's acquaintance with the McLean boys is described in "Pioneers of the Bonapart" by M. W. Boss, *Northwest Digest,* January, 1952: 4. Boss says Mrs. Veasey "thought they should have received leniency" and that one evening the boys came down a hill onto the Veasey farm on the Bonaparte. "It was dusk and she nervously pushed the children into the house and she went out to meet the boys. One of them shouted out to her, 'Do not be afraid, Mrs. Veasey. We will not harm you but we are starving.' That was sufficient for Mrs. Veasey, and although she said she knew she was breaking the law, she loaded them down with all the food they could carry. Years later she said, 'If they only knew how scared I was they could have had the farm.'"

p. 157. "I never aided and abetted them": Hector's Statement of the Accused, Kamloops, 15 December 1879, ibid.

## Chapter 48

p. 158. "The weather was very severe . . . ": Charles A. Semlin, Cache Creek, to G.A. Walkem, Victoria, 18 December 1879, BCARS, K/J/M22.

p. 159. Joseph Burr: A descendant of Joe Burr was actor Raymond Burr, who went from New Westminster to Hollywood as TV lawyer Perry Mason and police chief Robert Ironside.

## Chapter 49

p. 161. " . . . entirely too small . . . ": *Colonist,* 17 November 1866, cited in "New Westminster 1859-1871," thesis by Margaret Lillooet McDonald, 208.

## Chapter 50

p. 161. "We the undersigned . . . ": Archie, Charlie and Allen McLean, New Westminster Jail, to Hon. G.A. Walkem, Victoria, 27 February 1880, BCARS, K/J/M22, 14/80.

p. 162 . . . .he was prime legislative material: Theodore Davie later became premier of British Columbia, then chief justice. A grand-nephew, E. Davie Fulton, QC, was the member of parliament for Kamloops for many years, federal justice minister, then leader of the provincial Conservative party, and later a judge.

p. 163. "My father was killed . . . ": *Colonist,* 14 March 1880.

p. 164. "The shoes worn in this jail . . . ": Ibid.

## Chapter 51

p. 165. "It may invalidate the commission": Begbie, Victoria, to Humphrey, Victoria, 9 March 1880, cited in *Colonist,* 22 June 1880.

p. 166. "The deadlock . . . ": *Colonist,* 11 March 1880.

p. 166. " . . . a miserable bungle . . . ": *Colonist,* 12 March 1880.

## Chapter 52

p. 167. Seventeen-man grand jury . . . : Members of the grand jury were J.C. Armstrong, D. Withrow, W.B. Townsend, W.D. Ferris (foreman), H. McRoberts, G.C. Webster, John Murray, P. Arnaud, C.G. Major, A. Coulthard, J.E. Lord, J.W. Howison, N. Johnston, F. Eickhoff, W. Blackie, R.W. Deane and H. Elliott. *Colonist,* 14 March 1880.

p. 167. "The occasion which has called us together . . . ": *Colonist,* 16 March 1880; Crease, Legal Papers, BCARS, Add MSS 54, vol. 6, f. 33: 3,500-3,511.

## Chapter 53

p. 170. The court, on behalf of "our Lady the Queen . . . ": AG Documents, BCARS, GR 419, vol. 18, f. 59.

p. 170. " . . . in the vicinage . . . ": *Colonist,* 17 March 1880.

p. 170. "The plain point is . . . ": Ibid. Following dialogue based on same report; Facts, AG Documents, BCARS, GR 419, vol. 18, f. 59; Trial notes, ibid; Crease Bench Book, BCARS, GR 1727, vol. 698.

## Chapter 54

p. 173. "Can you identify this coat?": Ibid.

## Chapter 55

p. 174. "Those look like Ussher's . . . ": Ibid.

## Chapter 56

p. 180. "To the Grand Jury empanelled at New Westminster . . . ": Witnesses to the Grand Jury, New Westminster, 19 March 1880, BCARS, Add MSS 54, vol. 5, f. 32.

p. 181. "They are charged in the first count . . . ": Crease's charge is based on the *Colonist,* 20 March 1880; Crease's Bench Book, BCARS,

GR 1727, vol. 698; Crease, Legal Papers, BCARS, Add MSS 54, vol. 6, f. 33: 3,544.

## Chapter 57

p. 184. "Allen McLean, do you have anything to say . . . ": Ibid.

p. 184. "Alex stole a five-shooter from Bartlett Newman . . . " The *Colonist* reporter called this man Barclay Sherman, but it was likely a result of poor note-taking. Bartlett Newman was, at the time of the murders, ranching with his sons at the north end of Trapp Lake. They later sold to John Peterson, and the property became known as the Willow Ranch.

p. 185. " . . . After a long and patient trial . . . ": *Colonist*, 21 March 1880.

## Chapter 58

p. 186. "We think it would be both unfair and unjust . . . ": Trapp, New Westminster, to Walkem, Victoria, 20 March 1880, BCARS, K/J/M22.

p. 187 "How is the boy?": Allen to Angele, cited in the *Daily Standard*, 20 March 1880.

p. 188. "I cannot admit the accuracy . . . ": Crease to Walkem, 12 April 1880, Crease Legal Papers, BCARS, Add MSS 54, vol. 5, f. 32.

p. 188. "I am not instructed . . . ": Ibid. Davie to Crease, Victoria, 7 April 1880.

p. 189. Back in Kamloops . . . : Baptisms 1867-1882, Catholic Mission Records, Oblates of Mary Immaculate, KMA.

p. 189 . . . ."a rule directing the issue of a writ of *habeas corpus* . . . ": *Colonist*, 5 June 1880.

## Chapter 59

p. 193. "The Supreme Court, by the acts constituting it, has full jurisdiction . . . ": Dialogue in this chapter based on *Colonist*, 5 June 1880.

## Chapter 60

p. 194. "The horse commenced to buck . . . ": Crease's Bench Book, BCARS, GR 1727, vol. 710: 126.

p. 195. They fired him when he "made such a fuss" . . . : C. F. Cornwall Diary and Farm Record (vol. 1), 17 November 1866–7 June 1869, BCARS, Add MSS 759: 231. The entry 23 April 1869 states, "In the morning saddled the brown colt for H. McLean to ride but he made such a fuss about mounting him that I discharged him on the spot." Hector was fifteen at the time.

p. 195. "Don't care if there is . . . ": Crease's Bench Book, BCARS, GR 1727, vol. 710: 90.

## Chapter 61

p. 196. The Supreme Court issued its judgment: Since the publication of the author's original book, 'We've Killed Johnny Ussher!', an excellent article has been published examining the legal argument over commissions. The article is "The Kamloops Outlaws and Commissions of Assize in Nineteenth Century British Columbia," by Hamar Foster, which appeared in *Essays in the History of Canadian Law*, 1983: 308-364.

p. 196. "Indeed, it has been shown by the affidavit of the provincial secretary that no less than ninety-six assizes . . . ": McCreight and following dialogue from *Colonist*, 9 June 1880.

p. 197. "I have suffered some of this same experience . . . ": *Colonist*, 10 June 1880.

p. 198. "I felt much embarrassed . . . ": *Colonist*, 12 June 1880.

p. 198. "The prisoner says . . . ": *The Queen vs. Allan* [sic] *McLean*, etc., 110, cited in Rothenburger, 'We've Shot Johnny Ussher!', 164; Foster, *The Kamloops Outlaws and Commissions of Assize*, 352.

p. 199. "All the law and learning . . . ": Ibid, 164.

## Chapter 62

p. 199. "The decision of the Supreme . . . " *Colonist*, 29 June 1880.

## Chapter 63

p. 202. " . . . Very pleasant, great favorite with all . . . ": This and following quotes from Sarah Crease, "Notes of a trip with my dear husband on circuit to Cariboo, Kamloops and New Westminster, 1 September–7 December 1880," BCARS, A/E/C86/C861.1.

p. 203. "Don't let nobody catch you": Crease's Bench Book, BCARS, GR 1727, vol. 710: 84. Other quotes from witnesses in Hector McLean's trial from same source, 76-138.

p. 203. " . . . the father of cattle stealing . . . ": Crease wrote, "John Vesey [sic] was the father of cattle stealing in that district. That is a crime which has been very frequent among the vast rolling hills and bunch grass slopes of the district of Kamloops. It is one almost impossible of detection − for it is generally done thro' the agency of some of the finest riders in the world − the halfbreeds who know every mile of the country . . . . I have reason to believe that the convict was the principal instrument in leading the McLean youths into similar offenses − which ended at last so fatally. It is a greater mischief in a white man of position to employ halfbreeds to consummate these offenses than if they carried them out alone − for in addition to the offense they are prostituting their position and influence to lead the ignorant into crime." Crease, Victoria, to Minister of Justice, Ottawa, 27 February 1881, Correspondence Outward, 1881, BCARS, A/E/C86/C86J.

p. 204. The jury agreed . . . : The foreman, according to Crease, was "Mr. Pringle," but it's not known whether it was Alex Pringle, who ranched at Monte Creek east of Kamloops, or John Pringle, a packer turned rancher.

## Chapter 64

p. 205. The grand jury having found true bills . . . : The indictments were as follows: All four for participating directly in the murder of Ussher; Archie and Alex for doing the deed, with Allen and Charlie aiding and abetting; all four for the murder of Kelly; Allen for shooting with intent to murder Palmer, the rest with aiding and abetting; Allen for intent to resist lawful apprehension, the rest for aiding and abetting; intent to commit grievous bodily harm on Palmer; all for intent to murder John McLeod; all with stealing Palmer's horse and with receiving a stolen horse; all with stealing a shotgun and rifle from Trapp. Crease, Legal Papers, BCARS, Add MSS, vol. 6, f. 33: 3,478-3,498.

p. 205. "Who cares for the prisoners?": Dialogue in second trial from *Colonist*, 2, 5, 12-13, 17

November 1880; Crease's Bench Book, New Westminster Circuit Fall 1880, BCARS, GR 1727, vol. 533: 22-228.

p. 206. "The youth of the country . . . ": Ibid.

## Chapter 65

p. 206. "My duty is doubly painful . . . ": Ibid.

## Chapter 66

p. 207. "How far did you say . . . ": Ibid.

## Chapter 67

p. 209: "After a very careful but painful consideration . . . ": Ibid.

## Chapter 68

p. 211. "Get back in your cell, Allen . . . ": *Colonist*, 1 February 1881.

p. 212. "There only remains . . . ": Crease to Secretary of State, 24 March 1880, BCARS, Add MSS 54, vol. 6, f. 33; Governor general's aide to acting Minister of Justice Sir Alexander Campbell, 18 May 1880, PAC RG 13 C-1, vol. 1418, cited in Foster.

## Chapter 69

p. 213. "You would oblige me . . . ": Horris, New Westminster, to Crease, Victoria, 4 January 1881, Crease Legal Papers, BCARS, Add MSS 54, vol. 6, f. 33: 3,468.

p. 213. "I cannot conceive . . . ": Crease, Pentrelew, to Horris, New Westminster, 19 January 1881, Crease, Correspondence Outward 1881, BCARS, A/E/C86/C86J.

p. 213. "I think I can undress myself . . . ": Dialogue quoted in *Mainland Guardian*, reprinted in *Inland Sentinel*, 3 February 1881.

## Chapter 70

p. 217. "When you get out of prison . . . ": Allen McLean to friend, cited in *Dominion Pacific Herald*, 2 February 1881.

p. 217. "I have a favour to ask of you . . . ": Alex Hare to Nick Hare, ibid.

## Chapter 71

p. 218. " . . . That's a fair piece of work . . . ": *Colonist*, 2 February 1881.

p. 218. " . . . Under here we'll meet again . . . ": Ibid.

## Chapter 72

p. 221. "What's your name?": Dialogue based mainly on *Colonist*, 2 February 1881.

p. 223. "Remember me to little Willy": *Colonist*, 3 February 1881.

## PART 4 – SHOOTOUT ON THE RESERVE

## Chapter 74

p. 227. "Let's go home and turn our horses loose," said Alex . . . : *Sentinel*, 5 November 1887.

p. 228. "When I saw Oxime drop I was alone. Alex made for me and I ran . . . ": Ibid.

## Chapter 75

p. 230. "Who is it?" Louis asked: Ibid.

## Chapter 76

p. 231. " . . . Good men of this district": Ibid.

p. 231. "The court room presented quite a picture . . . ": Ibid. Other quotes regarding inquest this chapter from same source.

p. 232. A "friendly" arrangement . . . : George Rose Innes and Son and Crick to Freshfields and Williams, Billiter Square Building, London (E.C.), 16 December 1886, HBCA, A.10/122, f. 561-562.

## PART 5 – THE COWBOY AND THE OUTLAW

## Chapter 78

p. 237 . . . Charlie killed a young Boer . . . : Incident related by Laurence Bauman, letter to Pat Spiers, 17 March 1968.

p. 237. " . . . highly irregular conduct . . . ": SACA, 151, file 1731.

## Chapter 79

p. 239. " . . . confined to his house by his injuries": *Sentinel*, 5 May 1887.

p. 239. " . . . an experienced whiteman cook . . . ": *Sentinel*, 26 March 1887.

p. 241. "I've got to go and see Mother": Bauman to Spiers, 29 July 1970.

## Chapter 80

p. 242. "What the hell do you want?": This and other quotes in exchange between Stout and the posse members are taken from *Kamloops Standard*, 23 November 1907.

p. 243. "I fired almost as soon as the flash came": Ibid.

## PART 6 – FAMILY HONOUR

## Chapter 82

p. 247 . . . .Kamloops was no longer "a one-horse town . . . ": *Sentinel*, 7 January 1908.

p. 247. "For conspicuous gallantry . . . ": Citation, No. 688302 Private, G. McLean, London Gazette No. 30234, 14 August 1917.

p. 249. "There were two machine guns playing on us . . . ": *Kamloops Telegram*, 11 October 1917.

## Chapter 83

p. 251. He was "a likeable type . . . ": Interview, William Pearson Philip, 1992.

p. 251. "Me go England . . . ": *Merritt Herald*, 14 September 1934.

---

# SELECT BIBLIOGRAPHY

## ABBREVIATIONS

BCARS: B.C. Archives and Records Service
HBCA: Hudson's Bay Company Archives
HCRA: Hat Creek Ranch Archives
KMA: Kamloops Museum and Archives
NAC: National Archives of Canada
NVA: Nicola Valley Archives
PAM: Public Archives of Manitoba
SACA: South Africa Constabulary Archives

## PUBLISHED SOURCES

Akrigg, G.P.V. and Helen B. *British Columbia Chronicle 1847-1871, Gold and Colonists.* Vancouver: Discovery Press 1977.

Balf, Mary. Kamloops, *A History of the District up*

to 1914. Kamloops: Kamloops Museum Association 1969.

Ballantyne, Robert Michael. *Hudson's Bay or Every-day Life in the Wilds of North America, During Six Years Residence in the Territories of the Honorable Hudson's Bay Company.* London: Thomas Nelson and Sons 1902.

Bancroft, Hubert Howe (et al). *History of British Columbia 1792-1887 (The Works of Hubert Howe Bancroft),* Vol. XXXII. San Francisco: History Company 1887.

Boss, M.W. "Pioneers of the Bonaparte," *Northwest Digest,* January, 1952.

Bowsfield, Hartwell, ed. *Fort Victoria Letters 1846-1851.* Hudson's Bay Record Society, Winnipeg, 1979.

British Columbia, Supreme Court. *The Queen vs. Allan [sic] McLean, Charles McLean, Archibald McLean, Alexander Hare, Indicted and tried for murder, Judgment of the Court, June 26, 1880.* Victoria: McMillan & Son, Job Printers 1880.

Brown, Jennifer S.H. *Strangers in Blood.* Vancouver and London: University of British Columbia Press 1980.

Brown, R.C.L. *Klatsassan and other Reminiscences of Missionary Life in British Columbia.* London: Published under the direction of the Tract Committee, Society for Promoting Christian Knowledge 1873.

Bryce, George. *The Romantic Settlement of Lord Selkirk's Colonists.* Toronto: The Musson Book Company 1909.

Bulman, T. Alex. *Kamloops Cattlemen.* Sidney: Gray's Publishing 1972.

Carroll, Campbell. *Three Bar – The Story of Douglas Lake.* Vancouver: Mitchell Press 1958.

Champness, W. *To Cariboo and Back in 1862.* Fairfield, Wash.: Ye Galleon Press 1972.

Crease, H.P.P. *Judgement of the Supreme Court of British Columbia. The Queen vs. Allan [sic] McLean, Charles McLean, Archibald McLean, Alexander Hare.* Victoria, June 26, 1880.

Cronin, Kay. *A Cross in the Wilderness.* Vancouver: Mitchell Press 1961.

Deccar, Walter. "The Last Stand of the McLeans." *Vancouver Sun,* 16 November 1935.

Duff, Wilson. "The Impact of the White Man." *The Indian History of British Columbia.* Vol. 1 of *Anthropology in British Columbia* Memoir No. 5. Victoria, 1964.

"Extracts from the depositions respecting the Bute Inlet Massacre made before J.L. Wood, esq., Acting Stipendiary Magistrate for Vancouver Island, which may lead to the identification of the murderers." *Government Gazette,* 25 June 1864.

Farrand, Livingston. "The Chilcotin." *Reports on the North-Western Tribes, 1892-98.* London: British Association for the Advancement of Science (12th and Final Report), Bristol Meeting 1898.

Foster, Hamar. "The Kamloops Outlaws and Commissions of Assize in Nineteenth-Century British Columbia." *Essays in the History of Canadian Law.* David H. Flaherty, ed. 1983.

Glavin, Terry. *Nemiah, The Unconquered Country.* Vancouver: New Star Books 1992.

Hawthorn, H.B.; Belshaw, C.S.; Jamieson, S.M. *The Indians of British Columbia.* Toronto: University of Toronto Press 1958.

*Henderson's British Columbia Gazeteers and Directories, 1889 & 1890.* Victoria.

Howay, F.W. "The Bute Inlet Massacre and the Chilcotin War 1864-1866." *British Columbia from Earliest Times to Present.* Vol. 2. Vancouver: S.J. Clarke Publishing Company 1914.

Hussey, John A. *The History of Fort Vancouver and Its Physical Structure.* Washington State Historical Society 1957.

Jackson, James A. *The Centennial History of Manitoba.* Toronto: McClelland and Stewart, 1970.

Kopas, Cliff. *Bella Coola.* Vancouver: Mitchell Press Ltd. 1970.

Le Jeune, Father J. M. *Chinook Rudiments.* Kamloops 1924.

MacEwan, Grant. *Cornerstone Colony, Selkirk's Contribution to the Canadian West.* Saskatoon: Western Producer Prairie Books 1977.

MacLean, J.P. *A History of the Clan MacLean.* Cincinnati: Robert Clarke & Co. 1889.

McLean, John. *John McLean's Notes of a Twenty-Five Years' Service in the Hudson's Bay Territory.* Edited by W. Stewart Wallace. Toronto: The Champlain Society 1912.

Martin, Chester, editor. *Red River Settlement, Papers in the Canadian Archives Relating to the Pioneers.* Archives Branch 1910.

Mayne, R.C. *Four years in British Columbia and Vancouver Island: an account of their forests, rivers, coasts, gold fields, and resources for colonisation,* London 1862.

Merk, Frederick. *Fur Trade and Empire.* Cambridge: The Belknap Press of Harvard University Press 1968.

Morice, Adrian Gabriel. *History of the Northern Interior of British Columbia.* Toronto: William Briggs 1905.

Nesbitt, J.K. "Old Homes and Families." *Victoria Colonist,* Mag. sect., 26 February 1950; 29 October 1950; 28 January 1951; 18 May 1952.

Newman, Peter C. *Caesars of the Wilderness.* Markham, Ont.: Penguin Books Canada, 1988.

Ormsby, Margaret A. *British Columbia, A History.* Vancouver: The MacMillan Company of Canada Ltd. 1958.

Palmer, Henry Spencer. *Report of a Journey of Survey from Victoria to Fort Alexander via Bentinck Arm.* New Westminster: Royal Engineer Press 1863.

Poole, C.E. *Queen Charlotte Islands, A Narrative of Discovery and Adventure in the North Pacific.* West Vancouver: J. J. Douglas 1972 (First published by Hurst and Blackett, Publishers, London, 1872).

*Prospectus of the Bentinck Arm and Fraser River Road Company Ltd.,* Victoria, 1862.

Rich. E.E., ed. *Colin Robertson's Correspondence Book, September 1817 to September 1822.* London: Champlain Society for the Hudson's Bay Record Society 1919.

Roberts, John A. *Cariboo Chronicles.* Williams Lake, 1979.

Rothenburger, Mel. *The Chilcotin War.* Langley: Mr. Paperback 1978.

——. *'We've Killed Johnny Ussher!'.* Vancouver: Mitchell Press 1973.

Saunders, Frederick John. "Homatcho." *Resources of British Columbia, March, April 1885.*

Seymour, Frederick. "Speech of His Excellency the Governor, At The Opening of The Legislative Council, 12th December, 1864." *British Columbian,* 14 December 1864.

Shaw, George C. *The Chinook Jargon.* Seattle:

Rainier Printing Co. 1909.

"Sir Henry Pering Pellew Crease, Knight," *The Advocate*, January-February 1949.

*Statement Respecting The Earl of Selkirk's Settlement Upon the Red River, in North America, Its Destruction in 1815 and 1816; and the Massacre of Governor Semple and His Party, With Observations Upon a Recent Publication, Entitled 'A Narrative of Occurrences in the Indian Countries,' etc.*, John Murray, London, 1817. Reprint. Toronto: Canadian House 1969.

Stonier-Newman, Lynne. *Policing a Pioneer Province, The BC Provincial Police 1858-1950.* Madeira Park, B.C.: Harbour Publishing 1992.

Teit, James Alexander. *The Shuswap.* Edited by Franz Boaz, Vol. 4, Part 3 of *Memoirs of the American Museum of Natural History.* Reprint from Vol. 2, Part 7 of *The Jessup North Pacific Expedition.* E. J. Brill Ltd. 1909.

Waddington, Alfred. *The Fraser Mines Vindicated, or, the History of Four Months.* Victoria, 1858.

Wade, Mark S. *The Cariboo Road.* Victoria: The Haunted Bookshop 1979.

Walkem, W. Wymond. *Stories of Early British Columbia.* Vancouver: News Advertiser 1914.

Watts, Alfred, Q.C. "Mr. Justice George Anthony Walkem." *The Advocate*, September, October, 1967.

——. "The Honorable Mr. Justice Alexander Rocket Robertson." *The Advocate*, July-August 1967.

——. "The Honorable Mr. Justice John Foster McCreight." *The Advocate*, May-June 1967.

——. "The Honorable Sir Matthew Baillie Begbie." *The Advocate*, September-October 1966.

Whymper, Frederick. "The Inlet," memorandum in the *Colonist*, 9 May 1864.

——. *Travel and Adventure in the Territory of Alaska.* New York: Harper & Brothers 1871.

Williams, Glyndwr, ed. *Hudson's Bay Miscellany, 1670-1870.* Hudson's Bay Record Society, Winnipeg, 1975.

*Williams Official British Columbia Directories, 1882-83, 1897-8.* R.T. Williams, Victoria, B.C.

Woolliams, Nina G. *The Story of the Douglas Lake Cattle Company.* Douglas & McIntyre, Vancouver, 1979.

## NEWSPAPERS

*British Colonist*, Victoria

*British Columbian*, New Westminster

*Dominion Pacific Herald*, New Westminster

*Inland Sentinel*, Yale

*Kamloops WaWa*, Kamloops

*Mainland Guardian*, New Westminster

*Meritt Herald*, New Westminster

*Province*, Vancouver

*Sentinel*, Kamloops

*Standard*, Kamloops

*Standard*, Victoria

*Sun*, Vancouver

*Telegram*, Kamloops

## UNPUBLISHED SOURCES

Alexander, Richard Henry. Diary April 29–December 31, 1862, transcribed by W. Macintosh 12 June 1961. BCARS, E/B/Ae3.1A.

Atkins, E.A. "History of the Chilcotin War." Tanscript, n.d. BCARS, F/56/At5A.

Bauman, Lawrence. Letters to Pat Spiers 1968-1984.

Begbie, Matthew Baillie. "Notes on Proceedings, British Columbia Supreme Court," Quesnellemouth, 28-29 September 1864.

Blair, George. Diary 17 February 1862–29 December 1863. BCARS, Add MSS 186.

British Columbia. Attorney-General, Correspondence Inward, 1872-1910. BCARS, GR 429, vol. 1, f. 8-10.

——. Attorney-General's Documents. Depositions, warrants, testimony re: the Queen vs. McLeans and Hare, recognizance to prosecute, misc. correspondence, inquests. BCARS, GR 0419, vols. 18, 22; GR 431.

——. Census 1881, 1891.

——. Department of Interior, Dominion Lands Branch, B.C. Lands. Correspondence. BCARS, GR 436, f. 1613.

——. Governor. "Despatches from Governor Seymour and Administrator Birch to the Colonial Office, 26 April 1864 to 20 December 1865." NAC, photostat UBC Special Collections.

——. Lands and Works Department. Ferry contracts, mining licenses, free miner's certificates, records of pre-emption claims, miners and storekeepers occupying Crown lands as gardens, trading licences, ground rents, liquor licences, 24 February 1859–15 May 1870. BCARS, GR 833.

——. Record of Land Acquisitions, 2 August 1902–10 July 1908. BCARS, GR 1374, vols. 15305, 15505.

——. Supreme Court (Victoria). Probates 1859-1941. BCARS, GR 1304, vol. 25.

——. Supreme Court. Probates 1884-1946. BCARS, GR 1562, vols. 43, 47, 80.

——. Supreme Court. Wills 1859-1948. BCARS, GR 1417, GR 266.

Brough, John. Diaries of John Brough in British Columbia c. 1864. Edited by Sheila MacIntosh. BCARS, Add MSS 2797.

Colonial Correspondence. BCARS.

Correspondence of Archibald McDonald relating to Fort Colville, 1838-1842. BCARS.

Correspondence, Forts Dallas and Berens, extracts. HBCA, A.11/76b, copy in BCARS, A/C/2/D16.

Correspondence of the Government of the Colony of Vancouver Island, 1849-1866 and the Government of the Colony of British Columbia, 1858-1871. BCARS, F127/19a; F367/1; F515/28; F739/14; F920/40; F936/25; F955/21/26; F1063; F4856/3.

Correspondence, London Inward General 1856-57, Hudson's Bay Company. HBCA, Reel 92, A10/40.

Correspondence, London Outward General 1865-66. HBCA, Reel 45, A6/40.

Cornwall, C.F. Diary, May 1862-July 1864; Diary and Farm Record vol. 1, 17 November 1866-7 June 1869. BCARS, Add MSS 759.

Cox, William George. Papers. BCARS, C2229.

Crease, Henry Pering Pellew. Bench Books, 15 March 1880–6 July 1880, BCARS, GR 1727, vol. 698; Cariboo Circuit, 19 October–5 November 1880, BCARS, GR 1727, vol. 710; New Westminster Circuit, 10 November–19 November 1880, BCARS, GR 1727, vol. 533.

——. Correspondence Outward 1881. BCARS, A/E/C86/C86J.

——. "In the Matter of Regina vs. McLean, McLean,

McLean & Hare." Legal Papers, 1880. BCARS, Add MSS 54, vols. 5, 6.

——. "Notes on Special Assize holden at New Westminster on 3 & 4 July, 1864." BCARS.

Crease, Sarah. "Notes of a trip with my dear husband on circuit to Cariboo, Kamloops and New Westminster, September 1–December 7, 1880." BCARS, A/E/C86/C861.1.

"Donald McLean 'C'." Research paper done for the author and Pat Spiers. Information contained therein published by permission of The Hudson's Bay Company.

Fawcett, Edgar. "The Bute Inlet Massacre – The Adventures of a Surveyer's Rodman in the Wilds of British Columbia." Typescript, n.d. BCARS.

Fort Alexandria Journal 1845-48, HBCA, B/5/a/6,7; 1849-56, HBCA, B/4/a/f05-1; 1858-64, HBCA, B/5/a/10.

Fort Babine. Correspondence Outward, Hudson's Bay Company. BCARS, A/B/20/B11.

Fort Chilcotin, Miscellaneous information relating to. Typescript, n.d. BCARS, MM/C43.

Fort Kamloops Journals, 1859-62. KMA.

Fort Victoria, Correspondence Books 1864-1866, Hudson's Bay Company. HBCA B/226/6/48.

Governor-General's Office. Records from the Lieutenant-Governor's Office, Governor to Colonial Office, 1864-67. NAC, RG7/G8/C, vol. 23.

Hewlett, Edward Sleigh. "The Chilcotin Uprising: A Study of Indian White Relations in Nineteenth Century British Columbia." M.A. Thesis, University of British Columbia, 1972.

Kamloops. Assessment Rolls, 1902-1922 (KMA).

Hills, Bishop George. Diary, 1838-65. BCARS, Add MSS 1526, vols. 1-12.

Howse, Albert Elgin. Interview, n.d. NVA, E/E/84.

Hutchinson, G.M., ed. "The Kamloops Murder, copies of original letters, telegrams, newspaper excerpts." Typescript, n.d. BCARS, K/J/H97.

Laing, F.W. "Colonial Farm Settlers on the Mainland of British Columbia, 1858-71, with a historical sketch." Victoria, typescript. BCARS, Add MSS 700.

Lane, Robert Brockstedt. "Cultural Relations of the Chilcotin Indians of West Central British Columbia." Ph.D. thesis, University of Washington, 1953.

Leighton, James Buie. Papers (KMA).

London Inward Correspondence, General 1856-57, Hudson's Bay Company. HBCA A10/40.

McDonald, Margaret Lillooet. "New Westminster 1859-71," M.A., University of Britihs Columbia, 1947. New Westminster Library, R971.1/M145n.

McLean, Donald. Miscellaneous papers. BCARS, E/B/M221.9.

McLean Family Bible. KMA.

McLean Murder Correspondence 1879-80. Typsecript, n.d. BCARS, K/J/M22; K/J/H97.

McLeod, John. Diary and Notes, 1876-79. KMA.

*Nereide*, Ship's Logs 1833-1834. HBCA C/1/609.

"Proceedings at an Inquest held at Murder Camp before C. Brew and T. Elwyn on the 25th of May, 1864 on the bodies of William Brewster, John Clark and Jem Gawley." Typescript. UBC Special Collections.

Robson, Ebenezer. "Notes from the Diary of the Rev. Ebenezer Robson, D. D., Pioneer Wesleyan Missionary at Fort Hope, B.C. 12

March 1859–13 May 1860." BCARS, H/D/R57/R57.2A.

——. "An Old Timer's Diary – Rev. Ebenezer Robson." Edited by William Lashley Hall. BCARS H/D/R57H/vol. 1.

Shannon, William. "Chilcotin Massacre of 1863." Typescript, n.d. BCARS, 57/Sh1.

Selkirk Papers. NAC, MG19.

Smith, J.F. "McLean Bros.," Crimes and the Administration of Justice in B.C. of which I have personal knowledge – from 1873. Dictated to J. J. Morse, 1931 (KMA).

Tait, John. Letters 1872-1880. KMA.

## ADDITIONAL READING

Bertrand, Lugrin, N. de (Mrs. E.B. Shaw). "Murder Runs Amuck." Unpublished, BCARS.

Clark, Cecil. "McLeans' Outlawry Led to Gallows." Victoria Times, 17 March 1951.

——. "Murder on the Road to Long Lake," *Victoria Colonist*. 8 October 1967.

——. "The Fighting McLeans," *The Shoulder Strap*, Summer Edition 1939.

LeBourdais, Louis. "Death at Murderer's Bar." *Vancouver Province*, 28 May 1933.

Lindsay, F.W. "The Wild McLeans." *The B.C. Outlaws*. Kelowna: by the Author 1963.

McKelvie, B. "Tales of Conflict." The *Vancouver Province*, 1949.

Pearson, John. "The Wild McLean Boys." *New Westminster Columbian*, 10 December 1969.

Spinks, William Ward. "The McLean Boys," *Tales of the British Columbia Frontier*. Toronto: The Ryerson Press 1933.

Swanson, Judge J.D. "Turbulent History's Bright Climax," *Victoria Colonist*, 3 May 1925.

"The McLean Gang." *Sagas of the West* magazine. April, 1971.

Shannon, William. "Chilcotin Massacre of 1863." Typescript.

# INDEX

Black Pines, 235-238, 241-244, 252
McLean, Charles 'Charlie,' son of Donald of
the HBC, 22, 66, 69, 86, 91-92, 96,
100-102; bites Baptiste's nose off, 104;
107-109, 113-118, 121-122, 124, 131,
142-143, 149-150, 152-157, 161-162, 170,
175-176, 182-187, 195, 203-204, 209, 212,
216-218; execution of, 220-224; 235, 253
McLean, Christina Pauline, daughter of
Donald of the HBC, 22, 111, 189
McLean, Christina, wife of Alexander of Red
River, 3-8, 10-12, 16-18, 29; death, 58
McLean, Christine Selpa, 175, 231-232
McLean, Clifford, 241, 251-252
McLean, Donald of Drimnin, 3
McLean, Donald of the HBC, son of Alexander
of Red River, vii, 4, 7; leaves for Chilcotin
War, 20-23; 27, 29, 31-32, 38-41, 44,
47-50; appointed chief trader, 51; 52; in
charge of Fort Kamloops, 53; 54-60; moves
to Hat Creek, 61; 62-69, 73, 76-80; death,
81-83; 86, 110-111, 131-133, 226, 240,
252-253
McLean, Donald Jr., son of Donald of the
HBC, 22, 52, 61, 66, 79, 110-111, 163,
175, 194, 204, 220, 226, 235, 240-241
McLean, Duncan, son of Alexander of Black
Pines, 241
McLean, Duncan Joseph, son of Alexander of
Black Pines, 235, 238, 241-244, 253
McLean, Duncan, son of Donald of the HBC,
22-23, 52, 61, 66-68, 79, 81, 111
McLean Gang, vi, 86, 91, 95-96, 132, 136,
144, 235, 238, 240, 253
McLean, George, son of Hector, 241
McLean, George Allen, 134, 187, 189-190,
246-251
McLean, Hector, 22, 94, 96, 111-112, 121,
149, 157, 160-161, 163, 169, 194-196;
trial, 201-205; 213, 217, 226, 230, 235;
death, 240-241
McLean, Hugh, son of Alexander of Black
Pines, 241
McLean, Hugh, son of Alexander of Red River, 7
Maclean, John of Coll, Anna McLean's
husband, 232
Maclean, John of Mull, 31
McLean, John, son of Alexander of Red River, 7
McLean, John, son of Donald McLean Jr., 111,
240
McLean, John Allen, son of Donald of the
HBC, 22, 52, 61, 64, 66, 111, 195, 240
McLean, John Donald, son of Mathias Allen,
189-190
McLean, Maggie, 226, 232
McLean, Mary, 4
McLean, Mary Angela 'Annie,' daughter of
Donald of the HBC, 22, 96, 112, 150, 185,
189, 219-220
McLean, Mary-Ethel, 112, 189
McLean, Mathias Allen, 22, 66, 69, 88, 91-92,
95, 99-106, 108-109, 111, 114-125, 131-134,
138, 141-142, 148; fight with Pablo, 149-150;
151-156, 159-162, 170, 174, 178, 182, 184-190,

194, 200-201, 210; attempts escape, 210-212;
214-219; execution of, 221-224; 251, 253
McLean, Matilda 'Tillie,' 241
McLean, Miles, 7
McLean, Minnie, daughter of Alexander of
Black Pines, 241
McLean, Minnie, second of that name,
daughter of Alexander of Black Pines, 241, 252
McLean, Peter Arthur 'Archie,' 88, 92, 96; kills
John Ussher, 102; 103, 105, 107-109,
111-113, 115-118, 121-123, 131, 140-144;
149-150; 157, 160-163, 169-170, 173-177,
179, 181, 184-188, 196, 200, 206, 208-215,
217-220; execution of, 220-224; 253
McLean, Sophia, see Grant, Sophia
McLean's Restaurant, 22, 28, 65-66, 68, 70
McLennan, F., 172
MacLeod, Archibald Norman, 18
McLeod, John, 98, 99-106, 110, 122, 127, 130,
158, 163, 174, 177, 180, 182, 209
McLeod, Malcolm, 24, 43
McLeod, Robert, 25, 46
McLeod, William, 99, 126-127, 129
McLoughlin, John, 40, 56
McLoughlin, Marguerite, 40
McMillan, James, 230
McQueen family, 204
McRae, George, 92, 104
McRae, Kenneth, 6

Makai, John Henry, 213
Manning, Nancy, 54
Manning, William, Nicola Valley settler, 119,
126
Manning, William, Puntzi Lake settler, 24, 35,
45, 53-54, 63-64, 66, 73, 82
Manson, Donald, 47-49, 52-53, 56, 61, 241
Manson, Donald Jr., 59
Manson, William, 59, 61
Mara, John Andrew, 98, 112, 114, 116, 128-130,
136, 138, 150-151, 157, 185, 219, 231
Martin, Reverend Father, 156
*Maude*, 136, 145-146
Maynard, Joseph, 172
Mayne, R. C., 60
Mellors, Jim, 92, 95, 97
Miner, Bill, 237, 242
Modderfontein, 236
Moody, Col. Richard, 71
Moore, Ben, 92, 156
Moore, Joe, 156
Moore, Sam, 92
Moresby, Mary Anne, 199-202, 212, 216, 218
Moresby, William C., 161, 200-202, 211-214,
220-224
Moresby, Willy, 212, 223
Morgan, Tom, 203
Morrison, James, 221
Mucado, Basilio, 150
Mull, 3, 29
Murray, John, 140

Nadetnoerh, 49-50
Nancootlem/Sitleece, 23, 25, 35, 43, 45, 75

# KEY CHARACTERS IN THE WILD McLEANS

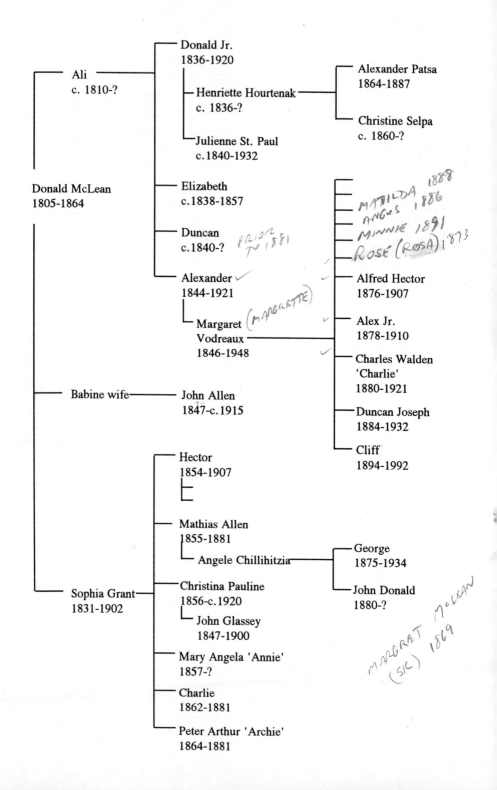

Donald McLean
1805-1864

Ali
c. 1810-?

Donald Jr.
1836-1920

Henriette Hourtenak
c. 1836-?

Julienne St. Paul
c.1840-1932

Alexander Patsa
1864-1887

Christine Selpa
c. 1860-?

Elizabeth
c.1838-1857

Duncan
c.1840-?     *PRIOR TO 1881*

Alexander ✓
1844-1921

Margaret *(MARGARITE)*
Vodreaux
1846-1948

*MATILDA 1888*
*ANGUS 1886*
*MINNIE 1891*
*ROSE (ROSA) 1873*

Alfred Hector
1876-1907

Alex Jr.
1878-1910

Charles Walden
'Charlie'
1880-1921

Duncan Joseph
1884-1932

Cliff
1894-1992

Babine wife

John Allen
1847-c.1915

Sophia Grant
1831-1902

Hector
1854-1907

Mathias Allen
1855-1881

Angele Chillihitzia

George
1875-1934

John Donald
1880-?

Christina Pauline
1856-c.1920

John Glassey
1847-1900

*MARGRAT McLEAN*
*(SIC) 1869*

Mary Angela 'Annie'
1857-?

Charlie
1862-1881

Peter Arthur 'Archie'
1864-1881